POLICY
AS
PRACTICE

POLICY
AS
PRACTICE

Toward a Comparative
Sociocultural Analysis of
Educational Policy

*Edited by Margaret Sutton
and Bradley A.U. Levinson*

Sociocultural Studies in
Educational Policy Formation and Appropriation,
Volume 1

ABLEX PUBLISHING
Westport, Connecticut • London

Library of Congress Cataloging-in-Publication Data

Policy as practice : toward a comparative sociocultural analysis of educational policy /
edited by Margaret Sutton, Bradley A.U. Levinson.
    p. cm.—(Sociocultural studies in educational policy formation and appropriation : v. 1,
ISSN 1530–5473)
    Includes bibliographical references and index.
    ISBN 1–56750–516–3 (cloth)—ISBN 1–56750–517–1 (pbk.)
    1. Education and state—Social aspects—Cross-cultural studies. 2. Educational
anthropology—Cross-cultural studies. I. Sutton, Margaret. II. Levinson, Bradley A.U.,
1963– III. Series.
    LC71.P565 2001
    379—dc21   00–020085

British Library Cataloguing in Publication Data is available.

Library of Congress Catalog Card Number: 00–020085
ISBN: 1–56750–516–3
      1–56750–517–1 (pbk.)
ISSN: 1530–5473

First published in 2001

Ablex Publishing, 88 Post Road West, Westport, CT 06881
An imprint of Greenwood Publishing Group, Inc.
www.ablexbooks.com

Printed in the United States of America

The paper used in this book complies with the
Permanent Paper Standard issued by the National
Information Standards Organization (Z39.48–1984).

10 9 8 7 6 5 4 3 2 1

Contents

Acknowledgments

We would like to thank Kathryn Borman for having the faith and gumption to entrust this new book series to us. We have learned a good deal from her work, and we hope this first volume carries forward her critical insights into policy formation. Several people have contributed to the development of this volume, through the example of their own work or through helpful commentaries on earlier drafts of the introduction. In this regard, we thank Kathryn Anderson-Levitt, Sheila Arens, Robert Arnove, Harbans Bhola, Mark Ginsburg, G. Alfred Hess, Amy Stambach, and the participants in the Educational Policy Seminar in the School of Education, Indiana University. For their help with communication and manuscript preparation, we thank Sandy Strain, Cindy Wedemeyer, and Ana Patricia Elvir. Finally, we thank our families for their forbearance in sharing the trials and tribulations that accompany a complex international volume of this sort.

Introduction: Policy as/in Practice— A Sociocultural Approach to the Study of Educational Policy

Bradley A.U. Levinson and Margaret Sutton

OVERVIEW

Over the past 20 years, approaches to educational policy analysis have gradually opened up to qualitative research methods and to sociocultural perspectives on schooling. The growing focus on policy implementation, in particular, has conferred legitimacy upon some constructs and approaches that derive more broadly from fields like anthropology and cultural studies. Still, we would argue, a more grounded sociocultural approach to educational policy studies, let alone a fully anthropological approach, has yet to be developed. Such is the project initiated by this book and the series that it launches. In this project, we ask: What would educational policy studies look like if they reconceptualized the notion of policy itself as a complex social practice, an ongoing process of normative cultural production constituted by diverse actors across diverse social and institutional contexts? In this inaugural volume, we bring together a collection of studies that view educational policy from a variety of angles and at different levels of social life. The studies share a common concern to explicate *policy as a practice of power*, and to interrogate the *meaning of policy in practice*. Drawing on work in anthropology (Douglas, 1986; Shore & Wright, 1997), sociology (Ball, 1990; Borman, Cookson, Sadovnik, & Spade, 1996), and feminist and critical theory (Bourdieu, 1991; Calhoun, 1995; Giddens, 1984; Habermas, 1984; Marshall, 1997; Mohanty, 1991; Smith, 1987)—and thereby anchored in qualitative, comparative research—this book seeks to expand our understanding of the cultural, contextual, and political dimensions of educational policy.

Our working definition of policy fails to privilege official governing bodies only, and includes unofficial and occasionally spontaneous normative guidelines developed in diverse social spaces. We thereby challenge an understanding of public policy as a necessarily legitimate representation of "public" needs and interests. Still, it is important to recognize the specific modes and impacts of government-backed—what we call "legally authorized," or "official"—policy. Authorized policy is a form of governance, to be sure, but one that is constantly *negotiated* and reorganized in the ongoing flow of institutional life, a political form "disguised by the objective, neutral, legal-rational idioms in which [it is] portrayed" (Shore & Wright, 1997, p. 8). Many authors in this volume examine official state policy as a discursive mode of governance absolutely central to the administration of modern societies. Policy serves at various levels of government as a legitimating charter for the techniques of administration and as an operating manual for everyday conduct; it is the symbolic expression of normative claims worked into a potentially viable institutional blueprint. Instead of separating them entirely, we prefer to examine policy formation and implementation (or, as we prefer, *appropriation*—see below) as a dynamic, interrelated process stretching over time. Thus, we investigate "moments" of official policy formation in relation to moments of policy appropriation to account for the negotiation of policy in daily life. One approach to official policy *formation* involves "researching the powerful" (Walford, 1995) and examining the specific social arenas where the interests and languages comprising a governing policy charter get negotiated into some viable form (see Anderson-Levitt & Alimasi, Chapter 1; Sutton, Chapter 3; Murtadha-Watts, Chapter 4; and Rosen, Chapter 12, this volume). Yet a sociocultural analysis of policy cannot end there. The study of official policy *appropriation* highlights other moments of the policy process, when the formulated charter, temporarily reified as text, is circulated across the various institutional contexts, where it may be applied, interpreted, and/or contested by a multiplicity of local actors (see Mantilla, Chapter 5; Street, Chapter 6; Quiroz, Chapter 7; Schwab, Chapter 10; Porter, Chapter 11; and Cade, Chapter 9, this volume).

Just as our definition of education includes intentional learning outside formal school settings (Levinson, 2000), so our approach highlights the validity of rather more local, nonauthorized forms of policy (see Street, Chapter 6; Cabral Félix de Sousa, Chapter 8; and Schwab, Chapter 10, this volume). Such a perspective can further challenge the division between policy "systems" or "arenas," on the one hand, and the range of sites where policy gets "implemented." We believe the now conventional distinction between policy formation and implementation as distinct phases of a policy "process" (Hill, 1993; Lewis & Wallace, 1984) implicitly ratifies a top-down perspective, unnecessarily divides what is in fact a recursive dynamic, and inappropriately widens the gulf between everyday practice and government action. When we pay close attention to the frameworks of cultural meaning people use to interpret their experience and generate social behavior, we see not only the recipients of educational policy but also its authorized formulators and purveyors as fully cultural animals as well. By highlighting the place and role of values, beliefs, and identities in the policy process, we provide analytic tools to range across the spectrum of sociocultural activity.

In reality, of course, processes of policy formation occur across many contexts of contemporary social life. After all, policy is a kind of normative decision making, and such decision making comprises an integral part of everyday life. On the one hand, public policy is conferred the status of official tool of governance. On the other hand, smaller-scale institutions, such as businesses and local schools, may enact their own policies to specify proper procedure and conduct. Our boss may explain the "company policy," our principal the "school policy." Even individuals have been known to refer to their "policies" on a range of matters, including the regulation of interpersonal relations. Though many societies and languages do not have such everyday analogues of policy, they do have well-developed moral discourses regulating human conduct. For these reasons, we believe a sociocultural policy analysis should link the discursive practices of normative control in any local-level community or institution with the discursive practices comprising larger-scale structures of law and governance.

A key term in our approach is the deceptively simple metatheoretical concept of *practice*. The idea of practice has emerged as a way of accounting for the situated logic of activities across a wide array of contexts. Practice gets at the way individuals, and groups, engage in situated behaviors that are both constrained and enabled by existing structures, but which allow the person to exercise agency in the emerging situation.[1] Qualitative sociocultural research into everyday practice thus promises to demystify the policy process and reconceive it in culturally reflexive terms. An emphasis on the purposeful practice of diverse social actors reinstates agency across all levels of the policy process, making it possible to see policy not only as mandate but also as contested cultural resource.

It is in this sense that we prefer to analyze policy in terms of how people appropriate its meanings.[2] Appropriation, of course, highlights the way creative agents "take in" elements of policy, thereby incorporating these discursive and institutional resources into their own schemes of interest, motivation, and action. Appropriation is a kind of taking of policy and making it one's own. With this term, we draw attention to how previously excluded actors lay claim to the right to create policy. Thus, Porter's study, in Chapter 11, of local actions in Kentucky shows that the state-mandated reform provided openings for action by newcomers and others who had previously been marginalized in educational leadership. Even outright resistance to a policy can be conceived as a kind of appropriation insofar as it incorporates a negative image of policy into schemes of action. Through this appropriation, new kinds of local normative policies may take shape. For instance, Street, in Chapter 6, shows how Mexican teachers, in their struggle for union democracy, reject the state's new modernization policy and thereby propose new local policies for school–community relations. In sum, we seek to link analytically the diverse domains and modalities through which people "make" policy through practice.[3]

We prefer qualitative, ethnographic research for elucidating the richness and complexity of the policy process. Ethnographic research highlights the lived experience of people in everyday life. On the one hand, it is a set of "methods" for viewing social reality. Researchers engage in "participant observation" and interviews for extended periods of time, attempting to get at patterns of social interaction and discourse. Yet ethnography is more than a set of empirical methods; it is perhaps more importantly a way of "seeing" (Wolcott, 1999), a practice of cultural interpretation that attempts to reconstruct the cultural logic, the embedded meanings, of discourses, institutions, and actions (cf. Wright, 1994). Though not every study in this book is fully ethnographic in the anthropological sense, each one helps us to "see" the way policy works as cultural practice.

As the following section will show, numerous social and intellectual currents have enriched and enlivened the field of policy analysis over the past 50 years. Yet, we maintain that in all the scholarly discourse around policy, there is little evidence of the sociocultural perspective: a locally informed, comparatively astute, ethnographically rich account of how people make, interpret, and otherwise engage with the policy process. We hope this introduction will make clear that a deeply cultural approach to educational policy has yet to be developed. Such an approach can and should develop in dialogue with existing studies to chart out new tools for research and change. Our primary goals in this volume are thus to build upon and extend previous work in the study of educational policy formation and implementation through the articulation of a critical sociocultural framework and the illustration provided by selected studies.

It is also our firm belief that a sociocultural approach to educational policy should not remain at the level of critique or analytic description. In our final section, we suggest the steps necessary for bringing ethnographic knowledge about policy into the policy process itself, to facilitate a more robust participatory dialogue and encourage a research practice that supports democratic action both in its execution and in its outcomes.

THE STUDY OF EDUCATIONAL POLICY: HISTORIES AND FRAMEWORKS

The notion of educational policy, like public policy more broadly, emerged over the course of this century as part of a trend toward greater rationality and efficiency in the administration of vast public enterprises. Like transportation, food supplies, sanitation, and health services, education today is a central arena of public policy. Public policy can take a wide range of forms, from broad statements of goals to more specific statements of intention (Pressman & Wildavsky, 1973), expressed in speeches, official statements, court decisions, and laws and regulations, all of which embody the authority to define goals and to command means. At the most basic level, all public policies specify priorities and procedures for distributing goods and services to the members of a society. As Bhola has observed, the intent of policy is "to *direct* and to *harness* social power for social outcomes" (1975, p. 1). In so doing, policies also express the authoritative allocation of values by a decision-making body (Ball, 1990).

In the United States of America, early conceptions of policy, trumpeted during the functionalist heyday of social science, celebrated a new administrative rationalism. Policy was often portrayed as a technocratic object, a kind of fuel rod for the body politic: put the policy in and watch the machine run. Policy analysis sought to apply the best of social scientific knowledge to the rational solution of perennial human problems. Indeed, the expansion of the Cold War lent a certain urgency to the tone of such analyses, which conflated national security concerns with the need to ameliorate "basic conflicts in our civilization" (Lasswell, 1951, p. 8).

Given the intent to assess and influence policy processes, it is perhaps not surprising then that policy analysis has historically been dominated by a "managerial perspective" (Bowe, Ball, & Gold, 1992, p. 7), which assumes a linear model of the policy process. In this model, "the policy process is divided into sequential steps and each is analyzed in turn" (Porter & Hicks, 1995, p. 8). Typically, the linear model assumes that policy processes begin with problem identification, then move through stages of policy formation and adoption, which is followed by implementation and ultimately by evaluation (Porter & Hicks, 1995). Until recently, the preponderance of scholarship in the field has focused on the extreme ends of the process—how policy is formed and methods for evaluating policy impacts.

In most contemporary *educational* studies, policy is conceived in terms of multilateral, national, state, or local directives that legislate institutional structures, proper codes of conduct, and academic standards for schools. Such directives are thought to originate in negotiations amongst the institutional actors and "stakeholders" who wield power at these various levels. Once formulated, policy then filters down to be implemented in the varying school contexts to which it might apply. However, in this conception, less powerful actors—students and their parents, and even teachers—are seen as adjusting their actions and expectations to a *fait accompli*, "challenging" the coherence of educational policy (Fuhrman, 1993; McLaughlin & Talbert, 1993), or at best "resisting" policy directives through footdragging or deliberate inaction. Other approaches counterpoise "policy" to "practice," conceiving the former as an instrument of governance and the latter as classroom instruction (Cohen & Spillane, 1993) or "political resistance" (Wells & Serna, 1996).

It is easier to define what public policy *is* than what policy *does*. Questions about the impacts and relative efficacy of specific policies define the better part of the field of policy analysis. In education, policy studies have grown from the academic study of school administration, which, along with educational psychology, formed the core subjects of schools and colleges of education as they developed in the early years of this century (Tyack, 1974). In the 1960s, federal civil rights legislation in the United States and similar state-sponsored efforts to induce social change in other countries spurred demands to assess the impacts of a whole range of social programs, leading to the creation of graduate schools of public policy (Wildavsky, 1987). Thus, since the 1960s, educational policy analysis has been informed both by changing theories in the field of education and by changing approaches to policy analysis in other social spheres. The techniques of policy analysis developed in North America, the United Kingdom, and elsewhere in Western Europe have become global sciences by their incorporation into practices of international assistance by development agencies.

Shaped by multiple contexts of theory and practice, educational policy studies defy neat categorization by theory or method. Bobrow and Dryzek note that the policy field is "marked by a variety of technical approaches" (1987, p. 5). Foremost among them, they maintain, is welfare economics, with an emphasis on cost-benefit accounting as a means of assessing welfare. This claim continues to hold true in particular for educational policy analysis in the Third World, the practice of which is strongly determined by the proclivities of external funders. With no less weighty an institution than the World Bank claiming intellectual authority over policy directions among nations that accept its funds, educational policy analysis applied to the Third World reduces to the "analysis of investment choices" (Psacharopoulos & Woodhall, 1985). To be sure, support by donor institutions for systemic reform of education has expanded the range of acceptable techniques for policy analysis in Third World contexts. However, with the fiscal center of gravity both for reform and for its study residing outside of national governments, educational policy analysis concerned with Third World settings remains more strongly technocratic than analyses produced by European and North American researchers about the policy processes of their own national societies.

Two trends of recent years have begun to change both the focus of policy analysis and the approaches to it. The first has been a growing concern with implementation as an integral part of the policy process, rather than what happens after policy is made. It is all too telling that the social turmoil of the 1960s, both in the United States and abroad, spawned a more critical and substantivist analysis of policy. Odden (1991) identifies the 1960s as the origins of "implementation" studies. The growth of federal initiatives gave rise to a generation of scholars who looked more closely at how policies generated through a rather distant political process were "implemented" in local settings. Lipsky and Wildavsky began writing about the "street-level bureaucrat" and the impulse to "speak truth to power." Greater attention was being paid to questions of scale—how policy moved across vastly different locales and levels of social organization—as well as to politics and power—how policy reflected distinct interests and thus was subject to different responses and scenarios. For perhaps the first time, policy was conceived as a "process" rather than a simple charter or political act (cf. Burstein, 1991; Burstein & Bricher, 1997; Weiss, 1982).

In education, this perspective on implementation is associated with Elmore and McLaughlin's (1988) study of educational reform in the United States, originally conducted in the 1970s (see McLaughlin, 1975). Taking seriously the notion that implementation shapes policy has led to a wide range of qualitatively informed case studies of policy in action, in education and in other fields such as health (Hill, 1993; Walsh, 1996). These studies implicitly challenge a simple linear model of policy processes and focus attention more closely on the meaning of policy in the lives of those affected by it. As Odden (1991) documents for the United States, studies of implementation, which fundamentally recognize the processual character of policy, have "evolved" over the past three decades to develop increasingly sophisticated mid-range concepts and theories (cf. Fitz, Haplin, & Power, 1994). A parallel literature on policy research, informed by concepts from critical and feminist theory (Ball 1990; Marshall, 1997), has emerged to complement, and in some ways to challenge, the implementation perspective.

Another important trend in policy analysis that has had special relevance for the study of educational policies in the Third World is the set of studies that focus on the development of social science research and the use (or as is often the case, nonuse) of expert technical knowledge in the formulation of policy (Apter, 1974; Böhme & Stehr, 1986; Eisemon, 1981; Knorr-Cetina & Mulkay, 1983). This branch of analysis brings the insights of the sociology of knowledge to bear upon policy processes. The literature on knowledge generation and utilization asks how research can be designed and undertaken so that researchers and policymakers "construct knowledge together" (Reimers & McGinn, 1997, p. 107). In some ways, this strain of work acknowledges earlier attempts to document the way policy was formed within government agencies. McGinn and Street's (1982, 1984) sociological study of the Mexican education ministry found that a "political rationality" emerging from organizational conflicts between technocratic politicians and the national teachers' union, rather than research-based knowledge per se, overwhelmingly determined the making of decisions and the allocation of resources. Research knowledge, if utilized at all, was applied selectively—and after the fact—to justify decisions made according to highly political criteria. Such studies force us to see that before research knowledge can substantially inform policy processes, the cultures of policy formation must be reformed.

Scholarship on policy implementation and knowledge utilization have opened the field of policy analysis up to some critical intellectual orientations, which influence our work in this volume. Both forms of study create dynamic models of policy processes and encourage a more contextualized understanding of policy as practice. Increasingly, ethnographic research approaches have been applied to understanding the power dynamics intrinsic to the formation of authoritative policy. "Institutional ethnography," a phrase coined by feminist sociologist Dorothy Smith (1987), has begun to yield important insights into the social dynamics of specific institutions that are central to the formation of official policy. Institutional ethnography has been especially revealing of the policy processes involved in internationally funded development projects, notably in James Ferguson's (1994) study of a rural development project in Lesotho funded by the Canadian government, and in Adele Mueller's (1986) analysis of the field of women in development.

Institutional ethnography shares intellectual ground with another set of approaches to the study of power and policy that are particularly critical to our sociocultural conception of policy. These are ideological analysis and discourse analysis, particularly those inspired by Foucault (1971, 1972, 1979) and by feminist and other critical epistemologies (Collins, 1990; Harding, 1987; Povinelli, 1991; Sutton, 1998; cf. Marshall, 1997). These approaches involve a cultural critique of dominant institutions and ideologies. In Thompson's (1990) critical survey

the analysis of ideology . . . is primarily concerned with the ways in which symbolic forms intersect with relations of power. It is concerned with the ways in which meaning is mobilized in the social world and serves thereby to bolster up individuals and groups who occupy positions of power. . . . *To study ideology is to study the ways in which meaning serves to establish and sustain relations of domination.* (emphasis added, p. 56)

Thus, to study the practices through which political elites formulate policy is to engage a cultural analysis of their "ideological strategies" (Eagleton, 1991). Phyllis Chock Pease (1991, 1998) has contributed a fascinating set of articles about how ideological discourses surrounding the issue of immigration shape policy discussions in the United States Congress. Carol Greenhouse's new volume, *Democracy and Ethnography* (1998), which compares the construction of identities in so-called "multicultural liberal states" (e.g., Spain and the United States), similarly explores the ideological terrain of elite, state discourses as these play themselves out in various realms of popular culture.

Finally, longstanding anthropological insights into myth, ritual, and the construction of social solidarity, coupled with critical discourse analysis, can be especially valuable for our understanding of the relationship between existing, codified policy and the conceptions of local actors. Three of the contributors to this volume invoke myth and other traditional anthropological concepts to elucidate policy formation and appropriation. Lisa Rosen, in Chapter 12, employs the categories of myth and ritual to analyze a local California debate on mathematics education policy as a focus for examining the broader relationships between policy processes and an underlying "moral order" in education. From her participant-observation of health educators in Sao Paulo, Isabel Cabral Félix de Sousa, in Chapter 8, reconstructs a set of myths that, she maintains, obstruct meaningful communication between these educators and their clients. In Chapter 11, Maureen Porter highlights a specific category of myth—the origin myth—and how in one Appalachian mountain community it provides a discursive frame for promoting educational change.

In relation to policy process in the Third World, these critical perspectives on the material efficacy of authoritative discourses have been elaborated by, among others, Escobar (1995) and Pigg (1992). Ball's (1990) work on educational policy reforms in the United Kingdom and Popkewitz (1991) in the United States develop analytically kindred approaches. Ideological and discourse analysis have particular relevance to a sociocultural approach to policy analysis, as they dissolve the lines between ordinary and authoritative meanings of policy by directing attention to the regimes of meaning which are constantly reinvented and reinforced through institutional practices.

STUDYING POLICY AS/IN PRACTICE: SOCIOCULTURAL CASE STUDIES

In relation to existing policy research, our sociocultural framework provides a number of key points. We urge a more fully historical, comparative, and localized view of policy processes. The need for a deeper historical grounding of policy studies should be clear. Especially because policy is such a relatively novel discourse on the world stage, the policy processes of the present moment can only be illuminated fully through a historical understanding of the rise of the nation-state as a political form and the subsequent formation of "international relations." More recent dynamics of globalization throw the historical importance of the nation-state into relief even as they challenge state sovereignty over national policy processes. The sociocultural studies in Part I, "Global and Nation-State Policy Processes," address this interplay in the historical context of the rising power of transnational capital, multilateral development institutions, and national and international non-governmental organizations.

In reviewing policy research, we find an existing division of labor and audience between those analyzing policy in liberal capitalist societies such as Great Britain or the United States, and those analyzing policy in or for the "developing" societies of the Third World that receive substantial aid from northern donors. While important differences exist between these types of societies in the ways policy is formulated and implemented, such a strict division of analytic labor seems not fully warranted, especially under conditions of increasing globalization. Indeed, comparative analysis of the political and institutional cultures across these different societies yields important insights into policy processes around the globe. For example, relationships between researchers and policymakers are more complex in situations that may include international as well as national actors and institutions. The added dimensions of hierarchy and authority illuminate the sometimes extreme differences in power between policymakers and the subjects of governing policy.

Nine countries are represented in this book, and in Part II, "Local Educators Appropriating and Forming Educational Policy," one can clearly see the valuable insights produced by such juxtaposition. For instance, across three different national societies, Murtadha-Watts, Mantilla, and Street analyze the interrelated meanings of *participation* and *autonomy* for local educators. Depending on the degree and nature of their participation in forming official policy, local educators appropriate and in effect form their own policies to deal with local conditions. In the same part, authors like Cabral Félix de Sousa, Quiroz and again Murtadha-Watts analyze how policy directives formed at district or even national levels get enacted in educators' practices.

Finally, in all of these studies we pay close attention to context-specific and localized elaborations of policy. The final part, "Community–Educator Negotiations of Policy Meanings and Practice," highlights the local view. Analyzing interactions between teachers, parents, and students across contexts such as offices, school board meetings, and town streets, Cade, Schwab, Porter, and Rosen portray the multiple ways policy is negotiated and thereby appropriated in local communities.

The goal of these authors is to enter into and interpret the logic of the sociocultural worlds constructed by policy actors across a variety of levels and sites. The kind of sociocultural approach we advocate here requires such attention to the multiple sites in which, and multiple modalities through which, policies are formed and appropriated. It is questionable, in fact, whether this attention to multiple sites can qualify as ethnography in the stricter sense of the term. To be sure, some of our authors have adapted a kind of "multisited ethnography" (Marcus, 1998; Ortner, 1997) to study intensively, and firsthand, the interconnected cultures of policy (see Anderson-Levitt & Alimasi, Chapter 1; Adams et al., Chapter 2; Quiroz, Chapter 7, this volume). Such multisited research may also become significantly longitudinal, attuned to different moments and cycles of the policy process as it unfolds in different sites. Seeking innovative means of interpreting the way policy gets produced, others— including Anderson-Levitt and Alimasi as well as Sutton—have concentrated their efforts on interviewing key policy figures and submitting key policy documents to a critical discourse analysis. In every case, the authors are concerned to elaborate a contextualized sociocultural analysis. Accordingly, they do not let individual documents or persons or laws stand in as the only expressions of policy. Rather, these authors interrogate what these documents and people have to say to and about one another, what kinds of suppositions they make about proper or desirable conduct, and how relationships and fundamental beliefs structure authoritative policy.

Each of the chapters attends more to one aspect of the policy cycle as we have conceived it. Those that focus on moments of policy formation draw on a variety of conceptual, theoretical, and empirical tools. They tend to highlight how policy formation in authorized governments shapes and constrains legitimate discourse on educational issues. In the processes of policy formation, problems are constructed for solution and thus the needs of individuals and society as a whole become subject to authoritative definition. Policy can also be a practice of constructing "political" subjects and identities, of creating a certain kind of public, a certain kind of citizen or "educated person" (Levinson, Foley, Holland, 1996). Among public policy arenas, educational policy is unique in its power to determine who has the right to become an educated person, as well as what bodies of knowledge and what cognitive skills count as properly educative. In no society that we know do the voices of all citizens weigh equally in the process, nor do such voices express uniform interests and values.

The first part of this book provides case studies that examine how educational policy is formulated at the national and, indeed, international level. Donald Adams and his colleagues begin this section by considering the relationship between researchers and policymakers in three countries, finding that for the most part researchers acted as information providers to their "clients," the policymakers. However, they also noted some exceptions to this model, which brought researchers and policymakers into a more collaborative role in two of the case countries, Mali and Ghana. In Mali, they found researchers working in a "research as collective practice" model, as they became directly and actively involved in the process of (educational) change through their involvement in teacher education and supervision. In Ghana, researchers uncovered policies concerning textbook provision that served to restrict rather than expand book availability to students by placing fiscal burdens on teachers. This finding ultimately led to an adjustment in the policies.

Looking at another instance of donor-sponsored research, Margaret Sutton, in Chapter 3, argues that the policy evaluation practices of international agencies are epistemologically constrained by models of acceptable research and by the specific practices associated with evaluation by development assistance institutions. Together, these features of "agency research" solidify an instrumental perspective that has the consequence of silencing the opinions, interests, and needs of policy subjects. The chapter illustrates the processes by which the range of relevant research concerns can become compressed in (commissioned) policy-oriented research, and challenges researchers to think strategically about ways to open up such research to more deeply interpretive and critical thinking.

Chapter 1, by Kathryn Anderson-Levitt and Ntal-I'Mbirwa Alimasi, underscores the problems that can result from policy analysis that is restricted to a narrow range of questions. While the questions may be framed in one particular manner, their underlying constructs may also be invested with diverse meanings by different actors, with only some of these meanings overriding others in the formation of policy. Anderson-Levitt and Alimasi's study of pedagogical ideals for reading instruction in Guinea shows how the same words mean very different things to teachers, the policy elite, and various external actors in Guinean education. In the process, the authors engage in a reflexive consideration of whether educational principles are imposed from outside of Guinean society, or are endogenous to it. Their analysis shows how such a simple question begins to dissolve under the weight of historical interactions of Guinean educators with myriad "outsiders." Ultimately, they pose the question of what it means to name an ideal or belief as authentic or imported.

Part II of this book looks at policy processes from a different set of perspectives, illuminating the ongoing dynamic between policy formation and appropriation in the lives of local educators. In her study of African American women school leaders in a midwestern U.S. city, Khaula Murtadha-Watts, in Chapter 4, argues that the life experiences of these women endow multicultural education policies with concrete meanings that go beyond a simple recognition of diversity. Thus, these leaders hold teachers accountable for implementing authoritative policies that discursively support multiculturalism—a form of accountability that is often in tension and at times even at odds with pressures for accountability in terms of (measurable) student achievement.

Looking from the perspective of teachers involved in a national reform process, Martha Mantilla, in Chapter 5, shows how new policies authorizing changes in pedagogy have been appropriated by a group of teachers in Guatemala. When an externally funded effort to improve education in rural, single-room schools was initiated in Guatemala, many teachers were skeptical. Those who became engaged, however, over time became both practitioners and advocates of active, non punitive approaches to teaching and learning. Ironically, their conversion to the practices promoted by *Nueva Escuela Unitaria* (NEU) brought them in conflict with local educational administrators, who insisted, for example, that passing and failing grades be reported, in contradiction to the self-paced learning approach of NEU. Despite conflicts of this sort, Mantilla shows that the teachers' participation in the formation and implementation of educational policies has made them more aware of the fact that they are viable contributors to the process of sociocultural change via educational reform practices and policies in Guatemala.

The activist Mexican teachers portrayed by Susan Street in Chapter 6 are also engaged in the appropriation of policy, on their own terms. Street describes how teachers in one of the "democratic" state sections of the national teacher's union resist most elements of the federal government's new policy for educational "modernization." Rather than implementing such top-down official policy, the dissident teachers portray it as an obstacle to union democratization and thereby encourage rank and file to question its authoritative status. Street examines some of the debates and conflicts over the meanings of democracy that ensue from this questioning. Should democratic teachers work primarily to pry open structures of union leadership, or should they work for more democratic relations amongst themselves, the students, and their parents? Democratic teachers' oppositional agency eventually reworks and reinvents official policy through a popular political project constituting a new kind of social subject. Street ultimately defines dissident teachers as producers of alternative policy.

Like the chapter by Murtadha-Watts, Pamela Quiroz's study of bilingual science teachers in Chapter 7 shows educators situated in conflicting demands of school policy and student needs. It is a story of eight language minority teachers who struggle to interpret and translate competing school policies within different school contexts while negotiating the demands made by their variegated student populations. Ultimately, the framework of a science education reform initiative enables them to create a niche within which they are able to access additional resources to augment their teaching practices and philosophies. Thus, this case study, like those that precede it, shows teachers as agents of change, generating a different vision of science and of schooling, with students at the center of this vision.

In contrast, the practices and perspectives of the Brazilian health educators studied by Isabela Cabral Félix de Sousa, in Chapter 8, constrain a meaningful sharing of knowledge about health between educators and their clients. Although the overarching policies that frame reproductive health education in Brazil call for the empowerment of learners and their treatment as autonomous beings, the myths that inform health educators' practices effectively block any appropriation by educators of an empowering approach. The structural conditions for the delivery of health education—in classes, with a fixed curriculum—reinforce a traditionalist pedagogy that ill serves its clients. Cabral Félix de Sousa's analysis suggests that a significant intervention into improved health education might begin by engaging the basic beliefs and attitudes of health educators.

In Part III, the perspective shifts again, cutting across institutional roles and settings to illuminate the active construction of meanings around education by actors in differing positions of power and authority. In Chapter 9, Sandra Cade studies the impact of disparate life histories and worldviews on the provision of education for new Latino immigrants in a small midwestern U.S. town. Her emphasis on one boy's ambivalent resistance to becoming "acquired by school failure" (cf. Varenne & McDermott, 1999) illuminates localized practices of policy formation. When Luis refuses to attend school, he creates a crisis for school authorities, who cannot easily abide his failure—despite their inability to meet his learning needs. The de facto existence of a policy of "no grade retention" gets appropriated in the reluctant negotiations between Luis's principal and his father over the issue of attendance, and, as Cade argues, the result is far from satisfactory.

The next chapter takes a different perspective on failure: that of an educational system that is failing its students, the Aboriginal citizens of Australia. R. G. (Jerry) Schwab explores the interaction of Australian Aboriginal people with the Western system of education in the remote community of Maningrida. In his study of the community school, he describes low levels of student performance, unwillingness by parents to enforce attendance, the government's inadequate provision of secondary or adult education opportunities, and the school's incapacity to somehow find and enact solutions to these problems. There is, against this backdrop, an extremely high level of concern about education throughout the community, and many people feel something is deeply and frustratingly wrong. That concern is manifest in the frequent use by Aboriginal and non-Aboriginal people in the community of terms such as "dysfunction," "decline," and educational "failure." But Schwab shows how assessing the success or failure of education in Maningrida according to state-defined performance measures such as student attendance, retention, and national performance tests masks some subtle and important processes. Instead, he focuses on the school's role in facilitating the acquisition of higher-level cross-cultural skills, conserving and reaffirming elements of traditional culture, and providing access to a range of vital economic and social resources. In his study, Schwab shows how Aboriginal people in Maningrida appropriate Western educational policy components and effectively create their own educational "policy," which they use to steer education toward their own particular ends.

Maureen Porter, in Chapter 11, looks at what happens in one community that has been declared, like similar small mountain towns in Kentucky, to be failing in its provision of education. The Kentucky Education Reform Act (KERA) called for massive restructuring of educational decision making, granting greater decision-making authority to the school and community level. As Porter shows, the appropriation of new authorities and approaches takes place within a cultural context shaped by local norms. She found that the local educators who emerged as leaders in the process were those who could successfully formulate their beliefs and actions in terms of the "origin myth" of the mountains.

The final chapter in this collection takes us back to the beginning, in a discussion of how certain questions become significant in policy processes. In a lively discussion of a California school board's review of curriculum policy, Lisa Rosen reveals the negotiations of local educational politics and their salience in framing policy debates. This is a process both similar to and different from the compression of issues that takes place within the halls of authoritative policymaking. Unfolding within democratic institutions, it is a messier process, but one that results nonetheless in exclusion of alternative definitions of problems. Drawing from theories in political anthropology, Rosen shows how authority is constructed in a public space and how this construction denies consideration of alternative perspectives and interests. She analyzes the creation and use of explanatory tales in education as a form of modern myth making, and demonstrates the relationship of these "myths" to cherished cultural ideals about education. The analysis also sheds some light on how, through cultural processes involving competitive storytelling, the narrower concerns of particular interest groups are transformed into "public problems" considered worthy of attention and redress. Rosen ultimately demonstrates how policies help to construct the very problems to which they are addressed. Those with the power to make local education policy collude in processes of myth making that result in the ratification of an existing policy, on the one hand, and the validation of a particular set of assumptions about education and achievement, on the other.

BEYOND CRITIQUE: ACTIONABLE KNOWLEDGE FOR POLICY DEMOCRATIZATION

Too often, research inspired by critical theory ignores the inescapable need for administrative techniques in modern societies. It is easier, and far too tempting, to raise a critique without venturing into the messy business of policy formation. We believe that the studies compiled in this volume suggest and illustrate ways in which critically informed, sociocultural policy studies can contribute to more democratic processes of educational policymaking. Spanning several continents, disciplines, and forms of education, these articles nonetheless pick up common threads in their analyses of policy formation and appropriation. Sociocultural approaches to policy formation and appropriation promise to expand and deepen understanding of policy processes and how they impinge upon the daily lives of diverse people. Underlying the theoretical agenda of opening up policy analysis to sociocultural constructs lies a pragmatic concern with contributing to improvements in educational policy. Authoritative state policy is likely to remain, for some time, a strong force defining educational experiences for children and adults around the world. Those who seek to understand the meaning and import of educational policy seek at the same time to inform it, as citizens and as professionals. By way of conclusion, this section lays out five ways in which sociocultural studies might contribute to democratizing policy processes.

In comparison to the average citizen, policy researchers are (relatively) privileged interlocutors in the process of policy formation. Although knowledge utilization research, as we previously noted, shows that research studies have only modest influence on policy formation, policy researchers often have access to the ears of policy designers. Sociocultural research into policy formation and appropriation can bring to light the diverse interests and perspectives of students, parents, teachers, local administrators, and others who shape and are shaped by policy processes. Being mindful of the dangers of speaking for others, policy researchers nonetheless are in a position to raise awareness in the policy formation process of the multiple sites in which policy manifests, as well as the multiple meanings that governing policy may acquire in daily practice. This point is illustrated throughout the volume, from Anderson-Levitt and Alimasi's explication of differences in pedagogical ideals for reading instruction, to Murtadha-Watts's and Quiroz's analyses of selective appropriation of conflicting policy mandates by educators, to Schwab's elucidation of the conflicting normative regimes in Aboriginal education.

In a related vein, policy research can be more or less well informed by the perspectives of its subjects. In the process of informing policymakers, policy researchers can construct research in ways that facilitate the voicing of concerns by those whom policy will affect. Participatory research methods, for example, are an effort to privilege the voices of subjects by providing a platform for subjects to define issues as they see them. In this volume, Street's long-term involvement as a researcher with teachers' unions provides one clear example of mutual engagement between researchers and "subjects" in the policy research process. Porter's reflections upon her efforts to construct participatory research illustrate some of the difficulties attendant upon such approaches. Through these and related techniques, and by providing a forum for the expression of the needs and interests of policy constituents, sociocultural policy research can contribute a counterbalance to managerial perspectives on policy (cf. Dryzek, 1987; Fitz, Haplin, & Power, 1994).

Cultural and critical perspectives on policy processes can also challenge fundamental assumptions behind specific policies. Adams and colleagues, for example, challenge researchers and policymakers to think more explicitly about the nature of their relationship and its consequences for policy formation. Sutton critiques the epistemological regime of policy studies, asking whether the current operational structures and procedures can be modified to accommodate more democratic purposes. Rosen's study of the debate processes of a California school board uncovers practices of silencing in public deliberation, which undermine free and open debate. Studies of appropriation in general can be a lever against unexamined assumptions in policy formation, because they show how policy in practice differs from policy as conceived authoritatively. The practices of research can put the researcher in a position of opening channels of communication among those who participate in different moments of policy formation and appropriation. Porter, Cade, and Schwab all speak of ways in which their presence as researchers created new and different venues for communication among and between parents and students, on the one hand, and teachers and educational authorities on the other (cf. Blackmore, 1995). Perhaps ironically, the nature of researchers as always in some sense outsiders—to the communities they study as well as to the policymaking process—provides a kind of cultural permission to initiate unprecedented meetings of people and ideas. Such possibilities should be maximized.

The final point is one that by definition will not be demonstrated by research studies, but rather by what researchers choose *not* to study. Democratization of policy processes calls for a retreat from purely technocratic, top-down approaches. In some cases, the best thing a researcher may contribute to democratizing policymaking is to advocate consultative alternatives to research. Such alternatives may in the end be more cumbersome or time consuming, but they will always be more effective in yielding beneficial and broadly endorsed outcomes.

NOTES

1. Practice has been articulated as a powerful heuristic corrective to the cultural and economic *determinisms* (which accorded little agency to individual actors and little power to historical-cultural particularity) and *voluntarisms* (which accorded little power to patterned social forces in constraining or enabling individual action) dominating the social sciences of this century. An emphasis on practice—what Giddens (1984) calls "strategic conduct" (p. 288)—has, moreover, challenged the reductive tendencies of materialism and idealism. Among the most prominent practice theorists have been the sociologists Pierre Bourdieu (1977, 1989, 1990), Bourdieu & Wacquant (1997), Anthony Giddens (1979, 1984), and R.W. Connell (1983, 1987). Bourdieu is the scholar who has most self-consciously undertaken to construct a general "theory of practices," and who uses the term most frequently. Similar and perhaps equally important theorists of practice for us would include Philip Abrams (1982), Norbert Elias (1978, 1991; Goudsblom & Mennell, 1998), Marshall Sahlins (1981, 1985), Mary Douglas (1975), Sherry Ortner (1984, 1996), Stuart Hall (1990; Grossberg, 1996), Michel de Certeau (1984), and Zygmunt Bauman (1973, 1992). Bourdieu, Connell, and Ortner provide the most helpful and explicit discussions of the methodological options entailed by practice theory.

2. The meaning of "appropriation" has links to practice theory as it has emerged in critical fields of scholarship like sociology (Corsaro, 1993), cultural studies (Johnson, 1986–87; Walser, 1997), social history (Chartier, 1997), and cultural anthropology (Gupta & Ferguson, 1997; Rockwell, 1996). The use of appropriation signals an active process of cultural production through borrowing, recontextualizing, remolding, and thereby resignifying cultural forms such as language, music, and dress. The appropriation of educational policy emphasizes the agency of local actors in interpreting and adapting such policy to the situated logic in their contexts of everyday practice.

3. Even informal educational practices outside schools may constitute "policies" based on alternative value systems or models of the "educated person" (Levinson et al., 1996).

REFERENCES

Abrams, P. (1982). *Historical sociology*. London: Routledge.

Apter, D. (1974). The role of the new scientific elite and scientific ideology in modernization. In S. P. Restivol & C. R. Vanderpool (Eds.), *Comparative studies in science and society* (pp. 398–408). Columbus, OH: Merrill.

Ball, S. J. (1990). *Politics and policy making in education*. London: Routledge.

Bauman, Z. (1973). *Culture as praxis*. London: Routledge and Kegan Paul.

Bauman, Z. (1992). *Intimations of postmodernity*. London: Routledge.

Bhola, H. S. (1975). The design of (educational) policy: Directing and harnessing social power for social organization. *Viewpoints: Bulletin of the School of Education, Indiana University, 51*(3), 1–16.

Blackmore, J. (1995). Policy as dialogue: Feminist administrators working for educational change. *Gender and Education, 7*(3), 293–314.

Bobrow, D. B., & Dryzek, J. S. (1987). *Policy analysis by design*. Pittsburgh, PA: University of Pittsburgh Press.

Böhme, G., & Stehr, N. (1986). The growing impact of scientific knowledge on social relations. In G. Böhme & N. Stehr (Eds.), *The knowledge society* (pp.
  7–30). Dordrecht, Netherlands: D. Rekiel.
Borman, K., Cookson, P., Sadovnik, A., & Spade, J. (Eds.). (1996). *Implementing
  educational reform: Sociological perspectives on educational policy.* Norwood,
  NJ: Ablex.
Bourdieu, P. (1977). *Outline of a theory of practice.* Cambridge, UK: Cambridge Uni-
  versity Press.
Bourdieu, P. (1989). *Language and symbolic power.* Stanford, CA: Stanford Univer-
  sity Press.
Bourdieu, P. (1990). *The logic of practice.* Stanford, CA: Stanford University Press.
Bourdieu, P. (1991). *Language and symbolic power.* Stanford, CA: Stanford Univer-
  sity Press.
Bourdieu, P., & Wacquant, L. (1992). The purpose of reflexive sociology. In P.
  Bourdieu & L. Wacquant (Eds.), *An invitation to reflexive sociology* (pp.
  61–216). Cambridge, UK: Polity Press.
Bowe, R., Ball, S. J., & Gold, A. (1992). *Reforming education and changing schools :
  Case studies in policy sociology.* London and New York: Routledge.
Burstein, B. (1991). Policy domains: Organization, culture, and policy outcomes.
  Annual Review of Sociology, 17, 327–350.
Burstein, B., & Bricher, M. (1997). Problem definition public policy: Congressional
  committees confront work, family, and gender, 1945–1990. *Social Forces,
  76*(1), 135–169.
Calhoun, C. (1995). *Critical social theory.* London: Blackwell.
Chartier, R. (1997). *On the edge of the cliff.* Baltimore: Johns Hopkins University
  Press.
Chock Pease, P. (1991). "Illegal aliens" and "opportunity": Myth making in congres-
  sional testimony. *American Ethnologist, 18*(2), 279–294.
Chock Pease, P. (1998). Porous borders: Discourses of difference in congressional
  hearings on immigration. In C. Greenhouse (Ed.), *Democracy and ethnog-
  raphy: Constructing identities in multicultural liberal states* (pp. 143–162).
  Albany, NY: SUNY Press.
Cohen, D., & Spillane, J. (1993). Policy and practice: The relations between gover-
  nance and instruction. In S. Fuhrman (Ed.), *Designing coherent educational
  policy* (pp. 35–95). San Francisco: Jossey-Bass.
Collins, P. H. (1990). *Black feminist thought: Knowledge, consciousness, and the politics
  of empowerment.* Boston: Unwin Hyman.
Connell, R. W. (1983). *Which way is up?: Essays on class, sex, and culture.* London: Al-
  len and Unwin.
Connell, R.W. (1987). *Gender and power: Society, the person, and sexual politics.* Stanford, CA: Stanford University Press.
Corsaro, W. (1993). Interpretive reproduction in children's role play. *Childhood, 1,*
  64–74.
de Certeau, M. (1984). *The practice of everyday life.* Berkeley: University of California
  Press.
Douglas, M. (1975). *Implicit meanings.* London: Routledge.
Douglas, M. (1986). *How institutions think.* Syracuse, NY: Syracuse University Press.

Dryzek, J. S. (1987). Discursive designs: Critical theory and political institutions. *The American Journal of Political Science, 31*(3), 656–679.

Eagleton, T. (1991). *Ideology: An introduction.* London: Verso.

Eisemon, T. O. (1981). Scientific life in Indian and African universities: A comparative study of peripherality in science. *Comparative Education Review,* pp. 164–182.

Elias, N. (1978). *The civilizing process, Vol. 1: The history of manners.* New York: Urizen Books.

Elias, N. (1991). *The society of individuals.* Oxford, UK: Blackwell.

Elmore, R. F., McLaughlin, M. W., Rand Corporation, & National Institute of Education. (1988). *Steady work: Policy, practice, and the reform of American education.* Santa Monica, CA: Rand.

Escobar, A. (1995). *Encountering development: The making and unmaking of the Third World.* Princeton, NJ: Princeton University Press.

Ferguson, J. (1994). *The anti-politics machine: "Development," depoliticization, and bureaucratic power in Lesotho.* Minneapolis: University of Minnesota Press.

Fitz, J., Haplin, D., & Power, S. (1994). Implementation research and education policy: Practice and prospects. *British Journal of Educational Studies, 42*(1), 53–69.

Foucault, M. (1971). *The order of things: An archaeology of the human sciences.* New York: Pantheon Books.

Foucault, M. (1972). *The archaeology of knowledge.* New York: Pantheon Books.

Foucault, M. (1979). *Discipline and punish: The birth of the prison.* New York: Vintage Books.

Fuhrman, S. (1993). The politics of coherence. In S. Fuhrman (Ed.), *Designing coherent educational policy* (pp. 1–34). San Francisco: Jossey-Bass.

Giddens, A. (1979). *Central problems in social theory: Action, structure and contradiction in social analysis.* Berkeley: University of California Press.

Giddens, A. (1984). *The constitution of society.* Berkeley: University of California Press.

Goudsblom, J., & Mennell, S. (Eds.). (1998). *The Norbert Elias reader.* Oxford, UK: Blackwell.

Greenhouse, C. (Ed.). (1998). *Democracy and ethnography: Constructing identities in multicultural liberal states.* Albany, NY: SUNY Press.

Greenhouse, C. & Greenwood, D. (1998). Introduction: The ethnography of democracy and difference. In C. Greenhouse (Ed.), *Democracy and ethnography: Constructing identities in multicultural liberal states* (pp. 1–24). Albany, NY: SUNY Press.

Grossberg, L. (1996). History, politics and postmodernism: Stuart Hall and cultural studies. In D. Morley & C. Kuan-Hsing (Eds.), *Stuart Hall: Critical dialogues in cultural studies* (pp. 151–173). London: Routledge.

Gupta, A., & Ferguson, J. (Eds.). (1997). *Culture, power, place.* Durham, NC: Duke University Press.

Habermas, J. (1984). *The theory of communicative action* (Vol. 1). Boston: Beacon Press.

Hall, S. (1990). Cultural identity and diaspora. In J. Rutherford (Ed.), *Identity, community, culture, difference* (pp. 222–237). London: Lawrence and Wishart.

Harding, S. G. (1987). *Feminism and methodology: Social science issues.* Bloomington: Indiana University Press.

Hill, M. (Ed.). (1993). *New agendas in the study of the policy process.* New York: Harvester.

Johnson, R. (1986–87). What is cultural studies anyway? *Social Text, 6* (1), 38–80.

Knorr-Cetina, K., & Mulkay, M. (Eds.). (1983). *Science observed: Perspectives on the social study of science.* London: Sage.

Lasswell, H. D. (1951). The policy orientation. In D. Lerner & H. Lasswell (Eds.), *The policy sciences* (pp. 3–15). Stanford, CA: Stanford University Press.

Levinson, B. (Ed.). (2000). *Schooling the symbolic animal: Social and cultural dimensions of education.* Lanham, MD: Rowman and Littlefield.

Levinson, B., Foley, D., & Holland, D. (Eds.). (1996). *The cultural production of the educated person: Critical ethnographies of schooling and local practice.* Albany, NY: SUNY Press.

Lewis, D., & Wallace, H. (Eds.). (1984). *Policies into practice: National and international case studies in implementation.* New York: St. Martin's Press.

Marcus, G. (1998). *Ethnography through thick and thin.* Princeton, NJ: Princeton University Press.

Marshall, C. (Ed.). (1997). *Feminist critical policy analysis: A perspective from primary and secondary schooling.* London: Falmer.

McGinn, N., & Street, S. (1982). Has Mexican education generated human or political capital? *Comparative Education, 20*(3), 323–338.

McGinn, N., & Street, S. (1984). The political rationality of resource allocation in Mexican public education. *Comparative Education Review, 10,* 178–198.

McLaughlin, M. W. (1975). *Evaluation and reform : The Elementary and Secondary Education Act of 1965, Title I.* Cambridge, MA: Ballinger.

McLaughlin, M., & Talbert, J. (1993). How the world of students and teachers challenges policy coherence. In S. Fuhrman (Ed.), *Designing coherent educational policy* (pp. 220–249). San Francisco: Jossey-Bass.

Mohanty, C. T. (1991). Under Western eyes: Feminist scholarship and colonial discourses. In C. T. Mohanty, A. Russo, & L. Torres (Eds.), *Third World women and the politics of feminism* (pp. 51–60). Bloomington: Indiana University Press.

Mueller, A. (1986). The bureaucratization of feminist knowledge: The case of women in development. *Resources for Feminist Research, 15*(1), 36–38.

Odden, A. (Ed.). (1991). *Education policy implementation.* Albany, NY: SUNY Press.

Ortner, S. B. (1984). Theory in anthropology since the sixties. *Comparative Studies in Society and History, 26,* 126–166.

Ortner, S. B. (1996). *Making gender: The politics and erotics of culture.* Boston: Beacon Press.

Ortner, S. (1997). Fieldwork in the postcommunity. *Anthropology and Humanism, 22* (1), 61–80.

Pigg, S. L. (1992). Inventing social categories through place: Social representations and development in Nepal. *Comparative Studies in Society & History, 34*(3), 491–522.

Popkewitz, T. S. (1991). *A political sociology of educational reform.* New York: Teachers College Press.

Porter, R. W., and Hicks, I. (1995). *Knowledge utilization and the process of policy formation: Toward a framework for Africa.* Washington, DC: Academy for Educational Development SARA Project.

Povinelli, E. A. (1991). Organizing women: Rhetoric, economy, and politics in process. In M. Di Leonardo (Ed.), *Gender at the crossroads of knowledge: Feminist anthropology in the postmodern era* (pp. 235–254). Berkeley: University of California Press.

Pressman, J. L., Wildavsky, A. B., & Oakland Project. (1973). *Implementation: How great expectations in Washington are dashed in Oakland; or, Why it's amazing that federal programs work at all, this being a saga of the Economic Development Administration as told by two sympathetic observers who seek to build morals on a foundation of ruined hopes.* Berkeley: University of California Press.

Psacharopoulos, G., & Woodhall, M. (1985). *Education for development: An analysis of investment choices.* New York: Oxford University Press.

Reimers, F., & McGinn, N. (1997). *Informed dialogue: Using research to shape education around the world.* Westport, CT: Praeger.

Rockwell, E. (1996). Keys to appropriation: Rural schools in Mexico. In B. Levinson, D. Foley, & D. Holland (Eds.), *The cultural production of the educated person* (pp. 301–324). Albany, NY: SUNY Press.

Sahlins, M. (1981). *Historical metaphors and mythical realities: Structure in the early history of the Sandwich Islands Kingdom.* Ann Arbor: University of Michigan Press.

Sahlins, M. (1985). *Islands of history.* Chicago: University of Chicago Press.

Shore, C., & Wright, S. (Eds.). (1997). *Anthropology of policy: Critical perspectives on governance and power.* London: Routledge.

Smith, D. (1987). *The everyday world as problematic.* Toronto: University of Toronto Press.

Sutton, M. (1998). Feminist epistemology and research methods. In N. P. Stromquist (Ed.), *Women in the Third World : An encyclopedia of contemporary issues* (pp. 13–23). New York: Garland.

Thompson, J. B. (1990). *Ideology and Modern Culture.* Stanford, CA: Stanford University Press.

Tyack, D. B. (1974). *The one best system: A history of American urban education.* Cambridge, MA: Harvard University Press.

Varenne, H., and McDermott, R. (1999). *Successful failure: The school America builds.* Boulder, CO: Westview Press.

Walser, R. (1997). Eruptions: Heavy-metal appropriations of classical virtuosity. In K. Gelder & S. Thornton (Eds.), *The subcultures reader* (pp. 459–470). London: Routledge.

Walsh, C. E. (1996). *Education reform and social change: Multicultural voices, struggles, and visions.* Mahwah, NJ: Erlbaum.

Weiss, C. H. (1982). Policy research in the context of diffuse decision making. *The Journal of Higher Education, 53*(6), 619–639.

Wells, A., & Serna, I. (1996). The politics of culture: Understanding local political resistance to detracking in racially mixed schools. *Harvard Educational Review, 66*(1), 93–118.

Wildavsky, A. B. (1979). *Speaking truth to power: The art and craft of policy analysis.* Boston: Little, Brown.

Wolcott, H. (1999). *Ethnography: A way of seeing.* Thousand Oaks, CA: Sage.

Wright, S. (1994). "Culture" in anthropology and organizational studies. In S. Wright (Ed.), *Anthropology of organizations* (pp. 1–31). London and New York: Routledge.

PART I

GLOBAL AND NATION-STATE POLICY PROCESSES: SOCIOCULTURAL STUDIES

1

Are Pedagogical Ideals Embraced or Imposed? The Case of Reading Instruction in the Republic of Guinea

Kathryn M. Anderson-Levitt and
Ntal-I'Mbirwa Alimasi

Sounds like Derrida

This chapter examines ideals of "best practice" or "good teaching," notions that are either explicitly or implicitly built into educational policy decisions.[1] We begin from the premise that pedagogical ideals represent cultural and social constructions, not the simple discovery of scientific truth. What people consider "good teaching" has varied over time and from country to country. For instance, the ideal that students should "pay attention" (Vincent, 1980) or the ideal that children should "participate" in class (Cuban, 1993; Vincent, 1980) entered received knowledge at distinct historical moments. The lecture/recitation method now considered "backward" has actually proven very effective in the right contexts (Delpit, 1986; Noblit, 1993; see also Baker, 1997; Wagner, 1993). Today, ability grouping is falling under attack in the United States just when France embraces it for the first time (Anderson-Levitt, in press).

But, if pedagogical ideals are culturally constructed, who constructs them, and when, where, and how? Where do notions of good teaching come from and how do people respond when they encounter a new notion? Within the comparative sociology of education, two grand theories offer answers to these questions. On the one hand, John Meyer and his colleagues argue that ideals belong to a global culture of "modern" schooling that flows across national boundaries (see, e.g., Meyer, Kamens, & Benavot, 1992). Originally the ideals moved from one European nation to another; now they flow from the "West" to the "rest." According to this "cultural ideology" argument, countries adopt

cultural ideals of "modern" schooling as part of the process of defining themselves as modern nation-states (see, e.g., Ramirez & Boli, 1987; Ramirez &
Ventresca, 1992). Local educational elites—in Botswana, for instance—pick
and choose from "themes of modern world educational discourse," which are
"packaged as general truths" (Meyer, Nagel, & Snyder, 1993, p. 467). Like
the "modernist" perspective that preceded it, the cultural ideology perspective
posits that countries embrace foreign ideals willingly. However, the cultural
ideology approach does not take for granted that imported ideals really are
more rational, efficient, and modern, as a "modernist" perspective would assume. The former approach assumes only that the borrowers *perceive* the imported ideals to be modern.

On the other hand, scholars who emphasize global conflict take issue with
the claim that, in today's world, countries embrace foreign ideals willingly.
Mark Ginsburg and his colleagues point out that it is naive to ignore the asym-
metrical power relationships within which such borrowing occurs (Ginsburg,
Cooper, Raghu, & Zegarra, 1991; see also Jones, 1992; Nagel & Snyder,
1989). They argue that countries adopt Western ideals under economic pressure from more dominant countries and from international organizations like
the International Monetary Fund and the World Bank.

Despite their differences on the important question of autonomy in adoption of Western ideals, both global theories beg two critical questions: What,
in fact, are "Western" ideals, and what does it mean for non-Western
policymakers to "adopt" them? Whether the macro-comparative theorists see
change as voluntary or coerced, they have not taken a close look at the actual
process by which pedagogical ideals get negotiated. Even the best studies of
changing pedagogical ideals in the West (see, e.g., Cuban, 1993; Vincent,
1980) track the changes through historical documents, not in live interaction.
Because scholars on both sides of the debate rarely look inside Ministries of
Education and never look inside classrooms, they miss the complexity of the
global flow of ideas and the contradictions among messages coming from outside.[2]

We have taken a closer look at what it means for educational concepts to be
adopted outside their place of origin, and specifically within a "developing
country," through a case study of the Republic of Guinea in West Africa. In
Guinea, we have focused on pedagogical ideals for instruction in reading and
language arts in the early grades. Guinea is a country making massive changes
to its educational system with the participation of many international donors.
What intrigues us about educational reform in Guinea is not what actually
works, a question we leave to Guinean educators. Rather, we are trying to understand how certain ideals of reading instruction, such as the "mixed
method" or the notion of teachers' professional autonomy, get defined as
good practice. We use the case of pedagogical ideals for early reading instruction in Guinea to ask the following questions: Which "Western" ideals play
into policy decisions? How do Guinean decision makers make use of "West-

ern" ideals? Do Guineans embrace foreign ideals voluntarily, do foreign donors impose them, or do we need a more complex model to describe what
happens?

After explaining our research methods, we will set the scene in Guinea and
identify the various actors involved, at one level or another, in negotiating
what counts as good reading instruction. We will also clarify what we mean by
"foreign" ideals in the context of an educational system originally imported
from outside Guinea. Then, we will show that the Guinean elite had occasion
and motivation for embracing foreign ideals willingly, but will also raise doubts
about how deeply Guineans accepted certain ideals. We will turn to evidence of
the donors' clear economic power over Guinean decision makers, but will also
illustrate the Guineans' far-from-passive responses to that power. Finally, we
will use the debates provoked by new language arts textbooks to illustrate how
difficult it becomes to distinguish purely strategic mastery of Western notions
from true appropriation of the ideals.

This chapter draws on a preliminary analysis of interviews and participant
observation conducted in the United States, France, and Guinea from November 1997 through November 1998. Our understanding of the points of
view of Guinean educational officials comes from several months of participant observation as well as many interviews and conversations. Anderson-Levitt was hosted by INRAP, the national Pedagogic Institute, from late
March through June and from late September through mid-November of
1998.[3] Alimasi spent the month of May in offices of the Ministry of Education.[4] Between them, Anderson-Levitt and Alimasi interviewed 34 staff members of the Guinean Ministry of Education and Pedagogic Institute (32 men
and 2 women), as well as two members of the Pedagogic Institute of Mali. Anderson-Levitt and Guinean sociologist Boubacar Bayero Diallo also observed
high-level educational officials and teacher educators in interaction with
teacher trainers and supervisors at two different seminars for the training of
teacher trainers, one of which is described here.

Although this chapter focuses mainly on the viewpoints of high-level officials, it is also informed by interviews and participant-observation with
Guinean supervisors and teachers. Anderson-Levitt, Alimasi, and Diallo interviewed 21 teacher educators and supervisors (19 men and 2 women), 10
school directors (6 men and 4 women), and 29 regular teachers (16 men and
13 women). Along with Sadialiou Barry of the Pedagogic Institute, Diallo and
Anderson-Levitt conducted classroom observations ranging from a half day to
five days in each class. We visited 21 different classes in 11 different schools in
the capital of Conakry, in three provincial towns, and in two rural villages.

Our understanding of donors' perspectives comes from interviews conducted by Anderson-Levitt in all three countries as well as observation of donor officers and technical advisors on the job in Guinea. Anderson-Levitt
interviewed 30 people (14 men and 16 women representing six different nationalities, including two African nationalities) at the international level—

educational officers and technical consultants working for the World Bank, the United States Agency for International Development (USAID), the Peace Corps, the French Ministry of Cooperation, French publishing houses, and nonprofit consulting agencies. In addition, Anderson-Levitt and Alimasi observed two coordinating meetings among the international donors in Conakry.

Throughout the chapter, we seek to protect the identity of our informants by keeping the quotations as anonymous as possible. In the case of donors and Ministry officials, we have tried to avoid mentioning gender or even nationality where it was not relevant. We hope this anonymous presentation does not give you the impression that we were talking with "faceless bureaucrats"; these were, in fact, fascinating men and women.

ACTORS AND IDEALS IN GUINEA

We chose to work in Guinea because the country is in the midst of a literacy revolution. Guinea is one of the least schooled countries in the world (World Bank, 1987, 1994), but the number of children attending its 3,500 primary schools has been rising dramatically. In 1991, just 31.8 % of an age cohort was attending primary school (44.4% of boys and 19.6% of girls). By 1997, the figure had risen to 50.5% (66.0% of boys and 35.5% of girls) (SSP, 1997), and the Ministry intends to push the attendance rate to 100% as soon as possible.

Guinean teachers operate under extremely difficult conditions. We have seen a teacher in a huge school on double sessions in Conakry facing nearly 120 first graders who spoke a variety of maternal languages. Another teacher we visited in a rural village stood before a combined second- and fourth-grade class in which the 51 students spoke only the local language at home. These teachers had blackboards and many of the children had notebooks, but until the arrival of new reading texts during our fieldwork, books had become exceedingly scarce. Yet the first and second graders had to learn to read and write—in French.

Under such difficult circumstances, you might mistakenly infer that specific teaching methods were beside the point. Yet Guinean educators were actively discussing and promoting ideals of good pedagogy. For instance, we heard both the elite and supervisors and teachers advocating "student-centered instruction" (*l'apprentissage centré sur l'apprenant*) and "active learning" (*la pédagogie active*). Elites raised the question of how much repetition and memorization was appropriate. Regarding our particular interest in language and reading, the Ministry of Education and its Pedagogic Institute were actively discouraging the "syllabic" (phonics-based) approach to reading instruction and encouraging a "semi-global" (mixed) method that combined reading for meaning with phonics (see, e.g., Diallo, 1993). The Institute had produced its own textbooks for reading instruction in first and second grades (IPN, 1992, 1994), and was completing revisions of their second editions during our fieldwork.

Actors

When you move from grand theory to the real situation in a particular country, simple categories like "Guineans" and "international donors" immediately break down into a complex array of actors. Before we can explain what it meant for Guineans to adopt ideals from outside, we must explain which Guinean actors were involved, at what levels, in negotiating what counts as good reading instruction. Likewise, we must clarify what we mean by "international donors."

We would like to underline from the start that both Guinean and international actors were people of good will. Everyone we spoke with had the interest of Guinea and its school children at heart as far as we could tell, whatever other personal or career motivations they might have felt as well (cf. Kaufmann, 1997). Complications arose, however, because not everyone defined the interest of Guinea and its school children in the same way.

Guinean Educational Elites

We will use the term "national educational elites" to refer to decision makers and educational experts in the Ministry of Education and affiliated institutions who participated in setting policy at the national level. The elites included the Directeur National de l'Enseignement Élémentaire (National Director of Elementary Education) and his staff, the Inspector General of Education and his assistants, and the eight Regional Inspectors (IRE, or Inspecteurs Régionaux de l'Éducation) who supervised Ministry policy in each region of the country (Table 1.1).[5] National elites also included the director and staff of INRAP, the Pedagogic Institute, which employed about 100 technical staff members to develop curriculum and teaching materials and to oversee continuing education of teachers for use of the new materials. In general, educational elites had begun their careers as teachers, usually as secondary school professors and in some cases as university professors, before rising in the administrative and technical hierarchy. Many had earned master's degrees and several held doctorates in the natural or behavioral sciences.

Guinean Supervisors and Trainers

A second layer of educational personnel mediated between the national elites and teachers. This second layer, glossed as "supervisors" in this chapter, included preservice teacher educators, the professors of Guinea's regional teacher-training institutions (Écoles Normales d'Instituteurs). More importantly for our purposes, it included a diverse group that Guineans sometimes referred to as *inspecteurs* (inspectors) or *le corps de contrôle* (the supervising corps). The supervising corps included Prefectural Directors of Education,

Table 1.1
Guinean Actors

National Educational Elites	• Ministry of Education, especially the National Director of Elementary Education and his assistants • Affiliated Institutions such as INRAP and the Statistical & Planning Section • Regional Inspectors of Education (IREs)
Supervisors	• Prefectural Directors of Education (DPEs) • Prefectural Directors of Elementary Education • Sub-Prefectural Directors of Pedagogy • Professors of Teacher Education (PENs) • Pedagogical Counselors (CPMFs) • Veteran teachers used informally as inspectors
Teachers	• School directors • Other civil-service teachers • Contractors (*contractuels*)

who had earned the official title of Inspector through training at a regional institution in Dakar. However, supervisors also included other personnel who, although not bearing the official title of "inspector," often assisted in the task of inspecting teachers. These supervisors included the Prefectural Director's assistants, pedagogical counselors (Conseillers Pédagogiques-Maîtres Formateurs or CPMF), and even veteran teachers (*maîtres chêvronnés*).

Guinean Teachers

The third layer of actors were school directors and classroom teachers. These were the people who actually determined what reading instruction looked like by following their own norms for good (or at least adequate) practice. In smaller schools, directors taught part-time or full-time, and all directors had the responsibility of signing off daily on the other teachers' written lesson plans.

International Donors Per Se

Asking who the international actors are turned out to be as complicated as asking who the Guinean decision makers are (Table 1.2). Donor agencies in-

Table 1.2
Donors and Technical Advisors in Guinea

Donors per se		Technical advisors	
global organizations	World Bank UNESCO UNPD (United Nations Program for Development) etc.	U.S. universities Canadian universities French universities etc.	**universities**
multinational organizations	European Union African Development Bank ACCT (Agence de la Coopération Culturelle et Technique) etc.	Washington-based consulting firms French-based consulting firms Canadian-based consulting firms Independent consultants etc.	**consulting firms & independent consultants**
arms of national governments	USAID U.S. Peace Corps Canadian Agency for International Development (ACDI) Coopération Française German Technical Assistance (GTZ) Japanese (JICA) etc.	Civil servants working for the French Ministry of Education	**civil servants**
NGOs (non-governmental organizations)	Save the Children World Education Aide et Action etc.	French publishers Belgian publishers Canadian publishers Ivoirian publishers etc.	**business corporations**

[Handwritten annotation: "wow so many layers" with an arrow]

cluded global organizations like UNESCO, UNICEF, and, most importantly
for our story, the World Bank. There were also regional and other multinational organizations such as the European Union (active in building schools in
Guinea), the African Development Bank, and Agence de la Coopération
Culturelle et Technique (ACCT), a multinational organization of
French-language nations. Donors also included the international aid arms of
national governments. Most significant here were USAID and "Coopération
Française," the French Ministry of Cooperation and Development.[6] However, the U.S. Peace Corps as well as the Canadian, German, and Japanese gov-
ernments also supported Guinean education in various ways.

When we talk about "donors," we really have in mind the educational officers of these donor agencies. The educational officers represented their respective agencies in negotiating and supervising loans, or grants for projects
involving Guinea's Ministry of Education. Many of the educational officers
had begun their careers as elementary or secondary school teachers; some had
become involved in international work through experiences like the Peace
Corps. Many now held master's degrees or doctorates in the educational sciences.

Technical Advisors and Other International Actors

Technical advisors from universities and private consulting firms were hired
by the donors' educational officers to advise them and to represent the donors
in the day-to-day work of collaborating with Guineans on particular projects.
For instance, USAID contracted work to a consulting firm that placed several
employees in Guinea for two years or more at a stretch. Most of France's
day-to-day work with Guineans was carried out by approximately 30 French
civil servants, employees of the French Ministry of Education, dispersed
throughout the country. These French advisors usually had begun their careers as elementary or secondary teachers in France. Some of the U.S. consultants had likewise begun their careers as teachers while others had entered
"development work" through other routes.

International actors including large and small non-governmental organizations (NGOs), such as Save the Children or the French-based Aide et Action,
also made contributions to Guinea's educational system. NGOs were invited
to coordinate their projects with governmental and global donors and some
subcontracted to carry out projects on behalf of donors. Finally, commercial
outfits—in this case, French publishing houses that produced textbooks for
the African market—played a role of particular interest to our research, serving
as supplemental sources of technical advice.

Inside or Outside?

Looking at this array of actors, you can see that any boundary between
Guinea and the rest of the world is a wide and nebulous zone. Being "inside"
or "outside" of Guinea was a matter of a degree, not an either-or proposition.

Most "inside" were those teachers and supervisors who had never traveled outside the country, although even they were exposed to foreign movies, television, and books. Many of the Guinean elite had often crossed the border for the sake of study abroad, as you will see. Meanwhile, many donors, too, were border crossers. Some of the foreign technical advisers spent months or even years collaborating with Guineans inside Guinea. Some consultants and some employees of donor agencies were Africans, even Guineans, themselves. Certain projects held an in-between status, financed by World Bank loans but officially run by the Government of Guinea.[7] The donor agencies themselves had one foot inside the country in the form of permanent staffs based in Guinea. In the case of USAID and the French Ministry of Cooperation, there were African education officers in Washington and Paris respectively, but also inside Guinea. Even the most "outside" of the outsiders, the donors based in their home countries, paid frequent visits to Guinea.

What "Ideals" Are We Talking About?

In the rest of the chapter, we will make reference to a number of specific ideals for good reading instruction. We focus on language arts and reading instruction because the Guineans themselves identified it as a high priority.[8] The ideals for reading instruction included a general philosophy on such issues as: What is the best language of instruction for beginners? Should teaching emphasize phonics or comprehension?

Events in Guinea led us to focus more specifically on ideals for the production of good textbooks in language arts and reading. As you will see, the country was in the process of adopting new textbooks, and this process provoked a great deal of discussion about what made for good textbooks. We should make clear that this chapter is *not* a case study of the actual adoption of the textbook. Rather, we are interested in the sources of various ideals that actors cited when talking about that adoption, as well as the uses to which they put those ideals. Ideals about the production or adoption of textbooks included answers to such questions as: How accessible and affordable should textbooks be? Ought they to be locally produced? Must broad learning objectives be redefined before new textbooks are produced?

The ideals we are examining also include specific criteria for evaluating textbooks, such as: What is the appropriate level of difficulty? Should textbook vocabulary be controlled and, if so, by what principles? In what sequence should sounds be introduced? What kinds of texts and exercises should be included? What makes for a well-illustrated textbook? What specifications ought the typeface follow? Is a detailed teacher's guide necessary?

Ideals, Not Practice

Keep in mind that this chapter considers only pedagogical "ideals," not practice. Concepts we mention, such as accessible textbooks or the ideal form of the mixed method, varied considerably from actual practice in some classrooms we visited. What a staff member of the Pedagogic Institute or a technical advisor contracting to USAID hoped to achieve in reading instruction might turn out to bear little resemblance to what actually happened in classrooms where the reforms got applied.

What Counts As "Foreign"

To ask "Are pedagogical ideals imposed or embraced?" implies that the ideals come from outside Guinea. That is a tricky assumption to make. On the one hand, it's true that the whole institution of formal schooling discussed here was introduced by the French and other Europeans during the missionary and colonial eras; in Guinea, people still refer to lay public schools as "French school." On the other hand, if people have eventually made the borrowed thing their own, is it still foreign? Not only may people lay claim to imported ideas as authentically their own (Sharrock, 1974, gives the example of baseball in different countries), but they may modify the introduced idea or reinterpret it in such a way that it becomes "indigenous" (see, e.g., Flinn, 1992). Hannerz (1987, 1992) makes the analogy to "creole" languages, which begin on the base of a borrowed tongue but become something new (see also Rogers, 1995, on "reinvention").

What people considered the "old-fashioned" or "traditional" way of teaching reading in Guinea reflected pedagogical ideals that had been imported in earlier decades, particularly from the colonial power of France. For instance, some teachers and most parents valued instruction in the French language, which had originally been imposed by French missionaries and then by French civil servants. Ironically, suggestions from World Bank and even French officials that Guinea consider conducting the earliest grades in local language represented a "foreign" ideal—and this even though Guinea had pioneered instruction in local languages during the previous regime (Bah-Lalya, 1991; Diallo, 1991). Only linguists and other experts who remembered the earlier experiments more positively than the general population were eager to consider new experiments with local-language instruction.

Similarly, the "syllabic" or phonics-based method represented the "traditional" Guinean way to teach reading. Again, the irony was that the textbook used in "the good old days" and still sold widely in the marketplace was a colonial-era text originally published in France (Davesne, 1950). Parents, a number of teachers, and quite a few supervisors looked to it with nostalgia.

Since mid-century or earlier, Guinean educators have made "French school" their own in some ways. Just as it was difficult to draw a sharp boundary between actors "inside" and "outside" Guinea, it could be misleading to try to distinguish "foreign" from "indigenous" ideals of good teaching within the formal school system.[9] It may be more useful to ask *when* an idea was introduced and what happened to it afterward. Therefore, in this chapter, when we write about the introduction of "foreign" ideals, we mean ideals relatively recently introduced to the Guinean educational scene and not (yet?) claimed by everyone there.

IDEALS EMBRACED?

Having set the scene and identified the kinds of pedagogical ideals we have in mind, we ask in the rest of the chapter how Guineans, particularly the Guinean elite, encountered and responded to "Western" ideals. First we consider what evidence we have that the elite willingly embraced foreign notions. It is difficult if not impossible to know with certainty what other people believe, particularly when fieldwork lasted only a few months, as ours did. However, we can cite two kinds of indirect evidence: the Guinean elites' multiple opportunities for exposure to "Western" ideals and their multiple motivations for adopting them voluntarily.

Exposure

Opportunities for study abroad had exposed many Guinean elites to the pedagogical ideals of one or more foreign countries. Experts at the Ministry and the Pedagogic Institute held master's degrees or, in some cases, doctorates, from France, the United States, Great Britain, Canada (that is, Quebec), Germany (the former East Germany), and the former Soviet Union. They had also taken shorter study tours to Morocco, Ivory Coast, the United States, Japan, and other countries. (Indeed, given Guineans' exposure to Japanese and eastern European ideas, it would be more appropriate to refer to the "North" rather than the "West" as the source of their borrowing. We keep the more familiar references to "Western" ideals simply because this chapter emphasizes influence from France and North America.) Even those who had pursued all of their studies inside Guinea had probably had occasion to work with professors from outside Guinea, and all of them had been exposed to Guinean professors who had had foreign training.

The experience of long-term collaboration with foreign technical advisors also made outside pedagogical ideals available to Guinean experts. For example, the first French-language textbook produced by Guinea, *Bonjour Fanta, Bonjour Fodé!* (IPN, 1983),[10] developed out of a collaboration between Guinean linguists from the Pedagogic Institute and two French linguists who had worked at the Pedagogic Institute in Guinea for some time. About 10 years later, when Guinea produced its own first- and second-grade readers, *Langage-Lecture* (Language-Reading), a different pair of French linguists collaborated on the development of the new text. In fact, one of the Guinean authors of *Langage-Lecture* went so far as to tell us that the French couple "were the real authors." During our fieldwork, staff members of the Pedagogic Institute who were developing a revised edition of *Langage-Lecture* again sought to collaborate informally with one of the French technical advisors stationed at the Institute. Meanwhile, Institute staff also collaborated with the USAID-employed technical advisors to develop radio scripts and language arts storybooks, and with French consultants to rewrite the country's educational objectives.

Motivation

Intellectual Conviction

We saw signs that certain Guinean elites adopted certain ideals whole-heartedly out of intellectual conviction based on their own extensive expertise in Western fields such as comparative linguistics or developmental psychology. One veteran actually cited science explicitly in justifying Guinea's shift from a phonics-based method to the mixed method:

La semi-globale privilégie la compréhension. . . . (KAL: Pourquoi la semi-globale?) C'était l'évolution de la science. [On a trouvé que] la semi-globale est plus rapide. Une langue n'est pas faite par juxtaposition de syllabes, [mais par le sens des phrases].[11]

The mixed method gives priority to comprehension. . . . (KAL: Why [did Guinea adopt] the mixed method?) It was scientific progress. They had found that the mixed method is more rapid. A language is not made up of the juxtaposition of syllables, but of the meaning of sentences.

This expert had studied in other African countries and in France. Another staff member of the Pedagogic Institute expounded with equal persuasiveness on the growing need for emphasizing comprehension in a situation where children do not understand French, the language of instruction, when they enter class.

Notre philosophie, c'était d'abord le langage, ensuite la lecture, et enfin l'écriture. L'enfant ne sait lire que ce qu'il sait dire, et il ne sait écrire que ce qu'il sait lire. Il faut créer l'intérêt, le besoin de communiquer. Ce n'est plus l'élite qui nous intéresse. Il faut faire du français un moyen de communication. Ce ne seront pas tous les élèves qui vont, plus tard, devenir des spécialistes en français, bien que certains vont continuer avec le français plus tard.

Our philosophy was first language, then reading, and finally writing. The child cannot read what he cannot say, and cannot write what he cannot read. You have to create an interest, the need to communicate. It's no longer the elite who concern us. You have to make French a means of communication. Not all of these students will become specialists in the French language later, although some will continue in French.

The phrase "The child cannot read what he cannot say, and cannot write what he cannot read" was a motto or slogan taken almost verbatim from the official national curriculum (Ministère, n.d.) and expressing the official rationale for the current reading method. However, the rest of what this expert said seemed to flow from personal experience with the development of new textbooks in collaboration with French experts. This staff member had also studied both in France and in the United States.

These intellectuals did not represent 100% of their peers. A few highly educated Guineans expressed intellectual skepticism about what they had learned from outside Guinea. We were asked, "Even if an idea has been proven in the West, would it translate to Guinea, where the context is so different?" For instance, the mixed method, with its stress on reading for meaning, works in France with native French speakers, one expert pointed out, but Guinean children do not speak the language of instruction at home. Could the mixed method truly be the panacea for Guinea that so many people claimed? Nonetheless, we had the sense that outspoken skeptics represented the minority among the elites. —✓

Western Concepts As Status Symbols

In addition, we learned that the allure of the West might motivate a person to espouse "Western" ideas even without deep conviction. A Guinean warned Alimasi that public professions and private practice wouldn't necessarily line up. Indeed, we saw traces on a blackboard in a house hinting that one educational official who surely promoted the mixed reading method in public might have his own children tutored with the phonics method in the evenings at home. Not unlike U.S. academics, who cite trendy French theorists, Guineans might cite "modern" ideals in public, claiming the scientific superiority of the West, simply as a status booster. Western science had prestige, and aligning oneself with it garnered a bit of that prestige. We—particularly Alimasi—noticed a certain cachet that surrounded us in Guinea merely because we represented U.S. universities.

The possibility that Guinean experts might have mastered Western ideals without deep conviction echoes James Wertsch's (1998) distinction between the "mastery" and the "appropriation" of a cultural tool. To "master" a tool or an idea is to know how to use it; to "appropriate" is to make someone else's tool or idea one's own. One can master an idea without appropriating it, as did Estonian intellectuals who mastered the Soviet version of Estonian history but maintained their own version of history for private use (Wertsch, 1998, Chap. 5). The possibility of mastery without appropriation does not necessarily conflict with the Meyer's "cultural ideology" perspective. What matters in the cultural ideology approach is whether the adopters see the new ideas as "modern," not whether they see them as true. However, if such cynicism existed, it does raise questions about the degree to which Guineans truly adopted Western ideals.

The "Same" Ideals Defined Differently

We also found another reason to doubt the penetration of certain "Western" concepts into Guinea. There were certain ideals on which everyone seemed to agree, but which different actors turned out to define differently in practice. For example, many people wanted to see "rich texts" in students' readers. However, for donors and some Guinean experts, "rich" referred to varied and imaginative stories, poems, and documents. In contrast, when certain teachers and school directors described textbooks as "rich," they meant that the books were full of exercises that teachers could use to reinforce the phonics taught in a particular lesson. For instance, one school director, showing Anderson-Levitt the new textbook series, said; "*Il est plus riche . . . en contenu, et en exercices. Par exemple, il y a même cette comptine pour faire répéter le [s]. C'est enrichissant*" (It is richer . . . in content and in exercises. For example, there is even this little rhyme for repeating the [s] sound. That's enriching). Similarly, different actors agreed that texts needed to be pitched to the students' level, but they apparently disagreed at times about whether a particular textbook was above or below the targeted students' level.

The ideal that a textbook be "culturally relevant" was another that actors defined differently. Everyone we talked with agreed that a textbook used in Guinea ought, at least up to a point, be "adapted to the Guinean context" (*être adapté au contexte guinéen*). Now, when Guinean elites talked about what one elite educator called "*matériel adapté aux besoins des élèves*" (material adapted to the students' needs), they emphasized that the children be able to recognize themselves in the pictures and the texts. Beyond that, they asked whether the texts built on "*le vécu de l'enfant*" (the children's lived experience). This is how a high-level supervisor at the prefectural level expressed the ideal for a good textbook:

Il doit utiliser des noms guinéens, les noms et contextes de villages, de fruits, et de zones guinéennes. . . . Si c'est un livre de calcul, dire que la maman achète un kilo de viande à 100 francs porte à confusion. Ce n'est pas possible: 100 francs guinéens, ce n'est rien; l'enfant ne sait pas faire le rapport. Quant à 100 francs français, là, c'est autre chose, et qu'en sait l'enfant? Il faut adapter le contenu aux réalités guinéennes. C'est comme quand on parle de bonbonnes de vin, est-ce que les enfants guinéens savent ce que c'est? Je ne dis pas qu'il ne faut pas leur en parler, mais il faut respecter la démarche où l'on va du connu vers l'inconnu.

It must use Guinean names, the names and contexts of Guinean villages, fruits, and regions. . . . If it's a math book, to say that Mama buys a kilo of meat at 100 francs will create confusion. That's not possible: 100 Guinean Francs is nothing; the child won't know how to make a connection. If it means 100 French Francs, that's something else—and what does the child know about that? You have to adapt the content to Guinean realities. For instance, when you speak of demijohns of wine—do Guinean children know what that is? I'm not saying that you shouldn't talk about them, but you must respect a sequence in which one moves from the known toward the unknown.

The Guinean Ministry had clear priorities and a clear rationale for deemphasizing text and illustrations on what was "not done here." As one Ministry official put it,

C'est bien beau dans l'enseignement de dire que nous allons parler de la neige, mais je crois qu'il faudrait mieux attirer l'attention sur l'avancée du désert et la reforestation, sur des questions essentielles de l'environnement. Voilà une manière où un manuel "serait"—je dis bien "serait" entre guillemets—adapté.

It's all very well in education to say that we're going to talk about snow, but I think it's more valuable to draw attention to the spread of the desert and to reforestation, to questions essential to the environment [in Guinea]. That's the way in which a textbook "would be"—I say "would be" in quotation marks—adapted.

Like the prefectural administrator cited above, this Ministry official acknowledged arguments that Guinean children need to be exposed to content beyond the borders of Guinea, and he commented during the interview that there could be no perfectly "adapted" textbook. (Yes, they should learn about wine containers and they should read about snow.) But both of these speakers emphasized that the first priority was to focus on Guinean realities.

On this point, North American donors seemed to agree with the Guineans. The donors, too, cited cultural relevance as one of the criteria by which they found French-written textbooks lacking. However, they sometimes defined cultural relevance differently from the Guineans. One North American donor complained of a new French-published series that it was too urban-oriented and, in fact, relevant only to the elite, citing as an example an illustration in one of the books of the TGV, France's high-speed train. We had not heard complaints about urban orientation from the Guinean educational elite. When we pointed this out, donors told us this was hardly surprising; since the educational elites are urban-dwelling and more or less members of the Guinean bourgeoisie themselves, they were not in the best position to recognize relevant problems like an urban bias.

More significantly, donors defined cultural relevance in terms of conformity to Guinea's cultural norms.

As an example of culturally inappropriate content, a North American donor told us of a textbook that included the story of a boy who wanted to go fishing. The boy's grandmother told him not to go because the weather would be bad. The boy went nonetheless and caught a whole lot of fish. Returning to his grandmother, according to the text, he said, "Voilà, Grandmother, I told you so." We didn't have to be told that the story illustrated remarkable disrespect and disobedience in the African context.

We did not hear the same kind of specific criticism from Guineans. It is true that one official commented, "*Il faut demander aux parents leur avis sur le contenu: quelles sont les valeurs que les parents aimeraient retrouver dans le livre?*" (We should ask parents their advice on the content: what are the values that the parents would like to find in the book?) However, supervisors who were examining the new, French-produced textbook for the first time during a training workshop came across a page in which two characters, a pair of boys called "*les farceurs*" (the jokers), overturn a market woman's vegetable stall.

The supervisors focused on the typeface and the purpose of the comic-strip style page rather than on the surprisingly disrespectful behavior depicted on the page.

Differences in definitions of "cultural relevance," "rich" texts, and appropriate level suggested that the Guineans were either redefining a donor-introduced word to suit their own values or borrowing an international "buzzword" to label a prior Guinean concern. In either case, they were confronting donors with a "creolized" version of the donors' own values, in Hannerz's sense of the word (1987, 1992), whether donors realized it or not. Despite surface appearances, donors and the Guineans were not really speaking the same language.

IDEALS IMPOSED?

So far, we have shown that the Guinean elite were exposed to Western notions of good teaching and that they had more than one reason to adopt those Western ideals. However, we've also raised doubt about whether certain Western ideals had actually been adopted at all, in their Western-defined versions, despite surface agreement between donors and Guineans. Now we turn to direct evidence of the exercise of power in the import of foreign ideals to Guinea.

Donors' Agendas Built into Projects

Donors arrived in Guinea with ready-made educational philosophies and priorities, whether they were aware of them or not. Sometimes donor concerns had little to do with the priorities Guineans expressed. For example, one North American technical assistant expressed concern that the vocabulary in Guinean readers was not introduced in a systematic way, an issue apparently important in France also judging from French textbooks (see, e.g., Debayle, Giribone, Touyarot, & Vitali, 1990), but one never mentioned to us by Guineans. Sometimes, as in the cases of "rich" texts and cultural relevance we've just cited, donor concerns did not mesh as smoothly with Guinean concerns as the donors might have thought.

The donors built their agendas into the reforms and projects they proposed to the Guinean Ministry and used them to evaluate Guinean proposals. One member of the Guinean elite put it rather bluntly: "They come with their documents already written. There is no negotiation. They've already decided in the United States or wherever what they're going to do." Technical advisors likewise arrived familiar with approaches said to have succeeded in their own country or approaches that they had recently applied in some other country. For instance, several technical assistants had participated in apparently successful efforts in other countries at teaching language arts through nationally broadcast radio programs. Not surprisingly, they were eager to try the same approach in Guinea. Similarly, French publishers who had already developed a template for textbooks in Mali or Senegal might seek to apply it when developing a book for Guinea.

We don't mean to imply that donors ignored Guinean wishes. On the contrary, the World Bank led other donors in allowing and encouraging the Guinean Ministry of Education to write its own objectives for the next 10–year round of coordinated funding from donors. Meanwhile, some of the technical advisors engaged in long-term collaboration actively elicited Guinean points of view and Guinean reactions to their proposals. One technical advisor from a consulting agency expressed the agency's philosophy: "We will, we hope, empower teachers in new ways through training and materials. But the sorts of things we promote must be what Guineans can and will want to continue for themselves."

However, ultimately educational officers and technical advisors faced the demands and deadlines of their own home offices or the employing donor. As a result, they might find it impossible to accommodate to Guinean desires. They might not even have had enough time to investigate the situation and find out what Guineans really wanted. A staff member of the same consulting agency, working in the field in Guinea, later described meetings the local consultants had been having with their donor sponsor: "[A donor official] also wanted us to put into the contract what we want to do, not what we think they [Guineans] want. [Our leader] told him that we were doing just that." Even if a donor encouraged its advisors to consult with Guineans, however, the very fact that the donors "allowed" the Guineans to develop their own objectives or that advisors elicited Guinean "input" indicated who held the more powerful position in the discussions.

Guinean Acceptance of All Projects

The high-level managers and experts we talked with judged that donors were willing to fund only projects that matched the donors' needs or interests. The Guineans feared not getting the funds if they didn't accept projects as defined by the donors. "We are a poor country," more than one educational elite told us, "and we cannot afford to say no to any offer." Here is how one decision maker expressed it in an interview:

Nous ne pouvons pas dire non à un projet, parce que nous sommes un pays pauvre. Quelque modeste que soit l'argent, nous lui trouvons une raison d'être. . . . Dire 'non' à un projet? Non, nous allons plutôt négocier. Nous allons lui trouver une place qui sert à nos objectifs. . . . Mais il faut le faire avec tact, avec souplesse. Est-ce qu'il faut prendre un marteau et taper? No. C'est eux qui apportent leur argent. Alors, il faut les prier.

We cannot say no to a project because we are a poor country. No matter how small the amount, we find a raison d'être for it. . . . Say 'no' to a project? No, instead we will negotiate. We will find a place for it that serves our objectives. . . . But it must be done with tact, with flexibility. Must one pound it in with a hammer? No. They are the ones bringing their money. Consequently we have to make polite requests.

The end of this decision maker's remark made it perfectly clear that money was power in the relationship between donors and Guinea.

Another high-level decision maker explained Guinea's position on textbook adoption by making an analogy to the construction of expensive, high-quality classrooms that the Japanese were funding:

Pour moi, ma préoccupation, ce n'est pas par rapport à un bailleur de fonds. C'est par rapport à l'intérêt de ce pays et à l'intérêt de l'école. . . . Un bailleur de fonds nous a dit ici que les classes que nous construisons sont chères. Or, . . . c'est un don que l'on offre à la Guinée. Nous avons une crise aiguë de salles de classe. Pour avoir le même effectif, le même nombre de classes offert par ce bailleur de fonds, nous sommes obligés de négocier avec un autre pendant deux ans avec des conditionnalités. . . . Le manuel aussi, c'est la même chose.

My concern is not the donors—it's the interest of this country and the interests of the schools. A donor told us that the classrooms we were constructing are expensive. Now . . . it's a gift that they [Japan] gave to Guinea. We have a dramatic classroom crisis. To serve the same number of students, to have the same number of classrooms as offered by this donor, we would have to negotiate with another donor for two years with all the strings attached. . . . With textbooks, too, it's the same thing.

In other words, according to both of these decision makers, when offered a "gift," take it.[12] If Japan offers to construct high-quality classrooms, don't turn them down just because they or another donor could have built a larger number of cheaper classrooms for the same cost. If the one donor offers a loan to buy textbooks, don't turn them down just because another donor plans to finance locally produced textbooks. Take what you can get, because whatever you get will still not be enough for a school system as needy as Guinea's.

COMPLICATIONS ON THE GROUND

We've painted a picture of donors who wittingly or unwittingly imposed their own concepts of good teaching through offers of loans and grants that the Guinean elite could not afford to turn down. However, this does not translate to a simple story of the West imposing its cultural ideals. Things were not that simple.

Conflicts among Donors

We have already hinted that the French publisher did not see eye to eye with North American donors on the value of cultural relevance. Indeed, the donors were not a monolithic group. Just as donors and Guineans gave different definitions to the same terms, so French and North American educators shared a common vocabulary ("student participation," "equality," "individualized instruction," "reading groups," and so on), but defined the concepts differently in practice (Anderson-Levitt, in press). Thus donors did not always speak with a single cultural voice to Guinea. They did not share a uniform version of "Western" ideals to present to Guineans.

Consider the question of how textbooks should fit into a national curriculum. Anyone concerned with producing or using textbooks had to face that issue. The current *programmes* or official national curriculum spells out in detail how teachers should carry out reading instruction. The French felt that it was important to build slowly but carefully from the ground up. Thus they were collaborating with Guineans in a long-term rethinking of overarching educational goals (*référentielles de compétence*). After the educational goals have been rewritten, they imagined development of a new national curriculum and a new set of textbooks to suit it. Donors like USAID, on the other hand, felt that the dearth of current teaching materials required getting materials (such as inexpensive storybooks we saw under development) into classrooms as rapidly as possible, long before the national curriculum could be rewritten. Thus they decided to adapt the projects they proposed to the existing curriculum.

Another minor but interesting difference among donors concerned the use of typefaces in reading textbooks. Textbooks in Guinea used varied typefaces—both cursive and detached scripts (with serifs) and sometimes uppercase sans-serif typefaces in a comic-book style. French donors considered the use of multiple typefaces normal, as it was in France (Anderson-Levitt, 1987), but the diversity of scripts worried anglophone donors. A World Bank officer first pointed out to us the varied scripts as a problem with both French- and Guinean-produced readers for first and second graders. Later, a U.S. donor made a similar complaint about the French-produced books, saying, "It's hard to figure out how to use it as a text. The print shifts from cartoon-style to typeface."

The fact that "the donors" did not represent a monolithic group had important implications for the way Guineans reacted to ideals imported by donors.

"Juggling" Donors

If the Guinean elite were accepting projects with donor agendas built in and if the agendas varied from one donor to another, how did the Guineans manage those diverse projects? A few of the elites used metaphors of "coordinating," "juggling," or "playing the game." For example, when we asked whether there weren't philosophical differences among donors such as the French and the Americans, one decision maker explained,

Il est difficile d'harmoniser les philosophies, parce que la philosophie est une expression d'une culture. Les cultures américaine et française ne sont pas les mêmes. . . . Mais nous n'avons pas eu de problèmes. . . . Notre rôle, c'est de cultiver l'amitié de tous les coopérants. Notre rôle est de coordonner. . . . On cherche une complémentarité.

It is difficult to coordinate the philosophies, because philosophy is an expression of a culture. The American and French cultures are not the same. . . . But we have not had problems. . . . Our role is to cultivate the friendship of all the assistants. Our role is to co-ordinate. . . . We seek a complementarity.

Another expert said less diplomatically, "*Nous sommes obligés de jongler, que les bailleurs de fonds fondent un peu de ce que nous voulons—mais ils sont têtus*" (We must juggle, so that the donors fund a little what we want—but they are stub-born). This metaphor of juggling, although we heard it from only one person, captured very neatly what we had been observing.

To illustrate "juggling," consider the development of various locally designed text-books. While we were in Guinea, there were at least four projects in progress at the Ped-agogic Institute that bore on the design of reading materials in one way or another. First, revision of the Guinean textbook *Langage-Lecture*, financed by the World Bank but informally aided by French advisors, was drawing to a close. Second, as we have mentioned, the French-funded project of rewriting the overarching objectives (*référentielles de compétence*) for the whole of elementary education was supposed to pave the way eventually for a new curriculum and new textbooks. Third, USAID-funded technical advisors were working with Guineans to develop little storybooks and other supplementary teaching materials on a dramatically different time scale, intending to distribute their new materials within months. Finally, the Insti-tute had just begun a fourth project funded by ACCT (the international organization of French-speaking nations), which involved rapid development of workbooks and other supplemental materials. Like the U.S. materials, these too were to be ready within a few months. Some of the same Institute staff participated in two or three of these pro-jects.[13]

Occasionally, a few Guinean elites suggested to us that they deliberately wanted to play one donor against another. For example, if the French presence was felt to be too "strong," the Guineans could invite a different donor to bal-ance the strength of the French. One of the educational elites recounted how, many years ago, the French expanded their presence beyond the central bu-reaucracy by establishing inservice training centers throughout the country. "I responded to this game," said the educator, by trying to get another country involved to develop other centers. "It was a game," the educator repeated. Even the decision maker, who had talked about "harmonizing" and coordi-nating donors, used a milder version of the game metaphor, saying, "*Même s'il y a des gens qui ne le reconnaissent pas, nous avons réussi. . . . On a joué le jeu, au profit de la Guinée*" (Even if there are people who don't recognize it, we have succeeded. . . . We have played the game, to Guinea's benefit).

Strategic "Adoption" of Specific Ideals

One reason it is difficult for us to say whether the Guinean elite truly em-braced Western ideals or merely mastered them under duress is that the need to juggle donors constrained which Western ideals they could publicly claim. Let us illustrate the perceived need to juggle donors and the strategic public "adoption" of certain ideals with the case of a newly adopted textbook series.

Since 1992, first- and second-grade teachers in Guinea had been using the language and reading textbooks developed by Guinea's own Pedagogic Institute (IPN, 1992, 1994). However, the local textbooks had become scarce in the marketplace, and official texts for third through sixth grade had likewise become harder to find. The World Bank was financing development of a second edition of the local book, and there was talk of extending the local series to the other primary grades. However, late in 1997 Guinea obtained a loan from the African Development Bank to acquire a series of French-published language and reading books (see, e.g., Vilette, Lalo, & Bouillon, 1994) for all six primary grades. By the end of the 1997–98 school year, the Pedagogic Institute was beginning to distribute the new French-published books in schools.

As a result of the decision to adopt the new textbook, Guinean decision makers found themselves "juggling" donors. The process by which Guinea negotiated the loan to purchase new textbooks risked alienating the country from other donors and endangered World Bank support for revision and publication of the local textbooks. Therefore, the Guineans needed to justify their decision and to woo back the Bank and allied donors.

A Question of Emphasis

Here, we do not examine institutional politics behind the adoption decision; rather, we ask how pedagogical ideals were cited to justify the decision. What matters to this chapter is not the acquisition of the textbooks per se, but rather how it created a situation in which the Guinean elite had to claim pedagogical ideals strategically. One strategy the elite employed was selective citing of ideals that the elite (and probably all Guineans) actually would have claimed to share with the World Bank and other donors under other circumstances. Guinea emphasized the ideal of textbook accessibility while downplaying the ideal that textbooks should be indigenously produced.

Accessibility: Donor Rhetoric Used for Guinean Purposes. In other contexts, both donors and Guineans readily agreed that textbooks should be accessible and affordable for all students. In reference to the newly acquired textbooks, the donors deemphasized accessibility, while the Guinean elite played it up. Since reading textbooks had become rare, the Guinean elite explained the acquisition of the French-produced series as a way to put textbooks into students' hands more quickly. "What we were trying to do, because books from the Bank were not supposed to be available until 2000 or 2001, was to get books for now, because the children don't have any," one official explained to us. Moreover, the Bank-funded, locally produced books covered only grades 1 and 2, whereas the French-produced series put textbooks in the hands of all primary students, grades 1 through 6. The Guinean elite thus argued for the overriding goal of accessibility. By taking advantage of the loan to adopt the new series, they argued, they would get reading books more quickly into the hands of students at all grade levels.

And what would happen when the new Guinean-produced books came out? Guinean experts called on the free market philosophy that they had heard from donors on other occasions. "*Il faut que les maîtres aient une choix*" (Teachers need to have a choice [among books]), as one Guinean educator put it. In other words, it would be good (not wasteful) to have more than one reader. Wasn't it true that in other contexts, donors advocated making multiple textbooks available? Why else would USAID be funding supplementary storybooks for the early grades?

Local Production: Deemphasizing Guinean Interests. In other contexts, donors and Guineans both expressed the ideal that, when possible, textbooks should be locally designed and produced. The World Bank and partner donors had committed to this policy by supporting the original development of the Guinean-designed language and reading texts and by funding the revision of that home-grown text. We are not sure how Guinean supervisors and teachers felt about local production, but we do know that the Guinean elite had an economic interest in local design and publication of textbooks. The Pedagogic Institute was affiliated with the national educational publishing house that might hope to publish textbooks locally. In addition, at least two past or present staff members of the Institute had founded private publishing houses that someday might hope to gain textbook contracts. Meanwhile, the pro-Western market reforms taking place in Guinea since 1984 meant that staff members of the Pedagogic Institute could gain individual remuneration as textbook authors and illustrators.

Yet, in spite of their own interests as well as their philosophical commitment to local control, Guinean educational elites chose to ignore the criterion of indigenous production when they adopted the new, French-produced textbooks. They quietly passed over the issue, except to acknowledge the hope that by the time the French-published series wore out, Guinea would be ready to go to press with its own home-grown series for all six grade levels.

Strategic Alignment with Donors in Opposition to Teachers

Guinean elite may have chosen their ideals strategically not just in the face they presented to donors, but in the messages about good practice they conveyed to Guinea's own supervisors and teachers. At least so it seemed from our observations of a 3–day workshop run by the Pedagogic Institute in Conakry to familiarize supervisors and teacher trainers with the new textbooks. Sixty-six supervisors and trainers from the entire western half of the country participated in this workshop, and they were then supposed to take its message back to teachers within their various districts. (A simultaneous workshop served supervisors in the eastern half of the country.)

During the workshop in Conakry, the participating supervisors raised potentially legitimate objections to the new textbooks. Given the circumstances in which the books had been acquired (the delicate balancing of one donor against others), the elite had to defend the new books against criticism. The interesting question is how they did so.

On the one hand, the supervisors raised certain concerns that seemed to have been completely invisible to the publisher and to foreign donors. Most dramatically, they examined the typeface in the new textbooks—not to comment on the use of cursive, as North American donors had, but to determine whether the typeface was large and readable. It happened that the new textbooks had been printed only in black and yellow rather than in four colors to keep the cost down. The sound to be studied in each lesson, such as the *or* of the word *porte*, had been printed in yellow in an effort to highlight it. Unfortunately, the yellow letters were pale against the white page. The supervisors perused the books and asked, "How do you expect a child to read that in the evening by the light of a kerosene lamp or a fire?" The Guinean experts running the workshop simply did not respond to these concerns.

On the other hand, the supervisors made different criticisms of the new textbooks to which the elite had a ready answer. One such criticism was that the new textbook would not be accompanied by a teacher's manual. This concern had emerged when the two experts running the workshops revealed that Guinea did not have enough funds to provide teachers' manuals for the new textbooks. Many of the supervisors and trainers reacted with consternation. They knew that many teachers wanted a detailed guide similar to the teacher's manual for the previous, Guinean-produced first- and second-grade textbooks, which had provided detailed scripts for different kinds of language and reading exercises.

The Institute staff had already argued during their opening presentation that the method should be in the teacher, not in the scripted lesson plans of a teacher's manual or textbook. They had even argued for teacher autonomy from the official curriculum. As one of them had phrased the issue on the first day:

On ne peut pas imposer. Si un maître utilise le syllabaire [not sanctioned by the official curriculum] et un autre *Langage-Lecture*, à la fin de l'année, si les objectifs sont atteints, c'est ça qui compte. Ce n'est pas le livre qui fait le maître.

You can't impose. If one teacher uses a phonics method [not sanctioned by the official curriculum], and another *Langage-Lecture* [the official textbook already in use], at the end of the year, if the objectives are reached, that's all that matters. It's not the book that makes the teacher.

Now faced with supervisors disgruntled about the absence of a teacher's manual, the elite held to their philosophy that teachers could function without such guides. A few workshop participants supported the elites' position, citing mottos like, "*Un nouveau livre ne veut pas dire une nouvelle méthodologie*" (A new book does not mean a new method), or "*À chaque maître correspond une méthodologie*" (For each teacher a [different] method). However, most of the workshop participants continued to insist on a guide that teachers could follow closely. In their final, written report on the workshop, the participants petitioned the Ministry and the donors to provide a teacher's manual.

At the same workshop, supervisors also raised a related set of criticisms that were bothering teachers (as we knew from our fieldwork in schools). They wanted to know whether the new textbooks conformed as closely to the official national curriculum as the old, Guinean-produced readers had. For instance, did the new books present lessons on sounds in the order prescribed by the official curriculum? Did the new books contain the kinds of texts and exercises (e.g., "text for fluent reading," "structural exercises") that the official curriculum suggested? Did each lesson contain an illustration that would lead the teacher and the students to produce the expected "key sentence" around which the lesson would be structured? Like the demand for a teacher's manual, these concerns reflected the desire for a text that teachers could follow closely with the assurance that they were teaching the official curriculum. Again, the elites of the Pedagogical Institute responded with the rhetoric of teacher autonomy. One of them commented in reference to complaints about the organization of the new textbooks, "*Le livre, [ce n'est] pas la Bible, [ce n'est] pas le Coran. . . . Si on sent le besoin, on modifie*" (The book is not the Bible, it's not the Quran. . . . If you feel the need, you modify [rather than following its sections in the order presented]).

A number of donors would have agreed with the Guinea elites' motto, "It's not the book that makes the teacher."[14] For example, one consultant for USAID told us, "[Guinean teachers] are not encouraged to think for themselves. They are not encouraged to seize the moment, the teachable moment. . . . That's why we hope to encourage supervisors to encourage teachers to be free to create." In the same vein, one master teacher in the United States commented to Anderson-Levitt, "I always say, 'I can teach reading with anything. Just give me a newspaper.'" French officials, too, discouraged fixation on the textbook. As one French donor said to us:

Quelque que soit le livre, ce n'est pas ça qui fait la qualité; c'est le savoir-faire du maitre. . . . On peut apprendre à lire sur le journal, sur un circulaire. C'est un esprit un peu infantilisant de dire que le maître va suivre un livre particulier.

Whatever the book may be, that's not what makes for quality; it's the know-how of the teacher. . . . You can teach someone to read with a newspaper, with a pamphlet. It's a bit like treating people as children to say that the teacher must use a particular book.

This French donor's words echoed the U.S. teacher's support of teacher autonomy in startlingly similar language.

Therefore, we are arguing that the two elite running the workshop defended the new textbook against criticism by citing the donor-favored ideal of teacher autonomy. Downplaying the supervisors' concerns and the teachers' anxieties suited Guinea's current need to defend the new textbooks. The elites' advocacy of teacher autonomy defused criticism of the new textbook, and defused it in the same "modernist" language that most donors would have used. Since donors, too, had been critical of the adoption of the new textbook (although not for the same reasons), it was in the experts' interest to deflect criticism. What better way to do it than by citing modern pedagogical thinking?

Now, from what we know of these two individuals, they probably believed what they told the supervisors. One of them had explained in an interview on a different occasion that "once you know the teaching method (*la didactique*) for a subject, you don't need a textbook." Both of them had demonstrated their own apparent commitment to student-centered instruction by organizing the workshop itself around small-group work rather than by lecturing. However, even if they had not appropriated Western ideals about teacher autonomy, they would have had good reason to claim such ideals publicly. In the case of the new textbooks, then, did Guinean elites adopt foreign ideals under duress (that is, out of the need to juggle donors in order to maximize aid to Guinean education), or did they embrace the ideals out of intellectual conviction? We could not tell. Both might have been true.

CONCLUSION

We began with the questions that the grand theories take for granted: What are "Western" ideals introduced into developing countries, and what does it mean for non-Western policymakers to "adopt" them?

The "West" Is No Monolith

In answer to the first question, in the case of ideals for reading instruction introduced into Guinea, the "West" was hardly a monolith. First, the term "West" fails to encompass the full range of outside influences, which came from other African nations, from Japan, and from eastern European countries as well as from Western Europe and North America. However, even when we restricted our gaze to North America and Western Europe, presumed uniformity dissolved. The French and the North Americans did not agree on the best process for developing new reading textbooks nor on what a good first-grade reader should look like. If we had expanded our inquiry into ideals for classroom practice, we would have found additional differences (Anderson-Levitt, in press). The elites who worked with donors and technical assistants from different countries and particularly those who had studied in two or three different countries themselves had had the opportunity to discover cultural differences and inconsistencies within modernist pedagogical thought. They could "shop" among alternative ideals and produce from them a personal synthesis.

What It Might Mean to "Adopt" an Ideal

Variation among Guinean Actors

What it meant for Guinea to "adopt" a Western ideal, whether French, North American, or other, turned out to refer to a whole range of possible events. First, it was crucial to distinguish between the national educational elites, regional supervisors and teacher trainers, and local school directors and teachers. The Guineans were no more monolithic than the "Western" donors. There was some variation within each category of Guinean actors, with a few skeptical elites demurring when most accepted the mixed reading method, or with supervisors disagreeing among themselves about the importance of teacher's manuals. More importantly for our analysis, different categories of Guinean actors aligned themselves differently depending on the ideal in question (Table 1.3). There were some ideals, such as accessible and affordable textbooks, where everyone in Guinea could agree with international donors. There were others where the Guineans seemed to agree among themselves (as in their understanding of "cultural relevance") but not with the donors. There were certain concerns, such as readable typeface or the sequence in which a textbook presented the sounds to be learned, that preoccupied supervisors and teachers but didn't even show up on donors' radar screens. There were likewise a few concerns, such as the notion of controlled vocabulary, raised only by donors. Finally, there were ideals where the Guinean elite seemed to align themselves with "Western" views in opposition to a significant number of teachers and supervisors. These included a belief in the mixed method of reading instruction and a preference for using local languages in the early grades. As we have just seen, the elite likewise aligned themselves with the "Western" ideal that "the method is in the teacher, not the text" in the face of supervisors' and teachers' concerns about the new textbooks. The shifting alignments illustrated by Table 1.3 reinforce two points we made earlier: You cannot identify a sharp boundary between people who are "inside" and "outside" Guinea nor between ideas that are "foreign" as opposed to "indigenous."

The Many Dimensions of "Adoption"

However, we asked not just who claimed what ideal, but exactly what claiming an ideal might mean. Just as there was a range of actors in Guinea, there was a wide range of reactions to Western notions. First we must distinguish as Wertsch (1998) does between mastery and appropriation. Mastery is a dimension that ranges from expertise to unfamiliarity. Mastery of foreign ideals in Guinea depended, first, on the opportunity to learn, and members of the Guinean elite who had studied in one, two, or three foreign countries could display expertise in one or several educational fields. At the opposite end of this dimension lay those teachers who, according to some of our informants, failed to master new ideas like the mixed method or teacher autonomy due to lack of training or to the interference of "traditional ideas."

Appropriation, on the other hand, depends on motivation rather than simply on the opportunity to learn. For Wertsch (1998), the opposite of appropriation—or the point at the opposite end of a continuum, perhaps—is resistance.[15] At one end of this second continuum, members of the elite might have truly "appropriated" a Western ideal, making it their own through intellectual conviction or through strong identification with the Western teachers or collaborators who introduced them to the idea. (Witness the expert who cited the scientific progress as support for the mixed reading method.) At the opposite end of the continuum lay the Guineans who refused to accept an idea at all, whether for scientific reasons or out of resistance to donor power, as in the case of the educator who questioned that the mixed method could work in Guinea. Closer to the appropriation end, we would locate the Guineans who mastered a foreign ideal, albeit without deep conviction, appropriating it for the sake of the status appeal of the West. Closer to the resistance end lay the elites who mastered without appropriating for strategic purposes, to maximize loans and grants from donors in the face of Guinea's desperate economic situation.

Our case study hints at yet a third dimension of contrast. Recall the pedagogical ideals that everyone seemed to share but that Guineans defined differently from donors in practice. We need to identify the degree to which borrowers modify the ideas they borrow. The Guineans may have adopted some notions "as is." However, at the opposite end of this continuum, we think there were cases where they adopted nothing more than the label for an idea ("rich" texts, cultural relevance) to attach to their own concerns. Somewhere in the middle of this third continuum would lie what Hannerz (1987) calls "creolized" ideas, borrowed ideas transformed to the point that they become something new. We gather from our classroom observations, not discussed in this chapter, that once Guinean educators put certain Western notions such as the mixed method into practice, they created a new, "creolized" version of it (Anderson-Levitt, 2000).

Finally, do not forget the dimension of time. Guineans long ago appropriated (and perhaps "creolized") once-foreign ideals like the phonics method or instruction in French. Ironically, these former imports now represent a Guinean orthodoxy sometimes opposed to newer ideals from outside. Which of the foreign ideals currently buzzing about the halls of donors' offices and Guinea's Pedagogic Institute will become the orthodoxy of the future and which will blow away with the next breeze from American and French research institutions?

Embraced, Imposed, or Strategically Selected?

In light of the complex picture our ethnographic study has revealed, what are we to make of the grand theories of a global diffusion of educational ideals? This case study supported the cultural ideology approach only to the extent that it demonstrated the intellectual allure and the status appeal of Western

Table 1.3
Pedagogical Ideals and Their Adherents: A Rough Guide

	Donors and advisors	National educational elite	Supervisors and teachers
Ideals accepted by all actors:			
Textbooks should be accessible and affordable.		Yes.	
Textbooks should be locally produced when possible.	Yes.		
Ideals claimed by all but defined differently:			
Textbooks should be culturally relevant.	Yes, they should *suit local mores.*	Yes, *children should see themselves in the books.*	
Textbooks should be at the students' level.	Yes, current textbooks are *too difficult.*	Yes, but are current books *too difficult or too easy?*	
Textbooks should contain "rich" texts.	Yes, texts should be "rich" *in ideas and imagination.*		Texts should be "rich" *in the sounds to be studied.*
Ideals where the elite tended to align with the donors:			
What language of instruction is best for earliest years?	Local languages.	Local languages, but parent resistance is strong.	Some preferred French.
What is the best reading method?	Some preferred "whole-language" but felt the mixed method made sense for Guinea.	Reading should be taught with the mixed (semi-global) method.	A significant number preferred the syllabic (phonics-based) method.

Question			Answer
Is a detailed teacher's guide essential?			Yes.
Must the national curriculum dictate the sequence of sounds in a textbook?	Method should be "in the teacher, not in the text."		Yes.
Must illustrations conform exactly to needs of the prescribed curriculum?			Yes.
Must texts and exercises in a textbook match the prescribed curriculum closely?	World Bank: Perhaps.	Others: No.	No.	Yes.

Concern unique to supervisors and teachers:

Typeface should be big, dark, and readable.

Concerns unique to donors:

Vocabulary in basal readers should be controlled.	Yes.	
Should multiple scripts be used in first-grade books?	French: Yes.	North Americans: No.
Must goals be redefined before new textbooks are designed?	French: Yes.	US: No.

ideas. It made a stronger case for the global conflict model by showing that the economic power of the donors gave their ideas leverage. When donors proposed projects, Guinean national educational elites accepted the projects and the philosophies that went with them due to the neediness of the Guinean system. They told us so outright. Money was power; money talked.

Outside ideals also exerted a subtler kind of influence when Guineans collaborated with technical advisors. As we mentioned, "Guinean-produced" texts had been developed under the heavy influence of technical advisors. One participant told us that the French advisors were the true authors. Now, you could interpret this kind of influence as voluntarily accepted guidance, as a voluntary embracing of the knowledge brought in by foreign experts. That is, in fact, how some of the Guinean participants portrayed it in conversations with us. Nonetheless, the technical advisors would not have been present in the first place, we suspect, if Guinea had not found it impossible to get textbooks at all without their participation. Even the intellectual persuasiveness of Western science is partly a matter of power at a deeper level. The economic power of countries like Canada, France, and the United States have allowed them to develop educational research industries—a huge one in the U.S. case—which in turn positions these countries as sources of "received knowledge" for the world (see Grillo, 1997).

Our case study thus tended to support the argument of Ginsburg and his colleagues (1991) that the power dimension controls the flow of pedagogical ideals. The cultural ideology model ignores crucial power differences between countries.

However, both the global conflict approach and the cultural ideology perspective miss two important points that the fine focus of ethnography made abundantly clear. First, as we have already underlined, the "West" did not present a united front. Second, Guinea hardly played a passive role; they went beyond playing "passivity as strategy" (Meyer, Nagel, & Snyder, 1993, p. 470). Accepting all donors, they took an active role in juggling the projects and the pedagogical ideals that came with them, even playing one donor against another if deemed necessary. We do not mean to say that the power game necessarily converted the elite into cynics. For instance, we think that the two young elites at the training workshop believed the ideal of teacher autonomy that they expressed so well. However, given Guinea's strategy of accepting and juggling potentially conflicting projects, the two experts had good reason to claim the ideal of teacher autonomy even if they had not believed in it. However much individual Guineans might be convinced of the value of certain "Western" notions and might willingly embrace them, at one level or another the transfer of ideas involved a power game. It was, however, a power game in which the powerful "player," Western donors with their Western ideals, turned out to be multiple players. They were powerful but not monolithic. And because they were in fact fragmented, the supposedly powerless players found them amenable to manipulation, juggling, and play.

NOTES

1. This study was made possible by a generous grant from the Spencer Foundation. An earlier version of this article was presented at the meetings of the Comparative and International Education Society in Toronto, April 1998. We thank John Schwille, Penelope Bender, Christopher Wheeler, Margaret Sutton, Régine Sirota, Seth Spaulding, Kathryn Borman, Daniel Moerman, and several participants in the research for helpful comments on earlier versions of this chapter. Gando Camara and Mme Camara helped with transcribing field notes, and Renee Bumpus, Régine Bernkopf, and Peri Weingrad coded the notes and interviews. We are deeply indebted to the Ministry of Education and to INRAP in Guinea, to the many Guineans who tried to help us understand the educational system there, and to the educational officers and technical assistants who tried to help us understand their work. What we present here is only our own interpretation of the situation, and we apologize for any inadvertent error of fact.

2. Fiala and Lanford (1987) did document regional variation in educational ideology, noting, for example, less emphasis on the individual development of the child in Africa than in the West. However, they studied only official policy pronouncements, not Ministry or classroom realities.

3. INRAP stands for Institut National de Recherche et d'Action Pédagogique (National Institute for Pedagogical Research and Action). Before 1996, it was known as the Institut Pédagogique National, or IPN (the National Pedagogic Institute). We will refer to it simply as the "Pedagogic Institute." Anderson-Levitt taught a postgraduate course on qualitative methods for INRAP staff, in the context of which INRAP supported her research as a model for its staff members.

4. By "Ministry of Education," we mean the Ministère de l'Enseignement Pré-Universitaire, or MEPU, the Ministry of Pre-University Education. It is distinct from the Ministry of Higher Education and the Ministry for Professional and Technical Training.

5. In the capital of Conakry, the equivalent of the Regional Inspector is the DEV, or Directeur de l'Éducation de la Ville (Directory of City Education).

6. Technically titled "le Ministère Délégué à la Coopération et à la Francophonie," Coopération Française was a separate French Ministry that was, during our fieldwork, poised to become the African Department of the French Ministry of Foreign Affairs.

7. We are indebted to John Schwille and Martial Dembélé for this and the preceding point.

8. For instance, a Guinean elite told us that, when given the chance to propose small school-based reforms, "80%" of the teacher teams that participated focused on problems of language arts and reading. A provincial school director told us that he did not let his students pass first and second grade unless they have an average grade in reading.

9. You might argue that formal Quranic schooling represents truly "indigenous" or "West African" teaching ideals, but it, too, was originally borrowed from outside Guinea. We presume that certain "indigenous" child-rearing practices, specifically the kind of respect due an elder and the kinds of punishments permitted, affect teaching practice in Guinean classrooms. However, even those patterns could have been influenced in the past by Muslim teaching from "outside" or by Christian missionaries. In

any case, in this study we were not able to examine Quranic schooling nor family child-rearing practices.

10. Fanta is a common girls' name and Fodé a common boys' name in Guinea.

11. Words in brackets represent places where we were not certain of a speaker's verbatim expression. Translations from French to English are our own, and any errors in the French represent our errors in note-taking or transcribing, not speaker errors.

12. It would take another chapter to distinguish how different actors conceived of grants, projects, and loans within the aid given by donors. For instance, although money given by the African Development Bank and by the World Bank came in the form of loans and therefore might be thought of as ultimately Guinea's own money, some elites seemed to refer to it as though it represented gifts.

13. Whereas this case illustrates four different donors working with a single Guinean institution, one might find other situations in which different units of the Guinean ministries of education allied themselves with different donor projects (J. Schwille and M. Dembélé, personal communication March 8, 2000). However, we did not conduct enough fieldwork to permit a close analysis of institutional decision making and institutional politics within Guinea.

14. Not *every* donor agreed completely. One World Bank official later pointed out that textbooks closely aligned with the official curriculum helped teachers prepare students for examinations driven by the official curriculum.

15. Although Levinson and Sutton note, in this volume, that you could think of resistance as a kind of appropriation insofar as it requires incorporating an image of the thing to be resisted into one's schemes of action.

REFERENCES

Anderson-Levitt, K. M. (1987). Cultural knowledge for teaching first grade: An example from France. In G. D. Spindler & L. Spindler (Eds.), *Interpretive ethnography of education at home and abroad* (pp. 171–192). Hillsdale, NJ: Erlbaum.

Anderson-Levitt, K. M. (2000). What counts as the mixed method of reading instruction in Guinea? Fractures in the global culture of modern schooling. Paper presented at the annual meeting of the American Educational Research Association, New Orleans, April 24.

Anderson-Levitt, K. M. (forthcoming). *Teaching cultures: Knowledge for teaching first grade in France and the United States.* Cresskill, NJ: Hampton Press.

Bah-Lalya, I. (1991). *An analysis of educational reforms in post-independence Guinea: 1958–1985.* Unpublished doctoral dissertation, Florida State University.

Baker, V. (1997). Does formalism spell failure? Values and pedagogies in cross-cultural perspective. In G. D. Spindler (Ed.), *Education and cultural process: Anthropological approaches* (pp. 454–471). Prospect Heights, IL: Waveland.

Cuban, L. (1993). *How teachers taught: Constancy and change in American classrooms, 1890–1990* (2nd ed.). New York: Longman.

Davesne, A. (1950). *Nouveau syllabaire de Mamadou et Bineta, à l'usage des écoles africaines* [Mamadou and Bineta's new syllabary, for the use of African schools]. Paris: EDICEF, Librairie ISTRA.

Debayle, J., Giribone, Cl., Touyarot, M., & Vitali, D. (1990). *Le Nouveau fil des mots: Lire au CP.* Paris: Nathan.

Delpit, L. (1986). Skills and other dilemmas of a progressive Black educator. *Harvard Educational Review 56*(4), 379–385.

Diallo, B. (1993). La lecture à l'école élémentaire: Aspects théoriques et pratiques [Reading in elementary school: Theoretical and practical aspects]. *L'éducateur: Trimestriel Pédagogique des Enseignants de Guinée*, 17, 12–14.

Diallo, M.L.P. (1991). *Enjeux et avatars de l'enseignement du Français en République de Guinée: Contexte historique, aspects pédagogique, et perspectives de renovation* [Competing interests and complications in the teaching of French in Guinea; Historical context, padagogical aspects, and perspectives in reform]. Thèse pour le doctorat de l'Université de Bordeaux II, Sciences de l'Education.

Fiala, R., & Lanford, A. G. (1987). Educational ideology and the world educational revolution, 1950–1970. *Comparative Education Review, 31*, 315–332.

Flinn, J. (1992). Transmitting traditional values in new schools: Elementary education on Pulap Atoll. *Anthropology and Education Quarterly, 23*(1), 44–58.

Ginsburg, M. B., Cooper, S., Raghu, R., & Zegarra, H. (1991). Educational reform: Social struggle, the state, and the world economic system. In M. B. Ginsburg (Ed.), *Understanding educational reform in global context: Economy, ideology, and the state* (pp. 3–47). New York: Garland.

Grillo, R. D. (1997). Discourses of development: The view from anthropology. In R. D. Grillo & R. L. Stirrat (Eds.), *Discourses of development* (pp. 1–33). New York: Berg.

Hannerz, Ulf. (1987). The world in creolisation. *Africa, 57*, 546–559.

Hannerz, Ulf. (1992). *Cultural complexity: Studies in the social organization of meaning.* New York: Columbia University Press.

IPN [Institut National Pédagogique]. (1983). *Bonjour Fanta, Bonjour Fodé! Manuel de Français, langue étrangère, à l'usage de la 3e année du 1er cycle.* Conakry, Guinea: IDEC (Imprimerie de l'Éducation et de la Culture).

IPN [Institut National Pédagogique]. (1992). *Langage et lecture en 1ère Année* [First grade language and reading]. Conakry, Guinea: Author.

IPN [Institut National Pédagogique]. (1994). *Langage et lecture en 2e Année* [Second grade language and reading]. Conakry, Guinea: Author.

Jones, P. (1992). World Bank financing of education. New York: Routledge.

Kaufmann, G. (1997). Watching the developers: A partial ethnography. In R. D. Grillo (Ed.), *Discourses of development: Anthropological perspectives* (pp. 107–131). New York: Berg.

Meyer, J. W., Kamens, D. H., & Benavot, A. (Eds.). (1992). *School knowledge for the masses.* Washington, DC: Falmer.

Meyer, J. W., Nagel, J., & Snyder, Jr., C. W. (1993). The expansion of mass education in Botswana: Local and world society perspectives. *Comparative Education Review, 37*(4), 454–475.

Ministère de l'Éducation Nationale et de la Recherche Scientifique, République de Guinée. (n.d.). *Programmes de l'enseignement élémentaire 1re & 2me années.* Conakry, Guinea: Institut National de Recherche et d'Action Pédagogique.

Nagel, J., & Snyder, Jr., C. W. (1989). International funding of educational develop-
    ment: External agendas and internal adaptations—the case of Liberia. *Com-
    parative Education Review, 33*(1), 3–20.
Noblit, G. W. (1993). Power and caring. *American Educational Research Journal,
    30*(1), 23–38.
Ramirez, F. O., & Boli, J. (1987). The political construction of mass schooling: Eu-
    ropean origins and worldwide institutionalization. *Sociology of Education,
    60,* 2–17.
Ramirez, F. O., & Ventresca, M. J. (1992). Building the institution of mass school-
    ing: Isomorphism in the modern world. In B. Fuller & R. Rubinson (Eds.),
    *The political construction of education: The state, school expansion, and eco-
    nomic change* (pp. 47–59). New York: Praeger.
Rogers, E. M. (1995). Diffusion of innovations (4th ed.). New York: The Free Press.
SSP (Service Statistique et Planification). (1997, July). *Données Statistiques,
    Enseignement Primaire, Année Scolaire 1996–1997.* Conakry, Guinea:
    Ministère de l'Education Nationale et de la Recherche Scientifique.
Sharrock, W. W. (1974). On owning knowledge. In R. Turner (Ed.),
    Ethnomethodology: Selected readings (pp. 45–53). London: Penguin.
Vilette, N., Lalo, L., & Bouillon, J.-P. (1994). *Le Flamboyant. Langage-lecture 2e
    année.* Paris: INRAP/Hatier.
Vincent, G. (1980). *L'école primaire française: Étude sociologique.* Lyon, France:
    Presses Universitaires de Lyon.
Wagner, D. A. (1993). *Literacy, culture, and development: Becoming literate in Mo-
    rocco.* Cambridge, UK: Cambridge University Press.
Wertsch, J. V. (1998). *Mind as action.* New York: Oxford University Press.
World Bank. (1987). *Education policies for Sub-Saharan Africa: Adjustment, revital-
    ization and expansion.* Washington, DC: Author.
World Bank. (1994). *World development report 1994: Infrastructure for development.*
    New York: Oxford University Press.

2

Linking Research to Educational Policy and Practice: What Kind of Relationships in How (De)Centralized a Context?[1]

Donald K. Adams, Mark B. Ginsburg, Thomas Clayton, Martha E. Mantilla, Judy Sylvester, and Yidan Wang[2]

INTRODUCTION

The 1980s and 1990s have witnessed heightened international concern about enhancing educational quality (Chapman & Carrier, 1990; Fuller, 1987; Hallak, 1990; Heyneman & Loxley, 1983). While the concern is almost universally shared, different conceptions of what constitutes educational quality have been adopted (Adams, 1993). Moreover, there have been debates on two issues related to the process of improving educational quality. The first concerns the alternative models for the relationship between researchers and policymakers/practitioners in efforts to link research and policy/practice, and the second involves arguments about the merits of centralized, linear versus decentralized, iterative strategies for reforming education. In this chapter, we summarize the issues raised in these debates and then explore them using illustrations drawn from documentation research of a USAID-funded project, Improving Educational Quality (IEQ), which operated in Ghana, Guatemala, and Mali during the years from 1992 to 1996.

MODELS OF RESEARCHER-POLICYMAKER/ PRACTITIONER RELATIONSHIPS

Much of the research on educational quality may be categorized roughly into two methodologically and conceptually distinct approaches: school effects (see, e.g., Hanushek, 1994) and effective schools (see, e.g., Lezotte,

1989). These approaches, however, have been criticized on a number of counts (see, e.g., Hargreaves, Lieberman, Fullan, & Hopkins, 1998; Riddell, 1989), including the fact that neither school effects nor effective school research have much to say directly about the process of improving education, that is, implementing and sustaining the policies and practices derived from such research activities (Adams et al., 1997). Too often research conceived of in relation to efforts to improve educational policy and practice is done by researchers in isolation from policymakers and practitioners, and the findings from such research are disseminated through conference presentations, research reports, articles, or books (targeted primarily to an audience of other researchers). The assumption seems to be that "good science" (Whyte, 1991, p. 8) will "trickle down to the level of practice and inform practitioners [and policymakers] on what to do and what not to do" (Gitlin et al., 1992, p. 25).

However, in recent years educational researchers, in conjunction with policymakers, administrators, and teachers, have sought to employ (and write about) strategies for strengthening the links between research and educational policy and practice. Here we describe three models for linking research to policy and practice: decision-oriented research, collaborative action research, and research as collective praxis. These models differ with respect to the nature of the roles played by researchers and policymakers/practitioners.[3] Thus, the models are built on different notions of what constitutes collaboration and empowerment (see Kreisberg, 1992) of researchers and policymakers/practitioners.

In their book on the subject, Cooley and Bickel (1986) describe *decision-oriented educational research* (DOER) as "research designed to help educators as they consider issues surrounding educational policy, as they establish priorities for improving educational systems, or as they engage in the day-to-day management of educational systems" (p. 3). A key element in this model from the researchers' standpoint is a "client orientation," operationalized through an "on-going educational dialogue" (p. 27) in which researchers "work hard at trying to understand the information needs of the client and to meet those needs" (p. 36). Within the DOER model, researchers interact with clients (usually defined as policymakers or administrators, though logically they could be teachers, students, parents, etc.) to provide "facts" about education and society, whether based on quantitative or qualitative data, which are needed by the clients to make certain decisions. The researchers are in dialogue with the (policymaker or practitioner) clients, but each group has its own specified and fairly distinct role. The researchers are not involved directly in policymaking or practice, and the policymakers and practitioners do not participate intimately in the research process.

Similar to the DOER model, *collaborative action research* (see, e.g., Stenhouse, 1975)[4] is concerned with enhancing the use of research by educational policymakers and practitioners. However, in contrast to the DOER model, the collaborative action research model entails not only dialogue about, but also joint participation in, research by "researchers" and "educators" (usually defined as teachers, though logically they could be educational administrators, policymakers, etc.). This model builds on the notion that educational practitioners normally engage in inquiry and that their practice can be enhanced if they devote more time and energy to a more systematically planned and implemented process of research (Brause & Mayher, 1991; Kincheloe, 1991; Wagner, 1990). Nonetheless, a division of labor still seems to exist. Even though the "practitioner" assumes rights and responsibilities in the research process, the "researcher" is involved primarily as a collaborator in research design, data collection, and data analysis, remaining somewhat detached from the "professional" and "political" activity of educational policymaking and practice (see Whyte, 1991).

The third model, *research as collective praxis*, shares some of the elements with, but is also framed in contrast to, the other two models. In her chapter on "Research as Praxis," Lather (1991) comments: "I am arguing for an approach that goes well beyond the action research concept. . . . The vast majority of this work operates from an ahistorical, apolitical value system" (p. 56; see also Bodemann, 1978; Carr and Kemmis, 1986; Gitlin et al., 1992). Similarly, McTaggert (1991) describes a "process of using critical intelligence to inform action, and developing it so that social action becomes praxis through which people may consistently live their social values" (p. 176). Core assumptions of the "research as collective praxis" model are that (a) researchers acknowledge and act upon their political commitments and (b) they do so in the context of theorizing and practice (i.e., praxis) with both professionals and nonprofessionals, such as students and community members (Fine, 1989; Gitlin et al., 1992; Reinharz, 1984; Vio Brossi & de Wit, 1981). In this way, the line between "researcher" and "policymaker" or "practitioner" becomes blurred as those who identify (or are typified) primarily as playing one of these roles, and in fact play both. Not only do policymakers, administrators, teachers, students, and community members participate in research, but "researchers" become active participants in various settings, working with others to understand *and* change schools and society.

(DE)CENTRALIZED CONTEXTS FOR RESEARCH-BASED EDUCATIONAL CHANGE

Paralleling and reinforced by the frequently unsuccessful attempts to translate studies of educational quality and effectiveness into policies and programs have been moves to reconceptualize the process of initiating and sustaining educational change. Traditionally in most countries and particularly in developing countries, there is a clear division of roles and responsibilities, wherein the central educational authorities are expected to initiate reforms and innovations and local schools are expected to participate, largely as implementers.

Although such top-down, centralized, linear approaches to reform have continued to be promoted, in recent years there has been increased rhetoric in favor of and experimentation with various forms and meanings of educational decentralization and center-local partnerships (Adams, 1994; Bray, 1988; "(De) centralization," 1993; McGinn, 1992; Tyack, 1993). This trend away from an exclusive reliance on detailed educational plans and mandates from the center is partly in response to the perceived weaknesses of top-down policies and attempts at expert-driven, programmatic development of educational reform. It is argued that although inputs of technology, equipment, curricular materials, and staff development designed and implemented in the center have in some cases improved school quality, often such center-orchestrated efforts have only marginal impact on the way teachers and students operate in classrooms and schools. It is also claimed that while reform defined exclusively at the national level may successfully obtain compliance, it often fails to gain commitment from administrators and teachers, let alone from students and parents.

Traditional planning of educational change has tended to ignore uncertainties and complexities and to focus instead on simplifying and standardizing innovations for universal dissemination. The newer approach draws from the extensive local and regional experiences of many countries in initiating and implementing school- and classroom-level innovations (see Buckley & Schubert, 1983). To be successful in educational change efforts, one must recognize the complexity of developing viable change and give less attention to rigid plans or outcomes. Such planned change is assumed to begin with a few readiness principles (e.g., adequate resources, acceptance of validity of the new practice), require pressure (from below), support (from above), and continuous negotiation (between system levels). Specific, detailed, centralized plans are devalued as initial guides to new practice because plans follow culture and mission follows (rather than precedes) enactment of principles.

It should be noted, though, that during the same period that decentralization has been increasingly stressed in the rhetoric and activity of educational reform, we have witnessed an intense process of globalization not only in the economy but also in the discourse and action of the field of education (Ginsburg, 1991). Thus, as we examine the (de)centralized contexts in which researchers establish relationships with policymakers/practitioners and pursue educational reform initiatives, we need to consider the degree to which international as well as national or local actors are involved in planning and implementing educational research, policy, and practice. For example, if much of the reform activity is shaped at the school-levels and local system-levels, but with significant input from bilateral agency officials, international organization representatives, or foreign consultants, should we label this as decentralization and/or super-centralization?

ILLUSTRATIONS FROM DOCUMENTATION
RESEARCH ON THE IEQ PROJECT

To explore further the issues identified above, concerning the relationships between researchers and policymakers/practitioners and the (de)centralized contexts for implementing educational reform, we draw on documentation research we conducted on the USAID-funded "Improving Educational Quality" (IEQ) project.

IEQ was initiated in 1991 as a five-year, USAID-funded project. IEQ's main objective was to design practical ways to improve learning in classrooms and schools within the context of national educational reforms in selected developing countries. In the three countries supported from 1992 until 1996 under the core contract—Ghana, Guatemala, and Mali—IEQ formed partnerships with one or more host-country institutions to: (a) assist in the enhancement of country research capacity and application; (b) collaboratively design and implement classroom research at the primary school level; and (c) link findings to practice and policy at various levels, from classrooms to national ministries, of the educational systems.

Following the ideal described by Clark (1988), but working within time and financial constraints, the documentation research we conducted provides a window for viewing the relationships established, the classroom research and other work undertaken, and the contexts in which such activity took place. Our documentation research involved analyzing a variety of documents and interviewing key participants in the IEQ project in Ghana, Guatemala, and Mali. The following types of documents and other artifacts were examined: technical proposals; weekly, monthly, semi-annual, and annual reports prepared by the Institute for International Research (IIR) with input from other (U.S. and non-U.S.) members of the project team; IEQ project newsletters; trip reports prepared by U.S. consultants upon their return from one or more of the core countries; and research reports, other documents, and videos of schools and classrooms produced by members of the Host Country Research Team in each core country. In addition, beginning in March 1994 and continuing beyond the project's official ending in October 1996, a series of interviews were conducted with the Project Director and the majority of U.S. consultants involved in IEQ and a sample of the key members of the Host Country Research Teams from the three host countries. These interviews were conducted face to face or by telephone, fax, regular mail, or e-mail. Through these mechanisms, information was gathered to clarify and augment what was included in the documents, to focus informants' feedback on drafts of the "stories" of IEQ in each country (see Clayton & Wang, 1996; Mantilla, 1996; Sylvester, 1996), and to identify new activities or themes to explore.

Prior to discussing what our documentation research says about (a) the relationships (i.e., division of labor) between researchers and policymakers/practitioners and (b) the (de)centralized nature of the institutional contexts within which efforts were undertaken to link research to educational policy and practice, however, it may be helpful to describe briefly the societal context of IEQ activity in each country (for further details, see Ginsburg & Adams, 1996; Ginsburg et al., 1999).

IEQ IN GHANA, GUATEMALA, AND MALI

Ghana

Ghana, a West African country with a population of 17 million, achieved its political independence from Britain in 1957. Ghanaians speak 44 indigenous languages, though English is the official language and the sole medium of instruction (beginning with the fourth year of primary school). Ghana is rich in natural resources—cocoa, gold, diamonds, and timber (Agbodeka, 1992), but following years of expansion, Ghana experienced a severe economic decline beginning in 1975. This led the government to negotiate loans from the IMF and World Bank as part of a structural adjustment program, including the reduction in public expenditures on education and other social services (Rothchild, 1991).

Up until the mid-1970s, Ghana had one of the most advanced educational systems in West Africa, but in the context of economic downturn, investment in education dropped drastically, plunging the system into a crisis (Yeboah, 1992). Because of this educational crisis, the government began pursuing a number of educational reforms. For instance, in 1991, the Primary Education Program (PREP) was initiated with funding from USAID. PREP focused on (a) distributing instructional materials; (b) developing criterion-based tests for primary school leavers in grade 6; (c) organizing a comprehensive inservice education program for primary school teachers; and (d) preparing and implementing an Equity Improvement Plan in the Central Region. When in April 1992 representatives of USAID/Accra, the Government of Ghana, and IIR, the prime contractor for the IEQ project, met to discuss where to focus IEQ resources, PREP was the consensus choice.

IEQ activity in Ghana centered on the efforts of a Host Country Research Team (HCRT), which was created and staffed by members of the Faculty of Education at the University of Cape Coast. In the first phase of the project, the team collected data—via observation and interviewing—in primary level (P1–P6) classrooms in six schools, focusing on the availability and use of instructional materials for the teaching and learning of English, math, and science. In the second phase, the team collected data in 14 (seven experimental and seven control) schools, studying the implementation of interventions (i.e., emphasizing teacher-pupil and pupil-pupil oral conversation in English, exposing pupils to English via print sources, and adopting a mastery learning approach) and their effect on English language proficiency of 1,032 P2–P5 pupils (using curriculum-based assessments developed by the HCRT and U.S. consultants). And in the third phase, P3–P6 classrooms in the 14 schools were studied to gauge implementation of the interventions (those introduced in the second phase as well as additional classroom management, remediation, and enrichment strategies) and their effects on pupils' English language proficiency and classroom behavior.

Key findings from the three phases of the research (1–3) include: (1) pupils were not interacting with the teachers, classmates, or written materials in ways that would promote English language literacy; (2) pupils in the interventions schools were more likely to be exposed to oral and written English (via textbooks and other instructional resources) and they evidenced higher levels of oral and written communication skills; and (3) teachers in the intervention schools more often used textbooks and other print materials (rather than the chalkboard) and reinforced pupils' use of English in class and outside of class, while pupils evidenced significantly greater improvement in their reading, writing, and speaking skills in English.

Between 1992 and 1996, various forums for dialogue about the research were organized from the national to the local level. The "Conference on Improving the Educational Quality of Primary Schools" was held annually in 1992, 1993, and 1994, and the IEQ National Advisory Board was convened in April and December 1995 and March, June, and September 1996. These national-level gatherings were attended by representatives of the Ministry of Education, Ghana Education Service, the Overseas Development Association, UNICEF, USAID/Ghana, the teacher's union, the University of Cape Coast, and a teacher's training college, as well as by circuit supervisors, school administrators, teachers, and parents. IEQ research findings were also discussed at the local level during monthly school visits by researchers (and head teachers and circuit supervisors) for purposes of training teachers in instructional and classroom management strategies as well as data collection.

Guatemala

Guatemala, a Spanish colony until 1821, is a Central American country with over 9.5 million inhabitants. Approximately 60 percent of the population are Indian, who speak 22 Mayan languages (Jona, 1991); the rest of the population are *ladinos*, descendants of white and Indian intermixing, who speak Spanish, the official language.[5] With coffee, bananas, cotton, and sugar supplying 62 percent of their export earnings, Guatemala is characterized as having a dependent economic status. Extreme poverty and malnutrition (Jona, 1991) juxtaposed with concentrations of wealth have led to long-term social and political unrest, including a civil war lasting three decades (1960s-1990s).[6]

In this political economic context it is not surprising that Guatemala has one of the lowest literacy rates in Central America and the world (Hayes, 1993). In an attempt to alleviate this problem, the Guatemalan government developed the Basic Education Strengthening (BEST) program, a seven-year (1989–1996) project supported by a grant from USAID. The *Nueva Escuela*

Unitaria (NEU) component of the BEST program became the focus of IEQ activities in Guatemala. The NEU model was based on an approach developed in Colombia and involved flexible promotion; active, collaborative learning; peer teaching; use of self-instructional guides; and participatory student government.

A Host Country Research Team was assembled, including a research coordinator, two regional field coordinators, and 10 field researchers. The original plan in 1992 was for the HCRT to become part of the Ministry of Education, but instead it functioned as a stand-alone organization until February 1996, when it was incorporated into the Universidad del Valle. Designed as a longitudinal evaluation study of the NEU component of BEST, the IEQ research involved testing of cognitive and socioemotional development, health status, and language proficiency, as well as classroom observations, and interviewing in five NEU or experimental and five control schools. The sample in the first phase included first- and second-grade pupils and a cohort who were studied as they moved up the grades during the second and third phases. Additionally, in the third phase the research agenda was expanded to collect data on the retention of students, and 20 NEU and 10 control schools were added to the sample.

Highlights of the findings by the research phase (1–3) include: (1) children in NEU schools evidenced significantly greater gains on several test measures, including reading comprehension in Spanish; (2) no significant differences were observed between children in the NEU and control schools in terms of gains in achievement; and (3) NEU schools had significantly lower dropout rates.

Dialogue activity occurred in conjunction with local or regional workshops organized by NEU program officials for supervisors, administrators, teachers, parents, and pupils. While discussion and reflection were emphasized, these periodic workshops functioned more to motivate and train educators to implement the NEU approach than to evaluate and refine the NEU program. The former type of interaction also characterized the workshops organized by some of the NEU teachers (termed *multiplicadores* or multiplyers) to orient teachers in other schools, where the nationally planned NEU program was to be expanded. At the national level, IEQ findings were discussed during a (February 1995) research methodology workshop conducted for Ministry of Education personnel and UNICEF staff; the long-delayed (September 1995) meeting of the IEQ National Advisory Committee, which was attended by representatives from the Ministry of Education, the Universidad de Valle, Rafael Landivar University, USAID/Guatemala, and UNICEF; and an (April 1996) IEQ-sponsored "Latin American Conference on Educational Quality," which was attended by representatives of the Ministry of Education, the two above-mentioned universities, USAID, UNICEF, and World Bank.

Mali

Mali, which gained its political independence from France in 1960, is a West African country of approximately 8.5 million people, comprising 15 major ethnic groups (Ouane, 1994) who speak 11 different languages (World Bank, 1988). Only about 10 percent of the population speak French, the official language (Bokamba, 1991). About 45 percent of the GNP in Mali comes from agriculture, animal husbandry, fishing, and forestry (Ouane, 1994), and its economic position is one of dependency with extensive poverty, particularly in the rural areas.

School enrollment rates in Mali are among the lowest in the world, and there are significant rates of repetition and dropout (see, e.g., UNESCO, 1991). To address this situation, in 1989 the Malian government launched its Basic Education Expansion Program (BEEP), a major national reform of primary schooling supported financially by USAID and the World Bank. This reform program became the focus of IEQ activities in Mali.

The HCRT in Mali was composed of eight members, four members each from (a) the *Institute Pédagogique Nationale* (IPN), the technical research branch of the Ministry of Basic Education, and (b) the *Institute Supériere de Formation et de Recherche Appliquee* (ISFRA), a research unit of the Ministry of Secondary and Higher Education. IEQ research in the first phase examined factors that affect French language learning[7] in first- and second-grade classrooms in 11 school communities, with ISFRA researchers highlighting health, nutrition, sanitary environment, sociocultural, and other characteristics of children and IPN researchers illuminating instructional practices during reading and language arts lessons. The findings from the first phase of the research, combined with professional judgments by host-country researchers and U.S. consultants, shaped the decision to implement two interventions: (a) using didactic materials, folktales, and small-group instruction in large classes, and (b) establishing community centers to provide supervised settings with good conditions for studying. Following training workshops that were organized by the researchers and local/regional administrators, a second phase of the research was conducted. This initially involved follow-up visits—including classroom observations and interviews—to 21 of an expanded sample of 42 "intervention" schools, of which 22 were employing a transitional, bilingual approach and 20 were using a "classical" French immersion approach.[8] During subsequent activity of the second phase of the research, the HCRT conducted a more indepth investigation, involving observations, language testing, and interviews in 12 of the 42 "intervention" schools.

The research findings were discussed at a national *Colloque* (April 1994), which was attended by both ministers of education, inspectors, regional educational directors, principals, teachers, parents, and representatives of bilateral agencies (including USAID) and international organizations. Regional workshops (one in August 1994 and three in November 1994) were also organized by researchers and attended by teachers, principals, inspectors, pedagogical advisors, community development technicians, regional education directors, and parents. And during the second phase of the research, school visits not only provided opportunities for researchers to gather information from the field, but also offered a chance for dialogue about the data gathered previously.

RELATIONSHIPS BETWEEN RESEARCHERS AND POLICYMAKERS/PRACTITIONERS[9]

The relationships between researchers, on the one hand, and policymakers, administrators, supervisors, teachers, and parents, on the other, varied across the three countries in the IEQ project as well as across time and system levels in each country. The Guatemalan case seems to best fit the more positivist, "decision-oriented research" model. Researchers consulted with policymakers and practitioners, including those working at international, national, regional, and local levels; collected and analyzed data viewed to be relevant to key decisions; and then reported on the findings. Particularly during the first phase of the project in Guatemala, it was the government authorities and educators who took charge of training for and implementing changes designed to improve educational quality (namely, the NEU component of BEST). Although the IEQ research coordinator increasingly played a role in training activities, this primarily consisted of reporting on the research findings and illustrating the differences between NEU and non-NEU classroom activities using transcribed excerpts of videos filmed during the research. In two cases, however, the relationships differed from that associated with the DOER model. The first was that the Colombian consultant who was heading up the NEU project (having been hired for the job by a U.S. consulting firm) was an active participant in designing the research and interpreting the findings. Through the role he played in the research activities, he stretched beyond what might be seen as the typical role for a policymaker or practitioner. The second case involved the teachers/*multiplicadores*, who became involved in disseminating the IEQ research findings in their efforts to promote the expansion of the NEU approach to instruction. While not involved in data collection and analysis, these teachers took on interpretation and dissemination roles traditionally associated primarily with researchers.

In Mali, the relationships between researchers and educational policymakers and practitioners were also in many ways similar to those associated with the DOER model. The HCRT, representing research units in the two ministries of education, consulted primarily with national- and international-level educational policymakers and practitioners prior to conducting research that they (and U.S. consultants) perceived to be relevant to improving educational quality. The research team then reported their findings to local as well as national and international audiences of policymakers and practitioners. However, the Malian researchers took a more active role than associated with the DOER model in training and supervising teachers to implement the instructional strategies and other interventions developed within the IEQ project.[10] Thus, in Mali the researchers' role was more in line with that implied by the "research as collective practice" model, in that they became more directly and actively involved in the process of (educational) change. However, the complementary stretching of policymaker and practitioner roles was not as apparent. Policymakers and practitioners at various levels of the system mainly related to the project as sources of data or audiences for reports of research findings. The interesting exceptions to this conclusion, though, involved the significant involvement in designing the research—albeit in contradictory ways—by two policymakers: (a) the USAID/Mali official at the beginning of the project and (b) the Minister of Education who was appointed just before the start of Phase II of the project. As noted previously, the former discouraged any research focus on schools using the transitional bilingual program, and the latter mandated such a focus.[11]

In Ghana, particularly at the beginning of the project, researchers' relationships with national ministry officials (and USAID and international organization representatives) generally resembled those that are associated with the DOER model. Researchers conducted research while ministry officials and agency personnel determined policies. Two notable exceptions to this characterization, however, were observed hinting toward collaborative action research or research as collective praxis models. The first involved a USAID/Ghana official, who had a major influence on the research design in the second phase of data collection in urging that the HCRT (a) expand the sample of schools to 14 (seven experimental and seven control schools) and include schools from more than one region of the country; (b) focus on identifying "new instructional strategies that might be used nationwide"; and (c) limit the study to the investigation of the teaching and learning of English (and not on math and science) in the upper primary grades only. The second exception was the fact that during the final year of the IEQ project the coordinator of the research team was appointed to be a member of the Ministry of Education's Executive Committee for Teacher Training, thus incorporating her more formally into a national policymaking role.

At the local and regional levels in Ghana, the relationships between researchers and educational practitioners (especially head teachers and circuit supervisors) developed in ways to make them even more in line with a "collaborative action research" model or a "research as collective praxis" model. For example, the HCRT assumed a fairly active role in promoting educational change, not only through participating in the organization and implementation of training workshops, but also in assuming quasi-supervisory roles in relation to teachers and, thus, quasi-collegial roles in relation to head teachers and circuit supervisors. This occurred as the HCRT members engaged in ongoing conversations about educational research, policy, and practice with teachers during training, monitoring, and data-gathering visits to schools. Additionally, over the course of the project, head teachers and circuit supervisors increasingly participated in the research efforts to document the activities of teachers and students, and they assumed full responsibility for conducting the research in the third phase after fiscal and time constraints prevented HCRT members from participating.

CENTRALIZED VERSUS DECENTRALIZED CONTEXT

In each country, the IEQ project operated in a relatively highly nationally centralized context, though aspects of the project's functioning sug-gested—and to some extent moved the dynamics to—a more regionally or lo-cally decentralized model. To begin with, in each of three countries IEQ research was focused generally on a major *national* educational reform initia-tive, which both predated IEQ and was (at least in part) funded—and, there-fore, shaped—by an extranational organization (USAID).[12] And in the case of Mali, the NEF reform introduced by a new Minister of Education just prior to the beginning of the second phase of the IEQ research was also a cen-trally—and in this case, a nationally—determined policy, on which IEQ re-searchers were required to focus. Moreover, in all three countries, many of the initial research design decisions were made based on the advice of—or at least with the approval of—officials at the "center," whether nationally (i.e., repre-sentatives of ministries) or internationally (i.e., representatives of USAID mis-sions and international organizations). In addition, prominent dialogue efforts were undertaken in a centralized context in which many participants were representatives of national and international agencies.

A somewhat decentralized structure for IEQ efforts to link research to edu-cational policy and practice in each country, however, is indicated by the fact that these national events—the conferences, colloquia, seminars, and advisory committee meetings—often included administrators, supervisors, teachers, and parents from the local areas in which the IEQ research and other activities were being conducted. Furthermore, many dialogue activities were organized on a regional or local school level, thus creating opportunities for a more de-centralized approach to developing and refining classroom teaching practices stemming from ideas generated by IEQ research or based on professional in-sights of HCRT or U.S. support team researchers. During the period of the IEQ project in the three countries (1992–1996) there was certainly an in-crease in the level of local participation in discussing and shaping educational practice.

With respect to educational policy, though, the IEQ project inserted itself into, and functioned generally as a part of, a centralized process of planning and implementation. In a sense, the IEQ activity at the regional and local level served to disseminate and promote the policy (and practice) reforms that had been determined centrally—whether at the national or international level. Generally, local input was sought mainly for identifying problems with and solutions for implementation of the nationally and internationally determined reforms in educational policy and practice.

One notable exception to this conclusion is worth mentioning, in that while it provides an example of "bottom-up" policy change, it clarifies how those at the top or center of the system retain considerable control over at least the timing of policy reforms. The case in point occurred in Ghana. In 1993, the HCRT reported at the "Conference on Improving the Educational Quality of Primary Schools" on the finding from the first phase of their research that Ghanaian pupils' English language learning was hampered because textbooks were not available in some schools and, when available, the texts were not being used by pupils. Moreover, the researchers found that (a) textbook availability was limited because head teachers did not have funds to travel to district distribution centers to obtain the PREP-sponsored books for their schools, and (b) even when the books were available, teachers did not distribute the texts to pupils to avoid having to pay for any damage the books might suffer in the hands of the pupils. The dialogue stimulated by these findings resulted in two changes in national-level policy, although not until 1995—approximately one-and-a-half years later and after the findings had been replicated in the second phase of the research. First, a new policy was adopted authorizing payment to head teachers for the cost of traveling to district offices to collect textbooks for their schools. Second, the policy that held teachers fiscally responsible for textbooks that were soiled or damaged by student use in class or at home was rescinded.

The fact that teachers' and head teachers' views about the negative effects that national policies had on educational quality led to changes in these policies suggests that the IEQ project facilitated more local participation in policymaking and, in this case, a bottom-up reform. We should note, however, that it took a centrally organized team of university-based researchers, who were collaborating with U.S. consultants in the context of a USAID-funded project, to communicate the message to national policymakers. And, indeed, even their message did not result in policy changes until after they reported the same conclusions based on findings from a second phase of the research.

CONCLUSION

Whatever longer-term lessons were learned from such experiences by researchers as well as local, national, and international policymakers and practitioners will have to await future research, as will the examination of the level of local participation in decision making about educational policy and practice that occurred after the first five years of the IEQ project—and the funding for the research teams—ended. Whatever the longer-term impact, the experiences of the IEQ project in Ghana, Guatemala, and Mali illustrate some of the opportunities and challenges in developing different kinds of relationships between researchers and policymakers/practitioners and in pursuing educational reform efforts in contexts that vary—across countries and over time—in their degree of national–local as well as international–national–local (de)centralization.

NOTES

1. The documentation research on which this chapter is based was developed as part of the Improving Educational Quality (IEQ) project (Contract # DPE-5836–C-00–1042–00), a five-year (1991–1996), centrally funded, USAID project, undertaken by the Institute for International Research (IIR) as the prime contractor, along with Juarez and Associates, Inc., and the University of Pittsburgh as subcontractors. A second, five-year IEQ project (Contract # HNE-I-97–0029–00) was undertaken, beginning in 1997, by the IIR/American Institutes for Research as the prime contractor, along with the Academy for Educational Development, Educational Development Center, Juarez and Associates, Inc., and the University of Pittsburgh as subcontractors.

2. We would like to thank other members of the IEQ Project team who provided feedback on earlier drafts of this chapter: Francis Amedahe, Yetilú de Baessa, Ray Chesterfield, Sékou Diarra, Rick Donato, Joshua Muskin, Alimasi Ntal-l'Mbirwa, Beatriz Okeyere, and Jane Schubert.

3. Arguably, these three models of linking research to educational policy and practice have close affinities with three scientific paradigms (see Ginsburg & Klopfer, 1996). Thus, although proponents of each model subscribe to some form of methodological eclecticism—usually framed as using quantitative and qualitative data—it seems like the decision-oriented research model fits best with positivist science, collaborative action research with interpretivist science, and research as collective practice with critical science (for descriptions of these scientific paradigms, see Popkewitz, 1981).

4. Although Stenhouse (1975) and his colleagues at the University of East Anglia in England popularized and legitimized collaborative action research in education, Corey (1953), drawing on the ideas of Lewin (1946)—who coined the term "action research"—may have been the first to promote this approach in education through his book, *Action Research to Improve School Practices.*

5. The main language of instruction in Guatemala is Spanish, although beginning in the 1980s, there have been increasing efforts to include the four main maternal languages for bilingual instruction in the indigenous regions.

6. Until the 1996 peace accord, Guatemala had the longest-running guerrilla movement of Latin America, starting in 1961. It is estimated that since 1954, following a *coup d'etat* and an invasion backed up by the United States, 100,000 people have died, 40,000 have disappeared, and 150,000 have been made widows and orphans.

7. The focus on *French* language learning was shaped by an official in USAID/Mali, who discouraged a focus on bilingual (French and a maternal language) approaches. He asserted that U.S.-funded projects should avoid actions that might be interpreted by the French government as interfering with French–Malian relations, particularly in the area of language policy. This is despite the fact that approximately 100 schools were implementing bilingual programs and that some Malian educators' views were in line with the favorable evaluation (conducted in the context

of the USAID-funded Advancing Basic Education and Literacy [ABEL] project in the late 1980s; see Hutchinson, 1990) of a national experiment in the use of maternal languages.

8. Despite discouragement at the beginning of the project from a USAID/Mali official, IEQ research ended up focusing on bilingual instruction because a new Minister of Basic Education, who took office in January 1994, specified that all education projects in Mali must be cohesive with his new educational reform initiative, *Nouvelle Ecole Fondamentale* (NEF), which was designed to promote the teaching of maternal languages.

9. It is important to note that in the three IEQ core countries, the role played by the Host Country Research Teams is complicated because of their collaboration with U.S.-based consultants, who helped to design the research, collect and analyze data, interpret the results, and (in the cases of Ghana and Mali) develop and train educators to implement reformed educational practices.

10. In Guatemala, the HCRT coordinator and others made presentations at training workshops, and IEQ and NEU staff jointly organized such workshops late in the project, but in Mali (and particularly in Ghana), the HCRT played a relatively active role in training activities from the beginning of the project.

11. In another sense, though, the Minister's *Nouvelle Ecole Fondamentale* reform could be seen (and perhaps was in fact) in line with the results of USAID-funded research conducted in Mali in the late 1980s (Hutchinson, 1990) that concluded that language proficiency in French (and indigenous language) was better achieved through a transitional bilingual education approach. Thus, at the same time he was stretching his role toward active involvement in research planning, he was also operating as a policymaker consuming the research findings of decision-oriented educational researchers.

12. While the influence of USAID officials—both in Washington and in the mission of each core country—cannot be discounted, it should be noted that Ministry of Education officials and IEQ personnel helped shape the decisions to focus on USAID-funded projects: PREP in Ghana, BEST in Guatemala, and BEEP in Mali.

REFERENCES

Adams, D. (1993). Defining educational quality. *Educational Planning, 9*(3), 3–18.

Adams, D. (1994). COPLANER: An exploratory model for decentralizing educational planning in Indonesia. Jakarta, Indonesia: Ministry of Education and Culture.

Adams, D.; Clayton, T.; Rakotomanana, M.; and Wang, Y. (1997). Implementing and sustaining educational changes in educational quality. *Educational Planning, 11*(3), 3–20.

Agbodeka, F. (1992). *An economic history of Ghana from the earliest times.* Accra: Ghana Universities Press.

Bodemann, Y. (1978). The problem of sociological praxis. *Theory and Society,5,* 387–420.

Bokamba, E. G. (1991). French colonial language policies in Africa and their legacies. In D. F. Marshall (Ed.), *Language planning: Focusschrift in honor of Joshua A. Fishman on the occasion of his 65th birthday* (pp. 175–213). Amsterdam: John Benjamin.

Brause, R., & Mayher, J. (Eds.). (1991). *Search and research: What the inquiring teacher needs to know*. Bristol, U.K.: Falmer Press.

Bray, M. (with Lillis, K.). (Ed.) (1988). *Community financing of education: Issues and policy implications in less developed countries*. Oxford, UK: Pergamon.

Buckley, J., & Schubert, J. (1983). *Demonstration programs and educational innovation: A review and synthesis of the literature*. Unpublished manuscript.

Carr, W., & Kemmis, S. (1986). *Becoming critical: Education, knowledge and action research*. London: Falmer Press.

Chapman, D. W., & Carrier, C. A. (Eds.). (1990). *Improving educational quality*. Westport, CT: Greenwood Press.

Clark, T. (1988). Documentation as evaluation: Capturing context, process, obstacles, and success. *Evaluation Practice, 9*(1), 21–31.

Clayton, T. & Wang, Y. (with Diarra, S., Ntal-l'Mbirwa, A., & Tounkara, B.). (1996). The IEQ story in Mali. In M. Ginsburg & D. Adams (Eds.), *Policy-practice-research-dissemination/dialogue spirals in improving educational quality* (pp. 104–137). Pittsburgh, PA: Institute for International Studies in Education, University of Pittsburgh.

Cooley, W. & Bickel, W. (1986). *Decision-oriented educational research*. Boston: Kluwer-Nijhoff.

Corey, S. (1953). *Action research to improve school practices*. New York: Teachers College Press.

(De)centralization and democratic wish [Special issue]. (1993). *The Forum, 2*(3).

Fine, M. (1989). The politics of research and activism. *Gender and Society, 3*(4), 549–558.

Fuller, B. (1987). Raising school quality in developing countries: What investments boost learning. *Review of Educational Research, 57,* 255–292.

Ginsburg, M. (Ed.). (1991). *Understanding educational reform in global context: Economy, ideology and the state*. New York: Garland.

Ginsburg, M., & Adams, D., (Eds.). (1996). *Policy-practice-research-dissemination/ dialogue spirals in improving educational quality*. Pittsburgh, PA: Institute for International Studies in Education, University of Pittsburgh.

Ginsburg, M.; Adams, D.; Clayton, T.; Mantilla, M.; Sylvester, J.; & Wang, Y. (2000). The politics of linking educational research, policy, and practice. *International Journal of Comparative Sociology, 41* (1), 1–21.

Ginsburg, M. & Klopfer, L. (with Clayton, T., Rakotomanana, M., Sylvester, J., & Yasin, K.). (1996). Choices in conducting classroom-anchored research to improve educational quality in "developing" countries. *Research Papers in Education, 11*(3), 239–54.

Gitlin, A., Bringurst, K., Burns, M., Cooley, V., Meyers, B., Price, K., Russell, R., & Tiess, P. (1992) *Teachers' voices for school change: An introduction to education research*. New York: Teachers College Press.

Hallak, J. (1990). *Investing in the future: Setting educational priorities in the developing world*. Paris: UNESCO/IIEP; Oxford: Pergamon.

Hanushek, E. (1994). Education production functions. In T. Husen & T. N. Postlethwaite (Eds.), *International encyclopedia of education* (2nd ed., Vol. 8, pp. 1756–1762). New York: Pergamon.

Hargreaves, A., Lieberman, A., Fullan, M., & Hopkins, D. (Eds.). (1998). *International handbook of educational change*. Boston: Kluwer Academic.

Hayes, K. (1993). *Effective multigrade schools: A review of the literature.* Washington, DC: USAID.

Heyneman, S. & Loxley, W. (1983). The effects of primary school quality on academic achievement across twenty-nine high and low income countries. *American Journal of Sociology, 88*(1), 162–94.

Hutchinson, J. (1990). *Evaluation of the experimentation in national languages in primary education in the Republic of Mali.* Washington, DC: USAID-ABEL Project.

Jona, S. (1991). *The battle for Guatemala.* San Francisco: Westview Press.

Kincheloe, J. (1991). *Teachers as researchers: Qualitative inquiry as a path to empowerment.* Bristol, UK: Falmer Press.

Kreisberg, S. (1992). *Transforming power: Domination, empowerment, and education.* Albany, NY: SUNY Press.

Lather, P. (1991). *Getting smart: Feminist research and methodology with/in the postmodern.* New York: Routledge.

Lewin, K. (1946). Action research and minority problems. *Journal of Social Issues, 2*(1), 34–46.

Lezotte, L. (1989). School improvement based on the effective schools research. *International Journal of Educational Research, 13*(7), 815–25.

Mantilla, M. (with de Baessa, Y., & Chesterfield, R.). (1996). The IEQ story in Guatemala. In M. Ginsburg & D. Adams (Eds.), *Policy-practice-research-dissemination/dialogue spirals in improving educational quality* (pp. 64–103). Pittsburgh, PA: Institute for International Studies in Education, University of Pittsburgh.

McGinn, N. (1992). Reforming educational governance: Centralization/decentralization. In R. Arnove, P. Altbach, & G. Kelly (Eds.), *Emergent issues in education: Comparative perspectives* (pp. 163–172). Albany, NY: SUNY Press.

McTaggert, R. (1991). Principles for participatory action research. *Adult Education Quarterly, 41*(3), 168–87.

Ouane, A. (1994). Mali: System of education. In T. Husén & T.N. Postlethwaite (Eds.), *International encyclopedia of education* (2nd ed., Vol. 6, pp. 3578–3586). London: Pergamon.

Popkewitz, T. (1981). The study of schooling: Paradigms and field-based methodologies in educational research and evaluation. In T. Popkewitz & R. Tabachnick (Eds.), *The study of schooling: Field based methodologies in educational research and evaluation.* New York: Praeger.

Reinharz, S. (1984). Dimensions of an experiential sociological method. In *On becoming a social scientist* (pp. 308–368). Brunswick, NJ: Transaction Books.

Riddell, A. (1989). An alternative approach to the study of school effectiveness in the Third World. *Comparative Education Review, 33*(4), 481–497.

Rothchild, D. (Ed.). (1991). *Ghana: The political economy of recovery.* Boulder, CO: Lynne Rienner.

Stenhouse, L. (1975). *Introduction to curriculum research and development.* London: Heinemann.

Sylvester, J. (with Amedahe, F., Harris, A., Okeyere, B., Pasigna, A., & Schubert, J.) (1996). The IEQ story in Ghana. In M. Ginsburg & D. Adams. (Eds.) *Policy-practice-research-dissemination/dialogue spirals in improving educational quality* (pp. 15–63). Pittsburgh, PA: Institute for International Studies in Education, University of Pittsburgh.

Tyack, D. (1993). School governance in the United States: Historical puzzles and anomalies. In J. Hannaway & M. Carnoy (Eds.), *Decentralization and school improvement* (pp. 1–32). San Francisco: Jossey-Bass.

UNESCO. (1991). *World Education Report 1991*. Paris: Author.

Vio Brossi, G., & de Wit, R. (Eds.). (1981). *Investigación Participativa y Praxis Rural*. Lima, Peru: Mosca Azul.

Wagner, J. (1990). Administrators as ethnographers: Schools as a context for inquiry and action. *Anthropology and Educational Quarterly, 21*(3), 195–221.

Whyte, W. F. (1991). Introduction. In W.F. Whyte (Ed.), *Participatory action research* (pp. 7–15). Newbury Park, CA: Sage.

World Bank. (1988). *Education in Sub-Saharan Africa*. Washington, DC: Author.

Yeboah, V. (1992). *Ghana's policy adjustment initiative: Opportunity for renewal*. (World Bank Paper #132). Washington, DC: Author.

3

Policy Research as Ethnographic Refusal: The Case of Women's Literacy in Nepal[1]

Margaret Sutton

The practices of educational policy research that are framed by international assistance agencies have been largely impervious to critical theoretical debates, which have so altered the landscape of sociocultural scholarship over the past 30 years. As argued in the Introduction to this volume, heightened reflexivity about both culture and power has conferred scholarly legitimacy upon a broad range of research questions and methodologies not only in disciplines such as anthropology, sociology, and history, but also in "applied" and cross-disciplinary fields including area studies, women's studies, and policy studies. The enterprise of international assistance itself has become an object of cultural and political analysis (Escobar, 1995; Ferguson, 1994; Mueller, 1986; Pigg, 1992). Meanwhile, in some fields or "sectors" of development assistance, such as rural development (Apthorpe, 1997), research spawned by the exigencies of development work has incorporated not only qualitative research techniques, but also analysis incorporating "the culture concept," as described by Wright (1994), and the ethnographic stance of viewing the world through the whole self (Ortner, 1995). This has not been the case for educational policy research linked to the workings of international assistance agencies—agency research, for short. Agency research in education remains both methodologically and theoretically conservative, tied firmly to a "managerial" model of policy analysis (Bowe & Ball, 1992, p. 7) and to "instrumental" knowledge (Habermas, 1971) as its base.

Many currents of thought and practice influence the policymaking processes of international donor agencies in the field of education. The World Bank, regional development banks, UNESCO, UNICEF, USAID, SIDA, JICA, and the many other agencies that fund educational systems across national boundaries are moved by both common and unique dynamics. Each "donor agency" maintains a distinctive institutional culture defined by its space of origin and accountability, its mandate, and its systems of finance and governance. As Anderson-Levitt and Alimasi show in Chapter 1 in this volume, these differences result in conflicts between donors on specific programmatic approaches. At the same time, as Samoff (1999) has pointed out, there has been for at least the last 30 years an astonishing convergence of policy trends and positions in international assistance to education. Since the late 1980s, a dominant trend across the spectrum of donor agencies has been the support of girls,' and to a lesser extent, women's education. This is an area in which the author has worked since 1988 both as a scholar (Sutton, 1998) and as a program designer, policy researcher and evaluator, in the direct or contracted employ of five bilateral and multilateral agencies.[2]

The fundamental conservatism of agency research is nowhere more evident than in the case of girls' education, an issue given discursive and programmatic weight by international assistance agencies, governments, and citizens over the past 10 years or so. Perhaps *the* cause célèbre of education and development in the 1990s, girls' and women's education has been promoted in the United States by no less a personage than the First Lady.[3] As a major policy trend, the field of girls' and women's education has engendered numerous studies and proclamations, most commissioned by donor agencies in support of their own policymaking and programmatic processes. A search for such works has yielded a total of 116 research reports and policy statements on girls' and women's education generated since 1970 by UNESCO, USAID, the World Bank, and UNICEF.[4] Ongoing analysis of these documents by the author suggests a high level of agreement not only on the importance of girls' and women's education, but on approaches to improving it. For well over a decade, a rather narrow set of ideas has circulated around girls' education and thereby framed policy and programmatic measures by international assistance agencies. These ideas include the need for adequate sanitary facilities, local women as preferred instructors for rural girls, the need to convince parents of the importance of girls' education, and the value of community contributions to school finance and management as a means of expanding access.[5] While not denying the creativity of specific programs and individuals involved in them, agency-sponsored interventions in support of girls' education over the past 10 years have favored a limited set of actions.

Underlying the narrow range of programs is a restricted policy perspective on girls' education, as a means to such ends as reducing fertility, improving child health (Ainsworth, Beegle, & Nyamete, 1995; Cochrane, 1979; Cochrane, O'Hara, & Leslie, 1980), and, less convincingly, spurring economic development (Schultz, 1993). The policy questions entertained by agency research have taken little to no account of either the meaning of education to girls and women, or to the politics of patriarchy as they shape and contest the educational opportunities and experiences of girls and women around the world. These questions, however, are vital to effective policy formation in the field of girls' education. Decades of thought on education and social change around the world make it a truism that educational attainment is both a product and a source of social power (Bowles & Gintis, 1976; Carnoy, 1975; Dore, 1976). Any large-scale change in patterns of educational attainment by girls becomes a matter of altering gender relations—and thus the dynamics of power between genders. The social and personal meanings of education also change in the process.

This chapter argues that the resistance in agency research on girls' education to the incorporation of interpretive and critical approaches arises primarily from structural constraints on policy research that are endemic to international assistance agencies. These constraints generate research driven by instrumental knowledge interests, in Habermas's terms (1971) and promote practices of "ethnographic refusal," as characterized by Ortner (1995). The structural constraints are illustrated here by the example of an impact evaluation of girls' education in which the author participated. The case study, of an evaluation of women's literacy programs in Nepal, substantiates Escobar's (1994) construct of the hegemonic discourse of development and echoes many of the points made by Ferguson (1992) concerning the institutional construction of projects by international development agencies. The chapter concludes by considering ways that those involved in agency research can contribute to richer and more democratic processes of educational policy formation in international assistance agencies.

WOMEN'S LITERACY, GIRLS' EDUCATION, AND THE NEPAL IMPACT EVALUATION

The notion that literacy among women will result in improved educational attainment among their children is a piece of folk wisdom among many literacy activists and supporters. Harbans Bhola (1989) reports that Tanzanian leaders observed this phenomenon as a serendipitous outcome of the 1970s literacy campaign of that country. Recent reports by non-governmental organizations (NGOs) in the field of literacy have highlighted the phenomenon.[6] Scholars of literacy processes, including Stromquist (1997), have written thoughtfully on literate mothers' engagement in their children's learning and schooling. However, the possible and distinctive impact of women's new literacy on children's schooling has been little studied from what has come to be called "a policy research" perspective.

The Kingdom of Nepal provides an excellent context for studying the outcomes of adult literacy programs. The government, external donors, and national and international NGOs have supported efforts in adult literacy for some time now. USAID support to literacy programs in Nepal began in 1977. In the 1980s, World Education assisted the government of Nepal in developing and field-testing a set of basic literacy texts, *Naya Goreto*, based in part on Freire's pedagogical principles.[7] Revised versions of these texts continue to be used widely in Nepal by the majority of organizations providing literacy programs. In the 1990s, USAID support has moved increasingly toward post-literacy efforts with specific themes, such as legal rights, health knowledge, and microenterprise creation.

Ongoing external support has also made Nepal's literacy efforts among the most-studied in the Third World. Nepalese and international staff of the larger NGOs involved in literacy provision in Nepal have written numerous reports and a handful of academic papers[8] assessing their impact. The work of Comings and his colleagues takes particular care to understand learning outcomes and behavioral impacts of literacy programs (Comings, Shrestha, & Smith, 1991; Comings, Smith, & Shrestha, 1995). In 1996, Burchfield (1997) undertook a study of attitudinal and behavioral changes among women who had participated in literacy and post-literacy courses. Her study included reports of newly literate women whose children were more likely to attend school now than they were prior to the literacy class. At present, World Education Nepal, under USAID's Girls' and Women's Education project, is concluding a long-term study of the impacts of literacy efforts upon women. These reports, articles, and ongoing studies provided the groundwork for the case study.

In June 1997, I joined in a policy evaluation effort directed by the Center for Development Information and Evaluation (CDIE) of USAID called *Focus on Girls: USAID Programs and Policies.*[9] CDIE is the unit responsible for agency-wide research upon and evaluation of USAID policies and their implementation. The ultimate purpose of the exercise can be surmised from the title—to determine how programmatic and policy actions of USAID have impacted the education of girls. This particular project sought to ascertain the effects of USAID education efforts upon the education of girls, through "field" or in-country studies of the outcomes of programs in five countries: Guatemala, Guinea, Malawi, Nepal, and Pakistan. The evaluation ultimately is intended to inform the next generation of USAID policy toward girls' education. Multicountry impact evaluations such as these are a primary vehicle of the research conducted by CDIE, intended to inform USAID policy and practice. Thus, an exposition of how one of these studies was enacted speaks to theoretical concerns with the way in which policy knowledge is generated in agency research.

The exposition begins by considering the study from the "natural categories" of contracting practices in international assistance agencies. It then describes the survey component of the Nepal study and its findings. Following the exposition, it is argued that agency research practices construct girls' and women's education as an exclusively instrumental affair.

Deep Structures of Agency Research

The *Focus on Girls* impact evaluation and the Nepal component of it were enacted through processes that are common across development sectors and agencies, beginning with the definition of research questions by CDIE staff in consultation with USAID staff, education contractors, and other educational specialists, and continuing through the processes of hiring researchers and formulating reports. If one thing distinguished the *Focus on Girls* from other agency policy research, it was the magnitude of resources devoted to field-based study. For each of the five country studies, teams composed of one to four expatriate researchers and one to five "local" or national researchers conducted an intensive in-country information and data collection process lasting from two to four weeks, each culminating in a country case study report published by CDIE (Benoliel et al., 1998a; Benoliel, O'Gara, & Miske, 1998b; Bernbaum et al., 1998; Stromquist, Klees, & Miske, 1999; Sutton, Tietjen, Bah, & Komanor, 1999). The country case studies were followed by a synthesis report on the findings of the field-based case studies as well as a "desk study"[10] of Egypt (O'Gara, Sutton, & Tietjien, 1999). This section details the research practices in the Nepal case study, employing the contractual terms that define commissioned research.

Management of the Project

Like most work conducted by USAID and to varying degrees by other international donor agencies, the activities related to *Focus on Girls* were contracted by USAID to a private organization, in this case a nonprofit institution. A senior CDIE staff member oversaw the study as a whole and participated in two of the five country studies. In the contracting organization, a senior technical staff member, who also participated in two of the field studies, was responsible for contributing to the technical agenda and identifying, hiring, and managing the research teams. Behind the task managers in both institutions are offices responsible for ensuring that all contracts entered into are legally and procedurally correct and that the contracts themselves are honored.

Terms of Reference

As in other policy arenas, the heart of any consulting agreement with an international assistance agency lies in the "Terms of Reference" (TOR) for the work to be done. Specific content can vary widely, as can the rigor with which the task manager enforces them, but the terms of reference spell out what contracting agencies and individual consultants are to do. As reiterated in each country study, the overall purpose of the *Focus on Girls* studies is "to examine the effectiveness of USAID policies and programs in increasing girls' access to primary education, improving the quality of education received and strengthening primary educational institutions" (Benoliel et al., 1998a, p. 2). This language is echoed and elaborated in the TOR defining each individual's work on the project. The author's TOR specified the hiring and management of a

Nepali research team, consultations with specific organizations, and the design, implementation, analysis, and reporting on a field-based survey of the impact of women's literacy programs upon children's education.

The Nepal study differed from the other four country studies in two ways. First, the programmatic focus was on literacy programs conducted for adult women who had had little or no formal schooling, rather than on formal education programs for children, as was the case for the other studies. Second, the Nepal study included an original data-generating effort in addition to synthesis of existing data, which was the norm for the other studies. The field study was conducted in four Village Development Communities (VDCs) in the Western Terai region of Nepal.

Designing the Nepal Field Survey

As noted earlier, the general research questions to be addressed by the survey were determined prior to the hiring of any researchers. For 10 days, the four Nepali researchers and a research assistant worked with the three expatriate researchers to elaborate the general questions into specific ones, and at the same time to hammer out the design of the study, identify samples, and construct a survey instrument. This work was conducted in two locations: a conference room in a five-star hotel, and the many offices and meeting rooms of organizations involved in women's literacy in Nepal, including the USAID mission, the Nepali Ministry of Education, the Center for Educational Research Information and Development, and U.S.- and Nepali-based NGOs. One NGO lent a pretested instrument for gathering demographic and household data,[11] while another shared its work-in progress on a longitudinal study of women's literacy in Nepal, and later, sponsored a meeting for sharing initial findings.[12]

Through these processes, the team designed a four-page survey to be administered verbally. Following the demographic data, the survey recorded the names, ages, and past or current school attendance (when relevant) of all children of the interviewee, as well as details concerning repetition and dropout occurrences. In cases in which primary-school age children were not in school, mothers were asked why they were not in school, who made the decision, and whether she agreed with the decision. The last section included two questions for school-going children of the interviewees.

Research Questions

In line with the overall purpose of the *Focus on Girls* study, the field survey was designed to assess the impact of women's participation in literacy programs upon their children's education. In particular, the team sought to determine:

1. Whether children of women who had participated in programs had higher *school participation rates* than children of nonliterate mothers who had not participated in such programs;

2. Whether participators' children had higher levels of *educational attainment* than children of nonparticipants;

3. Whether participators' children had higher levels of *educational achievement* than children of nonparticipants;

4. Whether children of literacy program participants received *greater household support* for their schooling than children of nonparticipators;

5. Whether the *gender gap in enrollment* is lower among children of literacy program completers than among others;

6. Whether participators' children *attended school more regularly* than children of nonparticipants;

7. Whether participators' children were less likely to *repeat grades* than nonparticipators' children.

Questions one through five were to be addressed exclusively through the survey findings, whereas responses on questions six and seven were cross-validated by examining local school registers.

Note that the study did not attempt to assess skills acquisition among literacy program participants. Rather, it took a "black box" approach to the programs themselves. We felt confident, however, that we were picking the right boxes, by considering within the two "literacy treatment" groups only women who had successfully completed the six-month basic program. We were interested in talking with women who had completed a program at least three years prior to the study, with the belief that behavioral changes in relation to children's education take time to unfold.

Research Design

While the basic research questions were explicit in terms of reference for the study, the quasi-experimental design of the survey component was assumed as the proper method for identifying impacts specific to literacy programs. Similarly, two factors that were assumed to influence schooling among the children of nonliterate or newly literate Nepali women also informed the final design. On the one hand, the financial well-being of families has plausible links with children's schooling experiences. Thus, the research team decided to contrast the schooling of children whose mothers were involved in income-generation with those of mothers who had completed literacy programs. At the same time, the concept of "group formation effects," or changes in values and beliefs arising from programmatically-defined collective experiences of women, had also been recently posited as a factor that changes parental attitudes and behaviors toward their children (Comings, Smith, & Shrestha, 1995). The research team thus chose to conduct a four-way comparison encompassing women who had completed literacy programs, those who were engaged in income-generation through microcredit,[13] a group who had completed a literacy program and were engaged in microcredit activities, and a "control" group of women who had not completed a literacy program and were not engaged in microcredit. These four groups provided—on paper anyway—an ideal matrix for teasing out such specific impacts for children's education as might derive from participation in a literacy program.

Defining the characteristics of the control group was one of the more difficult issues that the research team had to resolve. The research team judged it unwise to compare women who had and had not attended programs in the same village, as such a design might reflect not the impact of programs, but the reasons that some women did not participate in them. Rather, we choose to compare participants with a group who had not had an opportunity to select into or out of a program, that is, those living in a VDC in which no programs had been offered. In this group, we would interview women who had also not attended school themselves, and thus were presumed nonliterate. The very short time frame for survey administration dictated this approach, rather, for example, than matching of individual women who had and had not participated, but were similar in other relevant ways like residence, caste, age, prior education, or mode of livelihood. As we shall see, it proved even more difficult in practice than in theory to conduct a "control-group" survey.

Administering the Survey

The entire research team flew to the Terai (plains region) of Nepal for a period of 3½ days. Prior to departure, the team identified the three programs from which "treatment group" women would be sampled. The USAID/Nepal office assisted in contacting program administrators. Program administrators, in turn, helped to arrange access to the women whom we wished to interview. The surveys themselves were administered by the national researchers and a research assistant. The research assistant and lead national researcher were fluent in the local languages of the Western Terai, while the other Nepalese team members spoke some. The three U.S. researchers spoke no local language. The Nepalese researchers, with the assistance of local schoolmasters, also compiled data derived from school records, which proved to be an arduous task.

Survey administration was intense work. In each of the three "treatment" villages, local program administrators helped to locate women who were involved in the literacy and microcredit programs. Three to four of the national researchers simultaneously interviewed individual women, while children, spouses, other community members, and the expatriate researchers observed. Interviews took place in the open air or on the verandas of public buildings; straw mats and rope beds were brought from nearby residences.

Locating and interviewing members of a "control" group turned out to be no easy task. In the first place, it was planting time in the fields and people were extremely busy with their work. The research team talked with program administrators in the region about VDCs in which programs had not taken place, and chatted with vendors and shoppers at a market outside of town. Ultimately, a schoolteacher we met at the market suggested the village in which he worked. It took several visits to locate and interview a sufficient number of women. All worked for one landlord and had very little time to spare for conversation. The "control-group" interviews were also emotionally challenging for the national research team, as one woman after another asked whether a program would be offered soon in their village. One of the researchers made a point of communicating the high level of interest among the "control group" to literacy program personnel with whom we worked.

After disqualifying respondents who had not completed programs within the time frame in question, we ended up with responses from 93 women with a total of 219 children in the target age range, from 6 to 15. The women ranged in age from 20 to 50, with the average age around 33. The total sample is represented in Table 3.1.

Findings of the Study

The team analyzed differences in educational participation and attainment among children in the four groups from several angles, including numbers of children ever in school and differences in participation rates among older and younger children (assuming that younger children would receive larger im-

Table 3.1
Number of Subjects

	Mothers	**Children ages 6 –15**		
		Boys	*Girls*	*Total*
Literacy	22	22	18	40
Micro-credit*	24	32	32	64
Both	23	32	25	57
Neither*	24	26	32	58
TOTAL	93	112	107	219

*Nonliterate women

pacts). No matter what indicator was employed, however, no significant differences were found in participation among children from the four groups, or between girls and boys.[14]

While rates of school participation did not vary among groups, there was a marked difference in the incidence of grade repetition between the "control-group" children on the one hand and all "treatment-group" children on the other. Grade repetition is high in Nepal's primary schools, averaging around 23 percent. In the Western Terai region, though not in all parts of Nepal, girls are more likely to repeat primary grades than are boys. From the survey, we found repetition rates for both boys and girls in the "treatment" groups to be at or below the national norm, while the percentage of children in the control group who had repeated a grade was extremely high. A T-test found the difference statistically significant at the .05 level.

The last two survey questions yielded some interesting findings, especially considering the lack of a discernible impact of programs upon participation in schooling. The brief conversations with children yielded the most compelling findings in relation to the overall purpose of the study. At the conclusion of the interviews with mothers, national researchers asked to speak with one or more of the women's children who were currently enrolled in primary school. The children were asked two questions: "Does anyone help you with your homework?" and "Does your mother help you in any way with your schooling?" One hundred sixty-six children responded to these questions, 90 of whom were girls.

Children of both genders in all three program groups were more likely than children in the control group to report that someone helped them with their homework. That "someone" was also more likely to be an older sibling or uncle than it was to be the mother, but the high prevalence of academic assistance shows that children are being encouraged and supported at home in their learning. In a similar vein, children in all three program groups were three to four times more likely than children in the control group to report that their mothers help them with school work. The help that children in the three program groups reported that they received from their mother was less often academic assistance than it was paying of fees, providing time for homework, and asking about school. In both help with homework and any assistance from the mother, the differences were statistically significant between the control and all treatment groups at the .05 level. These findings concerning support for schooling provide a plausible rationale for explaining the relatively low repetition rates across groups.

In addition to looking at all data for boys and girls separately, the analysis contrasted educational participation between genders, by looking at the "gender gap" in enrollment and how it varied across groups. Though school participation rates *per se* did not vary significantly by group or by gender, the *gender gap*, defined as the difference in net primary enrollment rate between boys and girls, does differ across groups, totaling 15% in the literacy group, 28% for the microcredit group, 3% in the integrated program group, and 26% in the control group, as compared to 20% for the country as a whole and 26% for the Western Terai in particular. A chi-square test, however, shows no significant differences between actual and expected values for each group.

In short, the field study returned insufficient data to answer questions of exam performance, found no significant differences between the control group and any treatment groups concerning participation rates, years of schooling attained, gender gap in enrollment, or daily school attendance. The significant findings were those associated with all three programs: literacy, microcredit, and the integrated program. The children of women involved in all of these programs are more likely to receive support for their studies. They are also much less likely to repeat grades than the children in the "control group," a fact that may be explained in part by the perception of parental and other support for their efforts. The fact that this effect is consistent across all "treatment" groups indeed suggests that something in the nature of a "group formation" effect is at work.[15]

Culture as a Variable

The above section summarizes the findings reported in the case study. But the survey results raised as many questions as they answered. At this point there is no doubt that the alert reader is asking what *else* might be going on to explain the differences found by the study—as well as the nondifferences. Looking at culture as a variable, that is, glancing lightly at specific cultural features of the four groups of women and their children, suggests that a great deal that is relevant to children's schooling may be going on *outside* of literacy classes and microcredit programs. The research team was surprised at first to find such high levels of educational participation among "control" group children. One obvious explanation for this finding is that the control group was really not comparable in significant ways with the "treatment" groups. A convenience sample, the control group lived in a VDC that was much closer to the main town in the area and only a short walk to the main road and market. The microcredit and integrated program groups, by contrast, were some distance from the main road; during heavy rains, they can become inaccessible. The literacy group is in between as far as proximity to town and its amenities, including access to higher levels of schooling, to formal labor markets, and to mass media.

A second, "uncontrolled" difference among the groups lies in their caste/ ethnic mixture. As illustrated in the literature on Himalayan anthropology (see McHugh, 1992), Nepali society is quite diverse; Nepalese population data reports more than 40 ethnic categories. For the topic under consideration here, one of the most important differences among ethnic groups is the prevalence of the practice of child marriage for girls, a practice believed to be associated with low educational participation (Odaga & Heneveld, 1995). The research team was alerted to this aspect of sociocultural difference by the explanations of some women in the microcredit group for their daughters' lack of attendance in school. "She is married," they would say of an 11–, 12–, or 13-year-old girl. In an analysis based on national demographic data, Thapa (1996) identifies ethnic groups associated with early marriage, late marriage, and—the majority—no consistent pattern of age at marriage for girls by ethnic group. Applying his categories to our data set, we find that 48% of the children in the microenterprise group, and 36% of those in the integrated program group are members of ethnic groups associated with early marriage for girls, in contrast to only 12% in the control group and none in the literacy group.

A final contextual variable further complicates interpretation of the gender gap differences among groups. Although isolated and clearly not wealthy, the VDC from which the integrated program sample was drawn is relatively newly settled, compared to the other VDCs. Many of the residents were Gurkha soldiers in the British and Indian armies who were provided with land upon their return to Nepal. Although the entire Terai contains migrants from the hills and mountains of Nepal, the antecedents of this migration included men's experiences of military education and training as well as travel.

These few examples begin to illustrate the many levels of meaning left untouched by policy research practices in international agencies. More time and resources can surely incorporate finer cultural detail, as is the case for one analysis of women's literacy in Nepal that is currently underway. Simply including cultural attributes as variables, however, is unlikely to bring fundamental changes in perspectives on women and education.

Agency Constructions of Females and Their Education

The fact that the Nepal field survey inadequately accounts for the complexity of Nepali culture(s) and pays even less attention to gender, caste, and class politics will come as no surprise to people familiar with policy-oriented research, especially in international development. Both policymakers and scholars who are concerned with policy recognize a difference, at times a seeming chasm, between the knowledge created as scholarship and the knowledge sought after by policymakers. Regarding educational policy in the U.S., Borman, Cookson, Sadovnik, and Spade (1996) observe that there is a "gap between sociological research and educational practice" and consider its possible sources in the differences in norms, communicative style, and reward structures between higher education and state bureaucracies (p. xxx).

Speaking of the "underutilization" of educational research by Third World policymakers, Reimers and McGinn (1997) maintain that the "ethos" of policymakers, who "value research to the extent that it is instrumental in achieving policy objectives," leads to skepticism about the relevance of much research, which may be seen as "insufficiently conclusive to support decisions" (p. 20). In his detailed analysis of the discourse and practices of development in

Lesotho, Ferguson assumes "the incompatibility of 'development' discourse and academic norms" (1994, p. 29).

Policy research in general is more likely to be shaped by instrumental than by interpretive or critical interests. In part, this is a reflection of the pragmatic information that policymakers seek from research. Note, however, that in the field of girls' and women's education, the purpose of research is not only un- abashedly but doubly instrumental in focus. The rationale for educating girls and women is so that through their children, the economy will grow—both because their children are more productive and because there will be fewer of them. The *Focus on Girls* study—indeed, all agency-based work on girls and women's education of the past 15 years—asserts that the nonschooling of girls is a problem requiring a solution. It is *pro forma* in the agency-based literature on girls' and women's education to invoke the rationale for female education as a public good, as in the Foreword to a study of girls' education in three countries that was prepared by the World Bank for distribution at the 1995 Fourth World Conference on Women in Beijing:

Educating girls . . . reduces child mortality, fertility rates, and the spread of AIDS. It in- creases the duration of girls' own lives and the human potential of the children they will bear. And it has important environmental benefits. Ultimately, getting more girls into school is critical for reducing poverty. (EDI, n.d., p. i)

The Nepal field study was designed explicitly to demonstrate that educating women leads to better lives (through more education) for their children.

What makes the instrumental orientation of agency research so problematic is the near-total hold that it has on research in the field of girls' and women's education. It may be the case that more has been written in English about women and literacy in Nepal than in any other country in Asia. The ERIC in- dex of education journals and monographs lists 60 relevant entries for the pe- riod from 1966 to 1998. Of these, only two are published in refereed journals (Comings, 1992; Junge & Shrestha, 1984).[16]

To the extent that agency research carries the weight of defining the mean- ing, value, and desirable approaches to girls' and women's education, it is in- cumbent upon those who particpate in it to consider how such research can be opened up to more diverse perspectives and interests. Literacy program work in Nepal is tightly linked to the support of development assistance institutions; the written discourse reflects this fact. Adele Mueller's analysis of Women in Development (WID) literature finds a similar profile in the broader discourse on women in the Third World. She notes that "Much of what members of the North American intelligentsia know about women in the Third World is made available to us in the organization and procedures of discourse in the Develop- ment apparatus" (1986, p. 36). What is true of Third World women in general is true of the field of girls' and women's education in particular. The prepon- derance of written discourse on girls' and women's education emanates from the work of international assistance agencies. This "policy language and discourse," as Shore and Wright note, "provides a key to analyzing the architecture of modern power relations" (1997, p. 12).

QUESTIONS NOT RAISED, ANSWERS NOT SOUGHT

The study described above was well executed within the framework of agency research and yielded information of interest to USAID and other policymakers. At the same time, it contributed to a process of restricting the range of questions considered relevant to policy and consequently limiting the understandings of policymakers. This study, like so much of the research conducted ostensibly to inform policy in education and development, falls into Habermas's category of "empirical-analytic science." These sciences, he maintains, are driven by an interest to expand human control over nature and over people by identifying causal or lawlike relationships. This form of knowledge Habermas also calls "instrumental," in that it examines the means for reaching a specified end. Technical or instrumental knowledge stands in contrast to two other forms of knowledge: interpretive or hermeneutical knowledge, which seeks to expand mutual understanding among human beings by explicating cultural meanings and traditions, and critical or emancipatory knowledge, which raises awareness of "ideologically frozen relations of dependence that can in principle be transformed" (Habermas, 1971, p. 311).

There is nothing intrinsically wrong or evil about instrumental knowledge. The question here concerns its adequacy to policymaking. The instrumental perspective on the phenomenon of literacy in the first case masks the wide range of interrelated approaches to and meanings associated with the acquisition of literacy. The evaluation made no attempt to contextualize findings about mother–child educational links in the lives or viewpoints of the women who were interviewed. Indeed, despite their recent attainment of literacy, the research subjects were considered as themselves voiceless. This is a real loss for our understanding of how literacy and other education for women plays into the lives of their children, let alone what it means to the women themselves. In her study of women participating in literacy programs in Sao Paulo, Stromquist (1997) demonstrates the range of perspectives among women involved in literacy programs on their own learning and that of their children. Many of the women in her study showed a strong and active interest in their children's education. The relationship of women's pursuit of literacy to their children's education, however, remains ambiguous. It is unclear

whether the women's concern for their children's education was affected by the literacy classes or whether their concern for their children's education predated their literacy classes and in fact moved them to seek literacy. . . . What is important is that women who seek literacy also evince an interest in their children's education, thus forecasting that women's literacy skills will be applied in one way or another as their children move through the educational system. (p. 143)

As Stromquist points out, "Causality cannot be assessed here" (p. 143).

Besides neglecting to attend to subjective meanings, instrumentally-driven research processes can be quite blind to power dynamics. As Mundy argues in the case of Southern Africa, "Illiteracy is a fundamental manifestation of the unequal relationships integral to capitalism" (1992, p. 411). Women, and men, do not just happen to be illiterate. Rather, the incorporation of Third-World societies into the global system creates categories of people who are literate and nonliterate—and shifts the "problem" of nonliteracy to those who are its bearers.

In Nepal, caste and/or ethnicity is strongly determinant of the lifeworld in which women, men, and children live, yet its workings and salience are muted in agency-based work. In recent years, caste may be mentioned in the development discourse as a characteristic of individuals, but not subjected to analysis. The Nepal report, for example, states that "A Nepali woman's status and degree of freedom is established by the caste or ethnic group into which she is born" (p. 5). Other agency-based texts, such as a recent report on the status of women (Shakti, 1995), manage to summarize the status of Nepal women without ever employing the word "caste."[17] Contrast this to the images conveyed by Kumar's (2000) poem about the literacy and life of a low-caste Indian woman:

PRIMARY LESSONS IN POLITICAL ECONOMY

For every ten bushels of paddy she harvests
    the landless laborer takes home one

This woman, whose name is Hiria, would have to starve
    for three days to buy a liter of milk

If she were to check her hunger and not eat
    for a month she could buy a book of poems.

And if Hiria, who works endlessly, could starve
    endlessly, in ten years she could buy that piece

Of land on which during short winter evenings
    the landlord's son plays badminton. (p. 138)

This poem is a part of the project Kumar defines as "supplying critical contexts for the consumption of cultural texts as well as events" (p. 209). Such contexts enrich and sharpen understanding of the lifeworlds of others.

Hegemony of Agency Research

The substantial overlap of agency-based and academic writing on women's literacy is not unique to Nepal, to women, or to the field of education. Recent work on the discourses and practices of development show a similar profile for most fields of "development studies." Inspired by the work of Foucault,

Escobar analyzes the "system of relations" that determines "what can be said" about development (1995, p. 40). The social relations and the texts created through them constitute the "hegemonic worldview of development" (p. 17). As in Foucault's work on the rise of prisons (1979), and of institutions defining madness (1973), as well as Said's (1978) exposition of the creation of "Orientalism," Escobar finds intimate and inescapable links among those who study and those who enact programs of social change under the rubric of development. He argues that the institutionalization of the international development regime "brings the Third World into the politics of expert knowledge and western science in general" (1995, p. 45). This process includes

a set of techniques, strategies, and disciplinary practices that organize the generation, validation, and diffusion of development knowledge, including the academic disciplines, methods of research and teaching, criteria of expertise, and manifold professional practices. (p. 45)

Research and information-gathering practices are central to the workings of development assistance institutions. In the discursive field of development assistance, the norms and practices of scholarship interact with the norms and practices of program development and policy analysis.

Several authors have documented or commented upon the extent to which the bureaucratic mandates of development assistance institutions take precedence over scholarly mandates. Ferguson (1994) shows that major World Bank policy documents for Lesotho are void of historical knowledge about the country and its societies. The absence of history enables the donor discourse to promote credit programs, the development of markets, and cash economies as if they were somehow new to Lesotho. Programs designed in ignorance of existing institutions and practices inevitably yield less welfare than promised. Commenting on the inability of development bureaucracies to take effective account of social diversity, Pigg argues that "what comes to predominate in this institutional context is a kind of ersatz sociocultural knowledge encapsulated in the notion of the village" (1992, p. 594).

Development discourse is hegemonic not only in regard to scholarship but also in the richer sense of hegemony, as an ideology that informs ordinary as well as expert views of the world. In her article, Stacy Leigh Pigg (1992) argues that the ideology of development now shapes language and thinking about day-to-day life in Nepal. Embedded in the Nepali term "*bikas*" (development), she maintains, is "an ideology of modernization: the representation of society through an implicit scale of social programming" (p. 499). This is an ideological framework that defines the elite as "the developed" members of society, and implies the possibility of such "development" for all.

Escobar (1995) concurs that the hegemonic discourse of development casts socioeconomic difference into an apolitical framework. At the core of the discourse, he argues, is "the problematization of poverty" as a technical matter. The discourse proceeds by "creating abnormalities (such as the 'illiterate,' the 'underdeveloped,' the 'malnourished,' or 'landless peasants'), which it would later treat and reform" (p. 41). Ferguson (1994), in a careful study of a large-scale agricultural development project in Lesotho, argues further that the way in which poverty is problematized in development discourse serves to obscure the power relations that structure poverty and privilege. He thus dubs the development assistance system the "Anti-Politics Machine," a network of institutions and practices that generate "the ideological effect of depoliticizing both poverty and the state" (p. 256). In an intellectual history of the practices of development, Rist agrees, noting that political leaders "use 'development' as a pretext to . . . widen the gulf between rich and poor" (1997, p. 216).

Agency Research as Ethnographic Refusal

In her analysis of the so-called "resistance" literature in anthropology, sociology, and history, Ortner (1995) accuses these studies of practicing a form of what she dubs "ethnographic refusal." The concept holds promise for understanding both the constraints in agency research and the possible means to overcoming them. By ethnographical refusal, Ortner means "a refusal of thickness, a failure of holism or density" (p. 174), and she levels this charge at a number of studies that attempt to document subversion of, or noncompliance with, dominant cultural norms by people who belong to subordinated groups.[18] Ortner identifies a set of three qualities that characterize ethnographic refusal: (1) "thinning culture," or the reduction of complex cultural practices to simplistic categories like "religiosity"; (2) "sanitizing politics," by overlooking conflicts and power differentials within a category of subordinate people; and (3) "dissolving subjects," or reducing the lives of individual people to a set of culturally determined actions and reactions. The net result of ethnographic refusal, Ortner argues, is "a kind of bizarre refusal to know and speak and write of the lived worlds inhabited by those who resist (or do not, as the case may be)" (pp. 187–188). Viewing Ortner's analysis through Habermas's schema of knowledge-constitutive interests, what the studies in question "refuse" is (deeply) interpretive and critical knowledge.

It is not difficult to see the qualities of ethnographic refusal displayed in agency-based research. As already illustrated, the Nepal study takes little account of the cultural contexts of those studied and even less of the class, caste, and gender politics through which these contexts are enacted. It takes a conscious act of "bracketing," however, to view agency-based policy studies as ethnographic research. After all, international agencies rarely commission full-blown anthropological studies in support of policy and programmatic decisions. It can be argued, however, that most policy research supported by international agencies inserts researchers into the life-worlds of people who live very differently than they do, thus necessitating layers upon layers of cultural interpretation—whether explicit or assumed.

If the analysis of the hegemonic discourse of development holds any truth, then policy research by scholars is also and always ethnographic in the sense that it draws the practices of scholarship into the bureaucratic field of development assistance agencies. Researchers are operating in a different lifeworld than the one that trained them to conduct research. The extreme time pressures and peculiar lifestyle of development agency work heighten the difficulties for policy researchers to conducting deeply interpretive and critical analysis. The bureaucratic procedures for review of work differ substantially from those of the academy. The former is a hierarchical system in which institutional authority includes editorial powers. This contrasts profoundly with the principles of peer review and contributes in no small measure to the consistent levels of "ethnographic refusal" apparent in agency research.

Three features of work in education further reinforce instrumental definitions of policy questions and ethnographic refusal in agency research practice. Formal educational systems today are vast enterprises with a clear hierarchy of power, which naturalizes the "managerial perspective" on education policy. Second, it is in the nature of education systems to generate data. Practitioners of educational development regularly decry the inaccuracy of this data and urge its better collection and use, with the more critical calling for a reconsideration of the relative merit of data-based arguments (Samoff, 1999). Nonetheless, the numbers are there—of students, teachers, buildings, and books—and it is hard to resist their potential to rationalize planning. Finally, what makes policy research practices different in education than in other development sectors is that the "beneficiaries" of educational policy are children, who do not have a voice in policymaking at either national or international centers of power. For the case of girls' education, the fact that the intended beneficiaries will grow up to be women reinforces technocratic definitions of agency research.

REFUSING TO REFUSE: DEMOCRATIZING GIRLS' EDUCATION POLICY

Hegemony is large and researchers are small. How can individual researchers who value anthropological thinking employ our craft in a nonhegemonic or even a counterhegemonic fashion? Is it possible to "refuse to refuse" as practitioners of agency research? Ortner's formulation suggests two avenues through which contracted researchers can attempt to pry open the sphere of questions that inform educational policy formation in international assistance agencies.

The strategies that individual researchers adopt to "refuse to refuse" will of course depend both on the effective authority of the person and on her specific values. If those values include democratizing research and policymaking practices, then the basic strategy would be to work for the broadest and deepest possible involvement of the "beneficiaries" of development efforts into their definition, workings, and evaluation. A good starting point is in pushing the locus of control over research into the hands of national scholars. Although sharing citizenship with research subjects is no guarantee of greater empathy or mutual comprehension, the contextual knowledge of national researchers is likely to outweigh that of expatriates. There is also the matter of long-term interaction with research subjects, leading in the best case to a form of accountability. Being strategic in the process of shifting scholarship into the hands of national researchers requires knowledge of the current realities of researchers in a given setting.

The quality of "thickness" that is so strongly associated with good ethnography is a result, among other things, of mindfulness—of the ethnographer being aware of the worlds in which he or she lives and works, and how profoundly they vary. Thickness is built through attention to multiple facets of life and to the myriad perspectives of those who live them. Few actors in the agency world have any illusions that a policy that they are proposing to a Minister of Education will have the same meaning to parents and children all over that country. The intense time pressures of agency-based policy research, however, seriously strain the "absorptive capacity" of researchers to grasp the complexities of local institutions and practices and their relevance to policy formation. It is incumbent upon researchers in this context to be mindful not only of what they see and hear around them, but especially of what can't be seen or heard in a two-hour visit to district education offices, let alone from the windows of a five-star hotel.

The slowly turning wheels of international agency practices have, over the past two decades, been realigned by the growing presence and activism of people with highly diverse backgrounds and perspectives. The time might be ripe for a fundamental reexamination of policy formation processes within them. Researchers can do their part by agitating in small and large ways for movement away from technocratic decision making and toward democratic dialogue.

NOTES

1. The research process reported here was conducted under contract with the Academy for Educational Development for the Center for Evaluation and Development of USAID. This chapter has benefited tremendously from collegial feedback on two earlier versions presented at the Comparative International Education Society meetings in 1998 and 1999.

2. In addition to USAID, these include the World Bank, the Asian Development Bank, UNICEF, and the UNDP, on assignments in Washington, D.C., New York, Malawi, Guinea, Nepal, Pakistan, India, Indonesia, and China.

3. Hillary Rodham Clinton first pledged U.S. support to girls' education in developing countries at the Copenhagen conference on Sustainable Development, held in 1995.

4. Of these, USAID sponsored or conducted 28; UNESCO, 27; The World Bank, 45; and UNICEF, 16. The author is confident that figures are comprehensive for the first three agencies but not for UNICEF.

5. These interventions were widely publicized in the agency sphere through the USAID-sponsored monograph *Educating Girls: Strategies to Increase Access, Persistence, and Achievement* (Tietjen, 1991).

6. For examples relating to Nepal, see Dhakal and Sheikh (1997); Save the Children (1997).

7. See Comings, Shrestha, and Smith (1991).

8. See, for example, Dhakal and Sheikh (1997); Leve et al. (1997); Save the Children (1997).

9. The author worked on the Nepal and Guinea field studies and coauthored the final report.

10. In agency terms, a "desk study" is conducted by analyzing documents and consulting in person or by phone, fax, or e-mail with people who have been involved in program implementation.

11. The team is grateful to the Asia Foundation, Kathmandu, for this assistance. See Dhakal and Sheikh (1997) for the original study.

12. The author thanks the staff of World Education Nepal for their professional generosity.

13. The microcredit most widely adapted in Nepal and around the Third World is based upon small-group membership.

14. In the case of educational achievement, the very low numbers of comparable scores precluded analysis. Although exam scores were recorded for 85 children, only those from grade 5 exams, standardized across the district, could be considered comparable.

15. It is possible that the underlying effect is similar to what Burchfield (1997) identifies as "planning for the future" in her study of the changes in behavior and attitudes among more than 400 Nepali women who have completed literacy programs. Burchfield argues that when women actively work to improve their lives, it is likely that they also become more attentive to their children's futures.

16. In addition to the indexed literature, other texts have been produced recently by international NGOs (INGOs) that administer literacy programs in Nepal with donor funding. These include the report of a study on USAID-funded women's empowerment programs conducted by the Asia Foundation (Dhakal & Sheikh, 1997) and a monograph of individual women's testimonials compiled by the Centre for Population and Development Activities (CEDPA, 1997), another INGO involved in implementing literacy programs. In 1995, Shtri Shakti, a Nepali NGO, published a comprehensive review of the status of women in development, with a sizeable section on literacy. The study was financed by U.S., Danish, and Canadian bilateral aid programs. World Education, the U.S.-based INGO with the longest involvement in literacy programs in Nepal (and the source of both academic and agency texts), is currently completing a two-year study of the impacts of literacy on women.

17. No doubt this was a conscious choice on the part of the authors. Like gender, the category of caste is far more complex and dynamic than any simple rendition can convey. And in the Nepali context, with its multiple shades of Hinduism, caste is a particularly complex concept.

18. James C. Scott's *Domination and the Arts of Resistance* (1990) is the most widely cited.

REFERENCES

Ainsworth, M., Beegle, K., & Nyamete, A. (1995). *The impact of female schooling on fertility and contraceptive use: A study of fourteen Sub-Saharan countries.* Washington, DC: World Bank.

Apthorpe, R. (1997). Policy as language and power. In C. Shore & S. Wright (Eds.), *Anthroplogy of policy: Critical perspectives on governance and power* (pp. 43–106). London and New York: Routledge.

Benoliel, S., Ilon, L., Sutton, M., Karmacharya, D. M., Lamichhane, S., Rajbhadry, P., Kafle, B. D., & Giri, S. (1998a). *Nepal case study (Focus on girls: USAID progams and policies in education).* Washington, DC: Center for Development Information and Evaluation, USAID.

Benoliel, S., O'Gara, C., & Miske, S. J. (1998b). *Promoting primary education for girls in Pakistan.* Washington, DC: Center for Development Information and Evaluation, USAID.

Bernbaum, M., Fair, K., Miske, S. J., Moreau, T., Nyirendra, D., Sikes, J., Wolf, J., Harber, R. B., Hartwell, A., & Schwartz, B. (1998). *Promoting primary education for girls in Malawi.* Washington, DC: Center for Development Information and Evaluation, USAID.

Bhola, H. S., & International Bureau of Education. (1989). *World trends and issues in adult education.* London: J. Kingsley.

Borman, K. M., Cookson, B. K., Sadovnik, A., & Spade, J. (Eds.). (1996). *Implementing educational reform: Sociological perspectives on educational policy.* Norwood, NJ: Ablex

Bowe, R., & Ball, S. J. (with Gold, A.). (1992). *Reforming education and changing schools: Case studies in political sociology.* London and New York: Routledge.

Bowles, S., & Gintis, H. (1976). *Schooling in capitalist America: Educational reform and the contradictions of economic life.* New York: Basic Books.

Burchfield, S. (1997). *An analysis of the impact of literacy on women's empowerment in Nepal.* Washington, DC: USAID.

Carnoy, M. (1975). *Schooling in a corporate society* (2nd ed.). New York: D. Mckay.

CEDPA. (1997). *Women on the move.* Kathmandu, Nepal: CEDPA Nepal Field Office.

Cochrane, S. H. (1979). *Fertility and education: What do we really know?* Baltimore: Johns Hopkins University Press.

Cochrane, S. H., O'Hara, D. J., & Leslie, J. (1980). *The effects of education on health.* Washington, DC: World Bank.

Comings, J. P. (1992). A secondary analysis of a Nepalese national literacy program. *Comparative Education Review, 36*(2), 212–226.

Comings, J. P., Shrestha, C. K., & Smith, C. (1991). *Efficiency and effectiveness of a national literacy program: A case study of Nepal.* Unpublished manuscript.

Comings, J. P., Smith, C., & Shrestha, C. K. (1995). *Adult literacy programs: Design, implementation and evaluation.* Washington, DC: USAID.

Dhakal, R. M., & Sheikh, M. M. (1997). *Breaking barriers, building bridges: A case study of USAID? Nepal's SO3 women's empowerment program.* Kathmandu, Nepal: The Asia Foundation.

Dore, R. (1976). *The diploma disease: Education, qualification and development.* London: Allen & Unwin.

Economic Development Institute. (n.d.). *Leveling the playing field: Giving girls an equal chance for basic education—Three countries' efforts.* Washington, DC: World Bank.

Escobar, A. (1995). *Encountering development: The making and unmaking of the Third World.* Princeton, NJ: Princeton University Press.

Ferguson, J. (1994). *The anti-politics machine: "Development," depoliticization, and bureaucratic power in Lesotho.* Minneapolis: University of Minnesota Press.

Foucault, M. (1973). *The order of things: An archaeology of the human sciences.* New York: Vintage Books.

Foucault, M. (1979). *Discipline and punish: The birth of the prison.* New York: Vintage Books.

Habermas, J. (1971). *Knowledge and human interests.* Boston: Beacon Press.

Junge, B., & Shrestha, S. M. (1984). Another barrier broken: Teaching village girls to read. *Reading Teacher, 37*(9), 846–852.

Kumar, A. (1997). Translating resistance. In A. Cvetkovich and D. Kellner (Eds.), *Articulating the global and the local: Globalization and cultural studies* (pp. 207–225). Boulder, CO: Westview Press.

Kumar, A. (2000). *Passport photos.* Berkeley: University of California Press. Copyright © 2000 The Regents of the University of California.

Leve, L., & Leslie, K. D. (1997). *10 Year retrospective literacy and empowerment.* Kathmandu, Nepal: Save the Children.

McHugh, E. L. (1992). Dialogue, structure, and change in Himalayan anthropology: A review article. *Comparative Studies in Society & History, 34*(3); 552–560.

Mueller, A. (1986). The bureaucratization of feminist knowledge: The case of women in development. *Resources for Feminist Research, 15*(1), 36–38.

Mundy, K. (1992). Toward a critical analysis of literacy in Southern Africa. *Comparative Education Review, 37*(4), 389–411.

Odaga, A., and Heneveld, W. (1995). *Girls and schools in Sub-Saharan Africa: From analysis to action.* Washington, DC: World Bank.

O'Gara, C., Benoliel, S., Sutton, M., & Tietjien, K. (1999). *More, but not yet better: An evaluation of USAID's programs and policies to improve girls' education.* Washington, DC: USAID.

Ortner, S. (1995). Resistance and the problem of ethnographic refusal. *Comparative Studies in Society and History, 37*(1), 173–193.

Pigg, S. L. (1992). Inventing social categories through place: Social representations and development in Nepal. *Comparative Studies in Society and History, 34*(3), 491–522.

Povinelli, E. A. (1991). Organizing women: Rhetoric, economy, and politics in process. In M. Di Leonardo (Ed.), *Gender at the crossroads of knowledge: Feminist anthropology in the postmodern era* (pp. 235–254). Berkeley: University of California Press.

Reimers, F., & McGinn, N. (1997). *Informed dialogue: Using research to shape education around the world.* Westport, CT: Praeger.

Rist, G. (1997). *The history of development: From Western origins to global faith.* London, New York: Zed Books.

Said, E. W. (1979). *Orientalism.* New York: Vintage Books.

Samoff, J. (1999). Institutionalizing international influence. In R. F. Arnove & C. A. Torres (Eds.), *Comparative education: The dialectic of the global and the local* (pp. 51–90). Lanham, MD: Rowman & Littlefield.

Save the Children/US. (1995). *15 Years in Nepal: 1981–1996.* Kathmandu, Nepal.

Schultz, T. P. (1993). Returns to women's education. In E. M. King & M. A. Hill (Eds.), *Women's education in developing countries : Barriers, benefits, and policies* (pp. xiii, 337). Baltimore: Johns Hopkins University Press.

Scott, J. C. (1990). *Domination and the arts of resistance* New Haven, CT: Yale University Press.

Shakti, S. (1995). *Women, development, democracy: A study of the socio-economic changes in the status of women in Nepal (1995).* Kathmandu, Nepal: Shtrii Shakti.

Shore, C., and Wright, S. (1997). *Anthropology of policy: Critical perspectives on governance and power.* London, New York: Routledge.

Stromquist, N. P. (1997). *Literacy for citizenship: Gender and grassroots dynamics in Brazil.* Albany, NY: SUNY Press.

Stromquist, N. P., Klees, S., & Miske, S. J. (1999). *Improving girls' education in Guatemala.* Washington, DC: Center for Development Information and Evaluation, USAID.

Sutton, M., Tietjien, K., Bah, A., & Komano, P. (1999). *Promoting primary education for girls in Guinea.* Washington, DC: Center for Development Information and Evaluation, USAID.

Sutton, M. (1998). Access to education. In N. P. Stromquist (Ed.), *Women in the Third World: An encyclopedia of contemporary issues.* New York: Garland Publishing.

Thapa, S. (1996). Girl childmarriage in Nepal: It's prevalence and correlates. *Contributions to Nepalese Studies, 23*(2), 361–375.

Tietjen, K. (1991). *Educating girls: Strategies to increase access, persistence, and achievement.* Washington, DC: Office of Education and Office of Women in Development, U.S. Agency for International Development.

Varenne, H., and McDermott, R. (1999). *Successful failure: The school America builds.* Boulder, CO: Westview Press.

Wright, S. (1994). "Culture" in anthropology and organizational studies. In S. Wright (Ed.), *Anthropology of organizations* (pp. 1–31). London: Routledge.

PART II

LOCAL EDUCATORS APPROPRIATING AND FORMING EDUCATIONAL POLICY

4

Multicultural Curriculum and Academic Performance: African American Women Leaders Negotiating Urban School Accountability Policies

Khaula Murtadha-Watts

> If we lived in a democratic state our language would have to hurtle, fly,
> curse, and sing, in all the common American names, all the undeniable and
> representative participating voices of everybody here. We would not toler-
> ate the language of the powerful and, thereby, lose all respect for words,
> per se. We would make our language lead us into the equality of power that
> a democratic state must represent.
>
> —June Jordan, *On Call*

In a multicultural society that is classist and racist, June Jordan's invocation of power, language, and representation as the substance of democracy speaks to a concern for the diverse voices of all peoples, but especially those seldom heard—children, those who live in poverty, minorities—to make known their anger, pain, joys, and passions. From the largest U.S. city districts—Los Angeles, New York, Chicago, and Houston—to the smaller city corporations, differing linguistic, ethnic, religious, and class groups settle on city public schools and thereby rupture ideals of wholeness and homogeneity in community. Instead, cultural differences create a wide variance in educational curriculum programming, educator/student/parent relationships, and a range of contending social, ethical, and political values.

Leaders in urban schools cannot afford to be indifferent to diversity nor can they ignore the complexity of responding to calls for equality. African American, Asian American, and Latino "minorities" represent a majority in 51 U.S.

cities. Students of color comprise at least half of the population in the largest 25 cities (Gollnick & Chinn, 1998). The urban educator necessarily encounters a number of salient conditions of practice, including great variability within their student populations' languages, ethnicities, and socioeconomic backgrounds. According to the National Center for Education statistics report, *The Condition of Education 1997*, black and Latino children remain much more likely than white children to be living in poverty, a factor associated with poor school outcomes. Minority students are more likely to attend schools with a high level of poverty. Poverty rates average 18% in cities, compared with 8% in suburbs. New York had a 1990 poverty rate of 19%, while its suburban poverty rate was 7%; in Detroit, comparative figures were 30% in the city and 6% in the suburbs. In some cities, these disparities are even more extreme.

To address these ethnicity and class differences, the diversity challenge is not merely to celebrate or tolerate culture but to engage and interrogate assumptions of equity in city school learning environments. In an increasingly U.S. pluralistic society, cross-cultural encounters between teachers and students are intensifying as educators ask the perennial questions of what and whose knowledges are most worth engaging. What forms of inquiry and analysis as well as what kinds of experiences and ways of thinking should be encouraged? How should the limited time spent in city classrooms be best used to further the meaningful engagement of students, and toward what purposes? These questions persist as educational leaders grapple with multicultural sensibilities and increasing calls for accountability.

TENSIONS OF DIVERSITY, MULTICULTURAL EDUCATION, AND ACCOUNTABILITY

Since Giles and Gollnick's 1977 study of federal and state requirements related to multicultural education identified 28 states with provisions supporting multicultural education in some form, the number of states with requirements related to multicultural education has increased (Gollnick, 1995). In 1993, after reviewing policies, guidelines, and legislation of 47 states, Gollnick (1995) noted that by that year, 45 states had multicultural education requirements that varied in their focus on targeted groups, curriculum, textbooks, and staff development. This analysis of state initiatives clearly reveals a significant degree of difference in states' requirements for multicultural curriculum. Significantly, 14 states expected schools to make their curriculum multicultural, but only Maryland, Nebraska, Minnesota, and New Jersey required *accountability* through regular reports of plans and implementation. Also important to note was that only one state, Oklahoma, required regular reporting on staff development activities supporting multicultural education.

The current national situation surrounding multicultural education is therefore marked by symbolic policy statements and voluntary implementation, making it subject to fragmentation and localization, with few enforcement or monitoring mechanisms. Effective mechanisms of what may be called multicultural accountability are not only rare, but in most school corporations they are nonexistent. A broad vision of multicultural education, including an analysis of class, race, gender, and disability often becomes diminished because of the national focus on academic performance accountability.

A number of insistent publics—students, parents, school boards, local and state governments, public interest groups, private citizens, and the business sector—are making demands on urban schools to meet high standards, to increase academic performance, and to be accountable for student achievement. These calls for accountability result in high-stakes testing, teacher performance measures, and increased scrutiny of the day-to-day practices of teachers and principals. As city school administrators face these demands for academic performance, the countervailing imperative for responsiveness to culture, class, and race differences becomes a chronic dilemma. As Beyer (1998) notes, "The expectations others hold of teachers—students, colleagues, administrators, parents, and local and state policy-making agencies—are equally wide ranging and at times conflicting" (p. 245).

McCarthy (1990) suggests that current trends in government policies have directly influenced the increased drive for accountability in education and for state mandates directed "at raising standards and competence and for an approach that privileges the needs of the economy over minority demands for equality" (p. 107). Similarly, Kanpol (1992), in a study of a primarily Latino city district, pointed out that the educators emphasized

> testing, instruction geared to tests, autocratic rules, rigid assertive discipline measures, a top-down hierarchy, and a strict adherence to an official subject-based curriculum in which the teacher and texts are the main (and often the only) sources of knowledge . . . standardized teacher evaluation, rigid role definitions, unflagging administrative authority . . . control and stability. (p. 227)

Similarly, Carlson's (1992) description of the crisis in urban education portrays teachers who are rewarded for ensuring that students pass tests, so that administrators can demonstrate to the state that their district is winning the battle against poor inner city schooling.

THE STUDY CONTEXT: INDIANAPOLIS PUBLIC SCHOOLS

Like most urban school districts around the country, Indianapolis Public Schools (IPS) faces distinct demographic challenges. In the communities it serves, nearly one third of the children live in poverty and more than one third of the householders do not have a high school diploma. With 97 schools and 46,000 students, IPS is one of the larger urban school corporations in a tri-state area of the U.S. heartland. Thirty years ago, the number of students reached an all time high of 108,200. Since then, the student population has declined as a result of court-ordered busing to desegregate schools and as middle class black and white families followed the trail of urban sprawl and movement to the suburbs.

At the time of this study, 1995–1997, the district faced projections of more than $7 million in budget deficits and a state-legislated reform measure, specifically enacted to increase achievement in the city's schools. The law, in effect for several years now, holds schools, teachers, and administrators accountable for school performance. A series of indicators are used to evaluate the schools, including student performance on state assessments, staff and student attendance, and graduation and remediation rates. The mayor endorsed the legislation, the acting superintendent at the time of the legislation's passage used it as a criteria for school evaluation, and business interests lauded it as long overdue. The first year the law was in effect, about 90% of the district's schools were put either on warning or on academic probation by the superintendent. Central office administrators were reassigned to schools to perform the role of "academic monitor" and to report progress to the district administration. Twenty principals were subsequently transferred and contracts of four others were not renewed.

TWO AFRICAN AMERICAN WOMEN AND AGENCY

This study raises questions about the negotiated terrain of curriculum policy formation as district level decisions are made and state accountability measures are put in place. Several layers of policy formation processes are therefore discussed, as well as the agency of individuals central to policy implementation. Participant observation, document analysis, and interview data gathered over two years are used to examine a multicultural curriculum policy formation process within a larger systemic curriculum development process. Central to this study are the narratives of two African American city school leaders who pushed initiatives for curriculum change—one, an assistant superintendent of curriculum and instruction; the other, a director of an office of multicultural education.

In this chapter, I use Hill-Collins's (1998) work in critical social theory as a lens for examining African American women's leadership because it is useful for thinking about the practices that constitute racialized *and* gendered work. The struggle of African American women and other women of color, amid educational change within particularized contexts, is important to understanding how school policy is taken up as well as, at times, resisted. Johnson (1996) suggests, "[F]or finally it is individuals leading in context whose work we must understand if research is to constructively inform practice" (p. 19). The experiences that African American women have with the matrix of race, gender, and class oppression may make useful contributions to understanding how power relationships of marginalization and difference are negotiated in city schools. From the standpoint of these leaders, racial, cultural, and gendered inequities in our society merge, making it impossible to be neutral in their beliefs about what it takes to initiate change. These insights are dramatically different from the many administrators who claim that they are color- and difference-blind in their treatment of children who are unlike them in class, in ethnicity, or in ability. yes'

Hooks (1994) points out, "Fixed notions about teaching as a process are continuously challenged in a learning context where students are really diverse, where they do not share the same assumptions about learning" (p. 162). People of color are often aware of unequal power relations between disparate racial, cultural, and ethnic groups and critical leadership that recognizes the impossibility of cultural neutrality among fellow teachers, administrators, staff, and students is an outgrowth of that awareness. To understand urban educational policy formation requires not only a political analysis of power relations in city schools, but also a carefully constructed examination of the subjectivities and agencies of those who work in classrooms and in administration, those who react to change and resist when change is not seen as desired or beneficial. Black women's experiences as leaders in city schools are shaped by a wide range of discourses about organizations and change, by current as well as historical inequalities in education, and by ethics of caring, urgency, and risk.

Valverde and Brown (1988) describe the challenges and problems faced by people of color in school administration. Such administrators must demonstrate loyalty to superiors, fellow administrators, and teachers; explain dysfunctional practices of school districts in the education of minorities; and help district personnel understand what is important to minority groups. All the while they also serve as agents of enforcement on behalf of policies and practices of accountability considered appropriate to the enhancement of education for minority children and youth. This is an appropriate description of the director of the Office of Multicultural Education who worked with the assistant superintendent of curriculum and instruction of Indianapolis Public Schools (IPS) to develop a new multicultural education policy.

Born and raised in a family of educators (her mother, her aunts, and her uncles), "Barbara Johnson" is a middle-aged African American woman who speaks critically and with deep convictions about the lack of support given to urban public schools:

I love teaching, it's a passion and I believe children need to be taught the truth. . . . Many [middle class parents] have their children in private schools and look down on [Indianapolis Public Schools]. [They] don't understand how needed public education is. [They] don't understand that the masses of children come here. So that's why we've got to keep public education strong for all those who cannot pick and choose what they want. exactly,

Johnson, as the Director of the Office of Multicultural Education (OME) in Indianapolis Public Schools, helped to develop its mission statement, "to act as a catalyst of knowledge, scholarship, skills and resources for the teaching, learning and understanding of the experiences and needs of diverse populations."

The OME sponsors professional development programs, including "cultural competency" institutes, an annual conference on infusion of culture and history into the school curriculum; a youth summit, cultural events, and celebrations. The office provides three vital services. First, it organizes a district-wide cadre system drawing interested teachers and administrators together for professional development and dissemination of multicultural teaching strategies, curriculum, and information. Second, the office is responsible for creating issue importance and maintaining momentum—prioritizing diversity concerns throughout the school district. Third, it works in alliance with an alumni trust that established a historical museum celebrating the nationally renowned achievements of students and faculty of the formerly segregated black high school, Crispus Attucks.

According to Johnson, who has been the one administrator of the center since the 1980s, the Office of Multicultural Education was predated by the work of a small committee that began questioning existing curriculum and textbooks during a period of court-ordered desegregation:

We began raising hell about the textbooks. . . . These were black teachers. We started having exhibits down at the Ed center (the central administrative offices). During that deseg time we lost black teachers. And a lot of those black teachers went to the township (surrounding suburbs) schools.

As she learned more about black history and social movements, her work intensified but lacked fiscal resources:

As my information grew then the exhibits grew. . . . We didn't have a budget at first. We would go from division to division [at the education center] begging to get money. "Black history shall be taught from September through June, kindergarten through twelfth [grades] and integrated into the entire curriculum." Now this was in 1979. The policy was passed with no budget. And was not changed till we did the revision in '97.

One factor that hampered Johnson's work was a lack of strong, consistent leadership in the school system.

When addressing issues of curriculum reform, accountability, and the ability of teachers and principals to bring about substantive change, the role of the superintendent cannot be understated. A significant problem in urban education is the rapid turnover of superintendents and the effects that this succession has on reform. Teachers in city schools are usually subject to a whirlwind of often contrary administrators who believe it is important to get their agenda in place as soon as possible in order to demonstrate their authority, power, competence, and value. A new superintendent can affect the commitment levels of school board members and parents, teachers, and principals and set priorities in district-wide fiscal management. In these and other ways, he or she can also affect the uncertain hopes for academic advancement of students (Hess, 1999; Kowalski, 1995).

During the superintendency of an African American male, the Office of Multicultural Education was fully supported:

> The importance [given to] our work all depended upon who the superintendent was . . . when [a specifically named superintendent] was here this department flourished. There were ten PBA days (professional days) and he mandated that at least five of those days be on multiculturalism. . . . And the teachers were grumbling. . . . Multicultural education was on the agenda of every administrative council meeting.

Superintendent support also made it possible to engage controversial topics and to explore the pains of racism and exclusion:

> One of those PBA days we showed, district wide, *Eye to Eye*, the Jane Elliot Blue Eye Brown Eye film. We always had discussion questions and different things that the school had to do after the presentation. On one of those days we connected with faculty from the University of Wisconsin. They had to listen to Gloria Ladson Billings. . . . We _Awesome_ had teachers at the studio. The schools could call in. So on those days the whole faculty had to be there [in their school] sitting and watching something that was [related to culture] and they didn't like it one bit. It was like [the superintendent] was trying to get in everything he could dealing with black people. We maintain that one of the reasons he got into trouble was because he said he was going to look out for black children in this city.

When asked what she hoped to accomplish with the multicultural policy, Johnson expressed both consternation that it was too expansive (including issues beyond race to linguistic, ability, religious, and ethnic group differences) while also acknowledging the policy's worth. She expressed concern that the focus on black children not be watered down, and yet she saw it as a way of being responsive to the changing cultural context as well as to accountability demands. Multicultural education policies can successfully produce an active discourse that provides a language of engagement to leaders. However Cornbleth and Waugh (1992) acknowledged that although encouraging pluralism can be a means of widening and deepening the multicultural conversation, it "may not change anything; it may only dissipate the energies of difference" (p. 33). Yet in a democracy, Gunn (1992, cited in Cornbleth & Waugh, 1995), tells us "we do not have a better choice" (p. 33). Similarly, Johnson believed that there were problems with the policy as formulated and yet she saw it as valuable:

> I use it. . . . In April we had the diversity panel. Only this time I added two new voices. There were nine members on the panel. Those new voices were multiracial children and gays and lesbians.

Johnson anticipated the eventual conflicts leaders encounter when they surface the problems of homophobia and other acts of oppression:

I knew it was going to happen . . . I started getting all these e-mails from this principal at [a specific school] whose cadre member was there. And they were saying this is against the Bible and how this was not any part of multicultural education. And what was I doing teaching it. This is a principal. We e-mailed each other back and forth until I said no more. I said, 'This is it.' I faxed him the article in *Education Today* where the high school students had sued the school district and won because their needs weren't being addressed and he was still saying, 'This is against the Bible.' And I told him, 'It is not your place to judge the values or the lifestyle of these young people. It is your job to make sure they have a safe place in which to learn.' Period. But I love little battles like this.

Johnson was able to use the policy as a means to expand the discourse and at the same time to require the engagement of her colleague. She also saw herself in battle, fighting for her vision for multicultural education and against those who refused to see how their prejudice affected students. African American women, historically, have been ambivalent in dealing with links between race, gender, and sexuality (Hill-Collins, 1998). However, Johnson saw it as part of moral and ethical leadership. She was clear about the need for superintendent support and noted that the assistant superintendent for curriculum and instruction was vital in her fight for curriculum change. She succinctly states that she could not have gotten the multicultural policy formed and passed if she had not had the backing of the assistant superintendent for curriculum and instruction: "It wouldn't have happened without 'Judy Watts.'"

Curriculum Leadership of Resistance to Institutionalized Apathy

Hurty (1995) described seventeen women leaders (principals) in her study, who were emotionally "committed to the education of the children in their care, competent in curriculum and instruction, energetic . . . and creative in their abilities to work with people toward needed change . . . they agonized . . . they had dreams of what could be, while working with what is" (pp. 384–385). These desires are similar to those of the assistant superintendent for curriculum in Indianapolis Schools, Judy Watts, who was born in Arkansas but has lived in Indianapolis all her life.

Watts describes Indianapolis as provincial and conservative, yet slowly maturing as diverse populations come to the city because of employment opportunities. She is also quick to point out that the city is not a community-focused place, that people are expected to "pull up by the boot strap" and that the city "has the reputation as having the worst health and worst schools in the state."

One of the pervasive trends that she fights against in schools are the low expectations for children who live in the city. Like many multiculturalists, Watts argues that the potential for the public school success of children of all ethnicities who live in poverty is often undermined by racism and other forms of subtle discrimination. In her many years as a school leader, she has observed relationships between white teachers and students of color and she dismisses the excuses of educators who say they care but don't change how they work with black children: "The facade is sympathy and [as an administrator] you can't just say 'have high expectations . . .' " Watts's observations of many white teachers' relationships with black students have been that: "there were not positive interactions between teachers and many students . . . many have a fear of the males, fear of aggressiveness."

Falvey (1995) points out that leadership in school reform requires courage. Leaders of reform most call upon others to rethink their assumptions and accept an unknown future, while they themselves will need to collaborate, strategize, and negotiate. As her administrative team planned district-wide curriculum changes, Watts's spiritual conviction was critical:

I could see where we were headed—that vision guided everything. If you have something in life that's guiding you, things will fall in place. . . . It keeps me from being daunted by nay sayers, and I mean that seriously. It's part of my greatest strength.

Policy Amplification -

An important function of the leadership role is to establish alliances, collaborations, and coalitions that serve as survival strategies in bureaucracies that often work too slowly and ineffectively. Watts operates from what I call an ethic of risk/urgency that is impatient with hierarchical separations of curriculum policy formation from teaching and impending improvements. As she works to build collaboration, she also urges teachers and other administrators to make decisions and take decisive action:

I've tried things the old way, trying to think everything through—plan, plan, plan. You never get anything done. I'm more apt to say "Let's do it." Urgency, we're losing kids every year that goes past. I'd rather have something in hand. My urgency is fueled by what I know our kids don't know.

nullification

Watts's leadership can perhaps best be described as resistance to institutionalized norms of mediocrity. She intentionally brought into curriculum deliberations the special education and multicultural education directors, so that central office administrators in elementary and secondary curriculum would collaborate with them to develop an instructional policy. For Watts, special education and multicultural education are both a part of education. These programs were not to be marginalized or added on to the curriculum.

Watts argued against giving empty praise for efforts that bore little fruit and said it misleads educators to accept mediocrity.

When you say to teachers and principals, "You're doing an outstanding job." "Thank you for working so hard." Then it sends the wrong message that what "I'm doing is okay." But look at where our students are. They're not reading. They're not computing. . . . What I've said to people is [this]: I use a terrible example of a water faucet.

These days we make them so differently. I've gone to a lot of water faucets and turned the water faucet the way I'm used to turning them for all my years of living and get no water and I keep turning and turning but the water didn't come out. And then I figured out that I've turned it in the wrong direction. And then I flip it this way. Less energy expended and I get water. That's what we do in schools. Working hard, spending time and energy, in meetings, dealing with kids and parents. We are working hard but we're doing the wrong things.

The task of explaining to others why they are being asked to do certain things, why they are meeting with success and failure, is important to her leadership. Watts clarifies educational purposes with individual central office administrators, teachers, principals, and with policy planning groups. For Watts, however, the issue isn't explanation alone. She is aware that many of her colleagues have become comfortable with business as usual, preoccupied with the procedures and routines of the present. So she offers critique and examples for change. She was instrumental in bringing in curriculum and instruction specialists, consultants, and university faculty to work with the district on curriculum change for reading and mathematics improvement.

Watts has also changed her approach to multicultural education from doing single day workshops and additions to curriculum about diverse ethnic groups:

I've grown. Back in the 80s, when I had a job here as a multicultural consultant on a federal grant, our task was to do lots of research on lots of different cultures because the textbooks were void of that kind of stuff and we actually wrote things that were supposed to be included in the social studies curriculum. And it was good work.

Today, Watts's work emphasizes systemic thinking and more critical approaches to multicultural curriculum.

Sleeter and Grant (1994) have a useful topography of the various approaches to multicultural education. Much of the literature, they suggest, is useful yet problematic. It presents a "liberal rhetoric" that is most often concerned with focusing on specific interventions, such as educational programs for culturally different groups, workshops on eliminating bias, how to celebrate heroes, heroines, and holidays, while not being critically concerned with the U.S. society's structural inequities. Social and economic disadvantage, poverty, racism, and sexism go unquestioned. Watts mirrored some of this thinking in her planning for professional development:

When people say they don't see color, many times I think they don't, or they don't see religion, they don't see gender. They just see some*body*. "I have to teach pages one through thirty today." Not understanding that that whole child was there to be taught. That child's culture, that child's values, that child's religion, that child's everything. And they were totally blind to it sometimes. That created problems with interaction, that created problems with the kid being able to be connected to what was going on because there was no connection often. And that's when we were doing our professional development. . . . We discovered that when we listened to those teachers talk about the kids, they really didn't know them as people. That's when we started putting them on school buses and driving them through our kid's communities. We took them to every one of the housing projects just to begin physically to see, "Here's where the kids come from."

Watts strongly urged her colleagues to avoid cultural deficit thinking. Her desire was to advocate for the complexity of cultural identity and its multiplicity of locations. There was a clear commitment to the dignity and worth of children from impoverished families. Watts refused to indulge ignorance as an excuse for not teaching in culturally responsive, intelligent, and engaging ways: "So what we tried to talk about then was that it wasn't a matter of trying to create sympathy . . . but understanding from whence children come, from poverty."

Ricardo Stanton-Salazar (1997), in a thoughtful discussion of social capital, posits that most schools present actual barriers to minority student learning by presenting dominant middle-class values with which most students are unfamiliar. Therefore, institutional agents are needed to be advocates and to bridge these differences. Teachers can, in addition to teaching subject matter and technical skills, provide the means for students to decode the larger social system beyond their communities. Watts saw a need for teachers to respect difference, to understand cultural norms that are not their own, and to examine how culture may influence learning and therefore achievement in school:

So I think of multiculturalism as bunches of lenses through which you can see the world, through which you understand different views. And the ultimate goal is that people come to understand that I have a lens and my lens has been influenced by my color, by my gender, by my religion, by my socioeconomic status, by my value system, by my lineage, by my heritage—all of that shapes how I see everyday. It shapes how we see political elections, it shapes how I see Columbine (or) Georgia. It shapes how I see whatever happens around me.

Cornbleth and Waugh (1995) assert, "How we 'see' the world or some part of it—our assumptions, conceptions, explanations—influences how we think about and act within or on it" (p. 29). For Watts:

ultimately if we are going to live in this world in harmony and if I'm going to be the best I can be and you will too, I need to first of all, understand my lens. So I need to understand my heritage and my lineage and all of that and understand what makes me a person. I need to understand yours too to the extent that I can. . . . And if I'm a teacher I really need to understand that so I can make connections.

As Lesko (1998) argues, it is not enough to plan field trips for teachers to explore their personal understandings about a majority black student population. Sonia Nieto notes, "Accepting differences also means making provisions for them" (1992, p. 137) Therefore, leaders must recognize their colleague's commitment levels, limitations, and resistance to multicultural education.

Watts's career has for so long been linked to the educators of IPS that she recognizes the need for different strategies for different educators in the corporation. Nevertheless, she feels that teachers must realize that they are all accountable for multicultural pedagogy, just as all students should be receiving a multicultural education:

If we had a [school] system that's 99 percent white, the professional development ought to be grounded in multicultural education and there ought to be a solid multicultural education component for the students because we are not just trying to teach respect for white and black and brown and white, we're trying to teach a respect for the way you see the world. . . . It's so absolutely critical. It goes beyond festivals. It goes beyond holidays. It has to start in preschool. That's why a goal of mine for the next two years or so is to ensure that we get our benchmarks. Make sure that in the first grade you ought to have learned about these things relative to culture and family. There are certain things you ought to know.

How she interpreted it. She appropriated it.

Policy, for Watts, was the backing she needed to draw serious attention to necessary action. She took her arguments to the school board thinking, if you get a board to say, ". . . that's our policy," then you've got something to hold onto:

It's the teeth. Now the hard work begins. You can always go back and say "Dear Board, you have a policy that says we believe in multiculturalism and that it ought to be an integral part of the curriculum and instructional process." So because of your belief you have in your policy, *your policy*, here's a recommendation of how we move from this point. We have these benchmarks. We have assessment.

Most writers about leadership agree that it involves a reciprocal process of social influence between leaders and followers. Watts's leadership was intentional in directing professional development efforts toward teacher perceptions of students and toward organizational learning, working to develop those shared orientations that hold a unit together and give it a distinctive identity. She wanted to influence individual and organizational cultural beliefs and to have the district respond through policy. These desires manifested in Watts's leadership for the development of an instructional framework for IPS.

THE INSTRUCTIONAL FRAMEWORK POLICY AND THE MULTICULTURAL EDUCATION POLICY

After more than three months of weekly, early morning meetings attended by central office administrators—including the instructional coordinators for elementary and secondary education; directors for gifted and talented education, special education, and Title I programs; elementary and secondary school principals; teachers on special assignment to the central office; and university faculty—an instructional framework began to take shape. The group of educators drawn from the classroom, from the central office, and from the university was both black and white and was mostly women. They debated what the instructional policy must reflect and the beliefs they held: Are learning styles to be included? Where's the research? What is constructivism? We've heard about it, but how will classrooms look different? What's wrong with talking about skills? Don't the children need skills? How can we be sure if we don't give tests? What gets tested gets taught. Reams of chart paper filled with points and counterpoints, ideas and issues, hung from the walls of the large meeting room. The group, after much deliberation, with Watts urging decision, listed nine principles of instruction that served as the foundation for the instructional framework policy:

WE BELIEVE CHILDREN LEARN BEST WHEN . . .

1. Instruction reflects high academic expectations that raise the level of understanding in all subjects for all students.
2. Instruction provides for active involvement, and collaborative and integrated student centered activities.
3. Instruction consistently reflects a focus on thinking, reasoning, problem solving, and higher order questioning.   .
4. Instruction allows students to see themselves and their culture mirrored in the learning process.
5. Instruction addresses the student's learning style.
6. Instruction builds on the student's prior knowledge.
7. Instruction reflects a process of incremental learning.
8. Instruction is flexible and responsive to the student's construction of knowledge.
9. Instruction allows the student to view concepts, issues, events and themes from the perspectives and experiences of diverse ethnic/cultural groups.

The group was clear that cultural difference must be responded to and built upon. In terms of the school curriculum and instruction, students were to be engaged in an education that could be used to improve their lives. The instructional framework represented an explicit statement of these beliefs as policy.

But the work of Johnson and Watts was yet to be completed. They criticized the old multicultural education policy and said it no longer met the needs of the district. As leaders who held positions of formal authority, they could leverage power to further purposes they considered important. They talked to individual board members, made sure that the superintendent agreed with the need for policy change, and were assured they would be supported. In response to the initiatives by the assistant superintendent and the director of multicultural education, the school board passed its Multicultural Education Policy in 1997, stating (in part):

Whereas, we believe that the educational process should prepare all learners to serve as social change agents in a democratic society;

Whereas, we believe that academic performance is enhanced when the curriculum is inclusive of the cultures of all learners;

Be it resolved, that Indianapolis Public Schools, by adoption of this resolution, hereby ratifies a policy of education that is multicultural and commits itself and resources to providing an education to achieve the following objectives [15 in total]:

1. To promote and foster intergroup understanding, awareness, and appreciation by students and staff of the diverse ethnic, racial, cultural, and linguistic groups represented in the Indianapolis Public Schools, the United States, and the world.
2. To help students develop more positive attitudes toward cultural diversity especially in early grades by dispelling misconceptions, stereotypes, and negative beliefs about themselves and others.
3. To identify the impact of racism and other barriers to acceptance of differences and,
4. To develop the life skills needed in interpersonal and intergroup relations as well as conflict resolution, with a special emphasis on conflict arising from bias and discrimination based on race, color, religion, national origin, gender, age, and/or disability.

Among its resolutions, the policy states:

It is, therefore, resolved that all IPS educators have an ethical, moral, and professional obligation and responsibility to prepare students to live in a culturally diverse society by providing an authentic education whose foundation rests on truth and a belief in the ability of all students to achieve.

These statements serve to highlight the significance of culture, race, gender, class, and ability to the framers of these policies. They link academic performance with multicultural education. Moreover, there is a strong call for the primacy of the political and the ethical as a foundation for democratic public life. The words draw attention to the need to struggle for the conditions and values that make democracy a substantive reality for all people.

TOWARD DEMOCRATIC NEGOTIATIONS OF DIFFERENCE

Hill-Collins (1998) suggests that African American socially critical thought may be useful for delineating an "ethical or ideal vision of humanity for all people" (p. 65). Rather than trying to form policies that are responsive to mythical unified communities, leaders may articulate a notion of shared space for sharing diverse concerns and affairs, without imposing notions of a false universalism. The school as a negotiated community of difference may be a site where trust is not taken for granted but struggled over and at times earned because of honesty and demonstrated long-term commitment to student learning. A negotiated community of difference may be where openness to critique is available but not seen as dangerous and hurtful. When crossing borders, from different positions of class, ability, ethnicity, and gender, issues of trust and comfort cannot be assumed. This suggests that over time, with frequent sharing, some small steps of successful alliance building may lead to a sense of shared purpose, which has an impact on policy formation. It also suggests the needed courage of conviction on the part of school leaders, to not be intimidated by nay sayers or be afraid to take the risk of acting across difference. As an African American woman superintendent pointed out after her first 100 days in a new urban superintendency:

One of the reasons that I have been able to do [this] is that I don't have any fear of failure—because there is really no failure. You may not be able to achieve as much as you had hoped to achieve, but generally you do make some inroads. I've already made them . . . in the short time that I've been here. And it's my responsibility to keep making those inroads. I am humbled by the responsibility of this job. And I cannot let down, through my actions, this community. I can't. I have to do everything I can to ensure that what they thought was going to happen with new leadership, is going to happen.

Positional authority can never be enough to bring about the commitment needed to reflect critically on bias, prejudice, or beliefs—for example, of white supremacy. Therefore, socially critical leaders are needed and crucial for organizational change "because they act as a constant source of pressure to think in ways that deviate from the current culture" (Louis & Kruse, 1995, p. 39). Leaders can stimulate a slow-to-change staff with the seriousness of dialogue about curriculum that necessitates examining the impact of cultural beliefs—both explicit and implicit—on content and instructional strategies that are planned and in place.

This study asserts that a more inclusive policy formation process that draws on different leadership resources—in this case, women of color—can accommodate a broader variety of educational interests and needs, particularly in city school settings. It is easy to understand that the current work of curriculum and instruction revitalization can be derailed by calls for accountability, which in part may reduce teaching in many schools, to a directive, controlling pedagogy that does not effectively engage students. Many reformers involved with urban schools have promulgated change strategies that deal with accountability and curriculum policy changes but have failed to carefully consider the issue of a culturally responsive pedagogy essential to the thoughtful and meaningful involvement of culturally, socioeconomically, and linguistically diverse students and educators (Carlson, 1992). In schools that fail to take a critical look at curriculum policy formation and implementation processes, the real losers become the children, the educators working with them, and ultimately, the families and communities where they live.

Multicultural sensibilities and academic accountability in city schools are both important if we believe that building a learning community creates a "climate of openness and intellectual rigor" (hooks, 1994, p. 40), "shared values, purposes and commitments that bond" (Sergiovanni & Starratt, 1993, p. 47), or where "individuals and their social systems can develop a kind of powerful interdependence" (Beck & Foster, 1999, p. 344). The example of African American women in leadership positions in a midwest urban school corporation demonstrates that it is possible to develop policy formation processes responsive to cultural diversity, yet applying academic performance criteria. It is possible to negotiate the terrain of communities of difference.

CONCLUSIONS

Increasingly, city schools are being led by women (Mertz & McNeely, 1994). Despite the growing numbers of women holding urban school administrative positions, however, the experiences and theoretical perspectives informed by women of color are sparse in the educational leadership literature (Murtadha-Watts, 1999). Capper (1993) points out that organizational theory is in the process of being reshaped to better meet the needs of our increasingly pluralistic society, and that those who are marginalized are entering the conversation. I argue that the voices of women of color are only faintly heard. Moreover, the question I ask, along with other womanist/black feminist researchers, evolves from this study: Are the existing theories—founded upon a positivist epistemology that separates the body from the mind, feeling, spirituality, and emotion from the material—adequate for understanding schools and the policies that impact practice?

In this case, state-imposed academic performance accountability and district-imposed multicultural education accountability are examined as negotiated on the terrain of personal, culturally informed commitments and public disposition. There are many ways to interpret the Indianapolis Public School's accountability policies. As to the academic performance policy, it may be seen as a modernist tool for state-legislated reform measures, impinging upon teacher professional authority. It may be used as a law to specifically increase achievement in the city's schools, holding teachers and administrators accountable for school performance, especially in sites where teachers have maintained low expectations for students, where children are traditionally viewed as coming from culturally deficient homes. As a series of indicators, the accountability plan may be used to compare and evaluate schools, including student performance on state assessments, staff and student attendance, and graduation and remediation rates. Or it may be viewed as diluting the possibilities for teachers to embrace and take up a more culturally responsive pedagogy. Finally, the accountability plan could be seen as a way for some educators to avoid changing the mainstream dominant curriculum discourses with claims of needing to teach what gets tested. On the other hand, the multicultural policy and instructional framework may be seen as engaging these same issues. The leaders in this case saw the policies in relational ways, as possibilities for raising concerns over ways of practice and while being accountable to children and families living in city communities.

By asserting the primacy of culture, poverty, class, and gender, the leaders in this study are engaged in eminently political acts. Power is not seen as merely an oppressive tool of the majority. Examining the context of their work, I suggest that power can be understood as constituted productively and used to deepen the democratic possibilities within education.

I am arguing further that without socially critical leadership, educators may interpret accountability measures and multicultural education policies as conflicting policy purposes that may in turn lead to nonaction in implementing a multicultural curriculum that engages children in city schools.

The African American women leaders in this study have learned how to work around established racist and inequitable educational systems for possible democratic purposes. From the narratives of these women, we learn that resistance to harmful normative processes in schools is crucial work for those who would provide effective leadership for the education of youth in city schools. These socially critical leaders spoke and acted across difference. They identified and made the biases, prejudices, and stereotypes of those with whom they worked visible, and they used class and color consciousness as a means of pushing for policies that could be used for creating greater equity in schools. Future research will have to explore the effects of these policies on teaching and learning in Indianapolis classrooms.

Their work also creates a potential for achieving deeper understanding of policy formulation and leadership rooted in and appropriate for marginalized and oppressed populations. Policy developers interested in moving beyond cultural deficit models of teaching and learning and educational inequality need to hear from contemporary black women who live, work, and struggle within disparate educational settings. Social democratic processes must have leaders and groups struggling with courage, passion, and a strong sense of moral conviction to bring about change. In order to serve democratic purposes, city schools can be forums where educational issues of policymaking and teacher labor bring to the surface economic, cultural, political and moral tensions of society.

REFERENCES

Beck, L., & Foster, W. (1999). Administration and community: Considering challenges, exploring possibilities. In J. Murphy & K. Seashore Louis (Eds.), *Handbook of research on educational administration* (2nd ed., pp. 340–358). San Francisco: Jossey-Bass.

Beyer, L. (1998). *The curriculum: Problems, politics and possibilities.* Albany, NY: SUNY Press.

Capper, C. (1993) Educational administration in a pluralistic society. Albany, NY: SUNY Press.

Carlson, D. (1992). *Teachers and crisis: Urban school reform and teachers' work culture*. New York: Routledge.

Cornbleth, C., & Waugh, D. (1995). *The great speckled bird: Multicultural politics and educational policymaking*. New York: St. Martin's Press.

Falvey, M. (1995). *Inclusive and heterogeneous schooling: Assessment, curriculum, and instruction*. Baltimore: Paul S. Brookes.

Gollnick, D. (1995). National and state initiatives for multicultural education. In J. Banks & C. M. Banks (Eds.), *Handbook of research on multicultural education* (pp. 44–64). New York: MacMillan Publishing.

Gollnick, D., & Chinn, P. (1998). *Multicultural education in a pluralistic society*. Upper Saddle River, NJ: Merrill.

Gunn, G. (1992) *Thinking across the American grain: Ideology, intellect, and the new pragmatism*. Chicago: University of Chicago Press.

Hess, F. (1999). *Spinning wheels: The politics of urban school reform*. Washington, DC: The Brookings Institution.

Hill-Collins, P. (1998). *Fighting words: Black women and the search for justice*. Minneapolis: University of Minnesota Press.

hooks, b. (1994). *Teaching to transgress: Education as the practice of freedom*. New York: Routledge.

Hurty, K. (1995). Women principals—Leading with power. In D. Dunlap & P. Schmuck (Eds.), *Women leading in education* (pp. 380–406). Albany, NY: SUNY Press.

Johnson, S. M. (1996). *Leading to change: The challenge of the new superintendency*. San Francisco: Jossey-Bass.

Jordan, J. (1985). *On call*. Boston: South End.

Kanpol, B. (1992). *Towards a theory and practice of teacher cultural politics: Continuing the postmodern debate*. Norwood, NJ: Ablex.

Kowalski, T. (1995). *Keepers of the flame: Contemporary urban superintendents*. Thousand Oaks, CA: Corwin Press.

Lesko, N. (1998). (E)strange(d) relations: Psychological concepts in multicultural education. In R. Chavez & J. O'Donnell (Eds.), *Speaking the unpleasant: The politics of nonengagement in multicultural education terrain* (pp. 265–273). Albany: SUNY Press.

Louis, K. & Kruse, S. (1995). *Professionalism and community: Perspectives on reforming urban schools*. Thousand Oaks, CA: Corwin Press.

McCarthy, C. (1990). *Race and curriculum*. New York: Falmer Press.

Mertz, N., & McNeely, S. (1994). How are we doing? Women in urban school administration. *Urban Education, 28*(4), 361–371.

Murtadha-Watts, K. (1999). Spirited sisters: Spirituality and the activism of African American women in educational leadership. In *Yearbook of the National Council of Professors of School Administration* (pp. 155–167). Lancaster, PA: Technomic.

Nieto, S. (1992). *Affirming diversity: The sociopolitical context of multicultural education*. New York: Longman.

Sergiovanni, T., & Starratt, R. (1993). *Supervision: A redefinition* (5th ed.). New York: McGraw-Hill.

Sleeter, C., & Grant, C. (1994). *Making choice for multicultural education: Five approaches for race, class, and gender* (2nd ed.). New York: Macmillan.

Stanton-Salazar, R. (1997). A social capital framework for understanding the socialization of racial minority children and youth. *Harvard Educational Review*, *67*(1), 1–40.

Valverde, L., & Brown, F. (1988). Influences on leadership development among racial and ethnic minorities. In N.J. Boyan (Ed.), *Handbook of research on educational administration* (pp. 143–157). White Plains, NY: Longman.

5

Teachers' Perceptions of Their Participation in Policy Choices: The Bottom-up Approach of the *Nueva Escuela Unitaria* in Guatemala

Martha E. Mantilla

INTRODUCTION

In this chapter, I show the relationship between participation on the one hand and policy formation and appropriation on the other. More specifically, I address the issue of teachers' participation in the formation and appropriation of educational policies within the context of the *Nueva Escuela Unitaria*[1] (NEU) in Guatemala. NEU is an educational reform initiative that seeks innovative ways of engaging different actors such as teachers, parents, students, government officials, and program administrators in the decisions concerning the educational choices that affect their lives.[2]

I begin with a brief summary of the views of donor agencies and international organizations on people's participation in local affairs during the last five decades. I introduce the NEU educational reform initiative and provide background information on Guatemala's social and political conditions. I concentrate on the teachers' perceptions of their participation in the formation and appropriation of educational policies and conclude the article with a discussion of NEU's bottom-up philosophy on policy formation and appropriation.

Participation, according to the Oxford University Dictionary (1933), means "taking part, with others, in some action or matter." Two aspects of this broad definition are highlighted in this chapter: One of them is the notion of taking part with others, which gives us the idea of participation as a joint endeavor. The other one is the notion of participation in some action or matter, which gives us the idea of participation for a specific purpose. In this chapter, the teachers are the primary actors who participate with others, namely, parents, students, government officials, and program administrators. The action or matter in which the teachers take part is the formation and appropriation of educational policies. Educational policies, in the NEU context, should be understood as a course of action or a solution to a problem.[3] The concepts of formation and appropriation will unfold as we examine the NEU educational reform.

I am in agreement with Coombs's (1980) view that participation should be examined more carefully, recognizing that participation acquires concrete meaning only when it is considered in a specific context. Pigozzi (1982) contends that participation means different things to different people and it can be manifested in a variety of forms. I further argue that participation should be studied primarily from the perspective of the participant. The participant's (or nonparticipant's) perception of their degree of involvement in educational activities becomes the starting point from which to investigate the way participation acquires meaning. Therefore, I use an interpretive approach to examine how teachers perceive their role, as well as that of other actors with whom they interact, in the formation and appropriation of new educational policies. For this chapter I draw on data collected over a seven-year period (1993–1999), including written and audio visual materials,[4] open-ended and in-depth interviews,[5] and observations.[6]

PEOPLE'S PARTICIPATION IN LOCAL AFFAIRS

Current community participation approaches are based on a rich legacy of ideas and practical agendas that have been formulated over the last five decades. The community development movement of the 1950s and 1960s focused on small communities and sought to establish democratic decision-making institutions at the local level. This movement also tried to mobilize people to get involved in development projects directed to improve their social and economic conditions. In the 1970s, there was disillusionment with community development projects, in part because many governments failed to provide adequate financial support. In the same decade, the emphasis on popular participation was formalized by the United Nations with the publication of two major documents—"Popular Participation in Development," published in 1971, and "Popular Participation in Decision Making for Development," published in 1975—and the creation of major research programs by the United Nations Research Institute for Social Development (UNRISD). In the 1980s, through the influence of international agencies, the governments of many developing countries strengthened participatory elements in their social and development programs (Midgley, 1986).

During the 1990s, international agencies reexamined their approaches to development in order to respond to several concerns of the world community. The most pressing one was the lack of progress in improving the lives of the very poor. Such lack of success of development efforts was attributed, in part, to the failure of international agencies and national governments to adapt development programs to the context of the local culture. A study of 2,000 World Bank projects, for example, showed that a major factor in poor project performance was inadequate understanding of the local culture. This was attributed, among other things, to the lack of local participation in the planning, implementation, and evaluation of development programs, which in many cases showed an "a la carte" approach whereby a program was taken from one environment and placed in another where different conditions prevailed (Wolf, 1997).

As with other areas of development, educational reform efforts in the 1990s have emphasized the need for increasing levels of people's participation as a prerequisite for achieving educational quality. As a consequence, the focus of many regional-international conferences and research projects has been on the conditions that facilitate the participation of the people who are affected by policy choices. Throughout the 1990s, community involvement in education has been one of the central issues of concern. For example, on March 5–9, 1990, UNESCO, UNICEF, UNDP, and the World Bank cosponsored the World Conference on Education for All. At this conference, held in Jomtiem, Thailand, a major emphasis was on the promotion of more effectively participatory and decentralized education systems. It was also determined at the Jomtiem Conference that the most significant partners in educational projects are those directly affected by the educational practices and policies, namely teachers, students, parents, and other members of the community. In addition, it was also noted that governmental and private organizations are equally critical in the process of articulation and implementation of educational choices. Therefore, in the "Framework for Action to Meet Basic Learning Needs," endorsed at the World Conference on Education for All, we read:

> Because basic learning needs are complex and diverse, meeting them requires multisectorial strategies and actions which are integral to overall development efforts. Many partners must join with the educational authorities, teachers, and other educational personnel in developing basic education if it is to be seen, once again, as the responsibility of the entire society. This implies the active involvement of a wide range of partners—families, teachers, communities, private enterprises (including those involved in information and communication), government and nongovernmental organizations, institutions, etc.—in planning, managing and evaluating many forms of basic education. (p. 54)

Following the Jomtiem Conference, there were several summits and initiatives related to the implementation of the Jomtiem resolutions. For example, in the Education for All Summit in New Delhi, December 12–16, 1993, panelists from United Nations agencies, as well as representatives from nine highly populated developing nations, reaffirmed their commitment to make education universal and at the same time make it the heart of sustainable development. According to the delegates, one of the pressing issues affecting basic education worldwide was the need for community participation in educational practices and policies, along with mobilization of the masses and grassroots units to participate in literacy programs.

When it comes to policy issues and decision making, the views of the actors who have traditionally been involved—namely donors, national governments, development agencies, technical experts, and researchers—have usually been recognized. However, in today's world, the people whose voices have traditionally been missing—teachers, parents, students, and other members of the community—are claiming their space and are increasingly seen as legitimate partners and participants in the activities and decisions that concern their lives. The challenge of community involvement has become evident in recent years, and decision makers at the national and international levels have started to rethink their roles in the development efforts and have turned their attention to the participation and perspective of local people, whose views are as essential as any other "expert" contribution.

Taking the aforementioned issues into account, international agencies such as the United Nations Educational, Scientific, and Cultural Organization (UNESCO), the United Nations International Children's Education Fund (UNICEF), the Asian Development Bank (ADB), the World Bank, and the United States Agency for International Development (USAID), have redefined their approaches to participation and have strengthened their support for it. *Nueva Escuela Unitaria* (NEU) is an example of a USAID-funded project based on the assumption that the best or the most effective way to introduce both quality and quantitative change in education is from the bottom-up. Unlike the traditional philosophy of education where reform is believed to pass from the top to the bottom, in the NEU reform, experts and government officials are still in the picture, but not as pivotal actors. The priority and primacy have shifted to new actors, particularly teachers, parents, students, and other members of the local community.

NUEVA ESCUELA UNITARIA (NEU)

NEU is an educational initiative that began in Guatemala in 1992 as part of the Basic Education Strengthening (BEST) project. BEST was a seven-year (1989–1996) project undertaken by the Ministry of Education and funded through a $30 million grant by USAID, with technical assistance from the Academy for Educational Development (AED) (Improving Educational Quality, 1993). NEU's fundamental principles are based on the democratic pedagogical principles formulated earlier in the century by philosopher John Dewey and the prominent social psychologist George H. Mead (Guatemala Ministerio de Educación, 1996). NEU traces its history back to the UNESCO Geneva Conference recommendations of 1961, which served as the impetus for many countries in the world to concentrate on the pedagogical challenges posed by multigrade teaching—that is, a single teacher in a classroom, working with children of different ages and skills representing all six primary grades. As a result of the meeting in Geneva, Colombia started a Unitary School Program under the guidance of UNESCO experts. With the name of *Escuela Nueva*,[7] the program started in the early 1960s in isolated rural areas with low population density, and by the mid-1960s it had expanded to 150 pilot schools in one province. With financing from the World Bank, the program expanded at the national level to several thousand rural schools, and by 1989 there were 17,948 schools serving 800,000 students (Psacharopoulos, Rojas & Velez, 1993).

The emphasis of NEU in Guatemala is on the improvement of the quality of education by an active teaching–learning process, a flexible system of promotion, closer ties between the school and the community, and appropriate curriculum to meet the rural needs. NEU is an integrated package of activities to assist teachers of multigrade classes to manage their classrooms effectively. NEU schools are unitary schools in which one or two teachers attend to all six primary grades, working with 50–60 students. The NEU program is composed of two major interrelated dimensions: *school–community relations,* and *teacher–student relations.* The first one emphasizes the integration and interaction between different actors in the school and community, with expectations of collective collaboration among them. NEU schools are intended to be the focal point for community integration and development, and NEU teachers are expected to be the school–community links. Teachers are encouraged to reflect on their practice and to participate individually and collectively in decisions about how instruction can be enriched by gathering information relevant to their work and using community resources. Parents participate in different ways, particularly in activities related to their children's learning. Parents are consulted, by the teachers, about what they want their children to learn in the school. In Guatemala, the parents said they wanted their children to learn how to write letters to their siblings in the military, how to write stories and legends of the community, and how to speak Spanish. Equally important was to teach them to love the community and not to lose respect for the elderly.

The second dimension emphasizes a number of educational practices conducive to fostering student achievement and cultivating participatory democratic behavior.[8] Such school practices include active learning, peer teaching, use of self-instructional guides, and participatory student government. The objectives of NEU include providing students with the opportunity to complete sixth grade; creating flexible, life-long learners; and encouraging the formation of participatory, democratic practices.

The Ministry of Education in Guatemala provided physical space and offices for the NEU administrators. It also provided logistic support, including secretaries, motorcycles for government officials, and the means to send notices about meetings and workshops to the teachers. Communicating with the teachers was not an easy task, considering the lack of phones and almost nonexisting roads to access most of the schools. Equally important was the effort made by the teachers to attend these activities. The remote location of many of the NEU schools[9] and the difficulty in accessing them is particularly important in order to understand the teachers' efforts to participate in the activities developed as a result of their commitment to the new educational reform, as we will see later in the chapter.

The technical and administrative aspects of the project were coordinated by the NEU director, a specialist in unitary schools who implemented the Colombian *Escuela Nueva*. He moved to Guatemala and lived in Cobán, a town located in Alta Verapaz, in Region II. This was a condition stipulated by the Academy of Educational Development (AED) and Ministry officials, that the NEU director and administrative offices were to be located in one of the two regions where the program was implemented.[10] The reason for this condition was because "only if you live in the community can you identify the problems, not only of the community but also of the children and the teachers. These are complex and intertwined problems."[11] The positive reactions of the teachers about the NEU director living among them is reflected in a statement made by a teacher:

I learned to value people. One of the things that motivated us is that they [the NEU director and his family] were part of us. He was like a brother to us or a relative. He was someone very close to us. Because many times the authorities do not come to partake with the people. To value people is what I learned from them [the NEU director and his family] besides many other things that they taught us, and I am very grateful to them as are many of my fellow teachers.

GUATEMALA'S SOCIAL AND POLITICAL CONDITIONS

Before we proceed to examine the teachers' participation in the new educational reform effort, and in order to better understand the significance of the teachers' role in the formation and appropriation of the educational policies implemented in the NEU program, we need to have a general understanding of the country's social and political conditions.

Guatemala is considered one of the most culturally diverse countries in Latin America. Its population is composed of diverse ethnic groups, most of which are indigenous groups of Mayan ancestry. Fifty to sixty percent of the population are Mayan Indians and the rest are *ladinos*, that is, Spanish-speaking descendants of white and Indian racial intermixing. There are 22 linguistic subgroups of Mayan origin. Out of these, there are five major mother tongues that are spoken by 80% of the indigenous population—these are Q'eqchi, K'echi, K'aqchiquel, Mam, and Pocomchi (UNICEF, 1994).

Ruled by Colonial Spain until the 19th century, Guatemala has more recently struggled with economic, social, and political problems, which have been attributed to distorted capitalist-dependent development, external political intervention, and internal conflicts. Economic and political elites, along with members of the military, have dominated and ruled the country (Del Cid, 1996). With one of the oldest guerrilla movements in Latin America, Guatemala is an ethnically divided society, split among Indians and *ladinos,* affecting virtually all aspects of its social, economic, and political life. Efforts to democratize and modernize the country in the 1950s were resisted and portrayed by some of the national elites as a means to advance communism. After a *coup d'état* and an invasion backed by the United States in 1954, the country was led into almost four decades of unparalleled political instability and violence. It is estimated that during this time 150,000 were murdered, 454,000 disappeared, 1 million internally displaced, and 200,000 fled abroad as external refugees (Del Cid, 1996). — ωσν

At the political level, the dominant groups are constituted by *ladinos.* In the 1980s, there have been some steps toward the participation of the Indian population in the political life of the country. In 1985, Indians started to be elected to high positions in the government and to participate in top governmental units. In 1987, the constitution of the country was translated into the four principal mother languages, and in 1993, the first Minister of Indian ancestry was appointed to the Ministry of Education. Being the first indigenous Minister in Guatemalan history became a political issue used by some of the politicians of different parties (Mantilla et al., 1996). During the last two elections and governments in turn, there has been an increasing number of Indians holding different positions. For example, there are now 84 Indian mayors in Guatemala out of a total of 330 mayors (Del Cid, 1996).

Guatemala is largely an agricultural country with the principal crops of coffee, bananas, cotton, and sugar supplying 62% of its export earnings. The country's total population is estimated at 11 million (July 1995), of which 60% are rural dwellers engaged in agriculture as farmers and migratory workers. Official statistics indicate a rate of unemployment of 4.9%, while underemployment is estimated to be between 30% and 40% (Del Cid, 1996).

Of particular significance in Guatemala's current social and political life is the signing, on December 29, 1996, of the Peace Accords between the government and the Guatemalan rebels, which ended the country's 36-year civil war. The agreements were supposed to be followed by structural reforms to bring peace and changes that would benefit sectors previously excluded from social, economic, and political advances. It was also hoped that the agreements would facilitate the less privileged groups—among them, the rural teachers—to claim their space in the country's political and social arena, which would presumably take Guatemala into a new chapter in the country's history (Jonas, 1997).

GUATEMALA'S EDUCATIONAL CONDITIONS

Guatemala's illiteracy rate has been cited as the highest in Central America and the second highest in Latin America. According to the National Census, in

1993, the illiteracy rate in Guatemala was 58%.[12] Only a small portion of the indigenous population speaks Spanish, and illiteracy is concentrated in the rural areas. Seventy percent of the rural population is illiterate and this indicator is more severe among the indigenous population, particularly women. In largely indigenous areas, few girls attend schools. This in part explains the low overall percentage (35%) of children enrolled, compared to 82% of all children in nonindigenous areas. Even for those children who are enrolled in school, attendance is irregular and dropout and repetition are high, resulting in an average of 10 years of schooling to produce a sixth-grade graduate, and approximately 87% of the population without a complete primary school education (UNICEF, 1994). The high illiteracy rate, particularly among the Indian population, and the disparities in educational attainment by ethnicity, region, and gender, can be attributed to the convergence of different factors, one of them being pervasive poverty. According to CEPAL and USAID, 72% of the population in 1990 lived in extreme poverty. Guatemala has the highest number of infants with low birth weight in Latin America and malnutrition is common especially in rural areas (Jonas, 1991).

Based historically on the Spanish colonial structure, the educational system in Guatemala has more recently drawn from Latin American and European innovative models. Like most Latin American countries, Guatemala has a rigid and highly centralized educational structure in which decisions are made from the top by government officials and international consultants. These decisions are to be carried out by other actors at the regional, local, and community levels. Such technical and administrative centralization reflects the concentration of power and resources at the top, leaving very little space for participation from the actors directly affected by the choices made. According to UNESCO (1986), the highly centralized vertical structure of the educational system is one of the problems affecting the Latin American region. In general, the educational system is affected by excessive centralization and bureaucratization in the administration and planning of the educational process; curricular rigidity with identical plans and programs for the whole country; and a prevalent urban orientation in terms of educational coverage and educational content, to the detriment of the rural areas. In the case of Guatemala, these problems are compounded by lack of information, which contributes to decisions based not on reliable data but on political considerations, an absence of concrete and realistic plans for educational development, an absence of institutional evaluation, concentration of services and resources for the most privileged groups of the population, and excessive bureaucratization. Indeed, the latter especially imposes unnecessary formalism, deflects responsibilities from the periphery to the center, and encourages passive obedience from local actors (ASIES/PREAL, 1997).

Like most countries in Latin America, Guatemala has taken steps toward decentralization.[13] The process of decentralization was started by the Ministry of Education in 1986, based on the *Plan Nacional de Regionalización*

Educativa.[14] The country was divided into eight regions, each of them with a regional director. One of the purposes of the regionalization was to seek the participation of local actors such as parents, teachers, and members of the communities. To that end, Ministry of Education officials established *consejos asesores*[15] for those actors to participate at the regional, departmental, and local levels. The process of regionalization has moved forward with respect to the delegation of tasks and functions from the central government to the regional level. However, the decision-making process continues to be made by top officials in the government without the participation of actors at the local and community level (ASIES/PREAL, 1997). The long tradition of concentration of power at the center, inherited from colonial times, did not change with independence. It continues to prevail in modern times. Among the obstacles *one leads* that hinder decentralization are negative attitudes from certain political, bu- *the other.* reaucratic, and *gremial*[16] sectors that are not ready to cede sociocultural control. This resistance is reinforced by the reluctance on the part of the traditionally marginalized actors to begin to exercise their right to participate in the decisions that affect their lives.

The participation of different actors who have traditionally been excluded in the decision-making process is of particular significance in the country's struggle to consolidate its efforts toward democracy. The Peace Accords signed by the government and the rebels on December 29, 1996, are not legally binding. Rather, they are commitments on the part of the two forces toward specific goals, such as broadening the participation of different actors in the political life of the country. The future of Guatemala's democracy has been the concern of many researchers. According to Seligson (1995), promoting a stable democratic system corresponds to a certain extent to the prevailing political forces of the country. Nonetheless, the stability of a political system also depends on the masses' perceptions about it. As far as the educational system is concerned, particular emphasis has been put on the urgency for preparing educators to participate, in an effective and responsible manner, in a free society. Similarly, Indian groups have struggled to make the legal, economic, and educational system more responsive to their needs. In education, for example, instead of having bilingual programs oriented toward *castellanización* (the speaking of Spanish), Indian children are going to school to learn in their own native language. These changes are the result of negotiations that have been underway since 1985, and which resulted in the Agreement on Identity and Rights of Indigenous Peoples (Del Cid, 1996). *Effectively excluding than from civic life.*

In the face of these social and political challenges, the Guatemalan government, with the cooperation of various international organizations and financial aid agencies, notably USAID, has developed several reform efforts. First was the National Program for Bilingual Education (PRONEBI). It started in 1979 and was funded by (BEST)-USAID from 1979 and 1984/1985. Subsequently, it became a division of the Ministry of Education. Second was the Girls' Education Initiative, which was a five-year scholarship program that helped primary-age indigenous girls to stay in school. This was a pilot program in 36 communities, which tried different ways to promote girls' school retention, completion, and achievement. Third was the NEUBI program, which was a UNICEF-funded effort in multigrade schooling carried out by Ministry officials in 14 schools in the indigenous region of el Quiche. Fourth was the Don Bosco program, a Catholic project that has worked in Guatemala for almost 20 years in the Alta Verapaz Region. Its goal was to impart secondary education to indigenous youth who have completed sixth grade. After completion many of them were sent to work as bilingual teachers in isolated communities that requested this service. Fifth were the USAID-funded *Nueva Escuela Unitaria* (NEU) program and the Improving Educational Quality (IEQ) project, which I report on here.

TEACHERS' PERCEPTIONS OF THEIR PARTICIPATION IN THE NEU EDUCATIONAL REFORM

When the NEU program started in 1992, the expectations of the actors involved were many and challenging. Teachers were expected to have positive attitudes toward the new ways of teaching. They were to become facilitators of the learning process, that is, to be guides rather than mere instructors. They were also expected to become active leaders in their communities. In addition, they were expected to manage the components of the program efficiently (Guatemala, Ministerio de Educación, 1996). However, most of the Guatemalan teachers were disenchanted by the government's programs that were handed down to them. They were also distrustful of government officials and national or international "experts." One of the rural teachers shared with me her reaction when the NEU director asked her if she wanted to participate in the new educational reform: "I do not want to hear about new educational projects anymore! All of those projects are deceitful! The government officials get the funding and we are just used. They come here and give us a bunch of brochures that we do not know how to use. Then, they send us someone, who does not either, to guide us! So we are stuck again. All is a deceit!"[17] Resistance to new projects, plus distrust of ideas coming from the top, were very common among the teachers that I interviewed.

From another angle, government officials faced their own mistrust and misconception about the teachers' capacity to work responsibly. Very often the authorities pointed out the teachers' irresponsibility, instead of their virtues and good will to work with the limited resources they have (Guatemala, Ministerio de Educación, 1996). Project administrators, on the other hand, wanted to engage the teachers in all possible aspects of the program. According to the NEU director, "The participation of teachers was the most important component of the program." Very often, he says, "Educational reforms are perfectly designed; but, if the program is not appropriated by the teachers, they will not be able to use it. In such a case, it is not possible to get the effect that one wishes."[18] For him, therefore, crucial to the program was "to build, together with the teachers, the appropriate educational model for the unitary schools in Guatemala" (Guatemala, Ministerio de Educación, 1996, p. 33). These were, in general, the views and attitudes of the teachers, the government officials, and the program administrators when they decided to work together on the NEU educational reform.

The first step taken by rural teachers toward participating in the NEU educational reform was to respond to the invitation by NEU administrators and regional authorities to attend a first meeting, where the program was presented to them. Of all the 865 rural teachers of unitary schools where NEU was going to be implemented, 440 attended the meeting. After a process of selection based on the profile of the teacher, the school, and the community, teachers from 100 schools were chosen for the NEU pilot program. In June 1992, a second meeting was held by NEU administrators, with the teachers who had been selected to participate in the pilot program. This meeting was convened in order to ask the teachers to identify the needs and problems that they faced in their schools, and to identify possible solutions. A plan of action was drawn by the teachers and NEU administrators in the areas of teacher training, curriculum, community, and administration.

A widely diverse range of educational processes, activities, and policies were affected by the NEU educational reform. At the school level, for example, new ways of teaching, new ways of managing the classroom, and new curriculum were introduced. Outside the school, a new set of activities were implemented. Most of those activities required the interaction of the teachers with other actors, namely parents, program administrators, evaluators, and government officials. We focus next on a more detailed examination of those processes, activities, and policies.

One of the most significant changes that the teachers made with respect to educational policies in their schools was finding new ways to grade, evaluate, and promote their pupils. The new grading, evaluation, and promotion system that the teachers implemented in NEU schools was radically different from the existing system endorsed by the Ministry of Education. The official system consisted of the traditional pass–fail approach, where at the end of the academic year the child either passed or failed the grade of current enrollment. The main difference with the new system is that children in NEU schools never fail grades. A child who, at the end of the academic year, does not finish the instructional units that allow him or her to advance to the upper grade is considered "in process." That child is encouraged to come back the following year and continue working on the same instructional unit until its completion, at which time the child is promoted to the upper grade. This flexible promotion system is more consistent with the rural environment of the child than the system supported by the Ministry of Education. One of the reasons why the flexible promotion system is more responsive to the needs of the rural children is because it enables the students to advance at their own pace. With this flexible promotion system there are more possibilities for the child to be enrolled the following year. This is done knowing that the child will continue at the point where he or she left off instead of having to start the same grade all over again. Consequently, the chances of the child completing all six primary grades increase. The grading system, therefore, is consistent with the flexible promotion system. In NEU schools, the teachers implemented a grading system based on positive reinforcement. Children in NEU schools are graded "Good," "Very Good," or "Excellent," instead of the traditional numerical system, endorsed by the Ministry of Education, by which a grade below 60 means "Failed."

The policies on promotion and evaluation implemented by the teachers of NEU schools are not congruent with the official policies endorsed by the Ministry of Education. This discrepancy between NEU policies and the Ministry's policies affects the records kept by Ministry officials and has an impact on the administrative process. For example, supervisors who either are not familiar with or do not support NEU policies demand that teachers produce the traditional grades and present records showing children who failed grades. The tension between teachers and supervisors has increased over time. A teacher describes the tension: "The supervisor is not in agreement with our grading system. He does not agree with the flexible promotion either; he does not accept that. He even makes fun of it! All in all, he does not accept the new system!" This tension builds up when a child who has been attending an NEU school is transferred to a non-NEU school. As a result of the tension, NEU teachers, with the support of NEU administrators, presented their case to the Ministry of Education via government officials so as to work out a policy solution that would accommodate not only their interests but also the interests of their pupils.

In September 4–5, 1997, a meeting of approximately 30 people was organized by the teachers with the support of the NEU administrators. It was attended by government officials at the local, regional, and national levels.[19] In that meeting, the teachers explained to the government officials their new ways of teaching and the promotion and evaluation system that they had implemented. This meeting was, among other things, a historical event in which teachers petitioned government officials to accommodate their educational policies. The following statement, made by one of the teachers attending the meeting, shows his assessment of the situation:

One of the limitations that is affecting this program [NEU] the most is that there has not been a hundred percent approval by the Ministry of Education. On this occasion, we are meeting precisely to work on a document in which we will get a green light for our evaluation system. We use flexible promotion and the supervisors might agree with it. But, if the authorities use records that do not reflect our system, then the supervisors are not able to continue supporting us. We run into problems at the end of the academic year because the supervisors want a legal base for our evaluation system to be officially accepted. We have struggled with this problem for some years now and we have never had an affirmative answer.

The views of this teacher were shared by most of the teachers that I interviewed.

A way to examine the manner of appropriation of educational policies by the teachers is through their use of language. For example, when teachers referred to policies implemented in their schools they almost always referred to them as "our" evaluation system or "our" grading system. This expression was used not only when they referred to the promotion, evaluation, and grading systems, but also when they talked about their classroom activities. Most of the teachers that I interviewed made clear distinctions between the Ministry of Education's grading, evaluation, and promotion policies, and their own.

The teachers who were part of the NEU program perceived themselves as a distinct group with their own teaching methods, instructional materials, and evaluation and promotion systems. They perceived themselves as being different from teachers in non-NEU schools. Similarly, teachers in non-NEU schools perceived the NEU teachers as different. There was also tension between the two groups. Teachers who were not part of NEU resented not being part of "something good" that was taking place. A non-NEU teacher acknowledged, in an interview, that NEU schools had a very good reputation in the region and were making a positive impact on the children. She resentfully stated, however, that NEU teachers formed "closed circles" to which the non-NEU teachers had not been invited. Additionally, she said, NEU teachers were not sharing their new knowledge and information with non-NEU teachers.

The self-perception of teachers in NEU schools as a distinct group, contributed, in my view, to their cohesiveness and group solidarity. Such solidarity was also strengthened by their participation in the *Círculos de Maestros*.[20] The *Círculos de Maestros* were created, by initiative of the teachers, as a way to share their experiences with fellow teachers, to analyze different teaching methods and techniques, and to reflect on their role in the schools and their communities. The *Círculos de Maestros* functioned also as a way to facilitate individual and group reflection and work collectively in the areas related to their practice. In these meetings, for example, the teachers identified new methods of teaching and managing the classroom; agreed on trying new pedagogical methods; implemented them in their schools; and reported their experiences back to the group. These activities were supported and coordinated by NEU administrators. The decisions made in the *Círculos de Maestros* were conveyed to the NEU director who, together with the local and regional authorities, made the necessary arrangements to provide financial and technical assistance for the implementation of the initiatives.

The *Círculos de Maestros*, in some cases, faced opposition by the supervisors. One of the teachers says:

We had fellow teachers who did not want to continue attending the meetings of the *Círculos de Maestros* because their supervisors were bothering them and told them to stop attending those meetings. They told the teachers that they were wasting too much time on those meetings and they were abandoning the children. There is some truth to that but sometimes there is a need to do that because if one does not get trained it is impossible to work.

Another teacher expressed her frustration about the lack of support from the authorities and by contrast her positive feelings of being supported by her fellow teachers: "In the *Círculo de Maestros* what we do is support each other." However, she continued,

I am going to be very honest, there are authorities that make demands on us. They come here to ask for our teaching plans. Sometimes we feel frustrated because we see that all this has given us good results. But, the authorities suddenly come to demand the teaching plans. We do not have teaching plans because the teaching is done through self-instructional guides. I give thanks to God because when something happens to us, since we belong to the same *Círculo de Maestros*, we consult with each other. Sometimes there are disagreements but not so much as to give up the work.

Another example of the teachers' cohesiveness and collegiality is the *Plan Padrinos*.[21] With the *Plan Padrinos*, teachers in NEU schools invited teachers from neighboring schools to join the program. They sponsored new teachers, shared their experiences with them, and guided them in all aspects of the program. By 1994, teachers from the *Círculos de Maestros* informed the NEU director which schools they wanted to be part of the NEU expansion and the number of new teachers that needed training. Although the expansion of NEU in Guatemala was planned from the beginning, the way to carry it out was the teachers' initiative and responsibility. Using the *Plan Padrinos*, the teachers who had participated in NEU from the beginning planned and implemented the expansion of the program to other schools in the region. Ministry officials and NEU administrators provided technical and logistical support. The teachers visited their colleagues in neighboring schools, and invited them to observe them in their NEU schools and to attend the *Círculos de Maestros*. In these meetings, they had the occasion to share their experiences with the new teachers and encourage them to join the program. One of them describes the experience:

We think that the expansion should be done in two ways: one in which we are instructing the teacher that is nearest to our school and who comes to visit us to see how we work. That is very important. The other way is to tell all the teachers that even if they are too far from us they still can come and visit our schools even if they are not in the same region, so that they can learn about new ways of teaching. What happens is that we do not share the idea that the *licenciado*[22] is the one to teach us. They know the theory but we know how to apply it. So, there is more trust among the teachers; we understand each other better. If I have doubts, the other is my colleague, my *compañero*,[23] so I ask him. But when an authority comes one feels inhibited.

The *Multiplicadores*[24] was the way in which the training process was carried out for the expansion of NEU. The *Multiplicadores* was a process by which teachers who had implemented the new practices in their schools trained their fellow teachers on the new methods of teaching and managing the school. Teachers who served as *Multiplicadores* were selected by their peers to train other teachers. According to the researchers who were evaluating NEU, those teachers "felt fulfilled to be able to share their knowledge and experiences with their peers; they felt valued as persons and professionals" (Improving Educational Quality, 1995, p. 5). The transfer of the newly acquired knowledge was done horizontally, from teacher to teacher, instead of vertically, from "experts" to teachers, as it had been done in the past. Looking down

Another illustration of the teachers' collaborative work was the design, development, testing, and implementation of self-instructional guides for NEU schools. One of the main features of NEU was to adapt the curriculum to the rural environment. To do so, teachers, with the support of NEU administrators, worked together with parents and children in the design, development, and implementation of the curriculum. The following statement is a reflection of a teacher who participated in this process:

It was a little bit difficult at the beginning because we thought the guides had to focus on the content [material to be learned] and not much on the process [how to learn]. So, we arrived at a consensus with the other teachers from Region IV and Region II. We went to test the self-instructional guides in our schools and two months later we met again to see how it worked. We made the necessary corrections, printed them again, and went back to test them once more in our schools. After three or four tries we decided that the material was almost in good shape. It was not perfect because the active learning pedagogy tells us that there is constant change and we have to be innovative. That is what we did. We worked on the materials. We took them to the field and tried to see if they worked. We planned to meet again. What worked remained and what did not work was modified.

After that explanation, I asked the teacher: "Who made the decisions about the instructional guides?" "We, the teachers," she responded. "The NEU director gave us the guidelines and the first draft of the guides, but there is a huge difference between the first draft and the final document. Therefore, the decisions were made by us, the *docentes*.[25] We met in the *Círculos de Maestros* and made decisions about a document, modified it, expanded it, and determined which processes were involved."

SUMMARY AND CONCLUSIONS

This chapter has focused on teachers' participation in the formation and appropriation of educational policies within the context of *Nueva Escuela*

Unitaria (NEU) in Guatemala. The rural teachers that I interviewed said that they participated in different aspects of the NEU educational reform. The areas in which they participated included the design, testing, and implementation of new curriculum. They designed and implemented new grading evaluation and promotion systems. They also selected, sponsored, and trained their peers. My research findings have shown that the NEU teachers no longer saw themselves as passive recipients of educational policies that were handed down to them from the top by policymakers or "experts." On the contrary, they started to perceive themselves as viable contributors to the formation and implementation of the policies in question. This was done, in part, through a process of cognitive self-awareness and social integration. By cognitive self-awareness I mean a mutual recognition, by the actors involved, of being distinctive groups, with distinct interests, needs, and preferences. Cognitive self-awareness involved their self-perception, as a group, of being able to take part in and influence the educational reform initiative. By social integration, I mean the social process by which teachers, together with students, parents, authorities, donor agency representatives, and other members of the community work together to make decisions concerning the educational reform.

The teachers perceived themselves as a cohesive group working together with these other actors. In so doing, they all shared the responsibilities and commitments involved in the educational reform effort. Teachers shared their experiences, needs, and ideas with fellow teachers and authorities. In turn, the authorities participated in activities conducive to changes in the schools. The abovementioned actors identified common interests and coordinated their efforts in pursuit of meaningful educational reform. They constructed, articulated, and implemented new educational procedures leading to the formation and appropriation of new educational policies.

As is usually the case in human endeavor, the collaborative effort was not always smooth. In fact, there was tension and disagreement among various actors regarding the changes that were taking place. For instance, in one particular school, one of the teachers joined NEU and used the new methods; another teacher in the same school did not. The tension between the two of them resulted in the removal of both of them from the school. The parents, who were aware of the situation, requested that the newly appointed teacher not use the new educational policies. There was also tension between teachers and some of the supervisors who did not support the changes, either because they did not agree with them or because they were not aware of the philosophy behind them. The bulk of the tension with respect to the new educational policies occurred between the NEU teachers and authorities. The teachers realized that the new policies had to be approved by the Ministry of Education in order to be accepted by their supervisors. The teachers, with the support of NEU administrators, called a meeting with local and regional authorities as well as representatives of the Ministry of Education. In that meeting, the teachers voiced their concerns and informed the authorities about the changes that they had made in their schools. Moreover, teachers explained to the authorities the rationale behind those changes and the positive results that, according to them, were occurring in their schools. They expressed their conviction that the new practices and policies were beneficial to the children and had made a positive impact on their schools. More specifically, they shared their beliefs that the new methods of teaching and new policies had contributed to the improvement of their pupils' achievement, retention, self-esteem, and democratic behavior.

Being eager to voice their views and beliefs in issues related to their work is, in my view, the best example of teachers making a significant move toward effective participation in the decisions that affect their practices as teachers. Furthermore, teachers who have traditionally been less powerful actors have become an integral part of the formulation and implementation of policy choices. They have invested their time, energy, ideas, trust, and goodwill in the accomplishment of the intended goals.

Policy formation and appropriation in NEU was a collaborative effort by different actors that participated at different times and at various levels. They also recognized that each group depended on the other for the accomplishment of the reform effort. They shared their ideas and concerns, which contributed to the strengthening of their ties. In the process of sharing with their peers, teachers realized that they were not alone in dealing with problematic educational issues. Most of them were amid similar conditions, such as overcrowded classrooms, lack of resources, absenteeism and dropout, and pressures from the authorities, to name a few. With a sense of being stronger while being united, they joined their voices and channeled their concerns to the authorities. Although some of the teachers were skeptical of the authorities' response to their requests, they were convinced that, at last, they had contributed meaningfully to the formulation and implementation of educational policies that made sense in the rural setting.

Some of the sentiments expressed by the teachers that I interviewed were a strong sense of personal growth, change, and satisfaction. Such sentiments are reflected in the following statements made by some of these teachers:

We started this work, which is very good because it begins with the experience of the teachers. The opportunity to participate and to create a new methodology was given to us. This is the best thing that could have happened to me.

Before, I was tormented because I did not know how to attend to several grades in a multigrade school, but that has changed. My attitude changed. Before I used to teach by lecturing, now I am a facilitator.

[The voluntary participation] is the most beautiful thing about the program. You were given the idea. You also got the opportunity to go and implement it in your community. You had the opportunity to accept it or to change it according to your location. So, that is the most beautiful thing. They gave us the opportunity to change. You did not do it because there is an imposition. Because when things were imposed on the Guatemalan teacher then they did not do it. But if they came to sell you the idea then they have given you the opportunity. That is when the change really happened.

[My personal change in relation to the students] is the best thing that could have happened to me as a teacher. Because change has occured from within one's self. One, as a teacher, has to change, because if there is no change in the teacher how can one expect change in the children of the community?

On the basis of my interviews and interactions with the teachers, I came to the conclusion that they perceived themselves as being able to both initiate actions and influence processes, thereby prompting outcomes that affected not only their professional but also their personal lives. They also had a sense of individual-collective professional development and professional accomplishment, together with an increased feeling of group solidarity.

According to Paul (1987), participation in some cases contributes to capacity building through sharing in the management of the project and taking on operational responsibilities for segments of the project. Some forms of participation, he adds, lead to an equitable sharing of power and to a higher level of people's political awareness and strengths. Although teachers in NEU played a more visible role and assumed responsibility for different areas of the reform, the power remained in the hands of the actors who have traditionally made the decisions. In the case of NEU, the element of empowerment, in my view, was associated with the element of cognitive self-awareness and social integration, that is, teachers' self-perception of being able to initiate actions on their own and thus influence the process and outcomes of sociocultural development.

EPILOGUE: THE BOTTOM-UP APPROACH IN NEU'S EDUCATIONAL REFORM

What I have tried to show in this chapter is the link between NEU's education policy reform initiatives and the teachers' perception of their participation in education policy formation and appropriation in Guatemala. This linkage constitutes a nascent bottom-up philosophy. The bottom-up philosophy is presented as both a critique and replacement of the traditional top-to-bottom philosophy, which focuses on national elites, experts, and government officials. The bottom-up philosophy is quite the opposite. It offers a different and promising approach that emphasizes the involvement of diverse actors from different sociocultural contexts. These include teachers, parents, and other members of the community. The bottom-up philosophy, as noted previously, is presented here as a serious contending alternative to mainstream policy discourse. In other words, the bottom-up philosophy views the problem of educational reform policy not only from the perspective of critical thinking but also in terms of the need for effective democratizing administrative techniques. For one thing, the bottom-up approach employed here is an attempt to examine the NEU's educational reform policies and practices that give priority and primacy to the participants themselves.

Furthermore, the bottom-up philosophy is predicated upon and committed to the idea that any viable attempt at significant sociocultural transformation has to take into account such critical issues as empowerment, effective citizenship, and sociocultural democratization. All these entail the processes and practices of broadening the social contexts and thereby enabling a meaningful discourse and participation by various actors from diverse historical and cultural backgrounds.

As I understand it, the bottom-up philosophy initiated by the NEU project is not simply an ameliorative endeavor, but a serious shift from a traditional technocratic view of educational reform policy. By widening the sociocultural context, the NEU project, it seems, enacted a view of policy as a normative decision-making activity grounded, in part, in everyday life experiences. As such, NEU's project is a case study that, in my view, enables us to understand policy formation as essentially a kind of sociocultural practice—a set of activities embedded in and informed by certain cultural models and social relations. These activities are carried out by individual, organizational, community, national, and international actors, entailing collaborative effort toward the intended goals. In the case of Guatemala, the collaborative initiative was undertaken by actors from diverse sociocultural contexts. While various social actors were involved, my focus in this chapter was on the key actors, namely, the teachers. These are the actors whose voices and direct participation in policy formation are central to this case study. Furthermore, as key participants, they were also involved in the process of policy appropriation. This meant that they were the social actors engaged in discourse involving their own interpretation and perception of policy choices and uses within the context of their own sociocultural practices.

NOTES

1. Meaning "New Unitary School."

2. This manuscript is part of my ongoing research on teachers' perceptions of their participation in educational policies within the context of NEU. My interest in the topic started while I was working for the Institute for International Studies in Education (IISE) of the University of Pittsburgh as part of the IEQ documentation team. IEQ is a USAID project that evaluated the NEU educational reform in Guatemala. The IISE was a subcontractor to IEQ.

3. I use a generic definition found in Heslep (1987).

4. Documents such as audiovisual material depicting NEU schools, newsletters, trip reports, research reports, and semiannual and annual reports prepared by the U.S. consultant on the evaluation of NEU.

5. In Fall 1997, I spent a month in Guatemala collecting data for my research. I visited and observed NEU schools, deepened my knowledge about the program, and interviewed NEU administrators and researchers. I conducted open-ended and semi-structured interviews with different actors, including 33 teachers; 10 govern-

ment officials; 4 representatives of the Academy for Educational Development (AED), which provided technical assistance to NEU; 3 researchers; and 4 parents. In 1999, I traveled to Nicaragua and interviewed the NEU director from 1992–1996 in Guatemala.

6. Observations include the ones done by the evaluators of NEU and my own observations done during my field trip to the regions in Guatemala.

7. For a description of this educational model and its history, see Schieffelbein (1991).

8. Participatory democratic behaviors and attitudes are promoted by creating situations that allow children to demonstrate or express rational, empirical, and egalitarian beliefs about how to function in social situations; to interact appropriately with peers and adults; and to become involved in the social and political life of their school and eventually of their community and the nation.

9. During my field trip I used a four-wheel truck in Region II and motorcycle in Region IV to access the schools. Walking was also an option if one would be willing to walk, in most cases, for three or four hours, which some of the teachers do daily.

10. NEU was initially implemented in 100 schools in two rural regions of Guatemala: Region II and Region IV. Region II consists of the departments of Alta Verapaz and Baja Verapaz. Alta Verapaz is populated almost exclusively by Q'eqchí-speaking Mayans. Baja Verapaz has a population comprised mostly of Mayans who speak either Q'eqchí or Poqomchí. Region IV is made up of the departments of Jalapa, Jutiapa, and Santa Rosa, and primarily is populated by Spanish speakers.

11. Interview on September 16, 1997, in Guatemala with Myriam Castañeda, NEU coordinator and liaison to the Ministry of Education.

12. Illiterate, according to the Guatemalan National Committee for Literacy (CONALFA), is a person 15 years of age or older who is not able to write or read Spanish.

13. For information about educational decentralization in Latin America and Guatemala in particular, see De Lara (1997).

14. National Plan for Educational Regionalization.

15. Advisory councils.

16. Belonging to a union.

17. All the interviews were conducted in Spanish. The translation is mine.

18. Interview on February 5, 1999, in Nicaragua with Dr. Oscar Mogollón, NEU director (1992–1996).

19. I attended this meeting, which was held at the time I was collecting data for my research.

20. Teachers' circles.

21. Sponsorship program.

22. Someone with a professional degree.

23. Fellow-teacher.

24. Multipliers.

25. Spanish term commonly used to refer to teachers.

REFERENCES

ASIES/PREAL. (1997). *Reforma educativa en Guatemala*. Guatemala: Author.

Bhatnagar, B., & Williams, A. (1992). *Participatory development and the World Bank: Potential directions for change.* (Discussion Paper No. 813) Washington, D.C.: World Bank.

Coombs, P. H. (1980). *Meeting the basic needs of the rural poor: The integrated community-based approach.* New York: Pergamon Press.

Craig, H. (1998). Guatemala: Changing teacher pedagogy in the *Nueva Escuela Unitaria.* In H. Craig (Ed.), *Teacher development making an impact* (pp. 77–91). Washington, D.C.: USAID/ABEL.

De Lara, C. G. (1997). La Descentralizacion Educativa en Guatemala. In ASIES/PREAL (Ed.), *Reforma Educativa en Guatemala* (pp. 105–132). Guatemala: ASIES/PREAL.

Del Cid, S. (1996). *Ethnicity, political culture, and the future of Guatemalan democracy.* Unpublished doctoral dissertation, University of Pittsburgh.

Education for All. (1993, December). Summit of nine high-populated countries (Final Report). Paris: UNESCO.

Epstein, J. L. (1995). School/family/community partnerships: Caring for the children we share. *Review of Education Research, 67*(1), 3–42.

Framework for action to meet basic learning needs. (1990, March). New York: Inter-Agency Commission.

Freire, P. (1972). *Pedagogy of the oppressed.* New York: Herder & Herder.

Ginsburg, M. & Klopfer, L. (with Clayton, T., Rakotomanana, M., Sylvester, J., & Yazia, K.) (1996). Choices in conducting classroom-anchored research to improve educational quality in developing countries. *Research Papers in Education, 11*(3), 239–254.

Guatemala, Ministerio de Educación. (1996). *La escuela rural Guatemalteca en los albores del tercer milenio.* Guatemala: AID-BEST.

Heslep, R. (1987). Conceptual sources of controversy about educational policies. *Educational Theory, 37*, 423–432.

Imber, M. (1984). Teacher participation in school decision making: A framework for research. *Journal of Educational Administration, 22*(1), 25–33.

Improving Educational Quality. (1993). *Semi-annual report.* Washington, DC: Agency for International Development.

Improving Educational Quality. (1995). *Informe sobre capacitación para maestros en el proceso de expansión de NEU.* Washington, DC: Agency for International Development.

Jonas, S. (1991). *The battle for Guatemala: Rebels, death squads, and U.S. power.* Boulder, Co: Westview Press.

Jonas S. (1997, May/June). The Peace Accords: An end and a beginning. *NACLA Report on the Americas, 30*, 6.

Kvale, S. (1996). *Interviews: An introduction to qualitative research interviewing.* London: Sage.

Mantilla, M. (with de Barsse, Y. & Chesterfield, R.) (1996). The IEQ story in Guatemala. In M. Ginsburg & D. Adams (Eds.), *Policy-practice-research-dissemination/dialogue spirals in improving educational quality.* Pittsburgh, PA: Institute for International Studies in Education, University of Pittsburgh.

McGinn, N. (1996, October). *Resistance to good ideas: Escuela Nueva in Colombia.* Paper presented at the 1996 Conference of the Nordic Association for the Study of Education in Developing Countries, Copenhagen, Denmark.

Midgley, J. (1986). *Community participation, social development, and the state.* New York: Methuen.

Oxford University Dictionary. (1933). London: Oxford University Press.

Paul, S. (1987). *Community participation in development projects: The World Bank experience.* (Discussion Papers, 6). Washington, DC: World Bank.

Pigozzi, M. J. (1982). Participation in non-formal education projects: Some possible negative outcomes. *Convergence, 15*(3) 6–17.

Psacharopoulos, C., Rojas, C., & Velez, E. (1993). Achievement evaluation of Colombia's *Escuela Nueva*: Is multigrade the answer? *Comparative Education Review, 37*, 263–276.

Reimers, F. (1993). *Escuela Nueva.* In F. Reimers, *Education and the consolidation of democracy in Latin America: Innovations to provide quality basic education with equity* (pp. 18–21). Washington, DC: Agency for International Development.

Schieffelbein, E. (1991). *In search of the XXI century school: Is the Colombian* Escuela Nueva *the right pathfinder?* Santiago, Chile: UNESCO/UNICEF.

Seligson, M. (1995). *La Cultura Democrática de los Guatemaltecos.* Guatemala: Asociación de Investigación y Estudios Sociales.

Shaeffer, S. (1991). *A framework for collaborating for educational change.* Paris: UNESCO.

UNESCO. (1986). *La investigación-acción en el contexto de la regionalización educativa.* Guatemala: Author.

UNICEF. (1994). *Realidad Socioeconómica de Guatemala con Enfasis en la Situación de la Mujer.* Guatemala: Piedra Santa.

United Nations. (1971). *Popular participation in development: Emerging trends in community development.* New York.

United Nations. (1975). *Popular participation in decision making for development.* New York.

Vieira, P., & Junho, M. V. (1997). *The limits and merits of participation.* (Policy Research Working Paper No. 1838). Washington, DC: World Bank.

Wolf, J. (1997). *Planning for community participation in education.* Washington, DC: Agency for International Development.

World Bank. (1990). *Strengthening the Bank's role in popular participation.* Washington, DC: Author.

6

When Politics Becomes Pedagogy: Oppositional Discourse as Policy in Mexican Teachers' Struggles for Union Democracy

Susan Street[1]

As democratic union leaders, we have been thinking of the teacher as a subject in the schools, enclosed within the four walls of the classroom. We now realize that what we need to do is to define teaching as a permanent, all-encompassing function, as a role that goes way beyond the school itself. The scheme I now use when working with teachers is one that tries to correct this vision of the teacher as merely a worker, which ignores the other definitions as citizen and as educator.[2]

INTRODUCTION

A concept normally restricted to technical jargon has come to the fore in the social field of Mexican education. The recent centrality of *autonomy* does not derive solely from its increasingly important place in state policy. Indeed, and certainly not to the liking of government policymakers, the term itself has become contested precisely due to its subaltern origins as an explicitly political concept. The concept was made popular by the support the Zapatista Army of National Liberation has given since 1994 to the national indigenous movement, to "civil society" organizations, and to popular movements in general. Struggles of indigenous groups for state recognition of their right to be politically autonomous over cultural, social, and geographic territories has directed public debate to examine the concept itself. This debate has underlined the idea of autonomy as the self-determination of a collective people, a notion rescued from previous historical periods and made concrete by the autonomous municipalities established by Zapatista communities in Chiapas. The very existence of these autonomous structures confronts head-on the power of federal, state, and municipal governments, all of which for the most part have been historically inseparable from the dominant party, the PRI (*Partido Revolucionario Institucional,* or Institutional Revolutionary Party). This identification of *autonomy* with political struggle for voice and recognition by excluded and exploited groups has effectively linked the concept to organizational processes constitutive of a popular democratic subject[3] pushing to dismantle Mexico's authoritarian regime and thereby deepen a democratic transition.

Such recent popular politicization of the term "autonomy" in Mexico runs up against the more official governmental use of it as a characteristic of institutions (such as schools) that is granted or "delegated" by the state. In the educational systems of many countries worldwide, the concept has been key in "school restructuring" reforms. In the United States, for example, so-called "second-round" reforms have altered the meaning of autonomy: Once considered to be a property or capacity of teachers deployed in the classroom, it is now becoming understood as a goal of school management. Once a means, it currently appears as an end in itself, embodied in the push around the world for schools to be productive enterprises, based on "site-based management" (Contreras, 1997; Smyth, 1993). As educational policy has been globalized and transnationalized, and the national state thereby arguably diminished, the concept of autonomy has become technified, converted into a technology of control, thereby shedding its connotations of self-determination.[4] This is because autonomy comes to be part of a top-down devolution process within the centralized educational administration. As many authors have recognized and documented, "autonomy is an illusion" (Ball, 1993, p. 65): Schools are given more responsibilities, but less power, which is instead reconcentrated in those central government offices dictating state educational policy as normative criteria. Usually via decentralization processes, institutional units now operate programs designed in higher and even external offices; their "regulated autonomy" is only meant to adapt external, centrally defined criteria to local conditions or predefined situations.[5]

In Mexico too, the "rhetoric of autonomy" (Smyth, 1993, p. 2) has become the guiding light of educational policy, the prime conceptual instrument in the state's retreat from its historical responsibility of providing free education for all. Carlos Salinas's government (1988–1994) consolidated what had long been a trend by the technocratic group[6] to control the educational bureaucracy by initiating the dismantling of the welfare state (often called the "educator" state because of 70 years of involvement in school expansion) and inaugurating a new educational project more in tune with the market as the central stimulus for social organization. This "modernizing" project is said to depend on a "minimal" state, reducing its financial commitment to public education and designing ways to increase and supervise other social actors' participation in providing educational services (Aboites, 1997; Noriega, 1999). The Mexican state each day looks more like the "evaluative" state that David Hartley (1993, p. 101) has suggested is emerging in Scotland. This is not so much because of the success of "school restructuring" programs, but of a systematic policy favoring the wholesale "marketing" of a new "political culture of evaluation."[7]

My effort here is not to present in full Mexico's public education policy, nor do I wish to engage the issue of the degree to which this policy—as a normative document—manifests "neoliberal" tendencies. While the international literature seems quite conclusive about the nature of the reforms arising during the 1970s in the First World nations,[8] there is still little research in Mexico that permits us to categorically demonstrate the effects of what are now clearly transnational educational policies in countries undergoing International Monetary Fund structural adjustment programs.[9] In the educational sector, there does not yet seem to be a general consensus among researchers as to the nature and direction of the trends.[10]

Notwithstanding that public educational institutions themselves have not yet been privatized, important constitutional modifications have opened the door for Mexico's (re)integration into the global economy—via the North American Free Trade Agreement (NAFTA; Aboites, 1997). The technocratic strategy guiding educational policy has focused—following World Bank-propitiated trends—on an explicitly ideological plane, one that has been carefully guarded at the central level: curricula and textbooks. In effect, teachers understand "modernization," for the most part, as the requirement that they adapt their teaching methods to new curricular programs and textbooks (Jiménez & Perales, 1999; Pontón, 1997). While government officials avoid using the term "privatization" and deny it is an explicit policy directive, teachers perceive the state's lack of commitment to public education through a wide variety of indicators (deteriorating school maintenance, eroding union presence in school zones, intensified work days, increased administrative duties and saturated workloads, not to mention the devalued purchasing power of their inflation-controlled salaries). The new definitions circulating from the modernization policy subordinate everything and everyone to a notion of "educational quality" related to productivity and competitiveness. Such definitions have not been wholeheartedly received by teachers, who tend to adhere to their inherited collective identity as public employees and builders of national citizens.[11]

TEACHERS AS POLICYMAKERS

In this chapter, I use the concept of autonomy as a window framing the issue of how some teachers appropriate educational policy and how they transform state-granted autonomy so that it can be of real use to a democratic subject developing an oppositional project. An ethnographic approach[12] bringing subjects' voices to the forefront leads to transcending the oftentimes normative and descriptive character of educational policy studies that define the state as the sole actor and everyone else as implementers or clients (see Levinson and Sutton, introduction this volume). Indeed, teachers are usually predefined as objects of reform; reforms are designed to change teaching practices. When occasionally defined as subjects, teachers' subject status is still explored only by looking at the way they do or do not implement state policy, the way they act upon what is given to them from above. Many studies focus on the distance between policy discourse and practice, between intentions and reality (Pontón, Rangel, & Cedillo, 1996). Even studies of teacher resistance may still fall within this approach if resistance is understood only as a reaction to policy imposed from above. However, this is not the only possibility. I address the issue taking a slightly different slant. What if the social actors themselves view policy in this way, and thereby define themselves as policy designers? This is a real possibility if that collective actor aspires toward "social subject" status. A social subject, by definition, necessarily transforms sociocultural practices by virtue of policy formation designs and strategies. In a situation of active resistance, when a subject is created through a social movement to change reality and to embody transformed social relations, the question becomes: How do those people forming the subject think of themselves as autonomous producers of policy, as definers of strategy and as constructors of power for themselves? How do the participants theorize their actions as cultural production? How do they "live" policy?

In the case of Mexico's authoritarian political regime, of course, state policy does not simply disappear for those pursuing democratization. My research suggests that such policy becomes part of the "context" of struggle, the conditions favoring or obstructing the autonomous development of the democratic subject. Such an interpretation redefines policy away from its formal character as a legitimate charter, and even as an object of political dispute, and redirects our attention to how teachers mediate the impact of official policy directives over the course of their "policy" moves, that is, as teachers reorganize to enhance their capabilities to exercise power. Their everyday actions (as a social subject) confront top-down official policy, but to successfully challenge government programs threatening what are interpreted as Mexicans' educational rights, their practices and strategies must go beyond immediate reactions and be part of policy formation for an autonomous political project carried out by an autonomous subject.[13]

That this approach can be an analytic possibility in Mexico is due to the fact that teachers' democratic struggles have reworked and resignified the concept of autonomy; some teachers are beginning to understand the term as a product of the development of a specific social subject to which they contribute. It is precisely because the teachers' democratic struggles resulted from the affirmation of teachers as having a voice in union and school affairs that teachers came to conceive of themselves as policymakers, as the "real" educational authorities. This new role was self-ascribed as teachers organized themselves in collective bodies to exercise "rank and file power" (*poder de base*).[14] Because their agency came about in a democratization process working on the structures and social relations determining school practices, teachers were able to envision the government's proposal for school reform—with its promise of local, school-level autonomy enhanced by new participatory schemes—as, at best, partial, restricted, and inadequate and, at worst, yet another mechanism enabling the state to mediate and reproduce class domination.

"DEMOCRATIZATION FROM BELOW" HISTORICALLY SITUATED: TWO DECADES OF TEACHERS' STRUGGLES FOR UNION DEMOCRACY

As a form of capitalist domination and not merely a set of policies selectively implemented, neoliberalism closes rather than opens democratic spaces (Chomsky, 1992; Steffan, 1995). Because of this, the construction of democracy in Mexico and elsewhere necessarily stems from below, from spheres of resistance that generate struggles seeking to create autonomous actors who may join together to form democratic subjects intent on democratizing themselves and the state (Alonso, 1995; Casanova & Rosenmann, 1995). Democratization, then, refers to a process of social construction from below, whereby individuals and groups gain access to, and exercise, rights and responsibilities previously denied to them.[15]

Democratization has been an oppositional discourse and practice in Mexico, a social demand turned radical, first put forward in the 1950s and 1960s by workers rebelling against corporatist union structures and practices that effectively left the rank and file without a voice in union affairs. For their part, as creatures of the state, public school teachers have historically participated in educational expansion. Nevertheless, dissidence and opposition developed around the time the import-substitution model for economic growth touched bottom (Salgado, 1998) and the country was submitted to foreign debt commitments and eventually to the IMF's "structural adjustment programs." In the late 1970s, teachers intensified salary demands, but since the union bosses (called *charros* by dissident teachers) rarely defended these economically motivated protests, teachers would then respond by forming organizations parallel to those of the national union. By strengthening these new associations, they contested regime-dominated and imposed leadership. Still, such emerging mass movements affected mostly the central and southern regions of the country.

It must be said, then, that democratization was never a formal component of the government's educational modernization policy. Perhaps this was so because the dissident teachers had already taken this concept and, via protest, converted it into a major demand within a basically confrontational model of political action. Starting in the 1970s, for at least 10 or 15 years, ousting the union boss, Carlos Jonguitud Barrios, and destroying the monopolistic hold of his *Vanguardia Revolucionaria* (associated with the PRI-government) over the excessively vertical and centralized teachers' union *The National Union of Educational Workers—SNTE*), became synonomous with democratization.

Democratization as a goal of the political opposition translated into a parallel umbrella organization that is soon to celebrate its 20th birthday: the *National Coordinatorship of Educational Workers (CNTE)*. Teachers' struggles for union democracy have always been attempts to push the government and the SNTE to recognize the CNTE as a legitimate political actor. This has meant that regional movements identifying with the CNTE have favored political unity at the cost of ignoring teachers' efforts to confront exploitation at the worksite.

Notwithstanding fundamental gains of the democratic movement, the structural limitations of the model that democratization followed during the 1980s has tended to reproduce not only the gap between union leaders and those represented, but also the irrelevance for democratic subject formation of teachers' responses to changing working conditions in the schools. CNTE's difficulties in representing teachers' interests after the 1989 protests in the Federal District (which brought down Barrios, the power behind the SNTE) can only be seen as a result of exclusionary tendencies undermining the original inclusionary nature of the teachers' movement. In essence, rank and file teachers lost interest because they were not the real subjects of democratization; over the course of time, they lost their subject status as decision makers and "molders" of the majority consensus (*formadores del consenso*), even within their own democratic movement. Democratization, in its crudest form, had become an issue of belonging to a political group, a matter of displaying loyalty to leaders and of taking to the streets when movement leaders thought it best to do so. As I examine further below, democratization had little to do with the ways teachers' work was changing; it did not respond to teachers' sense of loss of control over their work, nor did it represent a solution to the daily pressures to educate their students and improve "educational quality."

This is not to say the teachers' movement did not create democratic practices. My point is that democracy became real where rank and file teachers actively defined the terms of their own participation. Democratization, in its most advanced form at particular historical conjunctures, radically transformed the relationship between the rank and file (*las bases*) and the leaders elected by that rank and file (*los dirigentes*). Out of a clear-cut relationship of domination–subordination, teachers fought to create more equitable terms based on new conditions for participation and debate among themselves. The democracy created from within the democratic teachers' movement in Chiapas, for example, became a matter of reaffirming culturally relevant values of "responsible solidarity," represented in transformed union practices as an "ethics of reciprocity." Rank and file teachers emphasized relational characteristics among teachers guaranteeing a regime of respect and inclusionary dialogue theretofore absent in the social relations of schools and unions (Street, 1994, 1996a).

To sum up, 20 years ago democratization was thought of simply as the substitution of *charros* by new union leaders democratically elected by the rank and file. There was an obvious enemy, personified in the figure of Carlos Jonguitud Barrios; and where teachers mobilized for better salary conditions, demands for democracy could be expressed in one simple demand (easily reproduced at local and regional levels): "Down with the *charros*." But today, the conditions and possibilities for democratization appear to be qualitatively different. Practically all the references for political action have changed: from a basically negative struggle to dethrone authoritarian leadership to a basically positive struggle to articulate social projects in order to confront a vague, misunderstood, and controversial form of domination—neoliberalism. The current conjuncture, from the point of view of teachers, could be broadly characterized as an ambiguous and uncertain moment, an impasse marked by an inability to conceive of an alternative educational project that would be neither a return to the state-dominated model nor an open endorsement of the free market project. Twenty years ago, the teachers created the CNTE as a national, political actor vying for state power (via control of the union); today, those who disagree with this proposition believe that, for democratization to become an issue in Mexican education, it will be up to the teachers and parents. If teachers and parents are to participate in democratization as a popular project—are to create democratic schooling practices—it will depend, fundamentally, on the way teachers conceive of their work. It will depend on whether teachers' critical thinking about "teachers' work" leads them to constructive action in transforming their teaching and their relationships with students, parents, and authorities. Until now, "teachers' work" and democratization have been completely divorced, separated by structural and conceptual gaps impeding teachers from becoming activists and political activists from becoming teachers. Until now, democratization always referred to some external structure—union or government hierarchy at the national or state level. Democratization depended on the assumption that policymaking was divorced from teachers' and parents' spheres of activity. Yet, recently, teachers have been developing new perspectives around a notion of popular self-government, whereby teachers' teaching practices themselves take center stage in local and regional organizations. In this proposition, teachers define themselves as producers of policy. Upon doing so, they are learning to turn from politics to pedagogy.

EMERGING DEBATES WITHIN THE DEMOCRATIC TEACHERS' MOVEMENT

My reading of the Mexican teachers' movement tells us that activists are questioning whether movement actions should be only part of a project to accumulate the power of a national political actor—the CNTE—imagined at some point powerful enough to take over the SNTE. Some activists are beginning to make teacher subjectivities problematic. These are becoming central to teachers' efforts to improve the CNTE as a democratic subject and to enhance dissident teachers' contributions to Mexico's popular movement.There has been a significant shift within the democratic teachers' movement in the use of categories employed to think about state educational policy and the dissident "alternative educational project." This shift corresponds with the intensification of a debate internal to the movement between those activists who continue to push for democratizing the national union, via mobilizing the rank and file, and a newer project led by activists pursuing the "construction of popular power." This latter position requires breaking the closed nature of the teachers' professional association in order to establish links with other social sectors, now reconceived as "the poor," that is, any and all groups excluded by "savage capitalism" from Mexico's uneven development.

Thus, a new division within the democratic teachers' movement is replacing the traditional split on the Left between reformist and revolutionary positions. The leaders developing the emergent project contending for political dominance within the CNTE are concerned with creating new ways to exercise power that cut across the profession and that cross different social sectors and move into the communities in order to form new (autonomous) "social territories." They purport to strengthen working-class resistance to neoliberal policies by building a broad-based "political mass movement" centered on a popular economic policy.[16]

The ideas about the educational component of each group's political project are strikingly different. The older group imagines "the educational alternative" as a kind of normative policy document—a sort of mirror image of governmental policy plans—elaborated in special commissions by the more intellectually oriented teachers who volunteer for the task. The newer group views the educational issue as an inherently political struggle to redefine teachers' work and teachers' identities as professionals and workers. Historically, the first conception has brought mixed results, varying from little activity of the educational commissions (as they are subordinated to the political needs of the movement), to elaborately designed plans involving classroom teachers, regional officials, and State-level unionists. The more developed educational planning experiences within the movement have occurred where the democratic teachers have controlled a State-level union within the Mexican federal system (especially in the states of Oaxaca and Michoacán).

The limitations of even the most advanced planning experiences derive from certain persistent problems nagging democratized union leaders. Efforts to construct the "Alternative Educational Project" have been top-down and have tended to reinforce the hierarchical nature of the relationship between schools and the various levels of union organization. Rank and file teachers' participation is reduced to ratifying decisions made by leaders; when consulted, teachers present their opinions on proposals that address macroeducational problems normally unrelated to their everyday teaching practices. Notably, then, the traditional conception of democratization still assigns policymaking to the enlightened few.

These limitations, and the fact that the educational issue is widely regarded as "nobody's terrain" (or, as one teacher described it, as the movement's "Achilles' heel"), have not gone unnoticed. The emergent group's elaborations are based on a critique of these attempts to formulate plans as mirror alternatives to government policy. In synthesis, these leaders are questioning the democratic movement's reproduction of the very vices teachers' struggles originally fought to eradicate within the union: the domination of rank and file teachers by disrespectful leaders, the inequalities in access to state benefits, the lack of social mobility for the majority of teachers, the lack of voice of individual teachers, and the dominance over professional interests exercised by political parties (Street, 1997).

The following testimony illustrates that the thrust of this self-criticism reveals a deeper critique of what is seen as the basic problem impeding movement development: the social distance between leaders and rank and file. During a discussion in September 1998 among democratic teachers from SNTE Sections IX, X, and XI in Mexico City, participants' interventions alternated between expressions of frustration with many democratic leaders' tendency to privilege negotiations with the government over and above rank and file pressures, and complaints about teacher passivity and the perennial difficulty of mobilizing their colleagues. In this context, the speaker I quote here turned attention to many leaders' mistaken suppositions, which exacerbated the separation between union leaders and teachers, between politics and pedagogy:

We are wrong: all the time worrying about how to get the teachers to participate in union struggles. . . . We shouldn't speak so negatively about teachers. It reveals a lack of respect for others. Nor should we speak of teachers' ignorance and cultural backwardness. This is why there is a separation between unionists who believe they are the only ones who see the light and teachers who are assumed only to care about ascending the social ladder. It is clear that classroom teachers do not appropriate the struggle for democracy as something profoundly theirs; likewise, clearly we want them to join us, and not the other way around. We shouldn't be thinking of ourselves as enlightened activists, but instead as participants of a whole, of a unity; instead of judging, we should learn to share. . . . It is time we reconceived ourselves as subjects. I propose that we talk about all of us as one body of the movement (*todos somos base*). We must not accept divisions and separations.

Leaders' rethinking involves a criticism of the general pattern of democratic organization that CNTE struggles have produced. In this model, CNTE strategies and tactics are directed to pressure the state to fulfill teachers' demands, which are conceived as inseparably economical and political. The organizational formula has been based on incorporating rank and file teachers into decision making about union affairs; movement actions are designed to reveal movement power to the state. Once the union structure is democratized (i.e., decentralized), information concerning proposals for action elaborated and negotiated by political groups represented in leadership flows back and forth from the school-level assemblies, which are supposed to be the major consensus-making bodies, but which oftentimes are bypassed or act as rubber stamps. The limits of this model are seen in the type of rank and file teacher that tends to develop: one that passively responds to leaders' initiatives, lends moral support to leaders, votes in movement actions, and participates in mobilizations around labor and union issues. Even today, many teachers understand "democracy" as the union leaders' use of decision-making and accountability procedures for enhanced transparency in union affairs.

However, now more leaders are quick to reject this version of democratization, in essence because it structurally condemns the rank and file to political underdevelopment by restricting teacher participation to electoral affairs within the union, thereby ignoring pedagogical or teaching issues and relegating teachers' daily work situations to near oblivion. Also, leaders wonder about the efficacy of their efforts to democratize the union, precisely when the union's power to defend labor rights at different levels of the educational system has been undermined and the national union weakened as a political actor in the national ruling bloc (Vega & Ramos, 1998). In addition, and perhaps most importantly, the more critical teachers recognize the State's relative success in implementing new control structures in the schools. Such control structures serve to directly link teachers to government hierarchies, bypassing and subverting the union's historical role as protector of teachers and as mediator in labor relations.

EDUCATIONAL POLICY AS A PRODUCT OF STRUGGLES TO REDEFINE TEACHERS' WORK

The goal of union democracy has thus lost some of its appeal and legitimation among teachers, who view CNTE struggles as having produced "elite democracy." The emerging project, as reformulated by some, rescues radical democracy's emphasis on generating argumentative and deliberative capacities of teachers *regarding their work*, regarding teaching itself. As one leader from Michoacán's Section XVIII wrote, referring to the local movement:

[Before 1994] the profound contradictions that developed within the movement's leadership were not expressed in the rank and file precisely because these teachers delegated all the deliberation and decisionmaking to the leaders in what was really a virtual vote of confidence. Rank and file democracy was never allowed to materialize. The logic that it was enough to have honest leaders and support them for everything to be fine was imposed (this is not a criticism of leaders who are honest). But, without a doubt, representative democracy has been an important factor in the depoliticization of teachers and should be seen as the major obstacle to attaining true democracy. (Sosa, 1998, p. 88)

This point is driven home even more by discussions among activists from Michoacán concerning the issue of how the mass movement sustaining democratic Section XVIII can develop its own educational project. I reproduce part of this discussion in order to show both sides of this ongoing debate that, in essence, is concerned about how to conceive of teachers as policymakers. In SNTE's democratic Section XVIII, people ask whether teachers must control and democratize the regional union locals and state-level sections before transforming teaching practices, or whether there is a different route for teachers to become convinced of the need to transform educational and school practices. The question becomes: Do we change ourselves first or must we take over institutional power to pave the way for new transformative possibilities? On the one hand, taking over union power through democratic struggle has eventually implied losing the democratic organization's original social base, once people become accommodated within the union structures. On the other hand, without the advantage of controlling the union locals, there is no power with which to set up new mechanisms to reach the teachers in their schools and to develop specific programs leading them to interrogate State policy.

What follows is a segment of a discussion between teachers, union delegates, and committee representatives following a public presentation of my research in April 1996:

Regional Union Delegate A: What counts is the democracy we have implemented in small groups of classroom teachers; later one can worry about how to unite the local powers. Of course, the support that our (democratized) executive committee has given us by designing the alternative educational project has motivated us to continue our critique of the government's educational policy from the schools. But, I insist, if we don't start from democracy as it is lived from below, it is not possible to convince people that we need to elaborate a project to transform our teaching practice.

Regional Union Delegate B: Our project here in Michoacán has remained at an explicitly political level; it has not permeated daily work habits and structures. I think that each teacher must adapt our overall political project to the classroom and school, but this depends on how politicized he or she is. It has been difficult to know how to break with the conservativism implicit in our teaching practices. And these practices seem entrenched because teachers do not want to lose their status, their authority over the community. It is this attitude that provokes the confrontation between parents and teachers, instead of both together constructing a unity based upon new principles, such as those being discussed currently in our union section. To continue to assume that teachers are *the only* educational authority makes the teacher–community relationship much too hierarchical.

Regional Union Delegate C: In my region, in 1989 we started out with five people and soon mobilized the entire region in order to destroy *charrismo* and take power away from the corrupt zone inspectors. Back then we didn't worry about handling teacher benefits (*gestoría*) as the union section does now. But since we won the union section's elections, teacher activism has dwindled: teachers are passive. They stopped criticizing; they delegate everything at the cost of losing their activism. So, we can't talk about democracy in this context.

XVIII Sectional Executive Committee Member: But we should not give up the struggle to control the union. It is only since we obtained SNTE-recognized union section legality in 1994 that we have been able to set up special structures close to the schools to implement our alternative educational project. This is because we have constructed a power base within the union. Before, we held hundreds of talks about educational problems, but lacked any structures to deal with these problems and to generate solutions. Now our union structures in the regions and in the schools go way beyond little groups imagining how to design "alternative education"; now we are discussing how to reeducate ourselves.

Regional Union Delegate D: One of the first rural schools in Michoacán was created in my region, which is why there teachers share a tradition of active participation sustained over time within the movement. In my school zone now we are currently trying to diagnose the situation of the schools in the communities. For quite a while now we have worked with parents, so we know how they think. We are familiar with their cultural and educational level, which is quite low. Even still, we have established a dialogue with them. And we see a need to question how we, as teachers, are doing things. We are involved in constructing new relationships through which, together with parents, we decide the paths to follow. This is reality, not utopia; this is real democracy.

I wish to underline several novelties in this exchange that attest to the emerging discourse and to the rethinking about teachers' work underway within the democratic movement. The critical tone of these interventions should be appreciated: activists seem fully aware of the difficulties teachers experience with stressful daily educational practices. Here, it is interesting to contrast the divergent opinions—perhaps due to regional disparities and differences—about the state of the movement and teacher subjectivities. Some see democracy as a reality at the ground level, in the communities, while others presume that democracy is a lost cause, based on the observation that teachers are not motivated to participate in union affairs.

I note another contrast in conceptions of democracy: one teacher expresses a position implying democracy as a fundamental recognition of others, as a feature of equality in direct relationships among teachers and between teachers and parents, as they discuss community educational needs. A different notion of democracy is involved in the suggestion that teachers need to be politicized (by leaders) in order to perceive the importance of transforming their own practice as well as the social relations structuring the schools. My interpretation of these ideas is that democracy must be fought for at both individual and collective levels and spaces; it requires individual transformations as well as collective processes initiated from positions of power. During this particular session, a common understanding, or consensus, seemed to revolve around the idea that democracy demands that all participants hold a critical attitude toward reality. Democracy was also seen as involving a dialogical process necessarily based on mutual recognition as subjects, notwithstanding differences.

Likewise, it is important to not forget that this process of intersubjective deliberation does not occur within a social vacuum, but is part of an overall confrontation with a government that refuses to recognize teachers' collective affirmation as policymakers, as creators of new social powers. SNTE Section XVIII is the only democratic union to have proposed a state-level educational law and to have mobilized to open up negotiations between the government and the union over state-level educational policy. But it must be said that this (temporary) "success" was imposed on the government by means of a complex and lengthy democratization process that has required committed teachers to periodically mobilize as they balance classroom duties with political action.[17]

TEACHER SUBJECTIVITIES TAKE CENTRAL STAGE IN ACTIVISTS' POLITICAL THEORIZING

The recent concern by activists for understanding teacher subjectivities is of upmost importance. The new theorizing around a different project, which tries to construct autonomous actors as a democratic popular subject, reveals a basic questioning of teachers' practical ideologies and entails reformulating the union's role as pertaining to teaching itself. Indeed, there seems to be increasing awareness to create an entirely new discourse that critically situates teachers in their schools at the center of proposals to "create democracy." Witness this intervention made by a CNTE-controlled Section IX leader during a collective discussion:[18]

Because we were so intent upon conquering the union, we forgot a terrain that we must now, with urgency, recuperate in order to reconceive the struggle. By abandoning this terrain, we lost sight of how the government started to restructure the school as a space of state power. It is precisely here where we are not fighting; yet it is this school microspace where we must generate a new discourse of struggle.

If activists related previously to rank and file teachers through the question of whether or not they would participate in the movement's political actions, now activists adopt a much more careful attitude toward registering teachers' feelings and opinions about school-based activities, particularly those affected by state policy dictates. In Michoacán, periodically throughout the school year, the union organizes training and "sensibility" seminars with teachers to discuss union *and* educational issues. Lately, the exchanges between teachers and union representatives have focused on the effects of the government-SNTE co-coordinated *Carrera Magisterial* (merit pay system), " . . . because this is what teachers are talking about." In several interviews I conducted with Section XVIII activists at the beginning of the 1997–1998 school year, leaders' comments turned to the surprisingly critical nature of teachers' remarks about the program. A Section XVIII Sectional Executive Committee member explained that teachers had apparently radicalized their perspectives: from a prevailing uncertainty about the program's effects while wanting to believe that the program would contribute to their professional development, they shifted to a feeling of disillusionment (*se sienten engañados*) and to opinions that discredited program objectives. Teachers even expressed a preoccupation with learning how to counteract the program's inductive process, which was pushing teachers to adopt more individual stances in school affairs. A member of Section XVIII's Sectional Executive Committee said:

Now there seems to be a consensus that *Carrera Magisterial* is not fulfilling its objectives. People are finding out that to be in the program implies not having the time to prepare classes, or to be with the students, and that what it pushes them to do is to be prepared for the program's examination. This leaves them with little time for their classes. They ask how it can benefit their practices in the school if they have to be studying for the exams. . . . This is where, they say, education gets put in second place; they believe that preparing students to pass exams is not real education.

REEXAMINING THE TEACHING ROLE AS KEY TO POLICY "FROM BELOW"

The emerging discourse raises fundamental questions about teachers and schools as state-dominated agents and sites. At issue is the very essence of "public space" and how teaching and schooling may be reconceptualized and reconstructed to attend to the popular democratic subject's requirement of political autonomy. Activists are seeking to problematize the teacher as a transmitter of the official state curricula and instead to transform that role into one of educator of the community at the service of the people. A document circulating among teachers in the democratized union locals contains the emerging conception:

The teacher must abandon his or her role as the depository of knowledge legitimated by the state and accept a role of stimulating and participating in the actual processes of knowledge construction alongside students and other community members.[19]

If union activity is reconceived as a series of mutual support networks to activate class solidarity in the struggle to satisfy popular necessities, then

. . . transforming the school implies mostly changing the relationship that the school has with its social context. Efforts by those participating in the educational act should be involved in constructing numerous relationships deriving from the task of linking education with the needs of that social context. Schools shouldn't appear as foreign institutions within the social textures molding them, but instead can be vital community centers for carrying out activities that directly relate to popular needs . . . [and they quote Henry Giroux when he says] "There exists an urgent necessity for developing pedagogical practices that unite teachers, parents, and students around more emancipatory visions of the community."[20]

Democratic activists are modifying the very notion of a teachers' union away from historically rooted state corporatism and toward a social solidarity function fulfilled by autonomous social subjects. They are trying to counteract the limitations of union democratization as they rethink the struggle in terms of transforming the organization of work such that it responds to political objectives democratically worked out by community members. Activists see their role now in terms of the critical support they give teachers as the latter struggle to educate their students and themselves.

In Michoacán, Section XVIII activists are discussing how to get teachers to question many of the premises of their professional training and how to make union practices responsive to teachers' everyday quests for answers to teaching and learning problems, while at the same time leading them to extend complaints beyond the schools toward the state's organization of the educational system. This is one activist's version of her strategy, as a member of Section XVIII's educational commission, to stretch "teacher reflexivity" beyond a functionalist perspective. Even though she does not make explicit her agreement with Section XVIII's political project, her thinking clearly stems from the commitment to build a popular democratic subject, as it has been endorsed by Section XVIII. She begins with teachers' criticisms of *Carrera Magisterial* and ends with a different idea of the teaching role. It would be hard to find a more fitting representation of the "teachers as policymakers" perspective developed in this chapter:

The first step is to help teachers see the program for what it is: a government imposition, as yet another control strategy. This is the easiest part of the process. The real problem is to motivate them to see education in a different way, to envision it as a real service for the people of the community. Teachers know they must carry out a critical process of reflexion about their work, their teaching, their role as teachers, because teachers are, in actual fact, asking these questions. They ask themselves, "What am I giving to the students? How am I teaching?" These questions are everyday pursuits. The problem is to help them to think about education from a perspective that is not based on the adaptation of curricular programs and study plans. . . . The moment teachers realize that they are "technicians" of education (an instrument in the hands of the government), it becomes easier to talk about education reorganized as a social benefit and about their role as a guide to knowledge creation and appropriation rather than as a transmitter of knowledge.

CONCLUSION

I have approached some of the ways democratic teachers are addressing anew the struggles that bring them together. Their emerging perspectives suggest that a whole new social field of "teachers' work" is becoming politically relevant for activists' organization of teachers. Some leaders have taken the theoretical leap to conceiving teachers as pedagogical subjects, capable of redesigning teacher training and of rethinking the teaching role. Thus, the title of this chapter refers to the democratic teachers' move from union politics to pedagogy. Their theorizing has abandoned simplistic political propositions for empowering teachers (by taking control of existing structures) and has problematized the issue of how to construct power by analyzing schooling's pedagogical function, a function whose realization depends on converting rank and file teachers into informed policymakers. They insist that real democracy may only happen if rank and file teachers actively assume control over their work lives, and if unions transform their (now predominantly defensive) focus on purely "labor demands" into support structures for community-based, bottom-up problem solving that reorganizes the work processes themselves.

The struggle to build an autonomous popular subject, paradoxically, seems to imply for teachers a conscious decision to relinquish their aspirations for an autonomous classroom practice where their individual exercise of power over students is imagined to be accomplished. Indeed, the Michoacán formulation of the project depends upon a teacher-elaborated critique of the dominant social relations in the schools as these are manifested and constructed between teachers and students, teachers and parents, and teachers and administrative authorities. Some teachers are indulging in self-criticism in order to rethink the hierarchical nature of their relationships with parents and community groups. Activists acknowledge that this is an extremely difficult step to take for most teachers.

In my discussions and interactions with teachers and activists committed to the notion of popular sovereignty as the core concept of real democracy, and as I observe teachers learning to dialogue with each other about how they would like schools and teaching to be, I notice that they are actively trying to modify both their educational categories and their political discourse. In effect, they are making a self-conscious effort to construct their own agency as producers of the social world. They resist the way state policy defines their agency as part of a preconceived, top-down process. This resistance is strengthened because they already imagine themselves as social producers of a project, with historical roots and utopian aspirations, that could possibly give hope for the present and future realization of human dignity and a better life for those who today survive with little hope.

It is from within this paradigm of radical democracy as an everyday struggle for a different way of life that teachers are able to distinguish between "regulated autonomy" used by the state to control the development of educational institutions ("steering from a distance"), and the political autonomy of subjects whose discussions focusing on democratic *ends* guide their appropriation of means. Autonomy for democratic teachers is not, and must not, be a purely rhetorical issue.

NOTES

1. This chapter was expressly written for this volume, though a first draft, titled "Teachers' Work and Democratic Struggle in Mexico: A Challenge to Neoliberal Policy," was presented at the Comparative and International Education Society Conference (CIES99) in April 1999 at the Ontario Institute for Studies in Education, Toronto, Canada.

2. Interview with a member of Michoacán's Section XVIII Executive Committee of the SNTE, Morelia, Michoacán, August 27, 1997.

3. I distinguish between "social actor," "social subject," and a "popular democratic subject." The first term refers to those groups, sectors, classes, organizations, or movements that intervene in social life to obtain certain objectives. An actor may become a social subject when it begins—usually in concert with other groups—a process of continual interventions in social life that imply a progressive development of its struggles, in particular, of its consciousness. By "popular democratic subject," I mean those actors joining together and articulating a plurality of structural and cultural interests in an effort to destroy authoritarian practices as a way of life. This new subject constructs democracy from within and for itself. A theoretical discussion of these terms may be found in both Rauber's (1995) and Zemelman's (1995) work. In recent publications, I analyze the way that the teachers' movement became a democratic subject, in particular, how teachers carried out "democratization from below" in order to subvert oppressive work situations and to involve the rank and file in union and schooling decisions (Street, 1996b; 1998b).

4. Rockwell (1998a) does a historical analysis comparing school zones in the state of Tlaxcala with those of the state of Chiapas, contrasting how years ago the local control of schools was characterized by autonomy understood as self-determination, a meaning that the nation-state destroyed as it used the educational system to build a homogeneous national identity. See also Rockwell (1994).

5. My earlier research into Mexico's decentralization policy (McGinn & Street, 1999; Street, 1989) and more recent studies (Miranda, 1992; Resendiz, 1992) point in this direction, by virtue of the central or federal control of the vertical line of authority linking different governmental levels. See Ibarra (1999) for a theoretical discussion of "regulated autonomy" as it applies to higher educational systems.

6. In my research, I find it useful to speak of three basic ideological orientations (patrimonialism, technocracy, and democracy), each providing a rationale for a particular political project organized to determine the educational system's role in Mexican development (see Street, 1988).

7. For middle and higher education, government policy has implemented a private association's (*Centro Nacional de Evaluación de Educación Superior*, CENEVAL) designs as obligatory tests for selection and distribution of students in schools (see Aboites, 1999). For basic education, a merit pay system called *Carrera Magisterial* has introduced primary and secondary teachers to new criteria that "measures" their teaching abilities. The year 1993 witnessed legislative changes that created the Social Participation Councils *(Consejos de Participación Social)* and that gave way to specific policies (such as *Proyecto Escolar*) designed to promote schools' adoption of new comanagement programs. It is general knowledge that the organization of the councils has been extremely slow and very uneven across the country (Guerrero, 1998). However, after much initial resistance by teachers, the *Carrera Magisterial* program appears consolidated, caught up in a dynamic of progressive expansion characteristic of incentive programs begun in higher education during the 1980s.

8. Grassi, Hintze, and Neufeld (1994, p. 65) use the term "conceptual destructuring" to characterize the impact of "global productive restructuring" and structural adjustment programs on Argentinian public school teachers. These authors are among the few who have examined the effects of multiple and juxtaposed crises

(from the state's "fiscal crisis," from its application of IMF adjustment programs, and from privatization policies) on Latin American educational systems.

9. Mexico is very definitively being submitted to privatization programs in practically all areas historically understood as national patrimony (electricity, petroleum, health care, state-controlled industries, monuments, pre-Columbian ruins, etc.), though obviously with varied implementation processes and different degrees of success. Public debate on these issues has intensified and spilt over into the educational field since the student-led strike at the National University (*Universidad Nacional Autónoma de México, UNAM)*, in its seventh month at the time of this writing.

10. Some research has been reported twice a month in the national newspaper, *LA JORNADA*, by the newly-formed *Observatorio Ciudadano de la Educación* (Citizen Observatory of Education), a group of researchers trying to establish a civil society-oriented ombudsman for education. Pablo Latapí's column in the weekly journal *PROCESO* is one of the few nonacademic sources for a critical, non-Left evaluation of educational policy. Researchers are just beginning to study, from an ethnographic perspective, the local processes of school reform as proposed by the 1992 National Accord on the Modernization of Basic Education (*Acuerdo Nacional para la Modernización de la Educación Básica*). For a review of Mexican school ethnographies, see Rockwell (1998b). Of special interest is Bradley Levinson's (in press) ethnography of a secondary school in central Mexico.

11. I have come to this appreciation after coordinating two long-term seminars begun in 1994 with researchers, activists, and teachers on issues relating teachers' working conditions with the national teachers' movement. The diversity of institutional affiliations and geographic locations of seminar participants gives me some access to sensitive issues. Likewise, my public speaking agenda helps me to maintain contact with many groups of teachers in different parts of the country. For more information on *normalismo* and the *magisterio*, see De Ibarrola, Ruiz, & Cedillo (1997), Salgado (1996), and Pontón, Rangel, & Cedillo (1996). The Fundación SNTE's monthly journal *BASICA* carries pertinent analyses.

12. For a reflective summary of my ethnographic research over time, see Street (1998a). The analysis I report here mostly stems from an emerging "dialogical" perspective (Rosaldo, 1991; Tedlock & Mannheim, 1995), enabled by more than a decade of connecting my investigations to the teachers' democratic movement, in pursuit of understanding democratic subject formation. This approach allows me to register dialogues between teachers in seminars, during movement actions and meetings, and in collective discussions on themes of interest to teachers. I combine contextually relevant discourse analysis with document analysis and participant observation techniques. In essence, then, my ethnography is subject-oriented more than institution-oriented. For a selection of relevant discussions in English, see Gitlin (1994).

13. I confirmed this "perspective" in a recent interview with one of Michoacán's long-time "historical leaders," Morelia, Michoacán, October 22, 1999.

14. An English-language summary of my research with Chiapas democratic teachers can be found in Street (1996). For an excellent English-language study on the teachers' movement, see Cook (1996). Foweraker (1993) reviews part of the Chiapas movement. See Monroy's (1997) brief description of CNTE-coordinated struggles in Mexico.

15. Stepan (1993) is among the few academicians who stress the specific situations of opposition groups within authoritarian systems. My general approach agrees

with Stepan when he states that "a richer understanding of how authoritarian regimes become democratized can be achieved if less attention is paid to the structures forged by the coercive elite, while more is accorded to the relationships of domination that pervade such regimes. In particular, it is important that scholars learn to identify the major parties to these relationships, and to analyze those processes that might serve not only to cut the ground out from under authoritarian modes and orders, but to lay the basis for a securely democratic future" (p. 69).

16. Many documents elaborating the new project have been discussed by the rank and file teachers in Michoacán, by Section XVIII's activists in educational seminars, and by activists from other regions meeting to discuss "educational modernization" in different types of forums. For one such document, see "Hacia una nueva economía," Pleno Estatal de Representantes, Sección XVIII, Michoacán, September 1996.

17. Just recently, the Michoacán teachers "occupied" the state-level education ministry in protest of the policymakers' strategy of nonrecognition of certain previously negotiated agreements. A few months ago, the Michoacán legislature unilaterally approved the government's Law of Education ("Las causas de la tensión entre la SEE en el Estado de Michoacán y la Sección XVIII del SNTE," SEC, XVIII, March 1999.)

18. Field notes from a debate following a talk given by the author to members of CNTE-SNTE Mexico City locals, September 5, 1998.

19. Study group from Iztapalapa, Mexico City, "Propuesta de construcción escolar," unpublished paper, March 1997.

20. Study group from Iztapalapa, Mexico City, "Propuesta de construcción escolar," unpublished paper, March 1997.

REFERENCES

Aboites, H. (1997). *Viento del Norte: TLC y privatización de la educación superior en México*. Mexico City: Universidad Autónoma Metropolitana-Xochimilco and Plaza y Valdes.

Aboites, H. (1999). La batalla por el financiamiento de la educación superior en los años noventa. *El Cotidiano* (Universidad Autónoma Metropolitana-Atzcapotzalco), 15(95), 35–48.

Alonso, J. (1995). Construir la democracia desde abajo. *Nueva Antropología, XIV*(48), 69–82.

Ball, S. (1993). Culture, cost and control: Self-management and entrepreneurial schooling in England and Wales. In J. Smyth (Ed.), *A socially critical view of the self-managing school* (pp. 63–82). Washington, DC: The Falmer Press.

Casanova, P. G., & Rosenmann, M. R. (Eds.). (1995). *La democracia en América Latina: actualidad y perspectivas*. Mexico City: Centro de Investigaciones Interdisciplinarias en Ciencias y Humanidades, UNAM.

Chomsky, N. (1992). *El miedo a la democracia* [*Deterring Democracy*]. Barcelona, Spain: CRITICA, Grupo Grijalbo-Mondadori.

Contreras, J. (1997). *La autonomía del profesorado*. Madrid, Spain: Ediciones Morata.

Cook, M. L. (1996). *Organizing dissent: The unions, the state and the democratic teachers' movement in Mexico*. University Park, PA: Penn State Press.

De Ibarrola, M., Ruiz, G. S., & Cedillo, A. C. (1997). *¿Quiénes son nuestros profesores?* Mexico City: Fundación SNTE para la Cultura del Maestro Mexicano, A.C.

Foweraker, J. (1993). *Popular mobilization in Mexico: The teachers' movement, 1977–1987.* New York: Cambridge University Press.

Gitlin, A., (Ed.). (1994). *Power and method: Political activism and educational research.* New York: Routledge.

Grassi, E., Hintze, S., & Neufeld, M. R. (1994). *Políticas sociales, crisis y ajuste estructural (Un análisis del sistema educativo, de obras sociales y de las políticas alimentarias).* Buenos Aires, Argentina: Espacio Editorial.

Guerrero, A. (1998). Democratización de la educación: participación social en el contenido de la enseñanza. *El Cotidiano* (Universidad Autónoma Metropolitana-Azcapotzalco), *14*(87), 31–37.

Hartley, D. (1993). The evaluative state and self-management in education: Cause for reflection? In J. Smyth (Ed.), *A socially critical view of the self-managing school* (pp. 99–116). Washington, DC: The Falmer Press.

Ibarra, E. (1999). Evaluación + financiamiento = autonomía regulada, o de cómo la universidad le vendió su alma al diablo. *El Cotidiano* (Universidad Autónoma Metropolitana-Azcapotzalco), *15*(95), 14–24.

Jiménez, M. de la Luz, & Perales, F. de Jesús. (1999). *La profesión docente.* Saltillo, Coahuila: Secretaría de Educación Pública de Coahuila.

Levinson, B. (in press). *We are all equal: The play of student culture at a Mexican secondary school and beyond.* Durham, NC: Duke University Press.

McGinn, N. & Street, S. (1999). Educational decentralization: Weak state or strong state? In N. F. McGinn & E. H. Epstein (Eds.), *Comparative perspectives on the role of education in democratization. Part I: Transitional states and states of transition* (pp. 117–142). New York: Peter Lang.

McGinn, N., Street, S. and Orozco, G. (1983). *La asignación de recursos económicos en la educación pública en México: un proceso técnico en un contexto político.* Mexico City: Fundación J. Barros Sierra, Secretaría de Educación Pública.

Miranda, F. (1992). Descentralización educativa y modernización del Estado. *Revista mexicana de sociología* (Instituto de Investigaciones Sociales, UNAM), (2), 19–44.

Monroy, D. (1997). *Mexican teachers and the struggle for democracy.* San Francisco, CA: Global Exchange.

Noriega, M. (1999). Financiamiento de la educación superior y proyecto de país. *El Cotidiano* (Universidad Autónoma Metropolitana-Azcapotzalco), *15*(95), 5–13.

Pontón, B. C. (1997). *La modernización educativa: una perspectiva regional desde la frontera norte de México.* Doctoral thesis, Universidad Iberoamericana, Mexico City.

Pontón, B. C., Rangel, J.A.R., & Cedillo, D. S. (1996). Docentes de los niveles básico y normal. In P. Ducoing & M. Landesmann (Eds.), *Sujetos de la educación y formación docente* (pp. 85–156). Mexico City: Consejo Mexicano de Investigación Educativa.

Pleno Estatal de Representantes, SNTE Union Section 18. (1996). Hacia una nueva economia. Michoacán, Mexico. (unpublished report).

Rauber, I. (1995). *Actores sociales, luchas reivindicativas y políticas populares.* La Habana, Cuba: Ciudad Alternativa.

Resendiz, R. (1992). Reforma educativa y conflicto interburocrático en México, 1978–1988. *Revista mexicana de sociología* (Instituto de Investigaciones Sociales, UNAM), (2), 3–18.

Rockwell, E. (1994). Schools of the revolution: Enacting and contesting state forms in Tlaxcala, 1910–1930. In G. M. Joseph & D. Nugent (Eds.), *Everyday forms of state formation: Revolution and the negotiation of rule in modern Mexico* (pp. 170–208). Durham, NC: Duke University Press.

Rockwell, E. (1998a). Democratización de la educación y autonomía: Dimensiones históricas y debates actuales. *El Cotidiano, 14*(87), 38–47.

Rockwell, E. (1998b). Ethnography and the commitment to public schooling: A review of research at the DIE. In G. L. Anderson & M. Montero-Sieburth (Eds.), *Educational qualitative research in Latin America: The struggle for a new paradigm* (pp. 3–34). New York: Garland.

Rosaldo, R. (1991). *Cultura y verdad: nueva propuesta de análisis social.* Mexico City: Grijalbo and Consejo Nacional para la Cultura y las Artes.

Salgado, A. A. (1996). *Historia de una profesión: Los maestros de educación primaria en México, 1887–1994.* Mexico City: Centro de Investigación y Docencia Económicas.

Salgado, A. A. (1998). *La federalización educativa en México: Historia del debate sobre la centralización y la descentralización educativa (1889–1994).* Mexico City: El Colegio de México y el Centro de Investigación y Docencia Económica.

Smyth, J., (Ed.). (1993). *A socially critical view of the self-managing school.* Washington, DC: The Falmer Press.

Sosa, R., (1998). Maestros, el conflicto por la democracia sindical: testimonio de tres experiencias. *El Cotidiano* (Universidad Autónoma Metropolitana-Azcapotzalco), *14*(87), 82–93.

State Executive Committee of SNTE Union Section 18. (1999). Las causas de la ténsion entre la SEE en el Estado de Michoacán y la sección XVIII del SNTE. (unpublished report).

Steffan, H. D. (1995). Globalización, educación y democracia en América Latina. In N. Chomsky & H. D. Steffan (Eds.), *La sociedad global: educación, mercado y democracia* (pp. 49–182). Mexico City: Joaquín Mortíz.

Stepan, A. (1993). On the tasks of a democratic opposition. In L. Diamond & M. F. Plattner (Eds.). *The global resurgence of democracy* (pp. 61–69). Baltimore, MD: John Hopkins University Press.

Street, S. (1998b). *Magisterio y democracia: investigaciones desde el sujeto.* Unpublished manuscript.

Street, S. (1998a). *Researching teacher activism in Mexico: Democratizing culture and culturizing democracy (from representational to dialogical ethnography).* Paper presented at the Comparative and International Education Society Annual Meeting, Buffalo, NY.

Street, S. (1997). Los maestros y la democracia de los de abajo. In J. Alonso & J. M. R. Saíz (Eds.), *Democracia de los de abajo* (pp. 115–145). Mexico City: La Jornada, Consejo Electoral del Estado de Jalisco, Centro de Investigaciones Interdisciplinarias en Humanidades, UNAM.

Street, S. (1996b, March). Democratization "from below" and popular culture: Teachers from Chiapas, Mexico. *Studies in Latin American Popular Culture, 15,* 261–278.

Street, S. (1996a). Democracia como RECIPROCIDAD: modalidades participativas de 'las bases' del movimiento magisterial chiapaneco. In H. Tejera (Ed.), *Procesos políticos en el México contemporáneo: una visión antropológica* (pp. 351–376). Mexico City: Instituto Nacional de Antropología e Historia y Plaza y Valdés.

Street, S. (1994). La cultura política del movimiento magisterial chiapaneco. In J. Alonso (Ed.), *Cultura política y educación cívica* (pp. 427–466) Mexico City: Porrua.

Street, S. (1989). Descentralización educativa en el Tercer Mundo: una revisión de la literatura. *Revista latinoamericana de estudios educativos, XIX*(4), 13–51.

Street, S. (1988). *Organized teachers as policymakers: Domination and opposition in Mexican public education.* Doctoral thesis, Harvard Graduate School of Education.

Tedlock, D. & Mannheim, B. (1995). *The dialogic emergence of culture.* Chicago: University of Illinois Press.

Vega, M. E. V., & Ramos, G. P. (1999, June–July). El XVI Congreso del SNTE y el aumento de mayo. *Trabajadores* (Universidad Obrera de México), *2,* 28–30.

Zemelman, H., (Ed.). (1995). *Determinismos y alternativas en las ciencias sociales de América Latina.* Mexico City: Centro Regional de Investigaciones Multidisciplinarias, UNAM and Editorial Nueva Sociedad.

7

Beyond Educational Policy: Bilingual Teachers and the Social Construction of Teaching "Science" for Understanding[1]

Pamela Anne Quiroz

INTRODUCTION

Current educational reforms have merged into systemic change processes whose focus is to transform U.S. public schools into places where all children can learn. Two areas that have received widespread attention in these efforts are science and math education. Systemic reform in math and science education has been funded by the federal government and widely adopted by state and local school districts. The assumptions underlying this complex approach to educational reform are being manifested in such things as the creation of national standards, evaluations of math and science education, along with new curricular materials and instructional strategies for achieving these goals. One component emphasized in this transformation process is the notion that teachers are a powerful source of school reform, that is, within the school context nothing has more impact on student academic and social development than the personal and professional development of teachers (Barth, 1990).

However, increasingly researchers argue that such reform efforts fail to assist minority students in their academic achievement and may in fact exacerbate existing inequalities. Such policies are typically developed at one institutional level (i.e., the federal government) and operationalized in ways that are often disconnected to the constituents whose educational opportunities they are designed to enhance. For example, not only researchers but also teachers and parents argue that the proliferation of statewide assessments results in being used as the "stick" rather than the "carrot" that is supposed to generate learning. Ostensibly these assessments are used to measure student performance or "learning." However, in reality they are also used as aversive techniques such as failure to promote or grant a diploma or as accountability systems for teachers and schools. A few researchers even go so far as to suggest that such reform practices are intentionally designed to exclude culturally diverse and disadvantaged groups in order to maintain the existing inequities to access and opportunity between groups (Apple, 1993; Giroux, 1992; McLaren, 1994; Walsh, 1993). Regardless of the intent of policymakers, the reality is that the lack of articulation between policymakers and policy practitioners results in activities that often look different to each set of actors at each level of implementation.

Although teachers are now included as important agents of change, they are still largely defined as recipients of professional development rather than as partners who bring knowledge, skills, and experience to the process of professional development. With teachers as a group treated in this fashion it is no surprise to find that bilingual teachers have been entirely omitted from discussions of systemic reform. Indeed, research on effective teaching in math and science has traditionally ignored the instructional strategies of language minority teachers, with the focus for bilingual education on students' development and proficiency in the English language rather than the mastery of subject matter (Garcia, 1997). Language minority teachers as a source of educational change have been neglected, and their professional development in academic subjects has been left largely unattended. Thus, we are left either to assume that language minority teachers are subsumed into the current systemic change initiatives without attention to their unique circumstances or that, once again, they have been overlooked.

This is a case study of eight bilingual elementary and middle school teachers from a northeastern urban school district who are engaged in science teaching reform. I describe how the policy of teaching science for understanding is initiated, interpreted, and ultimately practiced by bilingual teachers participating in a professional development science program called Quest for Knowledge. A unique program, Quest for Knowledge (QK) is dominated by a linguistic orientation to science teaching and learning, and half of its participants are language minority teachers. The participants' phenomenology of science teaching is situated within the intersecting contexts of the school, the cultural frameworks of their students, and the Quest for Knowledge program. It is in these contexts where language minority teachers integrate identities, expand their affiliations with bilingual colleagues while establishing new associations with monolingual colleagues, and focus intensively on science teaching and learning through the lens of language. Together, teachers negotiate policies, resources, and each other in a concerted effort to assist students to develop and sustain identities as ethnic group members as well as science learners and problem solvers.

Given the pseudonym *Camelot,* the school district in which these teachers are located is reputed to use progressive approaches to education, giving serious attention to issues of diversity and equity, with school policies such as bilingual education designed to address these issues. Nevertheless, like most school districts, Camelot juggles a multitude of educational policies, including those made at other institutional levels. These policies often generate competing goals and the tensions associated with those goals (e.g., juggling support for science teaching with professional development needed in other areas such as literacy). This story focuses on two intersecting policies: science teaching and bilingual education. Specifically, I look at the intersection of science teaching, the issues surrounding bilingual education along with how the state's new assessment of learning affects both policy practices. I describe how language minority teachers face challenges for science teaching that are distinctive from monolingual teachers. The challenges and how they are met are given special attention in this chapter. These language minority teachers tell us how the school context and the conflicting demands of school policy and student needs influence their science teaching practices. They also describe how Quest for Knowledge provides a niche within which they are able to access additional resources to augment their teaching practices and philosophies. Indeed, it is through participation in Quest for Knowledge and the emergence of a culture of science that teachers not only interpret science policies but initiate new practices as well.

A story emerges of eight language minority teachers struggling to interpret and translate school policies within different school contexts while negotiating the demands made by their variegated student populations. Just as students are not *tabula rasa,* teachers (and schools) are not passive receptors of educational policies. To the contrary, teachers interact with policies, with other teachers, and with their students to transform these policies into practices that are meaningful and useful to their efforts. The "efforts" themselves may be in tension or defined in different ways. One goal may be to promote a "learn-by-doing-and-sharing" approach to science or math (i.e., "teaching for understanding"), while another effort may involve developing the kind of skills that will enable students to excel on the state assessment. Oftentimes these two situations are not congruent. These bilingual teachers discuss how they engage and filter policies developed at the national, state, and local levels to enable them to work with the policies in appropriate and effective ways for their students. Thus, this case study offers a description of language minority teachers as agents of change, presenting their voices and the active role they take in shaping and generating a different vision of science and of schooling, with students at the center of this vision.

DILEMMAS OF POLICY FORMATION AND IMPLEMENTATION IN THE CAMELOT SCHOOL DISTRICT

As we move into the 21st century, the expectations of schools have clearly shifted. Schools are not only expected to provide a variety of services for students and for the community, but they are now also expected to educate every-one in our society (Natriello, McDill, & Pallas, 1990). Despite the fact that numerous policies have been generated to move schools in these directions, what actually happens in schools or classrooms, how does it happen, and how does what happens compare to what policymakers intend to have happen?

Regardless of where or how policies originate, their practice often looks quite different from the original intent. Despite California's recent adoption of Proposition 227, we're already aware of ways in which this policy is being implemented and through its implementation, subverted, with parents, teachers, schools, and even districts (e.g., the Berkeley school district) requesting and using waivers to maintain bilingual learning experiences. Thus, the process of making educational policies come to life involves *policy-to-practice* connections that often look very different at the school and classroom level.

And while certain educational policies tend to find some support at all institutional levels (i.e., learning of basic skills) others are often embroiled in controversy. Despite celebrating the 30th anniversary of the federal Bilingual Educational Act in 1998, we are witnessing attempts to dissolve bilingual education in our public school systems, with California's Proposition 227 the exemplar of these attempts. Regardless of their distance from the Camelot school district, the events in California are followed closely by Camelot teachers as possible indicators of what's to come. As controversial as California's antibilingual education law is to communities in California, Camelot's newly adopted state assessment has generated its own concern for teaching in general and for bilingual education specifically. Reviews of the state assessment this past year found that most school districts performed poorly on the test, with Camelot's schools also having performed unevenly. Since the test is projected to determine student promotions and diplomas along with teacher and principal accountability, more than a few teachers express concerns about the impact of the assessment on classroom practice. Language minority teachers add their concerns for bilingual classrooms and programs.

In addition to education policy is the recent change in the state's rent control law and Camelot's changing demography. According to some teachers and principals, socioeconomic diversity is the most difficult challenge with respect to diversity. The district's changing demography exacerbates the challenges for schools to meet these agendas. The state's decision to eliminate rent control has had tremendous impact on lower- and working-class families, particularly minority and immigrant families who have had to leave the district. Having experienced a large out-migration of such students, schools are facing the challenge of maintaining diversity. In addition, the local newspaper published the new superintendent's declaration of a projected reduction in teaching staff due to the already low teacher–student ratio. These political, educational, and demographic changes only add to teachers' concerns about the future of bilingual education in their schools, with some of these language teachers more concerned than others. Thus, various school, district, state, and national level factors coalesce to create a context within which bilingual teachers must negotiate a multitude of expectations, goals, and concerns.

THE POLICYMAKERS: THE DISTRICT, THE TEACHERS, THEIR SCHOOLS, AND THE QK PROGRAM

The District

Camelot is a northeastern urban school system that combines district management with school choice in 15 elementary schools, enrolling approximately 6,200 elementary students and employing approximately 300 teachers. Six of the elementary schools contain a bilingual program with bilingual education in the district existing in several forms (i.e., English as a Second Language, early-exit transitional, modified-transitional, and two-way) and representing no less than five different language groups, including Spanish, Chinese Mandarin, Korean, Cape Verdean, and Portuguese. Several schools have a variety of educational programs, ranging from gifted to multicultural programs, totaling 23 programs in all.

Teaching science for understanding is endorsed by the school district and manifested in its science curricula and materials. This pedagogical approach emphasizes the active construction of meaning grounded in student experience in order to gain indepth understanding of an idea or concept (Newmann, Marks, & Gamoran, 1996). Teaching for understanding has been referred to in a variety of ways, including "authentic pedagogy," "inquiry based teaching and learning," and "constructivist teaching," to name a few. This approach to learning involves collaborative learning experiences, the framing of problem-solving contexts that requires analysis and conceptual thinking, and questioning and ongoing discussions involving subject matter (Schifter, 1996).

Like most urban school districts, Camelot is a highly charged and politically complex school system with substantial variation between schools (e.g., curricular programs, instructional styles). It is also an unusual school district in several respects. Although most of the elementary schools do not share physical buildings, a few do. Middle schools are housed within most of the elementary schools and classrooms are multigraded, with middle school defined as Grades 6–8 in some schools and Grades 7–8 in others. Schedules (i.e., school hours) also vary by school, as do the types of academic programs offered by schools, with some labeled alternative, traditional, or gifted programs. Camelot is also a system that engages issues of equity. Indeed, part of the district's complexity is its attempt to satisfy school choice while keeping schools racially/ethnically, sociolinguistically, and socioeconomically, diverse.

Nevertheless, five elementary schools are designated as "target schools," meaning that they have disproportionately large enrollments of disadvantaged students, racial/ethnic minority students, and LEP students, and relatively lower scores on standardized tests. And despite the existence of school choice, these schools have the appearance of "neighborhood" schools.[2] The five target schools reportedly receive additional funds and assistance with the hope of raising the achievement levels of students in the schools.[3]

Alternative schools are at the other end of the spectrum. These schools tend to be clustered in a different part of the school district and have abundant resources. Racial/ethnic and socioeconomic diversity vary in these schools and a few of the schools have students from families with disproportionately higher incomes. With the exception of one school's bilingual students, students at these schools typically perform well on standardized tests and other achievement measures.

The Language Minority Teachers

The language minority teachers who are the focus of this chapter comprise half of the Quest for Knowledge program's 16 participants. With the exception of one teacher, these teachers have been teaching in the Camelot school district for more than 5 years. Other than one teacher, who recently moved from a bilingual program to become a middle-school math teacher, all of the teachers are in bilingual programs and two are science specialists.

These language minority teachers (each of whom are given pseudonyms) are located primarily in two schools, with one in a third school: Rosa Parks, Schmidt, and Roberts. Rosa Parks contains a transitional Cape Verdean program (the only alternative school with a bilingual program) and Roberts contains a two-way Spanish bilingual program.

The Schools

Rosa Parks is the oldest of the district's three alternative schools and one of the most popular schools in the district, meaning that families often list it as their first choice in schools. The school serves Grades K–8 and houses the Cape Verdean bilingual program. The Cape Verdean program is a transitional bilingual program serving a largely immigrant population of students. Support for this program has reportedly waxed and waned over the years; however, the school has managed to sustain the program and is currently attempting to increase the integration of monolingual with bilingual students. For example, the school recently adopted French as its chosen foreign language with the idea that both monolingual and Cape Verdean students could not only learn French together but also learn more about each other. Despite its ethnic/racial diversity, Rosa Parks has a lower than average proportion of low-income students, the majority of them in the bilingual program. Although the school has no written curriculum outline, it does have a reputation for innovative teaching and teacher turnover is very low. Parent involvement is extensive, as are after-school homework tutorials.

One of the largest of the elementary schools and also a "target" school, Roberts houses Grades K–8. Roberts also houses two types of educational programs: a standard program and a two-way Spanish bilingual program. Although the traditional program is not one of the more popular programs in the district, Roberts' two-way Spanish bilingual program has been in existence for over 10 years and is one of the most popular programs in the district. This program prescribes enrollment to include 50% native Spanish speakers and 50% non-Spanish speakers (including students from other minority backgrounds such as African American). Essentially, the bilingual program operates as a school-within-a-school. Although somewhat isolated from the rest of the school, this program is the larger of the two programs and reportedly has the younger, more innovative teachers. The school's standard program also exhibits a traditional organization of schooling (i.e., desks in rows, fewer collaborative learning experiences, and veteran teachers).

Schmidt is one of the larger elementary schools in the district and is currently undergoing a number of physical and organizational changes. This school consists of three academic programs; however, each of these programs falls toward the bottom of the district ranking system in terms of parent choice. Similar to Roberts, Schmidt has a slightly higher than average proportion of low-income students. However, Schmidt also serves special needs students and has a below average proportion of students with limited English proficiency. According to the principal of Schmidt, the majority of the teaching staff consists of veteran teachers, however, the school is reportedly moving in the direction of more developmental teaching methods and programs.[4]

The Quest for Knowledge Program

Over the past 5 years, the Camelot school district has formally embraced teaching science for understanding. District endorsement of this approach is manifest in its choice of curricular materials along with professional development sponsored and provided by the district. However, not all professional development programs are provided by the district. Teachers are encouraged to avail themselves of other professional development opportunities operating within and endorsed by the school district. It is one such program in which the language minority teachers, who are the focus of this chapter, participate.

Funded by the federal government, the Quest for Knowledge program (QK) meets for 2-hour sessions every 2 weeks at a central site throughout the school year. It also meets during three school release days (8:30 AM–2:30 PM) and for one full week in the summer. The program's purpose is to increase the effectiveness of science teaching to all students but particularly to linguistically diverse and disadvantaged students. In fact, it was originally created for language minority teachers and targeted for elementary and middle school children whose first language is not English. Only recently has it become heterogeneous. The goals of the seminar are three-fold: (1) to encourage school districts to foster professional development programs patterned after the inquiry-based approach toward science; (2) to generate a "national" con-

versation on issues of equity in science teaching and learning; and (3) to develop a support system (i.e., "an infrastructure of human, material, and
conceptual resources") for science education reform, both locally and nationally. To achieve these goals, the directors of Quest for Knowledge attempt to
integrate science and mathematics, teaching and learning, and culture and language.[5] Because the program's success is dependent upon the development of
trust among teachers, a 5-year commitment from teachers is requested. Participation in the program is voluntary; however, teachers are provided a stipend
and the option of receiving graduate credit for participation.

   One of the most impressive features of the QK program is that teachers are
encouraged to help shape the form and direction of the seminars. According to
the participants, unlike other professional development seminars, the directors
of the QK not only respond to but also encourage teachers to set the direction
of the seminar. Some of the QK teachers have also participated in illustrating
their seminar work at universities, national conferences, and workshops, and a
few have coauthored articles or book chapters. One language minority teacher
has translated a book for use in his bilingual program.

   Quest for Knowledge projects operationalize teaching for understanding
by treating teachers as *learners* and as *researchers*. The seminars combine the-
matic exercises (alternating between the biological sciences and the physical
sciences from year to year) and examination of classroom discourse using reading materials and videotaped segments of science or math classroom lessons.
In the first year, the seminar's focus was on the development of plants while the
second year focus was on gravity. Bimonthly sessions alternate between research exercises and small group discussions of reading materials or observations of teacher videotapes. All activities in QK are videotaped and audiotaped.
Teachers are encouraged to videotape and to transcribe (with the help of QK
staff) a classroom math or science lesson. The videos are then viewed and the
transcripts read in small groups, generating discussions and providing feedback to teachers. Through various iterations of experiments, readings, and discussions of science, bilingual and monolingual teachers engage in crossing
linguistic boundaries to create a common discourse and a common understanding of science.

HOW THE STORY IS DEVELOPED

   The fieldwork involved in telling the story of language minority teachers in
the QK program began in 1996 and ended in the summer of 1999. This process involved participant observation of the QK program, multiple interviews
with teachers, principals, and certain district administrators, reading newspaper articles on school events, and survey data provided by teachers (particularly in schools with QK participants). The indepth interviews with QK
language minority teachers provide one of the most important sources of data
in framing this case study. They also reveal that teachers were solicited for par-

ticipation in the QK seminar either through the district's bilingual coordinator, the QK directors, or the principal of the school. Consequently, it is no accident that the participants in the QK seminar emerge primarily from 4 of the 15 elementary schools. Since these approaches are repeated consecutively for three years, the opportunity for observing an evolution of perspectives, instructional styles, and a community of learners is evident.[6]

TEACHING "SCIENCE" FOR UNDERSTANDING IN THE BILINGUAL CLASSROOM

How do science and language policy become formulated and how do bilingual teachers reconcile the goals for each policy with student needs? Often at the forefront of educational innovations, Camelot has a history of working with researchers, university professors, and a variety of community groups to further its goals of meeting student needs. The district's application of federally generated and state mandated policies have taken creative or preemptive form. For example, this was one of the first school districts in the country to desegregate voluntarily. It has also been experimenting with school choice and with bilingual education for some time, with two-way bilingual programs existing in Camelot for more than a decade and Camelot's state the first in the nation to pass a state bilingual education law. Additionally, science development has been aligned with the inception of the voluntary national standards. Thus, it is fair to describe Camelot as a school district on the "cutting edge" not only of negotiating and implementing policy but also in creating new policy practices.

Nevertheless, there are clearly different policy practices not only within the district, but also within the schools and even within classrooms. Just as the district adapts federal and state policies, so too do the schools and their teachers adapt district policies. Indeed, not all policy is practiced, even at the institutional level within which it is generated. For example, the disproportionate numbers of low-income and racial/ethnic students in certain schools belies district rhetoric of "controlled choice," where an assigning office places students with respect to parent choice and diversity requirements of the district. One principal characterizes the situation:

I think we need to step back and ask, "How are children assigned to the city of Camelot?" There was some discussion a couple of years ago that maybe it should be racially balanced. You can imagine how that was received. People on ——street certainly ran to show their 1040s so that idea went down pretty quickly. If you look closely at some of the schools, there are schools where the composition is extremely aligned in terms of academic and socioeconomic background, in terms of color, in terms of race. There are definitely some schools that are far more likely to have minorities than others. And it has always been interesting to me that no one has ever asked the big question about that. There are also different interpretations of what balance should be. Should we balance within the school or within a program within the school? Should it be a balance within the classroom per se? Because you can have any situation within a particular building where the building is racially balanced but you have one program that is very white and one program that is not very white. But the building on paper is racially balanced. So that is a very technical question.

What sounds very impressive either in conversation or on paper can be at best confusing and at worst misleading. Another interesting explanation for why "controlled choice" operates differently than portrayed involves how information is disseminated. A parent information booklet, created by a district parent, condenses a vast amount of information about each school in the district. This booklet can assist parents in making their school choices. However, the opportunities to take advantage of this information (and hence the Camelot system) is limited by the fact that the booklet is sold for $17 in specific bookstores, is written in a style that targets a more educated audience, and is produced only in English. Perhaps one of the most important explanations as to why the Camelot system works better for some families than for others concerns the political acumen needed by parents in order to optimize their child's opportunities. As a principal describes the situation, "It is a highly politicized situation because at any time that parents want something they need to be political. It is calling the school committee, calling administration, signing petitions, having meetings, inviting folks to come and listen. So that is the rallying point where the politics are involved."

Clearly, a variety of factors shape the ways in which policies are practiced. It is no surprise then to find that although there is a district science policy, bilingual teachers negotiate this policy with respect to their own knowledge of the curriculum and the curriculum's heuristic value to their students. Adopted 5 years ago, Camelot's science curriculum consists of "science kits" that promote a "learn-by-doing" instructional approach. This curriculum largely reflects the efforts of the district's science coordinator, whose success acquiring federal grants has greatly enhanced Camelot's recent focus on science learning. This funding has also supported four staff developers, each assigned to a set of schools. Combined with district-sponsored professional development workshops, these staff developers provide support for classroom teachers to engage in teaching for understanding. In a novel attempt to provide science assistance to language minority teachers, one of the staff development positions was targeted specifically for a bilingual teacher. Like so many school districts, administrator and teacher comments convey that Camelot has tended to focus on students' acquisition of language facility rather than subject matter content:

We had bilingual meetings every other week, the whole team in the school, but we dealt more with the structure of the program, not with the substance. Last year we were trying a transitional bilingual program that was 25/50/75 [i.e., the percentage of time spent on English in order to transition from Spanish to English]. Last year we tried a 50/50 program because we realized that just doesn't work. I mean a lot of the meetings we had were over that. . . . Our bilingual teachers receive the same training that anyone in the district would receive. However, there was a time when they didn't. If it were a release day [for professional development], then the bilingual teachers would all have to get together and we could do whatever.

Still, with just one bilingual staff development person, whose time is divided between bilingual and monolingual teachers, the time available to assist language minority teachers is limited. Two teachers complained that although a staff development person was assigned to their school, there was never sufficient time devoted to learn how to use the science kits nor were the kits always suited to their classroom needs. One teacher even suggested that no assistance had been forthcoming at her school:

I can clearly say that we haven't had any extra help or assistance. No aids, no one. It is hard to teach these kids because they are all at different levels. There is no one in the school that I can go to. Well, there are the head of the district math and science personnel I could contact, but they are never there. And the science staff development person has never come to our school for the last 5 years. So we only see her at a workshop where she is preoccupied with all of these other things.

Teachers have also witnessed recent attempts by the district to coordinate science and math curricula. In its goal to standardize the science curriculum, the district has adopted different sets of curricula specific to particular grades. However, the science kits chosen differ by school as well as by teachers within each school. For example, one school may elect a biology science kit while another may choose a physics science kit. Dislike of the particular kits offered to a given grade level, or a perceived disjuncture between the kits and the class focus, often result in the kits not being used at all.[7] Nevertheless, bilingual teachers urge, "We cannot afford to wait, which is the district's traditional stance on this issue, until students have 'mastered' English until we teach them science. Nor can we afford to think that just because they don't know English that they don't know science or anything else. They do."

One last point must be made regarding science policy formation in the Camelot school district: Despite the genuine efforts of the district to support teaching science for understanding, district goals, while inclusive and responsive to educational researchers and university professors, were produced without teacher input then presented to teachers in the form of professional development. Interestingly, a science teaching policy based upon collaboration and learning-by-doing was formulated without the collaboration and participation of those who were expected to practice it. Neither bilingual nor monolingual teachers were regarded as an integral piece of policy creation.

Lack of familiarity, dislike of "kit" contents, or even lack of participation in the policy process are only some of the explanations for the ways in which science is taught in bilingual classrooms (or monolingual classrooms). Another factor becoming increasingly salient to teachers in Camelot is the state's new assessment of learning. During the 1997–1998 academic year, science was targeted by this assessment as it was being initiated in the district. One administrator describes the significance of the test, "In 4th, 8th, and 10th grades there will be assessments this year. And so the principals want to be assured that whatever is happening through a project like QK, that the children will do well, because the tests are high stakes for principals. If children do not do well, then eventually a school could be put on receivership and the principal removed. So it is more important now, I think, than ever."[8]

The implications of this statement are obvious, although clearly some principals feel more "at risk" than do others. Similarly, teachers are just beginning to react to the use of this assessment and to acknowledge how it is affecting their classroom teaching. Several voice a concern common to other reform environments, the lack of alignment between the science curriculum, students' prior learning, and the test. Others admit that although committed to teaching science for understanding, they now allocate a portion of class time to "teach to the test."

The test takes about 18 hours of class time (just to take it) and more to prepare them for it. It is significantly above grade level even though we're testing these kids at 8th grade. The vocabulary, and these are kids who come from homes where they hear words and know words, but the vocabulary in the test confounds them. Did you know that no high school student [in the district] passed the science component last year! Students must pass all three components [i.e., science, math, and reading] in order to pass the test. . . . I'm not sure whether this is accurate or not but for the bilingual students I hear that the situation is one that is going to shift. Right now we were told that students had three years from the time they enter the program to take the state assessment. Now I heard it will be changed to one year. This test not only affects the bilingual students who will not be prepared but the parents of the other kids, the English-speaking kids, who won't want these kids [the bilingual students] pulling their scores down further. I'm afraid it affects parent support [for the bilingual program].

Also influencing teaching for understanding is the fact that the objectives of Camelot's science policy, however inadvertently, often compete with the multiple goals embedded in Camelot's different bilingual programs. For example, compared to the transitional Cape Verdean program whose goal it is to educate students in all subjects and to mainstream students within three years of entering the program, the modified transitional Korean program serves as an enrichment program with the majority of its students already mainstreamed. Students in this program are removed from mainstreamed classrooms into tutorials where they learn about Korean culture and are taught math in Korean.

In addition to the formal goals of these programs, namely to teach English as well as subject matter, are the informal goals dictated by student needs. Student needs, and therefore the goals of a bilingual program, involve everything from learning basic skills to acculturation and the impact of these processes on identity. These goals and the dilemmas they present to teachers are implicit in all bilingual programs. How does one teach science for understanding and mainstream a student within three years, while attending to the fact that a 10-year-old student has just arrived in the U.S. having never attended school? This scenario is not uncommon in the Cape Verdean program, where a considerable number of immigrant children from Cape Verde arrive in the Camelot school district having little or no formal education despite being school age. Once here the student must be placed in the appropriate age-grade level despite needing to be taught basic skills. With the current social promotion policy still in place and the emphasis of this program on mainstreaming students, such students often leave elementary school without the requisite skills needed to succeed in high school or beyond.

For the most part, QK language minority teachers appear to have embraced this new approach to science teaching; however, they often describe the difficulties of accomplishing their instructional goals within the larger school context, particularly those who teach disadvantaged students. One of the more outspoken teachers describes the challenges of dealing with culturally and linguistically diverse students:

Bilingual teachers have unique situations and in some ways I think that they have a harder job than English speaking teachers. They not only have to deal with kids from different socioeconomic backgrounds, which every teacher has to deal with in this district. You know not every kid who speaks Spanish here is from a poor home. We have the poor Spanish speakers and then we have the wealthy kids from Latin American backgrounds, but we also have to deal with tremendous sociolinguistic differences. Bilingual teachers have to handle that. They not only have to handle socioeconomic differences, they have to handle cultural differences too. They have to acculturate kids. They have to teach them the ways here. We have to teach the culture, even though its not our culture and get the kid to understand it if he is to be successful. But we also have to teach math and science. It's very hard.

Some teachers perceive a general nonacceptance or lack of support for their bilingual program in the school, either by parents, colleagues, or administrators. Oddly enough, the increased demands of meeting the competing goals of school policies, and of meeting new state and district goals for science teaching and learning, are countered by the frustrations of having to convince either colleagues or administrators that their students can learn science. These language minority teachers offer descriptions involving different cultural styles that they believe lead some colleagues and administrators to conclude their students are incapable of learning science.

Yes, there is that assumed idea that people would say either minority students or especially Cape Verdean students, because of their language problem cannot learn, especially science. Also, they would believe that they can't do this or they can't do that . . . at least because of QK we are thinking about it. We are thinking about it and we are trying to see that it is possible to teach those kids even though they do not really speak English fluently because their mind is there and they can use it for all purposes. I mean just by talking about it and not only talking about it, but giving them proof that kids, whatever their background, really can learn science, can learn math. Wherever I go, when I talk, I always underline the fact that my Cape Verdean kids culturally, they are very self-reserved in the classroom. They are not students who are going to ask questions. They are not going to say 'no,' I mean they are not going to challenge what the teacher is saying, stuff like that. But they can and do learn science.

One teacher, in her frustration, points to the lack of recognition not only of her students' abilities but of bilingual teachers' knowledge as well:

Just because we speak with an accent, it does not mean that our brains have an accent. I am as smart and as knowledgeable as anyone else in this job. I know science, I specialize in science, but I speak with an accent. And therefore people often treat me as if I'm not [as knowledgeable]. And because these kids have an accent they assume that the kids cannot know science or math. They do.

While it is difficult enough to cope with the conflicting demands of different school policies, it is equally frustrating to bilingual teachers when the policy is modified for their students. One teacher characterizes the principal as "dumbing down" the school's science teaching policy for the language minority students.

They [referring to staff] do support it but they support it in a way. Okay, we have science. But he [the principal] came saying, "Okay, except for the bilingual classroom, you can modify what you teach here." But when you say that, what do you expect? You have said, okay, you don't really expect the bilingual kids to fully observe the framework. I would say we are not really accepted. There are two schools in one school.

How do teachers reconcile these policy conflicts with student needs? By bringing their personal and their professional experiences, their skills and their knowledge to the policy process. Teachers decide whether or not to use science kits, how to organize the classroom to enable and to empower students, and how to draw upon student knowledge to generate a common science language and a common understanding of science. For example, these bilingual teachers pay particular attention to student voice, or rather who speaks and who listens, always attending to the impact "voice" has on science learning. Which students have the power to present "scientific" meaning and therefore to shape other students' perceptions? How is language used to express voice and how do "privileged" students whose science language implies knowledge affect other students whose science knowledge may be comparable but whose science language is not? How do teachers manage those children seen as purveyors of information by other children? Do they encourage this role or not? How do teachers help students who are science "outsiders" to become "insiders"?

Some examples are offered in addressing these issues. One teacher discusses introducing the science topics with her bilingual students in advance of the pending class discussion (a science class integrated with monolingual students). In this way, she hopes to enhance bilingual students' familiarity with the topic, respond to any language difficulties, and establish a more equitable and comfortable learning environment for all students. Another teacher has created her own science curriculum, creating small-group learning environments for her students, because, she notes, Creole-speaking students "have something to say" in small groups but not in large ones. A third teacher describes personalizing science since she believes that it is the personal experiences one has that feed what students can understand and what they don't understand. In this class, personalizing generally involves taking added time to learn about the student's personal experiences and science experiences within his/her culture, then linking these experiences to the classroom science topic.

To frame their science practices, teachers draw upon the district curriculum, professional development, and the Quest for Knowledge program. The consequence of these various institutional filters and the multiple goals within each set of policies is that policies are shaped and reshaped, and in the process modified. Nevertheless, the processes of interpretation and practice do not occur in a vacuum. Transformation in "teaching science for understanding" is not an individual construction but a social one, with language minority teachers engaged in teacher groups and developing teacher communities. It is through their participation in the Quest for Knowledge professional development program and in their workplace communities that these teachers gather information, sort this information into systems of ideas, and share their ideas with each other, thereby interpreting and ultimately generating this new pedagogical approach to science learning. It is also in these contexts that teachers obtain access to and use organizational resources in their efforts to *practice* these policies. *implementation Discretion over how things get done.*

POLICY AS A SET OF SOCIOCULTURAL PRACTICES

How is science policy practiced in the intersecting cultures of the school, the bilingual classroom, and the Quest for Knowledge program? Some researchers argue that the ways in which schools are organized is not conducive to achieving the various goals and expectations set for them. Indeed, teaching for understanding is argued to be rare partly because schools are not organized to support it (Gamoran, Secada, & Marrett, forthcoming; Neumann and Associates, 1996). Rather, the existing infrastructure of schools, that is, their organizational resources, are typically dedicated to traditional teaching with little evidence that schools are able or willing to manage their resources in order to facilitate these transformations.

Schools in Camelot organize many of their resources in similar ways. The district coordinates three school schedules in order to facilitate the busing of students to schools outside of their neighborhoods. Efforts are also made with respect to assuring that all elementary schools have similar material resources, such as comparable physical structures, computers, or science kits. However, individual schools do vary with respect to access to resources and they organize their resources in unique ways. They also differ in the types of academic programs offered. Consequently, teaching is also organized differently.

This is just as true of the bilingual programs in Camelot, with bilingual programs differing in their structures, their goals, and in their access to resources. For example, similar to students in the Korean modified program, students in the Chinese modified transitional program are essentially mainstreamed, yet offered ESL and cultural enrichment courses, with the lower grades having integrated language courses (i.e., Chinese Mandarin for native English speakers and nonnative English-speaking students in grades K–2). The Portuguese two-way bilingual program, on the other hand, maintains a dual language/subject matter learning experience for its students. The size of a program and such material resources as curricula also influence program goals and instruction. Since the size of the Cape Verdean program is sufficiently large, one teacher is able to teach science to a classroom of two grade levels. However, the Spanish transitional program (which is different from the two-way Spanish program) is a much smaller program with fewer staff persons, therefore the science teacher must teach to four grade levels collapsed into one science class.

Clearly, bilingual education is not a single enterprise even within the same school district. It takes various organizational forms and these forms both reflect and dictate distinctive goals. Camelot's modified transitional bilingual programs organize learning with an emphasis toward mainstreaming, whereas the two-way bilingual programs teach subject matter content while encouraging the maintenance of language and culture. More importantly, bilingual programs and hence, bilingual teachers do not necessarily receive the same organizational support or resources, regardless of the more broadly defined goal of teaching science for understanding.

These teachers describe difficulties with resources that range from lack of staff development, to professional isolation within the school, to difficulty obtaining curricular materials. Indeed, bilingual programs can be regarded as a school-within-a-school. Regardless of whether a bilingual program is located in a target school or an alternative school, the program tends to be self-contained. In these cases, bilingual programs exist in a status hierarchy of nonequal students and teachers who often receive unequal access to resources. This is one reason that some advocate two-way bilingual programs with the hope that eventually the entire school will become a bilingual learning environment: "This is the crux of the deficit model, that the isolation of the teachers and of the staff is not healthy. It is just not healthy for the school. That is why we are doing all of this reform, so that we can open up programs for everyone so that there is no longer a bilingual program."

Despite all of this, and for a number of reasons that are embedded in the structure of bilingual programs, teaching for understanding has been adopted by these language teachers. Ironically, perceived isolation and nonacceptance by some language minority teachers combine with having to negotiate re-sources in order to accomplish one or more classroom goals. One consequence is that negotiations generate a professional community among some bilingual teachers as they struggle to accommodate their students and implement district policies. One Spanish language teacher characterizes team teaching as a problem-solving device to reduce the number of science lessons:

Actually, I had to teach four through eight science and being one teacher it was almost impossible for me to do it alone, so I did basically the four through eight, which I taught with Liza and the six through eight, which I taught with Renee and Liza. The reason we decided to do community teaching that way was because Renee was in charge of the seventh-grade curriculum while I was in charge of the sixth-grade curriculum, and since we couldn't teach science 10 times a week, we decided to come together as a group and do more of the unit type of science.

Teachers at Rosa Parks describe a culture of professional development pervading the school with a leader who actively promotes collaboration, professional development, and innovative teaching practices, not only through school organization but also through grant writing. Unlike the rest of the schools in Camelot, two of the three alternative schools (including Rosa Parks) have also been adopted by local colleges and universities as professional development sites. Collaborations with these universities results in added human resources (i.e., added staff via workshops and student teachers) and graduate courses, which presumably enhances the collaborative efforts of teachers, a necessary component in teaching for understanding.

These practices, however, do not necessarily translate to the bilingual program within Rosa Parks elementary school. One possible reason is that undoubtedly it is more difficult to find student teachers and paraprofessionals that are knowledgeable in Cape Verdean creole from the local colleges. Of all of the bilingual programs in the district, the Spanish programs may receive the most support with regard to paraprofessionals and teacher interns. The Spanish programs are also more likely to have broader choice in curricular materials, although teachers in this program also describe being limited in materials.

Added to the earlier mix of language focus and subject matter goals, bilingual teachers must often negotiate a heterogeneous classroom of academic ability or preparation as well as varying age levels, socioeconomic backgrounds, and cultural experiences. One Spanish language teacher describes working in teams to teach science to multigraded, multiability, multilingual, and multibackground students, sometimes with limited material resources:

It's not easy. Like for example the AP, they have translated everything into Spanish. The science, or whatever unit I chose to do, I make sure it's in Spanish before I even choose it. Because that's the worse thing to have to do, you know, not only to have to teach the unit but have to translate everything to kids . . . having the worksheet in English, and then have to translate it into Spanish. I mean to me that doesn't work. Also, maybe if we had a better department. I remember going to the social studies [monolingual] department once to get a map and they said, "Oh, you're bilingual, you should go to the bilingual department." You know, that kind of reception.

Lack of curricular materials is not unique to the Spanish programs. Unfortunately, the Portuguese and Cape Verdean Creole programs must rely even more on translation since curricular materials are difficult to find and their selection is more limited. Nevertheless, the time used for translating a lesson is time not used to teach the subject. A teacher who had translated for the Portuguese program was caught between policy switches (not an uncommon experience for teachers):

I was doing the Algebra Project for the past three or four years. But they came to me and said, "Oh, everybody in the system now is doing Connected Math." They said, "Well, you don't have to do it. But everybody else is doing it." And I said, "Well, you made me translate the Algebra Project and now it's clear, and all that time I went for two years in a row to seminars that would help me do that. I was very invested in that. So I won't do that anymore." She's presenting it as if I had a choice but in fact, I didn't have a choice. I now have to translate Connected Math too. The Connected Math is very difficult, so much language that kids don't understand. They have the book but they don't understand. So when I get to crucial points in the book, I do it at home, translate it, and then give it to them. It takes extra time. That is the problem with a bilingual education classroom. Math is a language that is already difficult to understand but now it has to be presented in a foreign language, so now in class I have to translate what is in the book and to make them understand and help them to reflect upon it. It's very difficult. Of course it effects how much I can cover in the class. We had a meeting and they told us that we should be to chapter four of the book but we had only gone to chapter two. It takes so long.

Lack of materials also includes simple teaching tools. While few of the QK teachers complain about the lack of curriculum materials or supplies, one language minority teacher who teaches math finds the lack of materials frustrating:

I couldn't even get an overhead. I couldn't get calculators. So he [the principal] sent me some but that took a while. Maybe because it was my first year of teaching, but I mean this bureaucracy of going through what you have to have, you have to order at the end of the year. I didn't even get emergency fund this year when I went into the classroom in September. So this whole year I went through without . . . unless I went out and bought them on my own or borrowed from other teachers. So those are necessary things.

Ironically, these teachers also mention resistance from parents or colleagues to implementing the program goals. At the same time that the goal of transitional bilingual programs is to mainstream students within a circumscribed period of time, two teachers describe resistance to this process from monolingual parents who fear that integrating classrooms will retard the instructional process, thus disadvantaging their children. One teacher offers an anecdote involving a monolingual colleague who complained about her student recently integrated into his classroom, claiming that the student was of low ability and could not understand English. After some discussion with the principal, this teacher was able to impress the monolingual teacher with the student's abilities. Nevertheless, she admitted to occasionally suggesting to parents of bilingual students to remove their child from the school rather than mainstream them. Her reasoning was that once mainstreamed, these students tend to be ignored by some classroom teachers.

They don't even know where the kids are. They don't even know what these kids are learning, what level the kid is. They are just put in the lower group. And this teacher goes to you and says, "This child doesn't know anything." It hurts the child. And it hurts you because the child knows things. They [certain monolingual teachers] don't care. I want to say to people look closer. Listen to a bilingual child. He has a lot to say. He has a lot to say. If I could say that to all teachers, I think it would make a difference in the way they treated the kids when they go to them from the bilingual program.

What becomes clear from teachers' comments is that while they maintain high expectations for their students and for themselves, they do not believe that the same standards are applied to them or to their students relative to their monolingual counterparts. For these teachers, there is an implicit assumption on the part of some monolingual colleagues, administrators, or parents about what their students' capabilities are, or what they are expected to learn. Yet these teachers are encouraged to attend professional development seminars and to engage in teaching for understanding. For many of the reasons previously stated, to some teachers this requires assistance from outside of district-sponsored opportunities. This is precisely what makes the QK seminar so valuable to these teachers.

The Quest for Knowledge program provides additional material and human and social support for science teaching to both monolingual and bilingual teachers. All teachers complain about the lack of time as a critical resource for meeting and collaborating with colleagues. However, because of the diverse issues facing language minority teachers, planning time for collaboration becomes even more crucial. All teachers also experience a degree of social isolation, particularly those who do not have teacher interns or other paraprofessionals assisting them in the classroom. However, the isolation described by bilingual teachers differs from the isolation brought on by the structural conditions of the profession and of the working environment (i.e., classroom teaching). This isolation is one of a more personal nature. Certainly it is structurally induced, but it is also an interpersonal isolation from monolingual colleagues and from administrators grounded in cultural or linguistic differences. This is still another reason why the QK program is so valuable to language minority participants. It is through this program that bilingual and monolingual teachers come together.

The Quest for Knowledge staff provides additional support and expertise along with valuable material resources such as experiment and measurement instruments, as well as reading materials and video equipment for taping classroom lectures. But perhaps the most important resource that the program offers is the time and opportunity for teachers to interact with one another in an ongoing and meaningful way. It is in the QK program that teachers can interact with their bilingual colleagues from the same school but also build a network with bilingual colleagues from other schools. Here too, bilingual teachers have the opportunity to work with monolingual teachers, establishing ties that the school context often fails to encourage. The QK context affords bilingual teachers a safe environment in which to engage new science ideas and to reinforce these ideas and practices. It also brings together a collection of bilingual colleagues that support language minority teachers as they build associations across linguistic boundaries with monolingual teachers and with each other. What has evolved in one school is not only a cohesiveness among the bilingual teachers, but a shared commitment to a style of science instruction. In another school, teachers describe greater contact between language minority teachers and monolingual teachers, where assistance and exchange of ideas around science topics now occur:

She is a science teacher at the junior high level but before she used to teach a few years ago, she used to teach grades 5 and 6 too. Then she used to come to my class and we shared things. And she was a QK teacher too. And then there were some projects that we taped together since we had to, we studied other things. For instance, ants. We studied mold, so we had a chance to work together. We have been doing that less in the past year, but we still communicate and because I have some of my students, when they are mainstreamed, they go to her class.

How is this professional community and culture of science accomplished? Having focused discussions on science language and using group research with discussion about that research to generate a common language facilitates the emergence of a common science language. Sustained participation where shared conversations involving classroom lessons, classroom discourse, or science experiments are just some of the many ways in which a common culture of science begins to emerge. An abiding respect exhibited by QK staff for teachers along with recognition of what teachers bring to this learning process also contributes to the development of a culture of science. Perhaps the most important ingredient needed to accomplish the trust needed for such a community is time.

Because we have been in the program for a long time I think that we share our thinking, because that is what we've been trying to do. We've been trying to understand and to discover and that takes time. . . . They [the QK staff] put us exactly in the same situations that students are. We have questions and we have to do the research and try to experiment. And so by doing it yourself as a teacher you'll be more able to understand how kids react, what kinds of difficulties they do have when they are confronted by a new task. By doing it together, you learn to understand how we as teachers think.

Unlike the monolingual participants in the QK seminar, six of the eight bilingual teachers recall entering the seminar with their "teacher teams" or their professional communities in their school. This is partially due to recruitment by the bilingual coordinator or the QK directors, but it has also been initiated by teachers. The goal was to find greater opportunities to focus on science teaching for understanding as well as increased time for collaboration. With two exceptions, these teachers also indicate that they already held the teaching for understanding philosophy and had been engaged in the practices associated with it for some time. "One of the reasons we joined the group was that we were already working as a team . . . . I think it has reinforced everything that I believed in, you know, which was more of the hands-on exploration, you know, discussions, kids leading, and the teacher more as a faciltator."

Therefore, perhaps the idea of transforming teachers is misguided. Rather than looking at how teachers should be *given* professional development we should be asking how teachers' knowledge both informs and reforms the policy process. Equally important is the insight into how school policies and practices are structured to facilitate or inhibit the accomplishment of certain goals. One example is the size of the Spanish transitional program and the lack of sufficient bilingual teachers that led to collaboration among the teachers and to grouping students to teach science for understanding. Another example involves how bilingual teacher teams entered into the QK program, in part because of professional isolation and insufficient staff development in science.

Nevertheless, the QK network of colleagues that has evolved does provide bilingual teachers with an expanded community of colleagues. Prior to the district's recent changes in its science curriculum, bilingual teachers received little if any professional development in science. Therefore, the QK program is perceived by teachers as the conduit through which both pedagogical and social transformations can occur, not only for them but for other teachers as well.

Although these overlapping communities have evolved into a common network or community, they represent a fraction of the total bilingual (or monolingual) teaching population, most of whom are left largely on their own to create similar types of connections. Moreover, teacher ties across schools and across language groups have taken some time to evolve and to produce social resources that continue to be utilized idiosyncratically outside of the QK seminar. That is, teachers who do exchange ideas are generally located within the same school. They do not express seeking their QK colleagues (from different schools) for advice outside of the seminar, nor do they indicate returning to their schools and "spreading the word" to school colleagues.

The benefits of a program such as Quest for Knowledge are sometimes also cited as the costs. For example, besides the fact that the seminar is separate from the district, one of the freeing aspects of the seminar is its relatively loose or flexible structure, with opportunity for teachers to direct and shape the seminar contents and format. This was both a welcomed experience and a perplexing one for teachers who describe being accustomed to having something provided for them (e.g., "This is what we will do"). Another example involves the nonevaluative character of classroom discussions, which initially generated uncertainty for teachers. Indeed, teachers are constantly commenting on the fact that participation in the seminar has caused them to reflect on what they *thought* they knew, consequently generating uncertainty regarding the teaching of science. This is described as both liberating and anxiety producing.

Still, with all of the QK teachers currently engaged in developing a language for discussing science teaching and learning, there is opportunity not only for teachers to share their own understanding of science problems, but also to cross the boundaries of linguistic differences that often separate them in the context of the school. Through their practice of developing a common language for science, they are creating science policy. Through their increasingly deprivatized practice of sharing their work, their frustrations and their questions with each other, they are creating science policy. The guide was set by the district and assisted by the QK program but the practice is the teachers'. The issue is a delicate one of balance, in creating an environment where teachers come to trust, to rely upon, and ultimately to prefer the collective or collaborative experience rather than the individual one.

EVERYTHING OLD IS "NEW" AGAIN

It is clear that the bilingual teachers in Quest for Knowledge (like their monolingual colleagues) are active participants in the policy process. They acknowledge, reform, and construct science policy in the school, in the Quest for Knowledge program, and in the classroom. If we are to understand these processes and the so-called problems with policies that appear to have gone awry, we must first understand that one of the defining features of educational policies in our country is their revolving-door character. Teachers can often be heard decrying the fact that policies come and go with the frequency of NBA basketball coaches. It is common to pick up a copy of *Education Weekly*, the *Chronicle of Higher Education*, or any city newspaper and read about teachers who are reticent to begin implementing new standards for fear that the new approach will soon become yesterday's news.

Another feature of educational policies is that they do not exist in a political vacuum, isolated from one another. Rather, they coexist and often compete with other policies. This fact has the unfortunate consequence of creating tensions between different policy goals. More often than not, policies, as they are practiced, often have results that impact on some other policy, however inadvertently. We have seen that with the changing from the Algebra Project (whose translation to Creole had recently been accomplished) to Connected Math, for which no translation exists. A math curriculum regarded as superior to another, and implemented to enhance math learning and test performance, has inadvertently placed a greater burden on bilingual teachers by forcing them to take added time to first translate and then teach material that is linguistically more complicated to their students.

The proliferation and use of assessments as the traditional means of determining the value of curricula, teaching, and possibly learning, is another example of the transformation of policies such as the voluntary national standards. Some argue that these standards will act as an incentive structure for districts, hence teachers, to adopt more professional approaches to teaching/learning. It seems worthy at this time to question whether the national standards and their operationalization (i.e., state assessments) is either incongruous with the concept of teaching for understanding or will be counterproductive to this instructional style. The institutional layer of state-wide assessments generates a tension to move toward the more "traditional" teaching practices or teaching toward the test rather than teaching for understanding. This, of course, might be mitigated by the fact that some state-wide assessments are aligned with the new instructional styles being asked of teachers. Camelot is not the only district, however, where this is argued not to be the case (see Hoff, 1999).

While much of the rhetoric promotes the "professionalization" of teachers, one cannot help but get the feeling that the subtext continues to imply a continued "top-down" approach of providing professional development to teachers rather than incorporating teachers as partners who have resources upon which to draw in this policy process. One characteristic of the professions is a fair degree of autonomy. Yet when we read descriptions of teachers becoming professionalized, we also read about deprivatized practice within the context of accountability and standards. Clearly, teaching for understanding (that is, constructivist teaching, authentic teaching) seems incongruous with the use of some aversive technique to coerce and enforce it.

In this chapter, it is also important to understand that bilingual teachers engage in these new reform practices in structurally constrained as well as highly politicized contexts. Consequently, it is also important to acknowledge our awareness of the tensions and countervailing forces operating in any policy situation and the relative ease with which political conflicts beyond the teachers, the school, or even the district can affect the success of teachers' (hence students') efforts.

Due to lack of curricular and other material resources, uncoordinated and systematic professional development in science, or social and parental support, science policy and bilingual education policies push against each other.

SUMMARY/RECOMMENDATIONS

A reasonable avenue for pursuit of broader and sustained outcomes for science teaching for understanding is to implement such a program as QK on a school-wide basis, particularly at the elementary school level, where such implementation is feasible. Camelot's adoption of a science curriculum structured for this teaching style is only a starting point. Professional development in this instructional style is an important next step. However, the recent focus on professional development has not reduced our difficulties in transforming American education. Like most policies in our decentralized system of education, its content, its purpose, and its design and format for conveying information to teachers (i.e., issued and mandated by district personnel and presented as formulaic) is as variegated as the school districts in which it is found. Its failure is inherent in the ways professional development is so often conceptualized, as something to be given to teachers. Nor will the proliferation and added layer of state-wide assessments assist in this process of achieving voluntary national math and science standards, since such tests are typically not aligned with curriculum and are used for political purposes rather than to further learning. Quest for Knowledge represents a novel approach to teacher professional development that embraces a segment of the population critical to our future. Peter Negroni (1993) points out that because of demographic changes in our population, the new jobs developed by U.S. industry will outstrip the number of persons to fill them. Moreover, those persons available will be predominantly female and ethnic/linguistic minority persons. Without the successful transformation of our educational institutions to serve the needs of these students, we will produce a workforce of "at-risk" employees. Thus, the long-term benefits to this country are to maximize our available human capital in order to sustain our economy and our democracy.

The QK program is an example of how a professional development program promotes pedagogical transformation (by addressing what is taught and how it is taught), and serves to promote the formation of a community of teachers and the emergence of a culture of science. It is this culture of science that promotes and hopefully sustains teachers in their efforts to construct science policy (i.e., teaching "science" for understanding). This program promotes the active participation of those who know the needs of the community and in so doing, promotes their investment in that community. In this way, the QK program is an example of how professional development is shaped to achieve social justice and educational equity for all children as well as for those who teach them.

NOTES

1. Research on this chapter was supported by the National Center for Improving Student Learning and Achievement in Mathematics and Science, Wisconsin Center for Education Research, University of Wisconsin-Madison, with funds from the Office of Educational Research and Improvement, U.S. Department of Education (Grant No. R305A60007).

2. These schools are located in particular areas of the Camelot school district, with these areas having larger concentrations of ethnic minority and low-income persons. Moreover, their student populations draw disproportionately from these areas.

3. Due to the protest of parents who regarded this label as stigmatizing to their children this label has recently been dropped by the district.

4. This information is gathered from interviews with school principals and district administrators, and from a parent information handbook describing the schools and published annually.

5. The goals/foci of the program have essentially been paraphrased from the program's mission statement.

6. (1996–1997) Structured, 1- to 2-hour telephone interviews were conducted with 10 of 22 participants in the QK program. The interviews address such issues as professional development and the QK program, teaching science for understanding, and professional community and teacher collaboration. In addition, a survey focusing on school organization and professional development in math and science was distributed to elementary and middle school teachers in the district. (1997–1998) As a participant observer, I participated in the QK seminars with teachers. This included science exercises and "homework" developed by QK staff, small group discussions revolving around readings of classroom discourse, or videotaped segments of teacher classrooms. I attended release days along with the weeklong seminar. I interviewed 13 of the district's 15 principals, along with two district administrators responsible for science and bilingual education. These structured interviews offer insights into how school leaders assist in the development of a *community of learners.* The QK directors were also jointly interviewed along with 8 of the seminar's 16 participants. Seminar observations were tape-recorded immediately after the seminars. In addition to these formal processes, informal conversations with teachers and with QK staff inform this case study.

A second survey was distributed to all 15 schools, with particular attention to follow-up with the four schools with QK participants. The survey was modified to include items specific to bilingual instruction. The purpose of this survey was to supplement fieldwork with contextual information from each school community. Finally, since the city's local newspaper regularly devotes a section to coverage of school district news, a third source of information regarding the Camelot school district emerges from reading the newspaper's coverage of school events. Again, particular attention was paid to the four schools with teachers participating in the QK program.

(1998–1999) I participated in the QK meetings as an observer and interviewed the principals of the four QK schools. Seven of the remaining 12 teachers were interviewed during this year, along with district administrators responsible for bilingual education and for professional development (a new position created during the year). A computerized textbase system (i.e., NUDIST) assists in making sense of all of this information by allowing interactive coding and management of large amounts of qualitative data. Finally, the survey was distributed for the third and final year, with this year's survey focusing explicitly on the four QK schools.

7. Two principals and three teachers estimated that less than half to 50 percent of the teachers in the Camelot district actually use the science kits. Indeed, a rumor was being circulated that the forthcoming "sabbatical" being taken by the district's science coordinator was due to his failure to accomplish implementation of the new science curriculum.

8. Teachers also comment that the city's largest newspaper has already used students' performance on the test to compare and market residential communities in the metropolitan area.

REFERENCES

Apple, M. W. (1993). *Official knowledge: Democratic education in a conservative age.* New York: Routledge.

Barth, R. S. (1990). *Improving schools from within.* San Francisco: Jossey-Bass.

Gamoran, A., Secada, W. G., & Marrett, C. (forthcoming).The organizational context of teaching and learning: Changing theoretical perspectives. In M. T. Hallinan (Ed.), *Handbook of education.*

Garcia, E. E. (1997). Effective instruction for language minority students: The teacher. In A. Darder, R. D. Torres, & H. Gutierrez (Eds.), *Latinos and education* (pp. 362–372). New York: Routledge.

Giroux, H. A. (1992). *Border crossings: Cultural workers and the politics of education.* New York: Routledge.

Hoff, D. J. (1999, September). Standards at crossroads after decade: high stakes testing is chief worry. *Education Week, XIX,* 1–2.

McLaren, P. (1994). Multiculturalism and the postmodern critique: toward a pedagogy of resistance and transformation. In H. A. Giroux & P. McLaren (Eds.), *Between borders: Pedagogy and the politics of cultural studies* (pp. 192–222). New York: Routledge.

Natriello, G., McDill, E. L., & Pallas, A. (1990). *Schooling disadvantaged students: Racing against catastrophe.* New York: Teachers College Press.

Negroni, P. (1996). The transformation of public schools. In C. Walsh (Ed.), *Education reform and social change: Multicultural voices, struggles and visions* (pp. 199–221). Hillsdale, NJ: Erlbaum.

Newmann, F. M. and Associates. (1996). *Authentic achievement: Restructuring schools for intellectual quality.* San Francisco: Jossey-Bass.

Newmann, F., Marks, H. M., & Gamoran, A. (1996, August). Authentic pedagogy and student performance. *American Journal of Education, 104,* (4), 280–313.

Schifter, D. (1996). *What's happening in math class?: Reconstructing professional identities.* New York: Teachers College Press.

Walsh, C. E. (1996). Introduction. In C.E. Walsh (Ed.), *Education reform and social change: Multicultural voices, struggles and visions* (pp. xi–xvii). Hillsdale, NJ: Erlbaum.

8

Health Education Policies and Poor Women in Brazil: Identifying Myths That Undermine Empowerment

Isabela Cabral Félix de Sousa

Health education for poor women sits at the intersection of several themes in the discourse on women's empowerment.[1] Education itself is strongly tied to notions of empowerment, on both commonsensical and empirical grounds (Conway & Bourque, 1995). The right of women to control their own bodies is a feminist principle that encompasses women's sexual and reproductive autonomy as well as their integrity as physical persons (Dixon-Mueller, 1993). As a kind of nonformal education, health education can empower women if it modifies awareness, values, and individual and collective behaviors (Darcy de Oliveira & Harper, 1985) and contributes to greater physical autonomy. The promise and potential for health education to contribute to the empowerment of poor women in Brazil led to the study that informs this chapter. Brazil may be a particularly revealing case because Paulo Freire's pedagogy for liberation is expected to be practiced by many nonformal educators in his native land. In addition, policies and programs concerning reproduction and contraception in Brazil have been influenced by the feminist movement and by other forms of activism aimed at empowering the poor. As the study reported here shows, however, the potential for empowerment of poor women in Brazil through health education has been compromised by both structural and ideological factors. Looking closely at the interaction between health educators and their clients, and probing through interviews and conversations into the thinking behind some of the observed behaviors, it is argued that health education in Brazil is mediated by myths that undermine its emancipatory potential.

The concept of "myth" is often defined as "the fictions or half-truths forming part of an ideology of a society" (Morris, 1981, p. 869). While they may
not be true, the power of myth has been well described by Portuguese poet
Fernando Pessoa: "O mito é o nada que é tudo [Myth is the nothing which is
everything]" (p. 72). Because of their very invisibility, commonly held myths
can form rigid supports of an unequal status quo. As envisioned by Freire, a
pedagogical process that brings myths to consciousness for active questioning,
debate, and analysis provides a cornerstone for empowerment. This is the underlying purpose of the present analysis: to identify the myths that rob health
education of its potential to empower poor women in Brazil.

Before proceeding to the identification of the myths through ethnographic
analysis, it is necessary to clarify the complex concepts and realities in which
they rest. This chapter therefore begins by discussing the concept of empowerment and its relationship to nonformal education in general, and health education in particular. The following section summarizes the evolution of
contraceptive policy and programs in Brazil, showing their gradual shift toward the language of reproductive health, with its implicit recognition of
women's empowerment as both a means and a goal. Following this conceptual
and historical clarification, this chapter summarizes the study of how health
education is practiced in one set of clinics in Brazil. This chapter concludes by
identifying a number of myths that underlie the beliefs and behaviors of those
involved in health education and arguing that these myths effectively promote
a practice of health education that is disempowering for the women who are its
students.

EMPOWERMENT AND NONFORMAL EDUCATION

Empowerment has carried different meanings and not all of them are necessarily emancipatory (Stromquist, 1993). An example of a purported strategy
for empowering women that can be questioned as not seeking to emancipate
them was given by Antrobus (1989), who stated that international agencies,
such as the World Bank and UNICEF, have used women's empowerment as a
way to endorse the withdrawal of accountability for government expenditures
on social services and thereby place this responsibility in women's hands.

In contrast, the liberating or emancipatory connotation of empowerment

is one which brings up the question of personal agency rather than reliance on interme-
diaries, one that links action to needs, and one that results in making significant collective change. It is also a concept that does not merely concern personal identity but
brings out a broader analysis of human rights. (Stromquist, 1993, p. 1)

Empowerment in its emancipatory meaning is not simply the meeting of gen-
der-specific needs created by the status quo. A distinction delineated by
Maxine Molyneux between gender interests that are practical and strategic is
of particular relevance. According to Molyneux (1985), while the practical

needs do not question the present unbalanced distribution of power in which women so often occupy a subordinated position, the strategic needs do aim at gender parity.

The discourse on women's health in the *World Development Report* (1993) provides a good example of addressing practical gender needs while speaking the language of empowerment. This document argues that women must be empowered through better education and elimination of social discrimination in order to improve their health and that of their families. This is necessary, according to the document, because women have greater influence on their families' health than do men. An emancipatory approach to empowerment would go further, addressing strategic needs such as changing the conditions of gender inequality that make men's abilities to give health care to their families inferior to those of women.

When empowerment is thought of as a strategy of change it implies reorganizing the distribution of power. Through attempts to empower the oppressed, it is possible to envision a more equitable society where all can share their decision making. In the context of classrooms, Shor (1992) explained that education can be empowering if it is negotiated among teachers and students. In summary, empowerment is a nonlinear process in which people seek alternative visions and solutions for changing any oppressive ideology and practice. Empowerment is also a process in which respect and visibility is gained for the aspects by which an individual or societies are discriminated against.

Within the field of education, nonformal and popular education have long been associated with notions of empowerment.[2] For the purposes of this article, nonformal education is understood, using Paulo Freire's conceptual framework, as having the potential for changes in both the individual and social spheres, which requires going beyond individual needs to become a device for social change. In this framework, awareness and action cannot be divorced from one another. For Freire (1987), a liberating education is one grounded in a social practice, aiming for the liberation of the oppressed classes. As elaborated in the *Pedagogy of the Oppressed* (Freire, 1993), the oppressed will become aware of the oppressive reality and transform it through praxis.

Some studies have indeed evinced women's empowerment through nonformal education (Lephoto, 1995; Sousa, 1995; Stromquist, 1994). However, despite its emancipatory potential, nonformal education for adults is not always democratic (Allevato, 1986). According to Freire (1994), the pedagogical dialogue between an educator and the students relates to both the content and the exposition made by the educator, and an educator who is progressive must be democratic in both the programming of the contents as well as in his/her teaching.[3] Thus, it is necessary to study the conditions under which nonformal education programs have operated by analyzing class contents, class interactions, instructional materials, personnel training, and criteria for selection, in order to understand in what forms and contexts nonformal education can be a tool for women's empowerment.

Even though the concept of empowerment is new in the field of health education, ideas similar to it have been present since the field began (Li & Wong, 1989). Wallerstein and Bernstein (1988) analyzed health education for empowerment and general education for empowerment according to Freire's framework. They found that empowerment in health education shares three important characteristics of Freire's model: (1) It begins with the problems of the community; (2) it utilizes active learning methods; and (3) it fosters community participation so that community members can realize their own needs. At the same time, these authors claimed that empowerment in health education is more limited than empowerment in general education. In the first case, they argue, the knowledge content may come from experts imposing information. The origins of health education are grounded in a narrow bioreductionist model of medicine, which has had a profound impact on the way health education programs have been carried out and in turn have achieved limited success (Laura & Heaney, 1990). In addition, the teaching/learning process of specific health programs do not necessarily involve social action. Nevertheless, this learning process involves action and reflection by assuming that people can make decisions regarding their health if they are provided with the necessary information, skills, and reinforcement.

Much of the literature on health education focuses on two topics: the relative "success" or impact of programs, and the thinking that informs them. On the matter of impact, many programs have been found to fall short of their own goals. Problems in health education programs have been related not only to the absence of a broad-based approach to health, but also to the way these programs have been conducted. Hubley (1986) described the failures in the implementation of health education in developing countries as stemming from the following factors: the planning and communications processes, the organization of health education, and the evaluation process. Stromquist (1986), analyzing nonformal educational projects supported by international development agencies, contended that those designed to promote the acquisition of skills in agriculture, health, population, and sanitation have often paid small attention to their educational activities. In addition, Laura and Heaney (1990) affirmed that the method of health education in past programs had not fostered autonomy for the community and individuals that are clients of the programs.

Some of these critiques have fed back into the thinking of policymakers and program designers in health education. Stambler (1984) has argued that despite the medical monopoly, health education in less developed countries has been changing to focus more on sociocultural decision making than on endorsing biomedical prescriptions. This shift was reported to have occurred since the 1970s in Brazilian health educational projects (Schall et al., 1987).

REPRODUCTIVE POLICIES AND HEALTH
EDUCATION IN BRAZIL

Few nations have explicitly formulated policies regarding health education. As in most countries, the space in which health education is practiced in Brazil is circumscribed by its particular configuration of population and contraception policies, which together manifest the reproductive ideology of a state. The population and contraception policies that create the context of health education for women in Brazil have followed international trends, though they are marked by the specific social and cultural context of the nation. For example, the rhetoric in Brazil has changed over time from that of maternal health for population control to reproductive health care. At the same time, Brazilian reproductive ideology has been marked by a dominance of contraception over population policy. Programmatically, health education in Brazil has historically had a strong private component, which exerts specific influences on public programs.

Health educational practices for women in public health clinics in Brazil are part of family planning programs. Since these health educational practices owe their emergence to family planning programs, the creation of these programs must be reviewed. Watson (1977) provides a historical overview of the birth of family planning policy and family planning program adoption in the Third World. According to Watson, the first country to adopt a family planning policy was India in 1952. Thereafter, there was a rapid adoption of family-planning policies so that over only two decades, by 1975, Watson claimed that 94% of 81 countries of the Third World had family-planning policies.

Family-planning policies have not necessarily preceded family planning programs. Family-planning programs in Brazil appeared in the 1960s, as in other Latin American countries (Stycos, 1971). However, only in 1974 did Brazil sign the Declaration of Bucharest, which supported: "the right of couples to control fertility and the public duty to provide the means of exercising this right" (Giffin, 1994, p. 355). At the same time, the existence of a family planning policy has not necessarily meant that the entire population of a country has had access to family-planning programs. Watson (1977) showed that in 1975, Brazil, West Asia, North Africa, and most of Anglophone Sub-Saharan Africa had national family-planning programs that were able to serve only 1 percent of women in their reproductive years.

Over time, the international trend has been a shift in family-planning models from a maternal and child health care (MCH) approach, to one of reproductive health. Maternal-child health programs have been sharply criticized for their approach. Heise (1993) alerted us to the fact that these programs have often neglected the mother's health needs and placed more emphasis on children's needs. The concept of reproductive health care arose in response to the limitations of the MCH model. As Sai and Nassim (1989) have explained, the reproductive health approach is broader than the maternal health approach in five ways. First, it relates the health problems that women experience regarding sexuality, pregnancy, and delivery to health problems in their child-hood and adolescence. The reproductive health approach pays explicit atten-tion to maternal morbidity and views maternal mortality not as the defining factor of women's health but as an indication of the existence of greater prob-lems in regard to sexuality and pregnancy. The audience of reproductive health programs encompasses women and men of all ages, rather than pregnant women alone, and thus the content links the whole range of sexual health to life-cycle health issues and risks.

Although family-planning programs appeared in Brazil and elsewhere prior to the defining of family-planning policies, it is important to note that repro-ductive health programs only appeared after the emergence of the concept of reproductive heath. According to Dixon-Mueller (1993), this notion became popular in the 1980s, based on the feminist idea that all women should have the right to control their sexuality and reproduction. Dixon-Mueller (1993) further emphasizes that reproductive freedom and rights cannot be divorced from other basic human rights, for reproductive freedom is anchored in indi-vidual self-determination. This author delineates differences among repro-ductive rights such as "the freedom to decide how many children to have and when (or whether) to have them; the right to have the information and means to regulate one's fertility, and the right to 'control one's own body'" (p. 12).

While studying family-planning policies in depth in Brazil, Alvarez (1989) identified three systemic factors that influenced population policies from the late 1970s to the late 1980s. The first was the shift of reproductive ideology within some parts of the State. From 1978 to 1983, the reproductive ideology became gradually antinatalist, as opposed to the pronatalist ideology that was supported until the late 1970s.[4] Second, the debt crisis of 1982 left Brazil with less power to resist pressures from the international aid community to adopt population control. Finally, a change in state–civil society relations made the State more susceptible to the influence of social movements, as a source of re-inforcing state legitimacy. According to Alvarez, with this strategy the State adopted the Brazilian women's movement ideology of reproductive rights to design its family-planning policy. Consequently, there have been changes in the design of family-planning policies at the State level that represent successes for the ideology of the Brazilian women's movement.

At the same time, it is recognized to date that these policy successes have not completely translated into national practice, for the reason, among others, that family-planning services are often private (Dixon-Mueller, 1993).

The private sector, in fact, is a historically dominant force in family planning in Brazil, and thus in health education. The Civil Society for Family Welfare (BEMFAM) is the organization that has had the most marked impact in Brazil. BEMFAM started its Brazilian action in the mid-1960s, funded by the Inter-national Planned Parenthood Federation (IPPF). BEMFAM endorses the view that the causes of underdevelopment rest in high birth rate and that this rate should be curtailed (Barroso & Bruschini, 1991). Schultz (1993) states that BEMFAM distributes oral pills to all women, seldom mentioning alternative methods. But BEMFAM's operation in Brazil has not been homogenous; it has encompassed both clinical and community-based delivery (CBD) systems, the latter differing from one another and being mostly encountered in the Northeast region of Brazil (Foreith, Rodrigues, Arruda, & Milare, 1983). Only the community-based delivery system of BEMFAM's programs has been described as involving information and education through teachers and volunteer community leaders (Rodrigues, 1977). Due to its long existence, BEMFAM's actions have been reported to have grown to incorporate more feminist ideas and those related to community participation.

According to Schultz (1993), today in Brazil there are many private organizations working with family-planning programs that are similar to ones launched by BEMFAM. Although there are some international organizations supporting sterilization programs in Brazil, (Branford, 1993), there are also, in addition to BEMFAM, several women's health centers and groups that emerged from actions of the women's health movement (Schultz, 1993). These groups encourage women to discuss the health information they provide, as well as providing incentives for women to exert political pressure for access to health care and for individual choice. As noted by García-Moreno and Claro (1994), "In Brazil, the National Feminist Network for Reproductive Health and Rights, founded in August 1991, has 65 organizational members from all over the country" (p. 49).

In addition, health programs for Brazilian women, if not private, often have the influence of private organizations. According to Ribeiro (1993), in 1991, with the notable exception of the municipality of Rio de Janeiro, women's health programs in more than 35 Brazilian municipalities received a combination of public and private support, the latter through BEMFAM. In general, such programs have not taken a comprehensive approach to the health care of women, concentrating on prenatal care directed primarily toward adolescents (S.O.S Corpo, 1991). Instead, these programs follow the traditional maternal childcare approach, which emphasizes contraception (Germain & Antrobus, 1989).[5]

THE STUDY: PRACTICES OF HEALTH EDUCATION IN BRAZIL

There are networks to promote women's rights and issues in Rio de Janeiro. However, during data collection for previous research work, the author noted a certain isolation and lack of knowledge among private programs that promote women's citizenship and public programs fostering women's health. This may be because the Municipality of Rio de Janeiro is the only one in which women's health programs are funded solely by the government (Ribeiro, 1993). At the same time, both private and public organizations are facing diminished economic resources to run their programs. Due to the temporary nature of programs intended for sustainable development and financed by other countries, it is important that these experiences be known so that they become rejected or adapted according to the needs of each institution. At the same time, it is important to improve the governmental attempts to educate poor women, such as the one developed by public health clinics. In these settings, Israel and Vellozo (1996) have found the need for strengthening the notion of health education as a transforming practice.

Thus, the rationale for this research was to learn both how civic and health education do interact, and how they might. The research context of this study of the Municipality of Rio de Janeiro had three initial objectives. The first was to learn about social actions of notable private and public health clinics working for the promotion of women's citizenship. The second was to select and evaluate the health educational programs offered for women by two public health clinics. The third was to investigate the existence and potential of collaborative efforts among private organizations working on gender issues and health educational programs for women operating in governmental health clinics. The research was conducted from May 1996 to July 1998.

The research method employed is qualitative, inspired by sociology and anthropology. This research included visits to 13 institutions, and the observations, interviews, and interactions with the subjects under study. In-depth interviews were conducted with 20 professional women (10 working at private organizations and 10 working at governmental organizations in Rio de Janeiro) and 57 client women (27 from one public health clinic and 30 from another public health clinic).[6] The interviewed women were selected due to their organizations' good reputation for the promotion of women's citizenship. Three-fourths of the organizations selected have projects focusing principally on women's health, because this is the area where more projects can be identified. The remaining projects have health as a second focus, and basically emphasized women's issues related to income generation, protection against violence, legislative changes, and the portrayal of gender messages in the media.

The health education programs tend to meet every week. All women joined the program after at least one medical appointment. The health educational programs are designed to be regular meetings of at least one hour. According to health professionals, most health education activities lasted from two to five weeks, though some women came just once. There was no incentive or penalty for coming more often. The number of meetings specified depended on arrangements between each woman, her physician, and the health instructor. During one class observation, a health professional, upset that few women showed up, told us that I should observe an ideal public health clinic, where women attend all five meetings. I asked why more women were compliant with that program, and she told me she knew that they were less permissive, since women could only get free contraceptives attending all five meetings. No client women said anything in regard to her statement. Of course, this ideal clinic can be judged to be coercive in terms of women's rights to attain contraceptives.

During the meetings, the women always sat in circles. Some health professionals used the blackboard to explain concepts. Other health professionals utilized visual health educational materials. The texts distributed were very simple, but had concepts that were not fully explained in class interactions. For instance, a brochure designed by a non-governmental organization and distributed in one of the public health clinics during classes was titled "Women: Reproductive Health and AIDS." An analysis of this brochure demonstrates that it explains AIDS well, in addition to women's increasing risk for its contraction, the danger of transmission to a newborn, and contraceptive practices. Nevertheless, it does not explain the concept of reproductive health, which was not known by any of the interviewed women. Furthermore, it does not emphasize that among women, those who are increasingly at risk to develop AIDS are the women who have stable unions (many times without knowledge, they have bisexual male companions). Another brochure given to women, designed by a social worker in the other public health clinic for prenatal care, contained the following statement: "Women to have healthy pregnancies and babies must avoid high blood pressure, diabetes and spontaneous abortion." In no part of this brochure is there any medical advice on the first two conditions nor explanation of how the last factor may be monitored to promote healthy pregnancies or babies. A physician should have revised this brochure.

Instructors were never observed to recommend a book, even though some women were able to read and write well and could afford to buy them. Most encounters relied solely on conversations. The less talkative women were not always encouraged to talk during class. On issues that were particularly sensitive (such as some women's violent partners and a daughter imitating with a doll an aunt's homosexual relationship with her companion), the instructor generally approached the situation by inviting private conversation after the group's session.

The approaches used on some occasions did foster interactive dialogue. However, most of the time they were rather descriptive and normative. Their contents tend to rely on contraception and alternative methods. They emphasized HIV/AIDS among the sexually transmitted diseases. They also discussed male and female sexual relationships in the context of the patriarchal society and emotional affairs. The health education practices are identified as disempowering because they tend to teach reproductive health practices as the norm. They also tend to reproduce educational values that privilege formal education, and thus those who have more access to this kind of education, the upper- and middle-class. Still, the relationships physicians have with patients tend to be authoritarian. While they are intended to give choices, they usually do not emphasize choice, but modern reproductive health practices or those available in the public health clinics.

Despite the fact that health educational policies are advertised as being modern, observations in the public health clinic settings reveal that modern and traditional views of reproduction are taught concurrently. This coexistence of values generated by rapid social transformation is expected and coherent. A problem arises from the legitimacy afforded to modern health practices, which denies the necessary confrontational space that people need to evaluate their own values and practices in order to accept, reject, or adopt new ideas and behaviors. This is also problematic in a country with a great attraction to modern health practices. For instance, the rate of caesarians in Brazil is one of the highest in the world (Rutenberg & Ferraz, 1988). Vieira and Ford (1996) note that the proportion of voluntary female sterilization is high, amounting to 27% of total family-planning use. While there are many factors behind these rates, in Brazil, the rate of modern medical choices tends to increase with higher family income. But among the poor, this appeal can have more serious implications. Vieira and Ford's (1996) study among low-income women in the city of São Paulo demonstrated that sterilized women had misconceptions about the procedure, with one-third of them unsure of its reversal potential or not realizing that reversal might be a problem.

It is important to note that the high appeal of modern health practices does not mean that traditional practices are always devalued or disregarded. A juxtaposition of modern and traditional practices was observed in the beliefs of both the health professionals and the client population. For instance, the health professionals know the concept of reproductive health programs and their educational attempts encompass modern views such as the need to discuss gender relations in regard to sexuality and the need to focus not only on female contraceptives. However, it was seen that health professionals also express traditional views of maternal health care, like seeing older women as irrelevant to group participation and promoting discussions primarily focused on women's pregnancy. This gap of views can be related to the fact that in reality, modern views are not easily accepted and/or replaced by the health professionals and the population in general; they coexist with traditional beliefs. Furthermore, this gap may reflect inadequacies in professionals' training, which was reported to depend much more on individuals' will than on institutions' initiatives. The coexistence of traditional and modern notions of sexuality and reproduction emerged from both the staff and the client population. An instance that demonstrated this was an observation in which a physician encountered audience approval while teaching when she stated being against sterilization and abortion in all circumstances.

Another sign of the endurance of traditional values is that the titles of the groups do not reflect any modern notion of reproductive health, despite being part of PAISM's programs. In short, they are either named family-planning groups or contraceptive groups. And the titles of the groups do reflect the contents usually most discussed. During group observations, debates were rarely on issues related to gender norms, sexuality, third age and reproductive health rights. The debate on these issues may demand contesting the status quo on social issues that most health professionals seemed ill prepared to engage in.

It was observed that health professionals' educational attempts to promote women's health were often inadequate. This inadequacy stems from the following factors. First of all, many health professionals stated not valuing the donated instructional materials they had on hand to use. Second, many health professionals affirmed they did not believe in the possibility that poor women could learn. Thus, their attempts often began with lack of enthusiasm. Third, there was an overall lack of educational materials. For some contents, the materials were nonexistent. Fourth, another problem was the requirement that health educational groups occur on a schedule that was difficult for the client population to follow. This is similar to Moser's (1993) statement that "health facilities in low-income areas are frequently under-subscribed because their opening hours are inappropriate for working mothers" (p. 48). Fifth, the space allocated for educational groups were often too noisy. A dispersed environment was prevalent. Sixth, both health professionals and client women were usually distracted by solicitations. While health professionals were asked by the staff to help other patients, the client population had constant requests to devote attention to their family members and children. Seventh, class contents tended to be very repetitive to make up for absent or late women. However, this bored those women who were usually present and on time. Still, in most classes observed, repeating seemed a strategy for the health professionals to revalidate their assumption that the client women would have difficulty understanding the contents exposed. Finally, there were very few attempts by health professionals to verify whether women learned accurately the knowledge to which they were exposed.

One of the analyses focused on the client population's concepts of reproductive health. Based on the study by Subbarao and Raney (1992), which concluded that schooling has a greater impact on women than do family-planning programs, in this study, formal educational attainment of the client population was analyzed in regard to reproductive health concepts expressed during interviews. The majority of the population who studied until the 6th grade had difficulty in explaining essential concepts of reproductive health, such as HIV transmission. Those who studied until the 8th grade were inclined to respond correctly to reproductive health concepts. However, only those who finished high school were able to discuss reproductive health rights. This research finding is not surprising, given that the health education groups observed were brief, encompassing only a few hours in a few weeks.

MYTHS AND THEIR CONSEQUENCES

It is necessary to search for educational solutions for both the client and staff populations. On the one hand stand the occasional visits of poor women to public health clinics. One the other hand stands the staff population (with inadequate pedagogical training and instructional materials). The challenge is to look for social spaces, where poor and uneducated women can be truly educated. This means not only informing them about any concept that is important to improve their lives, but it also signifies the need to change the interactions and educational attempts they have in the existent social spaces.

Thus, thinking on how to foster change for women's empowerment, some recommendations for staff are related to changes in their expectations in regard to women coming to health education meetings or medical appointments in the days prearranged by the professionals. Usually, health professionals get frustrated with the women's absence, failing to address the issue that no true time negotiation occurred with the population they serve. The client population usually does not have the habit of participating in educational groups and setting appointments. In addition, they live under precarious conditions, which restrain any endeavor that demands time and money.

The fact that the client population does not take part in the programs as health professionals can be seen less as a lack of motivation and more as related to the lack of appropriate criteria for the establishment of these programs. It cannot be too strongly emphasized that some women's lack of motivation to take part in these health education programs derived from their existing and accurate knowledge of the curriculum. Many women agreed to take part in health education groups only to obtain freely contraceptive devices and not because they needed or desired to learn about the issues raised in these groups. Thus, the current criteria for requiring health education programs are based on myths that need to be clarified.

Myth 1: Poor Women Are Not Smart

Health professionals should question if the level of schooling and information a particular woman has should exempt her participation in any educational program. Some health professionals during interviews said that their clients in public health clinics were mostly poor women and thus, would benefit very much from health educational programs since they did not know basic information. However, during interviews, some poor women complained that these educational meetings were meaningless to them. Some interviewed women did not even recall having taken part in these meetings when first asked. Only when the interview proceeded did they tell me that some time ago they had participated, even it was less than six months ago. Initially, I interviewed women only after program participation. When I noticed that a few health professionals were teaching in the waiting room—either for the lack of an available room or because more women were in the waiting room than in the group meetings—I changed my strategy. I then began interviewing women in the days after they listened to and discussed health information in the waiting room. I interviewed women either in a closed room or in vacant waiting rooms. The following statement shows a moment of discontent of a woman who did not want to be interviewed: " I have a small child and for me it is difficult to come every month to get the free contraceptive. The physician did not like the month I bought at the drugstore. But I cannot afford to stay here hours to get this gratis drug or to discuss anything with you. I have taken the family planning educational classes. Shouldn't that be enough?" Clearly, many women had health knowledge acquired through schooling and attendance at other public health clinics or by informal education (television, family, and friends). Indeed, many women complained of having taken part in health education programs in other institutions, and that this participation had no value in the public health clinics where I met them. Similar complaints were reported in terms of health exams. Those were not always revalidated and often repeated unnecessarily.

The social class division between health professionals and patients supports the myth that poor women are always ignorant. The social class division also generates cultural and political gaps, which reinforce values and practices of health professionals and poor women alike. Bridging the cultural gap would require health care professionals to learn the knowledge which poor women already possess. Politically, if health professionals admit poor women's knowledge they will have to lose status, privilege, and power. Culturally, if poor women believe they have knowledge they will no longer consider health professionals as experts and will be in a position to teach them about their experiences as patients or as people. Politically, if poor women recognize that health professionals lack some sort of knowledge, they will gain status, privilege, and power.

Myth 2: All Poor Women Need Group Lessons on Sexuality and Reproductive Health

Health professionals must also question if a woman desires to take part in health education programs. During class observations, it was noticed that some women did not participate in conversations, and indicated that they were not pleased by some of the issues discussed. When I asked during interviews how they felt about the educational groups and how they felt about the issues discussed, some stated that many times they did not feel at ease to discuss issues related to their sexuality and reproduction in a group situation. During interviews as well, two women told me that they felt uncomfortable discussing sexuality and family-planning issues with someone unknown to them. Thus, it should be seen as a matter of privacy and autonomy for a woman to select the situation in which she prefers to act. The myth of needing to be grouped to learn may relate to the ideal of schooling. Although in group interactions people do learn, this is also true in other situations. People learn by themselves and in the private conversations and interactions they choose.

This myth may also relate to the ideal of there being no taboo on questions regarding sexuality and reproductive health. Nevertheless, it can be very oppressive to anyone to discuss any issue that the person is not prepared or not willing to discuss.

Myth 3: Ideal Health Education Groups Are Formed by Couples

Health professionals must question if a woman desires to come to educational groups with her male partner. Some health professionals were observed saying that they did not know how to attract the male partner to their groups. I discussed this fact with a social worker, who for a short time coordinated one of the public health clinics because there was no physician available. She said, "It is often assumed that the ideal situation is for females and males to discuss together their sexuality and reproductive health." Thus, I decided to include this question in the interview with the client women. In this sample, mixed results were found. While some women stated that this situation was desirable, others felt it was an invasion of privacy. It is important to mention that those who did not desire the company of their partners in the group had different kinds of relationships. While some women reported having good relationships, others reported having bad ones. In addition, some reported having stable partners, while others discussed their occasional affairs. This myth may relate to the ideal of preserving the partnership and family unit as if the couple did not have individual lives as well as shared lives.

Myth 4: Only Personal Motivation Counts, Social Context Is Irrelevant

Health professionals must question if a particular woman's living arrangements impede her participation. Very few health professionals discussed the difficulties experienced by women to come to the meetings. Most complained that they were not motivated enough. On the other hand, many women reported not being able to come to the public health clinic or any other educational endeavor on a regular basis due to their work, to childcare tasks, and to the danger of being shot due to regular gunfights in their communities. Thus, public health clinics must offer night and weekend schedules for the client population they serve so that they can participate. At present, the hours serve the health professionals' needs more than those of the client population. This myth may relate to the ideal that the individual is the responsible unit with society lacking problems. In addition, some health professionals had no training on social issues.

Myth 5: Without Ideal Grouping Conditions to Teach, Educational Efforts Are Undermined

Health professionals must not expect ideal group situations in which to teach. Many health professionals expect to have as clients those who have first gone to a medical appointment and who then come to all health education appointments. A nurse who gave up teaching after I observed some of her class-rooms said,

The women do not come. When I have a group of eight women, only three come the next week. Many do not end up using the contraceptive chosen during group discussions. Sometimes they initiate a contraceptive practice but do not follow the procedure. I have been waiting many afternoons without any women coming to the group. You know women come more in the morning. So, I think it is best for me to do my usual nurse activities.

It is important to note that this nurse, as well as other health professionals, had sent women home when only two women came.

It was observed that health professionals were more effective when they took advantage of situations compelled by necessity; for instance, if the reserved room was taken, the waiting room was used instead. Despite the noise, it was observed that the waiting room is a privileged space for nonformal education purposes because while women wait for information and individual or group appointments, they can use their time to discuss important health information with one another and with health professionals. Finally, while instructional materials such as texts and videos based on health issues can aid these discussions, these may unfold without them. This myth may relate to the ideal of sequential learning and the ideal that learning occurs in group situations. Nevertheless, learning is not a linear process and may occur on unplanned occasions.

Myth 6: Learning That Is Not Health Specific Is Irrelevant

During the interviews and classroom observations, none of the health professionals mentioned how illiteracy and low levels of education might hamper the client population's abilities to understand essential health concepts and take care of themselves and their families. Nor did they ever suggest that women engage in any free educational opportunities available in their communities. On two occasions, I have seen client women ask for these opportunities, but the health professionals did not give any incentive because it did not deal with reproductive health. As a feedback procedure of this research, when I discussed with health professionals the need for both formal education and nonformal education for the client women, some claimed that it was difficult to teach the women due to their low level of understanding and reading. These women need more educational opportunities. Likewise, health professionals need as well to not only learn more about the health and social benefits of general adult education for poor women, but also about what is offered at the communities they serve so that women might take advantage of the few educational opportunities in existence.

This myth may relate to the ideal of specialized education that prevails in Western societies. It appeared to me that the health teaching practices disregard "teachable moments," because instructors are too attached to the health specific contents that they have planned to teach. For instance, a client woman complained that during the five years she used birthcontrol pills she had no sexual desire. Instead of acknowledging that this could be a side effect and discussing other factors in play, such as workload and the relationship itself, the instructor said that this was impossible and continued to advertise the good side of pill usage.

The line drawn around health education practices was recently reinforced in a meeting of health professionals and client women. The meeting was intended to discuss the past and the future of the work toward women's health. During this occasion, a client woman complained that she did not like that smoking was permitted in the clinic waiting room. A social worker replied that this issue was not related to the meeting, but should be discussed afterward, after the presentation of the clinic's plans. Any health professional present could have used this instance more effectively. It took a great while for the client women to start talking. When a few did so, discussion should have been stimulated. Perhaps in this case, discussions could have centered around the difficulties of public health clinics in being a health model, or the bad health effects of combining pills with smoking and of smoking during pregnancy.

Myth 7: Education Only Occurs Through Preestablished Settings and Trained Personnel

In feedback discussions on the research, health professionals tended to agree that the poor population would only learn by the interventions of the health education groups and those willing to teach in these groups. It was generally assumed that learning in educational groups was the path. Some expressed doubts about their abilities and the setting being inadequate due to the noise and the fact that it was not like formal schooling with requirements to fulfill, except for attendance. Although many interactions occur (among patients, health professionals, and administrative staff) and a lot of educational folders are displayed, these informal instances of learning were not taken into account. Interestingly, only the client population, not the professionals, clearly spoke about the medical appointment as an educational tool. The relationship of trust in these appointments and the time taken to explain were seen as factors that led to learning. This myth relates to the privilege that formal education has over other forms of education.

Myth 8: Health Education and Health Services Are for the Client Population

Although the overtly stated intent of health education and services are for the client population, both also serve the professional population. It must be recognized that work settings benefit the employees. In fact, sometimes these benefits are greater for the employees than for the client population. For in-stance, in both public health clinics studied, there were more brochures for nonformal educational courses designed for the health professionals' employ-ees than for the client population. And, the working schedule is structured much more around employees' hours than those of the clients.

CONCLUSION

As the literature review shows, family-planning programs in Brazil were ini-tiated without being a consequence of explicit policies. Thus, only by analyz-ing policy as practice can we identify the historical conditions that shaped the emergence of Brazilian family planning. An analysis of policy as practice can also identify where implementation falls short of specified or assumed goals, such as the present Brazilian policy intended to provide comprehensive health for women. This policy includes health education that is not accessible to all, and when there is access, there are instances that it may fail to address its prom-ises: proper health information and the health rights and educational concerns of poor women. At the same time, analysis of policy as a practice can evince concrete possibilities of change, such as the ill training of health professionals about social (and sometimes health) issues, education, and teaching; the lack of a standard curriculum to follow; and some health professionals' views.

It is important to stress that the studied health professionals' views are not necessarily internally consistent. There is also a gap in perceptions between health care professionals and the client women. But there are still three kinds of shared myths that were often, though not unanimously, encountered in both populations. The first myth was that physicians knew more than did other health professionals, even for issues upon which they were not experts. For in-stance, a social worker asked that she be interviewed together with the physi-cian in charge because he was more entitled than she to answer questions regarding the organization of the public health clinic and about the client pop-ulation. I agreed, and, during the interview, observed how the educator re-sponded to more of my questions than did the doctor. Furthermore, it was observed that the only female physician attracted many more women than do other health professionals for her group discussions. Third, it was observed that some health educational groups had two health professionals teaching. When the female physician was teaching with the nurse or social worker, the client women directed all questions to the physician. The questions were not always health-related, but some were of interpersonal relations. It is important to note that not all of these women directing questions to the physician had known her before.

The second myth was related to learning. Learning was not viewed as oc-curring through informal interactions among health professionals and client women. Although I observed some moments of informal interactions be-tween client women and health professionals, in no interview or observation were these interactions mentioned as learning moments. Informal learning can be difficult due to the use of technical vocabulary not often understood by the population, thereby making them afraid to ask questions. Once in the waiting room, a health professional made the following recommendation: "Now, we are revalidating exams. For that you must bring your transcription." I did not understand what "transcription" meant. So, I first asked the two women sitting next to me if they knew the word. Since they did not know, I asked the health professional if she could explain the word. She did so, saying, "This is a word that we often use. I assumed you all knew." In a later discussion, I remarked to her that we often use words that others may not understand. She responded that usually the clients are afraid to ask for meanings. However, even if specific content is not learned or information not understood, it is not possible to assume that no learning has occurred. The misinterpretation of a message is part of the learning process involving personal and social construction of meanings. And learning includes nonverbal messages and ways of interacting. Nonetheless, learning through nonformal education was sometimes devalued for lacking formal educational standards.

The third myth was that medical concepts related to health were always better than popular ones. The concepts of healthy women that were elaborated during interviews usually related to compliance with modern medical practices. A few times, other, more popular concepts emerged during interviews. These were related to having a good sense of humor, to talking about problems outside the family, and to using herbs. But perhaps because the women were interviewed in public health clinics, when they talked about these notions, they allied it to the primary need to follow the physician recommendations. During class observations, it was generally agreed that a healthy woman had this condition because she prevented disease by following prescribed exams and, moreover, that when infected by STDs she brought her companion for treatment, although some expressed difficulties in convincing their partners. The use of herbs to provoke abortions was discussed as devastating for women's health. However, no proper use of herbs was ever mentioned, such as the relief of menstrual nausea symptoms.

The myths identified restrain educational efforts. The myths are not only an expression of class divisions between female professionals and female clients, but also help to sustain these class divisions. The myths ascribe to all women lack of knowledge, independent of verifying individual levels of knowledge, not to mention the diversity of experiences among clients. The fact of seeing all women as ignorant resembles the concept of homogenous "Other" attributed to Third World women (Mohanty, 1991), in which they are seen as an equally destitute group. It is my impression that in reality, what we do not know we tend to see as homogeneous. The perception of the complexities and idiosyncrasies emerges out of deep knowledge.

For the empowerment of women in public health clinics, the possibilities lie in clarifying these myths. Learning about the other is more difficult than ascribing some values as a group. Nevertheless, for educational policies to work, they must address and reverse myths so that the few spaces already allocated for adult women's education are better utilized. Educational polices must disseminate the social benefits of formal education for social development, such as improved health of women and their families. These potential benefits need to be learned not only by poor women and health professionals, but also by the population in general. Nevertheless, this learning must be coupled with growing incentives for the education of poor women and girls. Both public and private organizations can work in alliance to offer these incentives.

In health education, concrete and critical knowledge can make a fundamental contribution to women's empowerment, given that the learning really improves life conditions. For this purpose, teaching health knowledge needs to be critical, discussing how health choices and options are grounded in ideological standards, medical specialization, market strategies, and consumerist values. In the specific case of the literature on reproductive health, empowerment is related to women owning their bodies. Germain and Antrobus (1989) argue that a liberating form of reproductive health education (with appropriate clinical support) enables women

the ability to enjoy sexual relations without fear of infection, unwanted pregnancy, or coercion; to regulate fertility without risk of unpleasant or dangerous side effects; to go safely through pregnancy and childbirth, and to bear and raise healthy children. (p. 18)

Yet the true possibility of women owning their bodies as a result of increased health knowledge has to be questioned. For example, Lefrève (1999) criticizes the fact that in consumerist societies, bodies are perceived as healthier the more they consume goods. Thus, it must be recognized that while reproductive health knowledge is essential to women's empowerment, this knowledge does not necessarily translate into women's empowerment.[7]

It is important to note that, in order to be emancipatory, not only do the contents of health education need to be relevant and critical, but also the methods used to teach must take into account the reality of those involved. The methods chosen to teach are at times even more important than the contents. For example, if the method of teaching about gender norms is authoritarian, then the lesson provides no vision of nonauthoritarian relationships with partners, physicians, children, and so on.

The limits for empowerment of women are anchored in myths. The social structure can be rigid in supporting and reinforcing these myths. Policy as a practice analysis can search for moments of divergence among actors, when their initiatives deviate from an imposed policy. In this research, the bending of the systems' rules was noticed twice. First, it was seen when health professionals did not require the client women to take part in the health education programs. Second, it was viewed when the coordinators of the program allowed the researcher to start conducting her work without warning about the needed bureaucracy involved. These cases of bending the rules share a logic. In the first case, the few physicians who did not adhere to the clinic coordinator ideas of sending their patients to health educational groups were those who did not see the purpose in these groups. They were following different criteria, which cannot be judged as incorrect, when they took time to teach women or verify if they had the necessary knowledge. The other health professionals explained this lack of association as related to financial reasons, since educational groups provide less money than medical appointments. Nevertheless, these were a few of the health professionals mentioned by the patients as taking the time to teach during the medical appointment. In the second case, the bending of the rules was done because the bureaucracy involved in undertaking research often impedes its course and is not helpful to the research. Thus, when the health professionals allowed it, they knew the unnecessary difficulties involved.

Nevertheless, it is not always possible to escape inflexibility and the limits imposed by institutions. For instance, a health professional can truly negotiate an adequate hour for a group with the client population only if he or she has a voice in the working hours of the institution and if he or she does not hold another job, which is not always the case. Still, a health professional could like to teach, if he or she can be equally paid to teach as he or she is to provide medical care. This would demand verifying the effectiveness of educational impact on health-protective behavior, which is more difficult than analyzing if a drug prescription worked on a given patient. Moreover, a health professional could feel familiar with instructional materials if he or she were trained appropriately to use them. To select educational materials is part of a process of owning them, and engaging in the initial step of any educational effort is to make a choice and plan. Nevertheless, since training to educate is dependent upon individual initiative, it is not fair to expect health professionals to be good teachers.

The educational myths identified in the settings studied might be generalized to other similar ones structured by the same sort of difficulties. Yet, more important than verifying the extent to which a given myth is prevalent or not, is the task to address any myth that undermines education. This should be a requirement for any educational policy implementation that attempts to empower poor women. This is a challenge that demands understanding the social function exerted by myths and how they help to secure the ideas and social fabric of a social system. The power exerted by myths cannot be denied.

NOTES

1. I am indebted to those who empowered me while pursuing this endeavor: (1) The interviewed women and professionals who shared their experiences; (2) Dr. Brani Rozemberg from Oswaldo Cruz Foundation for her valuable insights; (3) Dr. Ellen Hardy, president of Asociación Latinoamericana de Investigadores en Reproducción Humana, for her huge effort in bringing together medical and social scientists; and (4) Dr. Margaret Sutton, co-editor of this book, for her great work in this editing

process which was so encouraging and pedagogical. I am also grateful to the research support received from CNPq/FIOCRUZ (Process Numbers 30.0863/96-9 and 30.0863/96-3) and FAPERJ (Process Number E-26/170.390/98 INST).

2. Fink (1992) described differences between nonformal education and popular education, which have been used interchangeably, or with different meanings. According to her analysis, while both aim at individual behavioral changes, popular education is more associated with the connotation of aiming at social transformation.

3. Freire (1994) claimed that for a progressive educator, the use of small expository themes is not bad in itself as long as the exposition is accompanied by an analysis of this exposition, made by both students and professor.

4. Yet the segments of the State concerned with limiting population control had divergence over ways to conquer this objective. While some supported population control measures and thus women's fertility regulation as a means to foster economic development, others argued that population control could best be attained through the development of Brazilian educational and occupational systems.

5. This is a limited approach because it does not involve the discussion of women, sexuality, and conditions of quality of life addressing factors such as housing, sanitation, work, education, leisure, and so on (Oliveira, Carvalho, Frustock, & Luz, 1992). And structural conditions are so important that Hernandez (1984), studying whether family planning programs contributed to fertility reduction between the mid-1960's to the mid-1970's—through studies of individual Third World countries and a cross-national research for 83 Third World countries—came to the conclusion that family planning programs' success was limited depending on several socioeconomic conditions and changes.

6. The 20 professional women's educational backgrounds were described in a previous article emphasizing the role nonformal, informal, and formal education had in shaping their gender awareness and in leading to their professional positions (Sousa, 1998).

7. For instance, learning about contraceptive choices is essential, but this knowledge cannot be learned without a critical perspective. Berquó (1999) demonstrates how much more women from the Third World resort to modern and irreversible contraceptive choices than those women living in the First World. The pressure to sell contraceptives and the ideology of population control need to be discussed with poor women. Therefore, an appropriate health education program needs to include questioning about the extent to which health choices are shaped by cultural, political, and market pressures.

REFERENCES

Allevato, C. L. (1986). Mitos na educação de adultos. [Myths in adult education]. *Fórum Educacional, 10*(2), 31–42.

Alvarez, S. E. (1989). Politicizing gender and engendering democracy. In A. Stepan (Ed.), *Democratizing Brazil: Problems of transition and consolidation* (pp. 205–251). New York: Oxford University Press.

Antrobus, P. (1989). The empowerment of women. In R. S. Gallin, M. Aronoff, & A. Ferguson (Eds.), *The women and international development annual* (pp. 189–207). San Francisco: Westview Press.

Barroso, C., & Bruschini, C. (1991). Building politics from personal lives: Discussions on sexuality among poor women in Brazil. In C. T. Mohanty, A. Russo, & L. Torres (Eds.), *Third World women and the politics of feminism* (pp. 153–172). Indianapolis: Indiana University Press.

Berquó, E. (1999). Contraception and caesarians in Brazil: An example of bad reproductive health practice in need of exemplary action [Special issue]. *Revista Estudos Feministas.*

Branford, S. (1993). Introduction. In D. Green (Ed.), *Women in Brazil: Caipora women's group* (pp. 1–12). London: Latin America Bureau.

Conway, J. K., & Bourque, C. (Eds.). (1995). *The politics of women's education: Perspectives from Asia, Africa, and Latin America.* Ann Arbor: University of Michigan Press.

Darcy de Oliveira, R., & Harper, B. (1985). As mulheres em movimento. Ler a própria vida, escrever a própria história. In P. Freire, R. Darcy de Oliveira, M. Darcy de Oliveira, & C. Ceccon (Eds.), *Vivendo e aprendendo. Experiências do IDAC em educação popular* (8th ed.). São Paulo, Brazil: Brasiliense.

Dixon-Mueller, R. (1993). *Population policy and women's rights: Transforming reproductive choice.* Westport, CT: Praeger.

Fink, M. (1992). Women and popular education in Latin America. In N. Stromquist, *Women and education in Latin America: Knowledge, power and change* (pp. 171–193). Boulder, CO: Lynne Rienner.

Foreith, J., Rodrigues, W., Arruda, J. M., & Milare, J. (1983). A cost-effectiveness comparison of service delivery systems and geographic areas in Piaui State, Brazil. In I. Siradeglin, D. Salkerer, & R. Osborn (Eds.), *Evaluating population policies: International experience with cost-effectiveness analysis and cost-benefit analysis.* New York: St. Martin's Press.

Freire, P. (1987). *Ação cultural para a liberdade e outros escritos* [Cultural action towards liberty and other writings] (8th ed.). Rio de Janeiro: Paz e Terra.

Freire, P. (1993). *Pedagogia do oprimido* [Pedagogy of the oppressed] (22nd ed.). Rio de Janeiro: Paz e Terra.

Freire, P. (1994). *Pedagogia da esperança: Um reencontro com a Pedagogia do oprimido* [Pedagogy of hope: A meeting again with the Pedagogy of the oppressed] (3rd ed.). Rio de Janeiro: Paz e Terra.

García-Moreno, C., & Claro, A. (1994). Challenges from the women's health movement: Women's rights versus population control. In G. Sen, A. Germain, & L. C. Chen (Eds.), *Population policies reconsidered: Health, empowerment and rights* (pp. 46–61). Boston: Harvard University Press.

Germain, A., & Antrobus, P. (1989). New partnerships in reproductive health care. *Populi, 16*(4), 18–30.

Giffin, K. (1994). Women's health and the privatization of fertility control in Brazil. *Social Science Medicine, 39*(3), 355–360.

Heise, L. (1993). Violence against women: The missing agenda. In M. Koblinsky, J. Timyan, & J. Gay (Eds.), *The health of women: A global perspective* (pp. 171–195). San Francisco: Westview Press.

Hernandez, D. J. (1984). *Success or failure? Family planning programs in the Third World.* Westport, CT: Greenwood.

Hubley, J. H. (1986). Barriers to health education in developing countries. *Health Education Research*, *1*(4), 233–245.

Israel, G. R., & Vellozo, V.R.0. (1996). *Mulher e saúde: práticas educativas em 11 municípios* [Women and health: educational practices in 11 municipalities]. Rio de Janeiro: IBAM/ENSUR/NEMPP

Laura, R. S., & Heaney, S. (1990). *Philosophical foundations of health education*. New York: Routledge.

Lefrève, F. (1999). Mitologia sanitária. Saúde, doença, mídia e linguagem [Sanitary mythology: Health, disease media and language]. São Paulo, Brazil: Edusp.

Lephoto, H. M. (1995). Educating women for empowerment in Lesotho. *Convergence*, *28*(3), 5–13.

Li, V. C., & Wong, G. (1989). *Emerging terminology in public health related to people's action for health: A critical review*: Working paper. WHO Group on Health Promotion in Developing Countries.

Mohanty, C.T. (1991). Under Western eyes: Feminist Scholarship and Colonial discoarses." In C. T. Mohanty, A. Russo, & L. Torres (Eds.), *Cartographies of struggle: Third World women and the politics of feminism* (pp. 51–80). Bloomington: Indiana University Press.

Molyneux, M. (1985). Mobilization without emancipation? Women's interests, the State, and revolution in Nicaragua. *Feminist Studies*, *11*(2), 227–254.

Morris, W. (Ed.). (1981). *The American Heritage dictionary of the English language*. Boston: Houghton Mifflin.

Moser, C.O.N. (1993). *Gender planning and development: Theory, practice and training*. New York: Routledge.

Oliveira, M. R., Carvalho, P. H., Frustock, L., & Luz, A. M. H. (1992). Análise das condições sócio-econômicas e reprodutivas de mulheres de uma comunidade de Porto Alegre, RS [Analysis of socioeconomic and reproductive conditions of women from a peripheric community of Porto Alegre, RS]. *Revista Gaúcha de Enferm.*, *13*(1), 5–11.

Pessoa, F. (1965). *Fernando Pessoa: Obra Poética*. [Collected poems]. Rio de Janeiro: Companhia Aguilar Editora.

Ribeiro, M. (1993). Direitos reprodutivos e políticas descartáveis [Reproductive rights and disposable policies]. *Estudos Feministas*, *1*(2), 400–407.

Rodrigues, W. (1977). Brazil. In B. W. Watson, (Eds.), *Family planning in the developing world: A review of programs* (pp. 41–42). New York: The Population Council.

Rutenberg N., & Ferraz, E. A. (1988). Female sterilization and its demographic impact in Brazil. *International Family Perspectives*, *14*(2), 61–68.

Sai, F. T., & Nassim, J. (1989). The need for a reproductive health approach. *International Journal of Gynecological Obstetrics*, Suppl. 3, 103–113.

Schall, V. T., Jurberg, P., Rozemberg, B., Vasconcellos, M.C., Boruchovitch, E., & Félix-Sousa, I. C. (1987). Health education for children: The project "Ciranda da Saúde." Proceedings of the Fourth International Symposium on World Trends in Science and Technology Education. *Science and Technology Education and Quality of Life*, *1*, 115–118.

Schultz, S. (1993). Women and the fight for rights. Having children? That's our decision! The women's health movement and population. In D. Green (Ed.),

Women in Brazil: Caipora women's group (pp. 81–87). London: Latin America Bureau.

Shor, I. (1992). *Empowering education: Critical teaching for social change.* Chicago: University of Chicago Press.

S.O.S. Corpo. (1991). *Viagem ao mundo da contracepção: Um guia sobre os métodos anticoncepcionais* [Travelling to the world of contraception: A guide for contraceptive methods]. Rio de Janeiro: Rosa dos Tempos.

Sousa, I.C.F. (1995). Discussing women's reproductive health, religion, roles and rights: Achieving women's empowerment. *Convergence, 28*(3), 45–51.

Sousa, I.C.F. (1998). The educational background of women working for women in Rio de Janeiro. *Convergence, 3*(3), 30–37.

Stambler, M. (1984). *Health education for health promotion in less developed nations* (Report No. SO-015–678). (ERIC Document Reproduction Service No. E. 244 879) (unpublished).

Stromquist, N. (1986). Empowering women through education: Lessons from international co-operation. *Convergence, 19*(4), 1–21.

Stromquist, N. (1993). *The theoretical and practical basis for empowerment.* Paper presented at the International Seminar on Women's Education and Empowerment, Hamburg, Germany.

Stromquist, N. (1994). Education for the empowerment of women: Two Latin American experiences. In V. D'Oyley, A. Blunt, & R. Barnhard (Eds.), *Education and development: Lessons from the Third World.* Calgary, Canada: Detselig.

Stycos, J. M. (1971). *Ideology, faith, and family planning in Latin America: Studies in public and private opinion on fertility control.* New York: McGraw-Hill.

Subbarao, K., & Raney, L. (1992, November). *Social gains from female education. A cross-national study.* Women in Development Division, Population and Human Resources Department, The World Bank.

Vieira, E. M., & Ford, N.J. (1996). The provision of female sterilization in São Paulo, Brazil: A study among low income women. *Social Science Medicine, 42*(10), 1427–1432.

Wallerstein, N., & Bernstein, E. (1988). Empowerment education: Freire's ideas adapted to health education. *Health Education Quarterly, 15*(4), 389–394.

Watson, B. W. (Eds.). (1977). *Family planning in the developing world: A review of programs.* New York: The Population Council.

World Development Report 1993: Investing in health. (1993). New York: Oxford University Press.

PART III

COMMUNITY–EDUCATOR NEGOTIATIONS OF POLICY MEANINGS AND PRACTICE

9

The Impact of Life Histories on Local Policy: New Immigrant Education in the Rural Midwest

Sandra L. Cade

INTRODUCTION

By focusing on various stories impacting the life of a particular immigrant boy in a particular midwest USAmerican[1] town, this chapter reveals the importance of situational context in policy implementation. Gathered in connection with a larger ethnographic study of a rural town undergoing demographic change, the narratives illustrate the ways that the boy, who I call Luís, his family, and educators in Redbud School Corporation (pseudonym) appropriate federal and state educational policy to fit cultural and institutional stories.

I begin with a brief summary of U.S. federal policy for the education of children whose home language is other than English, as well as a sketch of state-level language policy for Indiana, where this study takes place. A portrait of the community in which these policies are implemented and appropriated, and a description of methodology, follow this introduction. A compilation of metanarratives from both the long-term residents and new immigrants whose lives come together in the town I call Beneville, informs the situational context discovered through ethnographic research. With this background, the reader then enters into a narrative illustration of the intersection of life histories and local policy implementation. The chapter concludes with a call for policymakers to consider the importance of the knowledge gained from such studies, particularly in light of changing demographics and regional notions of best practices for immigrant education.

POLICY CONSIDERATIONS

Federal Level

Article X of the USAmerican Constitution places control of education at the state level and, with the notable exceptions of teacher licensing and school accreditation, local control of curriculum and pedagogy is the norm throughout the nation. Nonetheless, the carrot-and-stick nature of both state and federal programs impacts the ways in which local schools operate.

Several federal laws and court rulings stand behind educational policies that allow and, indeed, require the use of languages other than English for some instruction in the public schools. Three of the most important are presented in Figure 9.1. Under Title VI of the Civil Rights Act of 1964, threat of loss of all federal funding sometimes has been effectively used to convince local school boards to address language issues as required by the Equal Educational Opportunities Act of 1974. English-Only and Official English proponents recently failed in passing federal legislation,[2] which would have raised a Constitutional challenge to the Supreme Court case *Lau v. Nichols*. This 1974 landmark ruling in favor of the parents of Chinese-language-dominant children in San Francisco schools has served as a rationale for bilingual education ever since.

State Level

In the wake of *Lau v. Nichols*, Indiana legislators established a bilingual/bicultural educational policy in 1976. Recognizing "the need for and the desirability of" programs to "aid students to reach their full academic level of achievement and preserve an awareness of cultural and linguistic heritage,"

Figure 9.1
USAmerican Federal Law Pertinent to Languages

Civil Rights Act. Title VI, 1964

No person in the United States shall, on the grounds of race, color, or national origin. . . be denied the benefits of, or be subjected to discrimination under any program or activity receiving Federal financial assistance.

Equal Educational Opportunities Act, 1974

No state shall deny equal educational opportunity to an individual on account of his or her race, color, sex or national origin, by . . . the failure of an educational agency to take appropriate action to overcome language barriers that impede equal participation by its students in its instructional program.

Lau v. Nichols, 1974

Equality of educational opportunity is not achieved by merely providing all students with the same facilities, teachers and curriculum: [because] students who do not understand English are effectively foreclosed from any meaningful education.

this progressive policy called for such programs "for all qualified students enrolled in Indiana public schools." Responsibility for program design and establishment was placed at the local level. The policy was reviewed and reaccepted in 1984, just two years before the single-line legislation establishing English as the official language of the State of Indiana. The bilingual/bicultural policy, which has never been funded,[3] remains on the books at the turn of the millennium.

As the official agency charged with directing the policy, the Division of Language Minority and Migrant Programs relies on federal funding to oversee officially approved bilingual and bicultural programs. The Division provides schools with guidelines for the development of local policy for students whose first language is other than English (see Figure 9.2). It also makes annual reports of efforts to record the numbers of students designated as limited and functionally proficient in English (LEP and FEP). Within budgetary constraints, it provides teacher training for school corporations that request it.

Figure 9.2
Guidelines for Language Policy from Indiana's Division of Language Minority and Migrant Programs

Indiana Guidelines to Satisfy Legal Requirements of Legislation Impacting Language Minority Students
(Title VI of the Civil Rights Act of 1964, Lau v. Nichols (1974), Equal Educational Opportunities Act of 1974, Indiana Public Law 218 and 511)

Establishment of Policies and Procedures

Home Language Survey

Student Language Fluency Assessment

Student Placement Standards

Minimum 10 hours of ESL (Variety of approaches allowed)/Student Placement Standards

Specific Placement Criteria for Exceptional Language Minority Students

Retention not Solely Based on English Language Proficiency

Sufficient Qualified Personnel for Appropriate Service Delivery (1:15 ratio)

Explicit Criteria for Termination of ESL Services to Limited English Proficient Students

Interaction with English-speaking Peers

School/Home Communication in Native/Preferred Home Language

Report and Review

Implementation Plan

Annual Performance Review

Training

Designed and Offered by Division of Language Minority and Migrant Programs

Local Implementation and Appropriation

Like many Indiana school systems surprised by recent demographic change brought about by an influx of immigrants, Redbud Corporation is slowly working to come into compliance with the guidelines. While the focus of the remainder of this chapter is the appropriation of one particular policy guideline ("Retention not solely based on English language proficiency"), I offer here a brief discussion of the entire set of guidelines as evidence of Redbud's efforts to comply with federal and state legislation and policy. Ten years ago, the corporation had no experience with language policy issues. As the specific policy discussion will illustrate, the life history experiences of local actors deeply influence the construction of local policy impacting children who arrive at school speaking a language other than English.

The presence of growing numbers of students from Spanish-speaking homes prompted a January 1998 Redbud School Board decision to establish an ESL coordinator position. Not having budgeted in advance meant insufficient funds for a certified position. A school board member noted that no bilingual applicants would take the position "at the salary we are offering and with the sort of tenuous nature of the program." The person hired for the position held only an elementary school certificate with neither an ESL nor a bilingual endorsement.

Upon her employment, the new ESL coordinator enrolled in an endorsement program at the state university. With corporation funding, she attended a summer 1998 workshop in Colorado sponsored by TESOL (Teachers of English to Speakers of Other Languages). In addition to regularly sharing her growing knowledge through individual communications with administrators and faculty, in fall 1998 she arranged for a day-long middle and high school consultation by a university professor with expertise in ESL, bilingual, and culturally relevant pedagogy and methods. The university expert's visit was scheduled as a lead-in activity for a county-wide multicultural conference. Still, other than the ESL coordinator and the director of Title I reading and parent outreach, no Redbud personnel attended.

Compliance with the state policy guideline for a minimum of 10 hours of ESL instruction and sufficient qualified personnel for a 1:15 ratio depends on how one defines qualified ESL instruction. The "variety of approaches" allowed under both *Lau v. Nichols* and Indiana's language policy is of concern to both practitioners and researchers experienced in ESL and bilingual education (cf. Cummins, 1998; Greene, 1998; Krashen, 1996; Willig, 1985). In Beneville, regular teachers with little or no background in methods or pedagogy for second-language learners are responsible for making decisions about appropriate practice within their classrooms. In 1998–99, only the ESL coordinator was officially assigned to deliver ESL services to nearly 80 students, grades K-12, in five separate buildings. There are, however, several volunteers, including a peer tutor program initiated by the ESL coordinator.

In addition to K–12 curricular responsibility, the ESL coordinator maintains program records and submits an annual performance review to the school board. Although the middle school principal reported that the school corporation was "really counting on the ESL coordinator position to help us make some decisions," none of the coordinator's fall 1998 or 1999 recommendations[4] were funded. The school board generally defers to the superintendent for curricular decisions and, while it "recognized the issue of LEP students" at both its March and August 1999 retreats, no written plan or specific strategies exist.

The home language survey, once an informal decision made by whomever enrolled a student, now includes paperwork that parents/guardians must complete. Similarly, a formal testing process using the Woodcock-Muñoz language fluency test has replaced classroom teacher-based decisions about student language fluency. The ESL coordinator reports that Language Minority and Migrant Program personnel agree with her own concern about the test's accuracy, but consider it a reasonable compromise given time and staffing limitations in local sites.

Students initially are placed with age peers in regular classrooms. Based on testing, the ESL coordinator informs teachers what they can expect students to do. Termination of whatever ESL services exist also is determined via this testing system.[5] Many Spanish language-dominant students have Individualized Education Programs (IEPs) and receive special education services to aid in what teachers describe as "overcoming their language barrier." Generally, these services are provided through pullout programs, but primary school children have been assigned to separate special education classes. In one case, an elementary-certified teacher working as an aide[6] reports that a student "probably doesn't need special education," but will be kept in the program at least another school year while "he makes progress in his English." There is currently no special education testing service in Spanish in the corporation, and no Spanish-speaking counselors are available within the county.

Most long-term residents believe that learning English as quickly as possible is a primary responsibility for new immigrants, but ESL and ABE (Adult Basic Education) classes sponsored by various churches, the community college, and local employers have low enrollments. New immigrant adults report long working hours, childcare concerns, and learning difficulties as attendance deterrents.[7] Few parents report understanding communications sent from school. The primary school principal purchased translating software for home–school communications, but there is no regular Spanish language communication process corporation-wide. The bilingual father of a first-grade child was unsure of the meaning of a message translated by the software program. Administrators and teachers attempt to find interpreters for school conferences. There is a concerted effort not to use older siblings for such meetings. Because the use of volunteer interpreting services impacts its quality and availability, parents and school personnel sometimes are unable to communicate easily.

Although the ESL coordinator is a monolingual speaker of English, she and some teachers are trying to learn some Spanish. While the school corporation has arranged for summer courses in conversational Spanish, some teachers report frustration that classes are not available within school buildings during the year. Middle and high school teachers have begun to consider the use of materials available in Spanish,[8] and some elementary teachers send home worksheets in both English and Spanish (the first language of all currently enrolled students).

For the last few years, most Spanish-language-dominant students have not received grades and are evaluated on effort alone. Teachers are aware of a dictum against grade retention based solely on English-language proficiency, so students who attend regularly and "try hard" are passed from grade to grade. The former director of a now defunct Hispanic advocate agency reported that the unwritten "no grade retention" policy for LEP students resulted from a threatened lawsuit over a 1994 attempt to withhold graduation from a Hispanic 12th grader because he "hadn't mastered the language yet." The policy is a source of irritation among faculty members who fret about "compromising curriculum." Many regular classroom teachers consider LEP student learning to be the responsibility of the ESL coordinator and look to alternative programs, rather than altering their own pedagogical practices to meet student needs.

Teachers often comment on the "very good behavior" of their Spanish-language-dominant students, who are praised for "sitting quietly." Parents, pleased at such reports on their children's behavior,[9] do not realize that social promotion does not necessarily indicate content mastery sufficient for the next level.

SITE DESCRIPTION AND METHODOLOGY

Beneville

The early 1990s intentional importation of a primarily Mexican and Salvadoran immigrant workforce by a local turkey processing plant has had significant impact in Beneville. With its four-block-square central residential area and a population of 5,242 (1990 Census Bureau figure), Beneville seems more like their small Mexican and Central American villages than the California or Texas metropolises to which many of the new residents first immigrated. The long-term residents were originally unnerved by the arrival of people of color in their county, which counted less than 1% of its population from other census race categories in 1990 (see Figure 9.3). Indeed, one of the biggest issues of diversity in this community, identified by other long-term county residents as "the Protestant town," had previously been intermarriages of Catholics with members of other Christian denominations.

Figure 9.3
A portrait of Beneville in 1990

Small Town

    Total Population   5242

Homogeneous ethnicity

    Primarily Northern European (notably German-American)

    White   5204

    Black   10

    American Indian, Eskimo, or Aleut   9

    Asian or Pacific Islander   11

    Other   8

Homogeneous religious affiliation

    Catholic = 1 church

    Other Christian = 8 churches

    Other Religions = 0

Low Unemployment (County)

  1.2% (August 1998) (Second lowest in state)

School Enrollments: (Percentage of school population)

	Minority		LEP	
1991–92	10	0.6%		
1992–93	8	0.5%		
1993–94	12	0.7%		
1994–95	22	1.3%		
1995–96	31	1.8%		
1996–97	37	2.1%	12	0.7%
1997–98	—	2.6%	18	1.0%
1998–99		5.2%	NA	5.0%

Sources: U.S. Census Bureau, Redbud County newspaper, Indiana Department of Education.

Unemployment in the county is historically low, with workers commuting from surrounding areas to work in the many wood processing and furniture fabrication plants. The school population of children from Spanish-language dominant homes grew steadily from 1992. The school corporation began counting the LEP students in 1996 and hired an ESL coordinator in January 1998.

Previous Research in Beneville

I first began visiting Beneville in 1994 in connection with a comparative study of academic and economic immigrant mothers' attitudes toward the English language. The former were either university graduate students or had accompanied their spouses to the United States for graduate study; the latter were spouses of Mexican and Salvadoran immigrants working at Major Meats, Beneville's largest employer. Not surprisingly, the study concluded that, no matter their self-perceived English-language proficiency, mothers familiar with school culture were better able to intervene on behalf of their children.

In fall 1996, a 3-month-long qualitative study (observation, interviews, and document analysis) of Beneville's primary school asked, "How do children learn English in Summitdale Elementary?" Findings indicated that pedagogy too heavily focused on self-esteem without knowledge of appropriate teaching strategies for LEP students limited the academic success of immigrant children. These two studies and frequent visits to the town over a 4-year period led to the ethnographic study, *Intercultural Dynamics of Power in a Midwestern Town: Stories of the Enactment of Local Education Policy* (Cade, forthcoming).

Methodology

From mid-June 1998 through early March 1999, I lived, worked, parented, and played with both long-term and new immigrant residents. As a participant observer, I experienced first-hand the local issues surrounding housing, medical and social services, consumer needs, and recreational opportunities. Formal and informal interviews also served the goal of discovering the meaning of these issues for individuals and groups.

The life history component of the study design included individual interviews, group discussions, and an intercultural sharing of stories within gender groups. Five mothers (two Salvadorans and three Mexicans) and five women educators (a primary teacher, two middle school teachers, a school board member, and a volunteer tutor), two male educators (an administrator and a high school teacher), and three fathers (two Mexicans and a Salvadoran) accepted the invitation to participate. Among the men, only the Salvadoran father went beyond the individual interview, joining four of the mothers at the end of their group discussion. I audiotaped the conversations as each group attempted to answer the question, "What do I want my gender counterparts to know about what it means to be a Hispanic immigrant mother/father or long-term resident male/female educator in Beneville?" Both groups discussed the similarities and differences in their histories and talked extensively about their perception of the Other. The two groups were to come together in late 1999 for a conversation designed to facilitate mutual understanding and, thereby, create change in the enactment of local educational policy.

LIFE HISTORIES AND POLICY APPROPRIATION

The ways in which both long-term residents and new immigrants come together (or not) within the community play important roles in the construction, implementation, and appropriation of educational policies. Data collected thus far indicate a wealth of both divergent and convergent intra- and intercultural experiences and beliefs. The two columns in Figure 9.4 juxtapose in-group stories distilled from various data sources. They are held congruously by some, rejected by others, and are apt to change by situation and context. It is beyond the scope of this chapter to provide full background explanations for all of the stories gathered here,[10] but the following brief discussion of sources is offered as ethnographic background through which the reader is invited to consider Redbud School Corporation's no-retention policy. Taken together, the group stories and Luís's particular story should serve as counsel for policymakers concerned about immigrant education in rural communities.

THE META-NARRATIVE "WHAT IT MEANS TO BE AMERICAN"

For new immigrants, choosing to settle in Beneville is a practical decision providing access to steady work and relatively safe living conditions. Similarly, some new immigrants believe the decision to seek USAmerican citizenship should not require significant changes in identity characteristics. Legal definitions of immediate family mean that, even with permanent resident alien status, new immigrants may wait years to unite with the people they identify as close relatives. If they become USAmerican citizens, they usually can bring in spouses and children very quickly and there are no limitations—other than financial—to whom else they can sponsor. Thus, even though Luís's father had purchased a Beneville home with money saved over a lifetime of migrant work, it was the decision to bring his entire family to Beneville that prompted an effort to pass a citizenship test. Although he studied the civics questions, he insisted that he should be allowed to take the test in Spanish, because "llevo muchos años de vivir aquí" (I have lived here for so long).

Long-term residents who accept the continuing new immigrant presence[11] expect assimilation, voicing the belief, "Everything will be okay as soon as they become just like us." For these USAmericans, choosing to settle in Beneville is a decision to embrace the English language and a history that began at Plymouth Rock before expanding westward across the continent.

A regular feature of Beneville's newspaper allows local pastors to write "From the Pulpit." Brother John Parrish offered white male heroes such as Davey Crockett and Ben Franklin, and his historical "monuments" included Bunker Hill and the Alamo. His "melting pot" pioneers "pushed the wilderness back to settle America" from East to West. Making no reference to indigenous peoples or the presence of other-than-Anglo colonizers, his patriotic sermon quoted Jefferson on "Equal rights for all . . . special privileges for

Figure 9.4
Long-term resident and new immigrant culture stories

New Immigrants	Long-term Residents
Hard work and individual sacrifice for the good of the family is expected and accepted.	Good character, hard work, and good schooling can assure individual success, but we take care of our own (meaning anyone who lives in Beneville) when they need it and are grateful for it.
Family includes all the people to whom I am related by blood and marriage.	
Owning my own home is very important.	Hispanics* send too much money home and don't invest in the local economy.
Living together with family is important for financial and spiritual well-being.	
Americans* don't respect our language and culture.	Being from another culture/country means • Traditions, including religions, that are different (but similar) to ours • Different (but interesting) history, art forms, decor, and cuisine • Natural disasters, war, and political upheaval
Teachers don't think we care about our kids.	
It is essential for my children to be bilingual so that they can • Know their grandparents • Interpret for me • Go to school back home if possible	
	Except for a willingness to work hard, Hispanic values are different from ours.
Teachers don't realize the challenges my children face.	In order to learn, one must speak English and children cannot learn in homes where other languages interfere.
I want my children to have a good education so they don't have to work as hard as I do.	Languages are learned by immersion and interaction.
Except for work situations, I am uncomfortable being around Americans.	Hispanic parents don't care about school and would prefer to have their girls stay home and their boys go into the workforce as soon as possible.
I don't learn English because • I don't have time • I'm not smart enough • My kids will learn English and interpret for me	
	Hispanics are here to stay, whether I like it or not. I will (*choose one*) accept, ignore, tolerate, or reach out to them.
Becoming an American citizen means I can • Unite my family more easily • Defend myself from harassment	Adults don't learn English because they don't try hard enough.
It *does not mean* that • I will stop being Mexican, Salvadoran, or Guatemalan. • My family will stop speaking Spanish. • We won't continue to travel back and forth from *home*.	To become an American means • Accepting a common heritage of pilgrims and pioneers with a recognition of the pre-presence of Indians • Speaking English • Remembering and celebrating ancestral culture and language

*New immigrants distinguish between *americanos* and *los negros*, and some use derogatory stereotypes to refer to the latter.

*Long-term residents in professional positions identify new immigrants whose first language is Spanish with this Census Bureau term. Some, but not most, long-term residents are aware that Beneville "Hispanics" include people from various nations and other USAmerican states.

none." Indians do appear within the school curriculum, however. Some elementary school units from the "Pioneer Times" theme characterized all indigenous Americans as teepee-dwelling, war-bonneted recipients of Pilgrim generosity. Others included classroom displays celebrating Iroquois poets and honoring the Five Nations as predecessors to USAmerican democracy.

THE META-NARRATIVE "OTHER PEOPLE'S CULTURES"

In addition to a USAmerican heritage of pilgrims, pioneers, and Indians, the county's predominant German heritage is evident at Octoberfest. Beneville residents are quick to point out, though, "We're not *all* Germans!" Newspaper reports of International Week celebrations in the school show Beneville students dancing in Bavarian costumes, folding paper cranes, and eating taco salad. The same newspaper regularly runs expository features about other cultures. A local family or national celebrity was included in most articles in a 1998 series about December celebrations including Hanukkah, Ramadan, Kwanzaa, as well as a Mormon and a vegetarian Christmas.

A front-page photo article reported on December 12 celebrations of Our Lady of Guadalupe at Catholic churches in two nearby towns, and the editor dedicated six pages to a Quinceanera[12] celebrated in a Beneville church that has an active Spanish-language ministry. Members of Redbud High's championship girls' basketball team were quoted in the newspaper about their experiences traveling in China:

"Rice for 10 days was just too much . . . I think that's pretty much how everybody else felt."

"I had a great time, and I really enjoyed the trip because it was so different over there. Just to see some of the sites was an experience. The Forbidden City was just awesome. I don't think I've ever seen something so pretty in all my life, and I never dreamed it would be that much fun."

"China was nice, but Australia has got to be a little nicer and the food probably tastes a little better."

THE META-NARRATIVE "THEY DON'T HAVE OUR SAME VALUES"

The newspaper regularly publishes a list of convictions for various crimes. Although long-term residents' names predominate, any Hispanic name connected to a DUI (driving under the influence) is taken by some as factual evidence that single Mexican men, "who understand a hell of a lot more English than they let on when they get caught," are hopeless alcoholics. Such stereotyping was further evidenced in a downloaded Internet joke version of "A

Mexican Christmas" passed around the Thursday night ladies bowling league by a long-term resident furniture factory worker.[13] My teammates (whose jobs ranged from blue collar to professional) laughed uproariously over the altered poem's main character drinking "saam tequila . . . preety damn queek" as he jubilantly considered, "He gon get heemself something for free" from the "pot-bellied greengo" (Humorspace, 1997).

Sharing the scoring table with a member of the opposing team, I found it difficult to maintain my composure as I read the references to Mexicans as drunkards and welfare frauds. "What do you think of this?" I asked. Eyes staring at the pins in the alley in front of us, she responded, "Some people will laugh at anything." Several weeks later, I met her son-in-law and daughter when they came to show off their newborn son, Jorge, Jr.

With a mixture of admiration and concern, city officials comment on long post office lines on Major Meats paydays, and a university student reports her father's disgust over "money that never gets put into the local economy." Meanwhile, a Beneville landlord cosigns so a Mexican family can purchase the house they are renting and a Catholic priest from a nearby town regularly translates at mortgage signings.

Friendships among Salvadoran families are strained when some proselytize for the Spanish language ministry of a fundamentalist church. The Evangelicals sponsor an Octoberfest booth that tempts long-term residents to try *pupusas*[14] while a *mariachi*[15] singer entertains them. Beneville's parish priest is bilingual, but since at least 1994, retired priests from a nearby monastery have celebrated Saturday night's *misas* (Catholic Mass). Until fall 1998, these Spanish-language worship services were not posted on the reader board in front of the church. That year, a bilingual *tejana*[16] nun was hired as religious education director. Sister Anita insists she was hired "to serve the whole community, not just the Spanish-speakers." She refuses to provide Spanish-language-dominant parents with the opportunity to purchase bilingual versions of the children's Catechism books because, "My people have got to learn that English is the language of power and Spanish belongs at home." A front-page newspaper photo shows her making straw Christmas ornaments with an Elderhostel class for folks who want to get in touch with their German heritage.

Complaints regarding lack of concern about "our laws" are a frequent theme in conversations with long-term residents. Beneville's police chief expresses understanding that it's tough to pay for car insurance, "when what they really want to do is send money back home to their families," but he "really wish[es] these guys would realize that leaving the scene of an accident just makes it worse." Concerns about new immigrants who allowed the oil from their cars to drain into the streets prompted an early 1990s newspaper article explaining that, "different laws in Mexico, not bad morals among Mexicans," was the reason for this apparent lack of environmental concern.

A court advocate confirms that new immigrants with limited English fluency are overrepresented in cases of driving without a license or insurance. A long-term resident married to a Mexican immigrant with USAmerican citizenship reports that the man who gives the driving tests, "won't even get in the car with them if they don't speak English well enough to satisfy him." Both she and the court advocate are frustrated because, "these guys have to get to work whether they can pass the test or not."

A Mexican mother insists that her middle school-age son come straight home from school each day. He and his sisters play at home all summer, their mother observing, "Pues, los americanos no cuidan a sus niños" (Americans don't watch out for their children). A Beneville minister tells a parishioner concerned about "all these dark-eyed, swarthy-skinned young men" that he's more worried about the boys' welfare than the "trash girls" who get them in trouble. A city official tells me, "Hispanics don't have the same moral code as we do."

LIFE HISTORIES MEET POLICY

The ways in which the sources of these metanarratives contrast, conflict, or coincide are reflections of the varied race/ethnicity, class, gender, age, and other defining experiences among both long-term resident and new immigrant groups. The life history intersections of Luís Arenas, his father, and Luís's middle school principal, in conjunction with Redbud's no-retention policy for LEP students, illustrate how the situational appropriation of a well-intended policy, designed to assure compliance with a well-intended law, can produce results quite contrary to the best of those intentions.

Annual performance reports printed in local newspapers tout Redbud's higher-than-state average performance on graduation and attendance rates, as well as on Indiana's standardized testing *ISTEP*[+], which eventually leads to a high stakes high school exit exam. A decision about Luís's frequent long-term absences required a school administrator to consider the best response to state policy structural requirements. The principal wanted to improve the attendance and graduation rates among new immigrant children, a population he believed was "raised to go into the workforce as early as possible to help the family out." The intersection of this belief, his own life history, and the state guideline for retention of LEP students resulted in academic failure for Luís and academic underachievement for others within the new immigrant student population.

MEETING LUÍS AND HIS FAMILY

I first heard of Luís from my eighth grade son, who described "how Mrs. Capton burned him in study hall." Robbie frequently was absent from school in Beneville on Mondays when my research assistantship required my presence at the university. On one such day he missed an English class quiz that Mrs. Capton brought to him during study hall the next day. As she waited for him to finish, she noticed Luís sitting nearby. Her loud warning, "Luís, don't bother Robbie.... He's taking a test. ... Some time you might know enough to take one," was met with a low "Ooooh" from the rest of the class. Luís continued working on his math while muttering something that caused Robbie to later ask me, "Don't a lot of swear words in Spanish start with *P*?"

Our first meeting took place in our living room when his father brought Luís along on a visit to look over a medical bill from the boy's visit to the emergency room for an infected ingrown toenail. In an effort to distract Mr. Arenas from his anger over what he perceived as an outrageous charge for "algo tan chiquito" (something so little), I asked if he were aware that his son had been published in a school journal. *Many Voices—One Dream* had been compiled for the second annual Multicultural Conference held at the county seat in nearby Uberville, and featured short prose entries, poetry, and drawings done by ESL students throughout the county.

Luís was unable to read even the first few words of his paragraph aloud without prompting from Robbie:

My father decided to bring me and my brothers to this country from Mexico because he wanted me to study and learn English. My mother stayed in Mexico and I talk to her on the telephone. I like Beneville, but I find learning English is difficult.

I was surprised that, although he had been attending Redbud schools for over a year, Luís stumbled over even the relatively common English words in the paragraph, which he claimed he didn't remember writing. Furthermore, he was unable to translate the paragraph's message to Spanish.

Luís's Mexican School Experiences

Robbie reported that Luís was "one of the most popular Mexican boys in school," but Luís himself insisted that he had no friends and did not like going to school. The connection of friends and school was long-standing in his life history. He said that as a 6-year-old in his home village, "seguí por el monte" (I went on up the trail) many days when his parents thought he was at school. In spite of spirited insistence and (I suspected) considerable disciplinary efforts, his parents could not change his mind. Repeating first grade the following year, "conocí a muchos amiguitos" (I met a lot of good friends), Luís affirmed with a smile. From then on he reported happily attending school where he was "bueno para las matemáticas" (good at math) and "me gustaba leer" (enjoyed reading).

Mr. Arenas's Youth

Orphaned at age 4, Mr. Arenas never attended school. He and his seven brothers and sisters all fended for themselves on the streets of their village in Guanajuato, Mexico. Eventually he was apprenticed to a plasterer and, in his late teens, crossed the USAmerican border to labor as a migrant in California's orange groves. A continuing transmigratory work pattern carried him back and forth between Guanajuato and fruit orchards throughout the Pacific Coast states.

In spite of his many years of binational residency, Mr. Arenas never learned to speak English:

Pues, allá en los files, no hay necesida'. Todos hablan español. Uno vive en los campos y no hay necesida' para ir a la ciudad. A mí no me gustaba estar entre los americanos y, como no se necesitaba, ¿pa' qué?

(Well, there in the fields, it wasn't necessary. Everyone speaks Spanish. You live in the camps and there's no reason to go to the city. I didn't like to be around Americans and since I didn't have to, why do it?)

In between border crossings, Mr. Arenas married. His youngest siblings and all of his children were sent to school and, except for Luís, all of the boys eventually joined their father to work in the States. Mrs. Arenas raised the family in Guanajuato with money her husband and the older sons brought or sent home.

Moving the Family to Beneville

The purchase of a duplex just one block off Main Street made the Arenas among the first new immigrant families to buy real estate in Beneville. For three years, Mr. Arenas and one of his brothers rented out one of the apartments as well as extra bedrooms from the one they occupied. When Luís and an older sister joined the men in the spring of 1998, the girl stayed home to keep house. Mr. Arenas enrolled Luís in school, "pa' que nos interpretara" (so he could become the family interpreter). Shortly afterward, Mrs. Arenas and the youngest daughter arrived.

All the men living in the two apartments worked at Major Meats. One, a Baptist *hermano* (preacher), reported that both father and uncle rejected Luís's constant pleas to quit school and join them in the poultry plant. Indeed, he was expected to become the family interpreter, but Luís's growing record of absences from Beneville Middle School did not hold out much promise of that happening.

A Potential Dropout

At age 15, Luís was a year older and considerably larger than most of his classmates. Very fearful of not being passed on to high school, he had decided to just not go back, "porque me dolió mucho el dedo" (because my toe hurt so much). The ESL coordinator was concerned about the principal's warning that continued absence could result, not in retention, but expulsion. Taking advantage of the father/son medical help visit, I suggested a school conference at which I volunteered to interpret.

A Principal in His Corner

Luís had long ago exceeded the number of absences allowed by state policy, but Principal Georgevits kept him on the record because he cared about Luís. The special place in Mr. Georgevits's heart for "problem kids" came from his personal experiences. As he recounted to me in his life history interview,

> I was not a nice kid there at all. I gave my parents a lot of problems growing up. I regret those things. I ran away from home a number of times. I got booted out of school a number of times. Those are not a good part of my life, but I think being involved in education gives me an opportunity to relate with those kids.

The conference to determine whether Luís would be allowed to continue at Redbud Middle School started off with some tough warnings: "Tell Luís that if he doesn't come to school, he can get his father in trouble and he could get sent to a youth detention program."

I couldn't decide if the tough act was meant more to impress Luís or his father. The ESL coordinator told me school personnel "had heard that his sister arrived with their mother a week ago and still hasn't been enrolled in school." Zaida actually had been in Beneville for nearly five months. Mr. Arenas asked me to enroll her the day immediately following Luís's conference!

As the meeting progressed, Mr. Georgevits's tone became more like that of the trusted sports coach he had been upon first arriving in Beneville over 20 years ago. The changed atmosphere evoked words the principal had shared with me in his life history narrative:

> I'm able to relate to some of those kids. You know, and maybe, as I was about the same as a kid, I can look back and say "Yeah, you can do something. You can make something of yourself even if you've come through some troubled times."

Luís opened up some about the pushing and shoving he had endured, prompting Mr. Georgevits to assure him, "You know, Luís, sometimes kids can be the cruelest. We know who those boys are and we'll deal with it." With Luís's permission, I recounted Robbie's story of Mrs. Capton. The principal countered, "I'm sure she didn't mean it the way it came out, Luís. All of our teachers want the best for you all." Finally, Luís's admission of his greatest fear—being held back as an even bigger, older eighth-grader—resulted in the assurance, "That's not gonna happen. I promise you, Luís. If you come to school every day from right now until the end of the school year, I guarantee you will go on to the high school." What he could not promise Luís was that Redbud's language policy would provide the faculty with the professional knowledge and impetus to extend the effort to meet his special needs as a second-language learner.

An Immigrant Himself

Although he enforced the no-retention policy and actively supported the ESL coordinator's efforts to teach English, Mr. Georgevits's life experiences caused him to question the wisdom of education that might capitalize on students' home languages:

I think as a country not only do we accept, but we also go out of our way to provide languages other than the English language for those people . . . which I have my own personal feelings on that.

Mr. Georgevits wanted new immigrant students to develop bilingualism, but believed that home languages belonged at home:

I value that from my parents that I maintained my home language, or my native language. It probably hurt in a different sense that it took a little bit longer for me to pick up the English language, but no, when we stepped in that house we took our shoes off and talked Hungarian.

He felt strongly about the fact that, "we need an amendment in the United States that English is our language, that *English* is our language."

In 1956, when 8-year-old Peter Georgevits arrived with his parents, who fled Europe during the Hungarian Uprising, he

started school in the United States as a third-grader not knowing any of the language at all. . . . You know, my situation, when we came out, I didn't pick up the language fast enough so I remained in third grade one more year. So my process of education took a little bit longer than my brother's. They took him down to kindergarten a couple hours a day so that he could pick up phonetics and try to learn the language from, I guess, base one. I think they maybe thought that a third-grader could do that in class. I never heard anything that he had any problem with that. I think it quickened his process of picking up the language probably.

Mr. Georgevits's intuition about what "probably" speeds up the second-language acquisition process should be weighed against research, which suggests that it may take from five to seven years for an English language learner to become fully proficient and that there is also no need to delay academic progress in the meantime (Ovando & Collier, 1998). Indeed, a challenging and appropriate curriculum appears to be one of the better ways of facilitating second language development, particularly for secondary students (Faltis & Wolfe, 1999; Ovando & Collier, 1998).

Appropriated Meanings

Until the conference, Luís had not known that he would not be retained. He did know that, other than not being able to read the textbooks and understand what the teachers said, his schoolwork was not challenging. Regular classroom teachers who wondered, "How can I teach them anything when they don't understand the language?" didn't require Luís to keep up with the regular curriculum. He chafed under the ESL coordinator's efforts to get him to work when he didn't understand her instructions about what to do: "Aquella vieja no habla español" (That old lady doesn't know how to speak Spanish). Of math class, he said, "Pues, estudiaba eso en México" (Well, we already studied that in México). Knowing that no matter what he did would earn him a checkmark, Luís interpreted his ESL teacher's urgings to perform "like the good student I know you are" as unwelcome and useless criticism. He made the same choice as he did at age 6—to play hooky. The infected toe became an easy excuse to give his father.

Mr. Arenas had never been comfortable "entre los americanos" and he had no experience talking with teachers. Although he and the other men in the house mouthed the benefits of education, they had no practical life experiences to support their assertions. Even though Luís's hooky-playing long ago passed the legal limit, his father didn't remember any communication from the school about the seriousness of the continuing absences. His avoidance of a confrontation with Luís over a two-week absence for an ingrown toenail fed right into Mr. Georgevits's perception that his school had "kids coming from cultures where education is not important at all and there is no age limit in regards to when you don't have to go to school anymore."

The principal's commitment to "problem kids" focused his attention on solutions that ultimately tracked LEP students away from academically challenging programs. Since they did not speak Spanish, regular classroom teachers had appropriated the no-retention policy to mean they couldn't do anything to motivate the LEP students. Mrs. Capton recalled faculty room conversations with colleagues who complained, "I can't assign grades so how will they know they have to work harder?" The teachers as well as Mr. Georgevits began looking to alternative programs to solve their problems with teaching new immigrant students. Linking his concepts of "problem kids" to the LEP population, the principal reflected:

I think we're starting to get to the point with the type of kids that we're seeing, just the small percent of our problem kids, that we need to continue to focus on alternative schools for some of those kids. . . . Our problem comes when we get 'em into middle school-age level and they don't know the language and then trying to get them to that point. . . . You know, not that we're looking at higher education.

OUTCOMES OF AN APPROPRIATED POLICY GUIDELINE

The various life history intersections with an educational policy guideline resulted in the effective foreclosure "from any meaningful education," as explicitly prohibited by *Lau v. Nichols*. Redbud's policy disallowing retention "solely based on English-language proficiency," was enacted in response to state guidelines for legal compliance. Yet it effectively resulted in noncompliance with the Equal Educational Opportunities Act by failing "to take appropriate action to overcome language barriers that impede equal participation by its students in its instructional program."

Mr. Georgevits's life history led him to appropriate state guidelines for second-language learners so that they led to limited policy alternatives of either vocational tracking or expulsion. These alternatives were directly connected to the teachers' appropriation of the no-retention policy as a means to avoid the responsibility to modify curriculum to successfully teach all students. Luís and his father appropriated the resulting ineffective learning experiences and lack of home-school communication as opportunities for Luís to place himself in jeopardy of expulsion. Ultimately, the policy "framed" a dropout (Fine, 1991). Luís stopped attending school just after his 16th birthday in mid-April. The school removed him from the attendance roles in early May. Without even an eighth-grade diploma, Luís is working with an uncle in Florida. He plans to return someday soon to Beneville's Major Meats, but does not intend to pursue the high school diploma that long-term residents consider the minimal certification of success.

CONCLUSION

Situated Policy Implementation

As McLaughlin (1991, p. 155) notes, the challenge of effective implementation "lies in understanding how policy can enable and facilitate it." Surely, the presence or absence of indigenous peoples in the Pioneer Times theme lessons, International Week curricula emphasizing "food, fun, and fiesta" without adequate attention to deeper cultural issues, and a school curriculum locked in an English-only pedagogy, all play a role in the construction of the kind of knowledge of the Other reflected in laughter over "A Mexican Night Before Christmas." Unaware of their construction of a hegemonic curriculum delivered through a similarly constructed pedagogy, Beneville's educators lack the knowledge to reform practices that underserve the most needy of their students.

The lack of attention given to rurally situated race/ethnicity, language, class, and gender cultures is a serious gap in educational policy. The study from which this chapter is drawn meets McLaughlin's challenge by listening to a variety of voices in order to provide policymakers a clearer understanding of the situations in which individuals and groups construct their schooling. It also strives to provide those same individuals and groups with the means to investigate that construction as impacted by the sociocultural expectations of both long-term and new immigrant populations.

Beneville's teachers read in the newspaper about a nearby university student who, not possessing a word of Swedish, became "virtually bilingual" through the immersion process during a year abroad. Unaware of language-learning theory, it is difficult for them to imagine why new immigrant children do not just as miraculously succeed academically in their classes. When continued absences "ruin our record" on statewide evaluations, it is easier to lobby for alternative schools for " kids that may have a difficult time in the environment that we're in" than to change the structure of that school environment.

Access to information about the effect of the sociocultural knowledge of participants in particular situations is absolutely essential for educational policy, which impacts the growing number of children whose linguistic needs are not currently being met in USAmerican schools. Levinson and Holland (1996) warn that the

historically specific models of the "educated person" encouraged in schools often represent the subjectivities which dominant groups endorse for others in society. . . . And just as school discourses and practices specify the properly "educated person," they may also reproduce inequalities by defining the "uneducable person." (p. 24)

Ultimately, the various life histories that came together over Redbud's unwritten "no retention" policy framed Luís as an "uneducable" dropout.

Call to Action

Indiana and other U.S. midwestern states crossing the threshold of demographic change must seize the opportunity to foster positive educational outcomes for their new immigrant residents. If curriculum is "the collective story we tell our children about our past, our present, and our future" (Grumet, 1981), then educators facing the challenge of broadening and deepening that story for both long-term and new immigrant residents in rural communities like Beneville need professional development for culturally relevant pedagogy (Ladson-Billings, 1994). Given the relative void of state-level policy for immigrant education in Indiana, it is vital for life history intersections such as those illustrated by Luís, his family, and Redbud's school personnel to be brought to the attention of policymakers. Agencies and organizations committed to education reform must provide funding for inservice professional development and collaborative research projects that provide means for local actors to consider the impact of sociocultural constructs on education.

Policymakers must consider the situational impact of life histories as local implementation appropriates educational policy for LEP students and deprives *everyone* access to the knowledge and skills for developing a democratic concept of what it is to "be American." Mr. Georgevits's words to immigrant parents could easily be addressed to Redbud's faculty and school board, as well as state, regional, and federal educational policymakers:

So, you know, some of those we have to educate that, listen, education is important. Whether you like it or not, you gotta work with us, until the age of 16 if that's when you want your child to quit. But, we really hope that you buy into that your child has more to offer than quitting.

NOTES

1. The term "USAmerica" is used to refer to the United States of America (USA) rather than "the United States" or "America," as these terms may also describe several unions of states within nations on the American continents.

2. H. R. 3892 (1999), known as the English Language Fluency Act.

3. HB 1001, the recently enacted bill for the biennium beginning January 1, 2000, allocates, for the first time, a modest sum of $75 per student enrolled in non-English-speaking programs.

4. Based upon a sixfold increase in LEP enrollment between January and September 1998, she recommended: (1) changing her position to certified, (2) hiring the volunteer aide who worked with her in the spring 1998 semester, and (3) purchasing a computer dedicated to the ESL program. The superintendent took the first two recommendations under advisement and approved pursuit of outside funding for the computer. Beneville's Community Foundation granted $1,200 toward the technology purchase. No regular volunteer stepped in when the aide found paid employment elsewhere. When an August 1999 meeting with the superintendent confirmed that her position would once again be designated as uncertified, the ESL Coordinator resigned. The position remains vacant as of this writing (October 1999).

5. Drawing on reviews of the Woodcock-Muñoz Language Survey, Grady (1999) notes that "even within the philosophical and empirical framework of the field of psychometrics, the Woodcock-Muñoz Language survey has been judged as inadequate, lacking validity, and problematic. What we have then, is an invalid test coupled with an inadequate theory being used to make decisions about the educational trajectories of the children least likely to be well-served by the public schools" (p. 47).

6. It is not unusual for Redbud teacher aides, who are paid minimum wage, to be certified teachers. A school board member noted the presence of "a lot of teachers that are very frustrated for not having teaching jobs."

7. Many new immigrant adults ended formal schooling in their primary years. Salvadoran mothers report nonexistent or interrupted schooling during the war years. Some parents have extremely limited literacy and numeracy skills. While the ABE class offers more individualized instruction, various levels of adult students are grouped together in ESL classes that rely heavily on written worksheets. Summer ABE classes meet at the library and churches within walking distance of many new immigrant homes, but during the school year few new immigrant women have access to the transportation required to get to most ESL and ABE classes.

8. Concerned about whether her students could understand or relate to *The Diary of Anne Frank*, a middle school English teacher reflected, "I know there are books out there and I could probably find them at the state because, ESL, they've got their own little department. But I have to do that a year in advance. You gotta do it a year in advance. And I'm going, 'I don't know from day to day if they're even gonna be in here.' I probably should start looking at acquiring Spanish versions of some of the major ones." The same teacher seemed unaware of the value of multimodal teaching

strategies for LEP students (Gonzalez & Darling-Hammond, 1997) when she worried about including LEP students on a field trip to see a live presentation of the play. "We're taking the whole 8th grade over to see the play of Anne Frank. And I'm thinking 'Okay, now here's Graci and Luís who sat here and watched this movie, bits and pieces, you know [laughs]. Are they getting anything out of it?' When we take them over there to see the play, which is gonna be much more difficult probably, because if it's like every other play, the actors, some of them aren't gonna, their voices aren't gonna carry. I don't know."

9. In the home countries of most new immigrants, parental responsibility is to assure that children are "bien educado," that is, clean, fed, dressed, and respectful of adults. The assumption is that children thus prepared will learn whatever is presented to them by education professionals.

10. Stories dealing with home-school relations and language learning are explored in a video by Cade and Strout (1999).

11. Evidence of long-term residents eager for new immigrants "to just go away" has diminished over the decade. A monthly radio talk show featuring mayors from various county towns has fewer callers that complain about "dirty Mexicans." In the early 1990s, new immigrants had difficulty finding rental housing, but some landlords now actively seek new immigrant renters. As one put it, "We've had lots of dealings with these people and can truthfully say we've not had the same good luck dealing with some of the locals."

12. Traditional 15th birthday celebration for girls in the home countries of the new immigrants.

13. All participants in the bowling leagues are long-term residents. Participation by new immigrants in organized recreation activities is limited. In the early 1990s, church and business leaders created a soccer field "to keep the young guys without families busy." The 1998 community summer youth soccer team had only one Mexican teenage player. Although no new immigrant children currently play on middle or high school sports teams, some were active in summer 1998 Little League.

14. *Pupusas* are puffy circles of dough on which Salvadorans serve a variety of foods, including meats, shredded vegetables, cheeses, or sweets.

15. Mexican musical style that features a variety of guitar-like and brass instruments. Beneville's Octoberfest *mariachi* wore a traditional full-length black *charra* (cowgirl) skirt and vest decorated with silver medallions.

16. Female Texan of Mexican heritage.

REFERENCES

Cade, S. L. (forthcoming). *Intercultural dynamics of power in a midwestern town: Stories of the enactment of local education policy.* Unpublished doctoral dissertation, School of Education, Indiana University.

Cade, S. L. & Strout, A. R. (1999). *Anhelos: An immigrant life in the USAmerican midwest* [Videotape]. (Available: School of Education, Indiana University.)

Cummins, J. (1998, February). *Beyond adversarial discourse: Searching for common ground in the education of bilingual students.* Presentation to the California State Board of Education, Sacramento, CA.

Faltis, C. J., & Wolfe, P. M. (Eds.). (1999). *So much to say: Adolescents, bilingualism, and ESL in the secondary school.* New York: Teachers College Press.

Fine, M. (1991). *Framing dropouts: Notes on the politics of an urban public high school.* Albany, NY: SUNY Press.

Gonzalez, J. M. & Darling-Hammond, L. (1997). *New concepts for new challenges: Professional development for teachers of immigrant youth.* McHenry, IL: Delta Systems.

Grady, K. (1999). *Being identified: The construction of limited English proficiency.* Unpublished manuscript, School of Education, Indiana University.

Greene, J. P. (1998). *A meta-analysis of the effectiveness of bilingual education.* Austin, TX: Thomas Rivera Policy Institute, University of Texas.

Grumet, M. R. (1981). Restitution and reconstruction of educational experience: An autobiographical method for curriculum theory. In M. Lawn & L. Barton (Eds.), *Rethinking curriculum studies: A radical approach.* New York: Halsted Press.

Humorspace. (1997). *A Mexican Christmas* [Online]. Available: http://www.humorspace.com/humor/Holidays/cmexican.htm

Krashen, S. (1996). *Under attack: The case against bilingual education.* Culver City, CA: Language Education Associates.

Ladson-Billings, G. (1994). *The dreamkeepers: Successful teachers of African American children.* San Francisco: Jossey-Bass.

Levinson, B. A., & Holland, D. C. (1996). The cultural production of the educated person: An introduction. In B. A. Levinson, D. Foley, & D. C. Holland. (Eds.), *The cultural production of the educated person: critical ethnographies of schooling and local practice* (pp. 1–54). Albany, NY: SUNY Press.

McLaughlin, M. W. (1991). The Rand Change Agent Study. In A. R. Odden (Ed.), *Education policy implementation* (pp. 143–156). Albany, NY: SUNY Press.

Ovando, C. J. & Collier, V. P. (1998). *Bilingual and ESL classrooms: Teaching in multicultural contexts.* Boston: McGraw-Hill.

Willig, A. (1985). A meta-analysis of selected studies on the effectiveness of bilingual education. *Review of Educational Research, 55*(3), 269–318.

10

"That School Gotta Recognize *Our* Policy!": The Appropriation of Educational Policy in an Australian Aboriginal Community

R. G. *Schwab*

INTRODUCTION

This chapter is an exploration of the interaction of Aboriginal people and the Western system of education in the remote community of Maningrida in north-central Arnhem Land.[1] Fifty years ago, the indigenous people of this region enjoyed relative isolation from the rest of Australia, but increasingly this is no longer the case. While ceremonial forms and traditional social structures remain largely intact, dramatic economic change has swept through the region and modern technologies such as telephones, satellite television, fax machines, computers, airplanes, and four-wheel-drive vehicles have delivered options and pressures never imagined a generation ago. Many of these options present fundamental challenges to the cultural underpinnings of daily life, and the indigenous people in the region are currently attempting to negotiate change and provide the best future for themselves and their children. Much of that negotiation is mediated by various institutions introduced by Europeans, and prominent among these is the community school. As in many Aboriginal communities, the school is perceived as one of the most significant institutions, yet there is continual anxiety over the degree to which education is succeeding or failing in Maningrida.

On a particular school day, one can see school-age children roaming the dusty, red dirt roads of Maningrida while many of their agemates are in classrooms.[2] Impassioned discussions among staff, both Aboriginal and non-Aboriginal, regarding how to increase and maintain attendance are endless, but the problem has proven to be intractable. At the same time, there is long-standing discomfort with the low—and some say declining—levels of student performance; with the inability of most children to progress beyond, or in many cases, even attain low-level literacy and numeracy skills, with the unwillingness of parents to enforce attendance; with the government's inadequate provision of secondary or adult education opportunities; and with the school's incapacity to somehow find and enact solutions to these problems. These concerns are wearily and continually voiced by Aboriginal and non-Aboriginal teachers, school administrators, the school council, and community members.

The basis for these concerns is not immediately obvious to the visiting observer. The children appear enthusiastic and the school looks much like other schools in its general levels of productive commotion and activity. The school staff are committed and caring, the building is mostly adequate, innovative approaches to learning are being attempted, many of the teachers are Aboriginal, and the structures for community consultation are in place. In spite of all this, the feeling of frustration is pervasive. Few children will attend secondary school, few will have literacy or numeracy skills beyond Year 4 levels (or Year 2 levels in the more isolated homeland centers), and practically none of the students can perform at levels that would allow assessment by the education department's standard battery of performance tests; consequently, very few are even tested. There is an extremely high level of concern about education throughout the community and many people, especially non-Aboriginal people, feel something is deeply and frustratingly wrong. That concern is manifest in the frequent use of terms such as "dysfunction," "decline," and "failure." In terms of the needs of Aboriginal children, families, and communities, it is often said that "education is failing."

In this chapter, I argue that Aboriginal people in the Maningrida region hold a far more complex understanding of and relationship with education than is often assumed. Their involvement with Western systems of education is mediated by a range of particular interests and desires. As I show, to interpret the interaction of Aboriginal people with this institution in terms of failure is to fundamentally misunderstand the social process of education in this community and the agency of Aboriginal people who are purposefully engaged, according to a system of situated logic, with a set of specific, Western-based education practices and policies. The chapter begins with a description and historical sketch of the region, followed by a brief depiction of the structure of the school today. Next, it explores some of the assumptions underpinning notions of failure. It is proposed that education (and what might commonly be perceived as educational "failure") can only be understood productively in its broad sociocultural context. In an attempt to begin sketching this context, I identify four cultural themes that pervade life in Maningrida and illustrate the way they reflect and reproduce social relations against the backdrop of "the school." These themes, I argue, explain much about the cultural context that underpins educational "failure," but more importantly, they focus on Aboriginal people as agents and provide insight into what people want and expect from Western education. The chapter concludes with a discussion of the ways in which Aboriginal people in Maningrida use Western education as a means to a variety of ends.

ABOUT MANINGRIDA

Maningrida is located in north-central Arnhem Land in the far north of Australia on one of several major rivers draining a vast stretch of savanna woodlands between the Arnhem Land escarpment and the Arafura Sea. The region is ecologically diverse, with eucalyptus forests as well as swamps and mangrove jungles, sand dunes, dense bushland, and mud flats. It is subject to the Asiatic monsoon cycle, with distinct wet and dry seasons, dramatic storms, floods, and occasional cyclones.

The region is remote and Aboriginal people in Arnhem Land have enjoyed long periods of isolation from the rest of the world, punctuated occasionally by interaction with Macassan trepangers from the 16th century, the arrival of European explorers and pastoralists in the 1880s, and crocodile hunters, Japanese pearlers, and missionaries from the early 1900s.

In 1949, the Australian Commonwealth's Native Affairs Branch established a trading post at the mouth of the Liverpool River, where Maningrida township is situated today. The original vision for Maningrida was that of a regional center where indigenous people in the surrounding area could come to trade goods, particularly crocodile skins and indigenous crafts, and receive medical care. The government was unabashedly trying to stem the flow of Aboriginal people to Darwin, about 375 kilometers (230 miles) to the west, where most jobs had dried up after the war but where people were content to remain. The original vision for Maningrida was not of a new town drawing people from the region into a permanent settlement, but that was the outcome.[3]

Maningrida is now the largest Aboriginal settlement in Arnhem Land and one of the largest Aboriginal communities in Australia. The Maningrida region is home to about 1,850 people. Of these, around 1,200 are Aboriginal residents of the town, while a further 500 reside in one of between 20 or 30 homeland centers on clan lands. Maningrida is also home to just over 100 non-Aboriginal residents. There is a tremendous amount of movement of Aboriginal people between Maningrida township and the homeland centers with the population of the township swelling significantly during the wet season when access to the homelands is impossible or difficult because of flooding. Maningrida is located on the traditional lands of the *Kunibidji* people; there are around 160 members of this language group. The remaining indigenous population, representing about 27 other language groups, reside as "guests"

on *Kunibidji* land. While these guests reside with the permission of the traditional owners, that is not to suggest an absence of tensions.

Maningrida is on Aboriginal land and a permit is required to enter the community or pass through Arnhem Land. A single road running from east to west
through Arnhem Land provides access to Maningrida, but that road is closed
during the wet season. Air access is possible year round and is provided by two
airlines with daily service. The community has the expected range of services
for a population center of this size: a health clinic, grocery store, two fast-food
"take-away" shops, a bakery, community bus service, police station, workshop, post office, and school.

Unemployment is high. While there are some opportunities for work, there
are few long-term positions. Central Arnhem Land, unlike other Aboriginal
communities to the east and west, has up to now had few options for enterprise
development. Mines and tourism provide employment and development options a few hundred miles away, but at the moment there are no such regional
development enterprises to provide employment opportunities for significant
numbers who may wish to work in Maningrida, much less the homeland centers. When jobs are available, the generally low skill levels of Aboriginal people
in the region are a chronic impediment, and lack of Aboriginal worker commitment is an ongoing problem.

There remains, however, a strong and continuing spiritual attachment to
the land, and north-central Arnhem Land is home to rich and vibrant cycles of
ceremonies revolving around economic exchanges, expression and validation
of land ownership, and sacred ritual cult activities linked to ancestral beings
(called The Dreaming). While ritual activity is a prominent and pervasive part
of life in the region, Aboriginal people have had enormous success in translating and exporting certain facets of their culture to a wider Australian and international audience; Arnhem Land's totemic dancers, musicians, and painters
are world renowned.

THE MANINGRIDA COMMUNITY EDUCATION CENTRE

The Maningrida Community Education Centre is a government facility
comprising the hub school in Maningrida and 13 homeland center schools. In
August 1997, it had three administrators, a mentor teacher, and 16 classroom
teachers (including five indigenous teachers) in the main "hub" school, and
five "visiting" teachers serving 13 homeland center schools. In addition, there
were 12.5 Aboriginal assistant teacher positions in the hub school and 13 Aboriginal homeland center teachers. There were 15 other individuals working as
technicians in the literature production center, as janitors, cleaners, and office
staff.

Classes in the hub school are organized according to level, with preschool,
primary (to year 7), and post-primary sections. The curriculum is predomi-

nantly "Western" in structure and content, though some teachers invest enormous effort incorporating local cultural content into what is taught in the classroom. Communication technologies and efficient transport have dramatically expanded the depth of Aboriginal understanding of the outside world, but classroom materials increasingly reflect the reality of life in Arnhem Land today. While 10 or 20 years ago one might have observed Aboriginal children struggling to make sense of drawings of Easter bunnies in texts written for children in Sydney or Melbourne, today, school children in Maningrida will find mainstream texts complemented by locally produced readers depicting Aboriginal rangers collecting crocodile eggs or Aboriginal women weaving baskets to sell to European tourists in Darwin.

The school has a bilingual program focusing on English and the two most prominent Aboriginal languages spoken in Maningrida: *Burarra* and *Ndjebbana*. The preschool is divided into *Burarra* and *Ndjebbana* sections. The primary section is divided into three units: *Burarra*, *Ndjebbana*, and English. The non-English-speaking children receive instruction in both English and their home language. By Year 4, emphasis has moved to classroom work based on English. There is no secondary school in Maningrida, but post-primary classes are offered in three streams to meet the differing needs of students: general studies, intensive English, and manual arts. After Year 7, boys and girls are separated for cultural reasons. Students who wish to study at the secondary level must leave the community or undertake correspondence courses.

The 13 homeland center schools vary considerably in terms of infrastructure and size, but a single instructional pattern is in place for all the schools. Each school is operated by a homeland teacher, typically a person appointed by the senior traditional owner of the country on which the homeland center sits. The day-to-day operation of the homeland school is the responsibility of the resident homeland teacher, but the educational program is under the direction of the visiting teacher based in Maningrida. The visiting teacher typically spends one day and night in each of his or her homeland school communities, arriving by four-wheel-drive vehicle or aeroplane. The visiting teacher delivers materials, provides and models lessons, and helps train the homeland teacher. This modeling and training is particularly important since few of these teachers have had opportunities for formal training and some do not read or write English. The homeland schools are mostly simple structures with open but covered work areas and a locked room for storing school equipment. Some have solar power, a toilet, and a gas stove and refrigerator, while others have only camping facilities. Enrollments in these schools range from as few as 8 to as many as 21 students.

The enrollment figures for both the hub school and the homeland center schools indicated a total of 557 students in August 1997; of these only about 12 are non-Aboriginal. Attendance over the year fluctuates markedly. Attendance typically rises in the hub school during the wet season as people move from the homeland centers to Maningrida, and then falls during the dry season as people disperse and become involved with hunting, gathering, and ceremonial activities. School attendance records show an average combined attendance for the hub and homeland center schools of around 64 percent, but some weeks the attendance can drop as low as 20 percent. While enrollment has grown by about 50 or 60 each year, attendance numbers have held steady for the last several years. In general, attendance at the hub and homeland center schools is roughly equal.

THE NATURE OF EDUCATIONAL "FAILURE"

Drawing on their backgrounds in anthropology and education, Ray McDermott and Hervé Varenne have written extensively on failure and success in the United States, and their writings provide a useful map for exploring what is regarded with considerable anxiety as educational "failure" in Maningrida (McDermott, 1974, 1987, 1993; McDermott & Varenne, 1995; Varenne & McDermott, 1999). Where anthropologists and educators have traditionally sought explanations for educational failure, Varenne and McDermott are concerned with "the *constitution* of failure" (original emphasis Varenne & McDermott, 1999). Their argument is most fully developed in the context of an analysis of disability, particularly learning disability, where they identify three distinct approaches to thinking about educational disability that can be translated to the context of "failure," which I discuss here (McDermott & Varenne, 1995).

First, they argue, it is possible to account for failure as a result of deprivation. The foundation of this perspective is the belief that members of groups develop differently enough that they can be shown to be measurably different from other groups in terms of particular developmental milestones. In other words, some people have developed the skills to perform particular tasks, other people haven't, and the presence and extent of those skills can be reliably measured. This is essentially a deficit model that explains the failure of minority children in school as a function of impoverished or impoverishing experiences at home (McDermott & Varenne, 1995, p. 334). It is also a model used to explain differences in various types of cognitive or motor tasks as a function of poor nutrition or inadequate pre- or postnatal care, and as such has relevance for analyses of educational performance.[4]

The second approach to educational disability (or, in this case, failure) focuses on difference. This perspective assumes that members of particular groups develop knowledge and skills that are well tuned to the requirements of their cultures. Comparisons of cross-cultural measurements in the performance of tasks employing those skills are thus meaningless or require heavy qualification. McDermott and Varenne (1995) summarize the political implications of this view: "Despite a liberal lament that variation is wonderful, those who cannot show the right skills at the right time in the right format are considered out of the race for the rewards of the wider culture" (p. 335). According to this perspective, cultural difference often accounts for school failure: Minority children are struggling because they are swimming against the cultural current in an educational system that is foreign and controlled by teachers from the dominant society, and they are forced to perform tasks that reveal their weaknesses.[5]

The third approach begins with an inversion of the traditional view of learning disabilities: the child does not acquire a disability, the disability acquires the child (McDermott & Varenne, 1995, p. 336). I can't do justice in this space to their complex and provocative analysis, but the kernel of that analysis is useful for interpreting some of the concerns that manifest under the notion of "educational failure" in Maningrida. This approach begins with the assumption that every sociocultural system frames and shapes options, hopes, and aspirations for individuals or groups, and provides the criteria for tagging those who are competent and those who fall short. In schools, those tags are particularly powerful in their identification of failure. At best, they provide efficient ways to channel individuals or groups along pathways of remediation, at worst they provide a means to sort the wheat from the chaff. In either case, such individuals or groups are categorized and identified as possessing "particular qualities that symbolise, and thereby constitute, the reality of their position *to others*" (original emphasis, McDermott & Varenne, 1995, p. 336). In this sense, competence and failure are relative constructions.

Competence is a fabrication, a mock-up and people . . . work hard to take their place in any hierarchy of competence displays. Being acquired by a position in a culture is difficult and unending work. The most arbitrary tasks can be the measure of individual development. Not only are cultures occasions for disabilities, but they actively organise ways for persons to be disabled. (McDermott & Varenne, 1995, p. 337)

Extending this theme from disability to failure, one can argue that failure, like competence, is a fabrication—a construction. Along these lines, one would ask to what degree the educational structures in Maningrida and elsewhere construct opportunities for educational failure: failure by students, teachers, administrators, the education department, and the community?

All three of these approaches can usefully be brought to bear on perceptions of educational "failure" in Maningrida. Children might "fail" in school because they suffer deficits as a result of organic damage through inadequate pre- or postnatal care; or perhaps they "fail" because they are simply culturally different and, as a result, powerless and unable to "achieve" in the unfamiliar educational system. The third approach suggests they fail because they are "acquired" as failures by a rigid educational system that focuses on a predetermined set of competencies that Aboriginal students almost invariably do not have.

While each of these approaches has some potential for explaining what is perceived by many as educational "failure" in Maningrida, the complex role of education in the community can only be fully understood if the agency of Aboriginal people is acknowledged and their engagement with the educational system is emphasized, if their intentions, goals, and desires are considered as part of a larger social process of which the school is but one part. Once the frame is shifted and choice, strategy, and action are considered, the school can be understood, not only as a site for predetermined failures, but as a site of active cultural production, where Aboriginal people in Maningrida accommodate, resist, and adapt to the Western system and structures of education (Levinson & Holland, 1996).

CULTURAL THEMES

As I argue below, the daily strategic engagement of Aboriginal people in Maningrida with institutions of Western education is in large part constructed, negotiated, and enacted against, around, and through four prominent cultural themes. These themes are not only the backdrop to education but they infuse the ongoing negotiation of social relations among both Aboriginal and non-Aboriginal people in the region. In and through these themes, Aboriginal notions regarding the nature and purpose of education are continually cast and recast. An examination of the recurring social forms and actions in these themes show Aboriginal people interpreting education in their own cultural context, but also steering it toward their own ends.[6]

Autonomy: "You're Not Boss for Me!"

Personal autonomy frames much of Aboriginal social action. As sentiment, rule, expectation, and practice, it is one of the most pervasive and powerful ordering structures in Aboriginal society. Yet Aboriginal notions of personal autonomy conflict deeply with many of the traditional structures of Western education. Assumptions of authority and expectations of procedure are subverted and inverted every day in the school in Maningrida by the enactment of Aboriginal notions of autonomy. Western education is based on the assumption that children will attend school—in fact, it assumes they must attend—but this is an assumption that does not hold up in day-to-day practice.

Child rearing in Aboriginal society can only be described as permissive, and adults make no demands on children for obedience. As soon as children can walk, they begin to exert their autonomy. They are fed, protected, and indulged, but they are perceived to be and treated by adults as fully autonomous individuals. In this context, children ultimately decide if and when they will attend school, and with rare exception, their choices are supported by the Aboriginal community. From a Western educational perspective this can look absurd. This was illustrated when, following a serious conflict in the classroom between an Aboriginal child and his white teacher, a meeting was held with the child's parent, the head Aboriginal teacher, the white teacher, the white administrator, and the child. The meeting was extremely tense: the teacher felt her authority had been challenged and her ability to manage her classroom threatened, while the parent was angry that her child's autonomy had been violated. Ultimately, the meeting achieved little more than a truce and as it concluded, the white administrator told the Aboriginal child to return to class. In quick response, the head Aboriginal teacher stepped in and asked the child, "Do you *want* to go back to class?" In this simple and purposeful intercession, the child's autonomy was reaffirmed and the limits of Aboriginal tolerance for an alien system of authority were sharply and clearly delineated.

Autonomy is fundamental to interaction away from school as well. A homeland center teacher, in discussing the difficulties Aboriginal parents have in telling their children to go to school, said: "It's too hard for Aboriginal people. To tell your kids to go to school. Mother and father, to tell kids 'Go to school.' And the kids say, 'No! I don't like going to school,' they say. 'You're not the boss for me!' "

Autonomy is a cornerstone of Aboriginal society, and that autonomy extends to all individuals, not just adults (Hamilton, 1981; Keeffe, 1992; Myers, 1991). In practice, many parents and Aboriginal teachers will speak eloquently of the importance of school for Aboriginal children, but they will not force their children to attend; they will not "be the boss" for their children.[7] For example, one recent day in Maningrida, a handful of primary school children were present in the classroom of an Aboriginal teacher, while a few blocks away twice as many children of this age were in that teacher's home, with that teacher's children, watching videos. In effect, children attend when they like, popping in and out of class on any particular day. In addition, many children seem to view school as a stage in life where engagement and participation is less important than physical presence. In this way, school is much like a stage in ritual initiation, and older children who drop out will remark proudly and dismissively that they have "done school."

In principle, the school and teachers have authority to require attendance and restrict the movement of children once in their care, but in practice that authority is an illusion and totally impractical.[8] Thus, the cultural theme of autonomy is manifest as the Aboriginal community both asserts its cultural values and resists the assumptions of Western educational structures. Aboriginal people agree, for the most part, that education is valuable, but feel decisions to participate must be left to the child. It is extremely difficult, however, for Western educators—even those who understand the centrality of autonomy in daily life—to view children who enact that autonomy in choosing not to attend school as not failing within or being failed by the Western educational system.

Shame: "Too Much Balanda"

Another prominent cultural theme is shame. Like autonomy, this is a pervasive theme in Aboriginal communities across the country. It is a complex concept incorporating notions of embarrassment, shyness, and respect, and it explains a great deal about Aboriginal comfort and discomfort with schools. Many, if not most, Aboriginal people in Maningrida are shy and self-conscious around white people, and school is for some children and adults a foreign and often uncomfortable place. Paradoxically, school is also considered a safe place by some children and community members because it is neutral ground. Yet, coming to school, with its arbitrary structures of time and space and unfamiliar people (both Aboriginal and white), is difficult for many children.

One Aboriginal woman described children's resistance to school:

Kids say, "I don't like going in the school because there's too much Balanda (non-Aboriginal people) watching and we don't like writing words and doing work, hard work for us, going school there teasing each other. Other kids teasing." That's why Aboriginal kids don't like to come in hub school. They stay out in their homeland and stay out there. Just stay out in the bush. Maybe, I think, they are too frightened.

Children say they don't like to be stared at and they feel out of place in school. They say there are too many non-Aboriginal people and they are teased by children from other language groups. Sometimes the discomfort is more subtle. One former homeland center visiting teacher tells of another teacher's frustration over his inability to get some children to leave a particular town camp and come to class in the hub school. It turned out that the children had no clothes and were too embarrassed to come onto the school grounds. Naked school-age children are hardly noticed on the beach or playing in the forests on the edge of town, he said, but they would attract uncomfortable attention in the school in the center of town. In this way, highly situated cultural notions of shame directly affected those children's capacity to participate in schooling.

Every day, Aboriginal children in Maningrida and the surrounding region struggle to make sense of an educational institution that the majority of Australian school children find familiar and comfortable. There is a seemingly endless stream of cultural subtleties and complexities that make schooling challenging, and often extremely problematic for Aboriginal children. For example, cooperative learning, a model of instruction in which children work together in groups, has been found to be an effective learning strategy in schools across the world, and in fact, Aboriginal people themselves have indicated this mode of instruction fits well with their cultural style. But there are times when it does not operate smoothly. Many schools will have experienced tensions between children of different ethnic groups who have conflicts outside the school, and that pattern exists in Maningrida, where children from different language groups sometimes harbor deep resentments that make it difficult for some children to work together. Equally problematic is the existence of a classificatory kinship system, which restricts interaction between different classes of kin. Avoidance relationships, for example, where one child is prohibited from speaking with or even being in close proximity to another child of a particular kinship relationship, can cause serious problems both for white teachers (who often have little or no understanding of the intricacies and complexities of Aboriginal kinship and are totally unaware of what has gone wrong) and students, who suffer the shame and embarrassment of being placed in situations they know they should not be in but about which they will not speak.

Notions of shame and shyness have a powerful impact on children's willingness to attend school, but it also affects their degree of participation and engagement. As Myers (1986) has observed in the Central Desert of Australia, Aboriginal people protect their autonomy by hiding it, and this pattern appears in Maningrida as well. Children and parents will go out of their way to not bring public attention to themselves, to avoid embarrassment, particularly in interaction with people other than close kin. The school is thus a place where one can be easily shamed and Aboriginal people are very careful when structuring interactions in that setting. Deference is shown, avoidance engaged in, and classroom behavior constrained; facilitating learning against this cultural backdrop is an enormous task for non-Aboriginal teachers. Western educational institutions have grown out of European cultures, and for Aboriginal people school is not merely an intellectual challenge, but a cultural one as well. In many Aboriginal communities, those who cannot meet that challenge are in danger of being sifted out or tagged for remediation. In this way, cultural notions of shame can have a powerful effect on children's willingness and ability to participate in the classroom.

Sharing: "We Just Came for Tucker"

Altman (1987) captures some of the complexity of contemporary economics in the Maningrida region when he refers to "hunter-gatherers in the welfare state." As he shows, there is no escape from the Australian state or the dominant Australian economy for Aboriginal people. Nonetheless, Aboriginal people in Maningrida as elsewhere operate in many ways according to traditional socioeconomic rules and expectations.[9]

Sharing, the cornerstone of hunter-gatherer economic and social relations, is alive and well in Maningrida and has a powerful effect on life in and around the school. It is, in fact, an Aboriginal cultural assumption that collides forcefully with education department policies. Teachers, other school staff, school council members, and even children are subject to the demands of kin within the context of school. Positions of authority in the school held by Aboriginal people provide access to resources that, in the Aboriginal community, are expected to be shared. Thus, food, cash through wages, vehicles, shelter, and school supplies are seen to be community resources that can be demanded and redistributed through broad links and obligations of kinship and affiliation. This causes enormous conflict where, for example, the school must account for the use of materials, vehicles, school funds, and work time. When expectations conflict, and the Aboriginal way persists, the Western system breaks

How do we reconal this especiely it accountably is poverty?

down—as, for example, when a school truck needing to collect freight at the barge landing disappeared for several hours when the driver was pressed by senior men of his clan to take them to a remote homeland center. Such breakdowns, and the subsequent frustration and disruption of the Western system, is seen from the non-Aboriginal view point as a failure; from the Aboriginal perspective, it appears as business as usual.   — *Hmm?*

Sharing and the principles of reciprocity frame other aspects of the educational experience as well. Life in Maningrida is focused on the here and now and there is still a tendency for most Aboriginal people in Maningrida to live a "feast and famine" lifestyle. When resources are available, whether food, money, alcohol, or any other material good, they are immediately called upon to be shared and consumed. Traditionally, there has been little reason to think about tomorrow, and people continue to struggle with the concept of money and notions of monetary value or worth; furthermore, Aboriginal people in Maningrida find little resonance with the white world's notion of earning, much less investing. In this context, the notion of education as an investment is not intuitively obvious to many students or parents, and this results in tension, misunderstandings, and frustration on the parts of both school staff and members of the wider Aboriginal community as they fail to share fundamental assumptions about basic principles that underpin Western education.

The life of hunter-gatherers in the welfare state has more immediate implications for many school children. Daily life in the region, as in precontact time, is shaped largely by the necessity of making a living, and particularly of obtaining food. People can get by through sharing and many would rather buy canned food or fried "take-away" chicken and chips with welfare money than hunt or fish; others, who would prefer traditional food, may not have reliable access to transportation or tools such as fishing lines or rifles.[10] In this context, the school canteen, known locally as "the tuck shop," with its carefully restricted menu of wholesome foods, has become a major food source for much of the community, proven by the fact that it cleared $100,000 in profits in 1996.[11] Ironically, this has proven to be a significant factor in getting children to go to school. In Maningrida, children are always hungry and food from the school canteen and fruit distributed in classrooms is the only predictable meal of the day for some children. Food, not the allure of learning, is what draws many students to the school.[12] While some school staff find this depressing, and others worry that food distribution might appear paternalistic, most are pragmatic and believe that anything that draws children into classrooms is a success.

While some limited employment exists and money comes into the community through various pensions and unemployment benefits, in the context of daily life, most Aboriginal people are poor. As is well known, poverty does not facilitate learning or parental involvement in schools and Maningrida is no exception to this pattern. In Maningrida, pervasive gambling has a powerful siphoning effect on community cash.[13] Card games run around-the-clock in the community and thousands of dollars change hands in every part of Maningrida every day of the week. Though some people do not and will not participate, the late nights, noise, and social disruption affects everyone, adults and children alike. One school staff member remarked on the prevalence of gambling and its impact on children:

When the siren sounds in the morning to call children to school, many are still asleep, unable or uninterested in getting up and going to school. Everybody's exhausted after the night's gambling. Children hang about the games all day and all night, waiting for a family member to "win" so they can get a $5 or $50 note to take to the school canteen for food. Some of these kids you don't see in the classroom, but there they are as soon as the tuckshop opens for morning tea. I asked some boys playing outside the tuckshop, "Hey, why aren't you kids in class?" and they just laughed and said, "We just came for tucker. We're not here today."

The continual economic and social demands placed on students, parents, and teachers can distract educators (and children) from what teachers perceive to be the core business of the school: the facilitation of learning. Similarly, poverty, economic vagaries, and the frequent chaos of life in the community can be disruptive and frustrating for those educators attempting to work within the boundaries of an institution built upon assumptions of constancy and predictability. Unlike their colleagues in private schools in the suburbs of Australia's major cities, Maningrida's teachers must contend everyday with children who are constantly hungry, who have not slept, and who suffer from various physical illnesses and chronic conditions such as otitis media. Non-Aboriginal teachers must attempt to explain to their Aboriginal "kin" who have adopted and protected them why the school truck cannot be borrowed to go hunting or to drive an old woman to the clinic. They have the unenviable task of attempting to make comprehensible school rules and education department policies, which no Aboriginal person can see as other than selfish and arbitrary. And in this context, they must attempt to win the support of children and parents, draw children into their classrooms, and teach. For these teachers, and for the Aboriginal community within which they teach, the potential for failure—of students, the educational system, and the efforts of parents and teachers—looms ever present.

Caretaking: "That School Gotta Recognize Our Policy!"

Maningrida has always been an artificial community. It has no real economic production base and exists only as a service center. It is also artificial in that it brings together language groups that would never normally reside together. The *Kunibidji* people are the traditional owners and spiritual custodians of the land on which Maningrida was built, but members of 27 or so other language groups reside there as well. The local council is structured to provide representation from the diverse community, but it is clear that some groups have more power and influence than others. Those differences create and per-petuate tensions in the community. But the more visible power differential is between the Aboriginal and non-Aboriginal people in the community, and while there is much attention paid to the fact that Maningrida is an Aboriginal community and white people are the guests, there is no question that a few non-Aboriginal residents wield significant power and influence. Each major organization, including the school, has a board of governance of some sort, of-ten with a majority of Aboriginal board members, but in many cases the deci-sions of these boards are shaped by non-Aboriginal people. This is not to suggest there is necessarily coercion involved or that Aboriginal board mem-bers are there in token capacity, though some would argue that is in fact the case in some organizations. Rather, Aboriginal people recognize that the vari-ous organizations are their conduits to the white world and white people are there to do their bidding. After all, no one knows the rules of the white game better than whites.

Aboriginal people in Maningrida see themselves as caretakers, as the "boss," responsible for the "country" and their culture, and in recent years, they have also come to see themselves as caretaker and as ultimately responsi-ble for the institutions—such as the school—that non-Aboriginal people have introduced to their world. The cultural theme of caretaker, carried in the con-ception of "boss," pervades life in Maningrida and structures many of the key interactions between Aboriginal and non-Aboriginal people.[14] As bosses for the country, Aboriginal people believe they retain authority (if not power) over non-Aboriginal institutions and the non-Aboriginal people who operate them.

Several years ago a group of Aboriginal people from Maningrida travelled to Indonesia as part of a cultural exchange program for artists. The Aboriginal guests observed the ways of the Indonesian people and enjoyed the hospitality of their hosts but eventually expressed their puzzlement: "Where are your *Balandas* (White people)?"

While most Aboriginal people consider the residence of white people in their community a fact of life, and there are many deep and strong friendships and enormous respect between some individuals, others are less tolerant and consider white people a necessary evil. No one, however, doubts that white people can be extremely useful. As many Aboriginal people are quick to point out, "This is our country. The *Balandas* work for us, we don't work for them." The idea that the Indonesian people had no *Balandas* to take care of the things *Balandas* take care of was incomprehensible.

In Maningrida, as elsewhere in Arnhem Land, there is an increasing move-ment toward self-determination. This is accompanied by a growing politicization of Aboriginal people, many of whom are articulate and deter-mined in their search for an appropriate way to contain and control the non-Aboriginal people, whom they view as guests in their country. This search is tempered by the struggle to find a balance between the costs of participating in the white world, and the costs of allowing non-Aboriginal people too much power. An Aboriginal school council member complained that the school seemed to operate on its own agenda, not an Aboriginal one. "That school gotta recognize *our* policy," he said. "That principal works for us!" This simple statement encapsulates the sense of responsibility and ownership Aboriginal people feel for the school as well as the frustration that overflows when they believe their interests are not being attended to. The statement is also indicative of the fact that a local Aboriginal education "policy" is indeed emerging.

There is growing Aboriginal input into the operation of the school, accompanied by a healthy amount of grumbling and conflict, some public, some private. Yet, ironically, the result largely has been the maintenance of the status quo and there is open frustration among some Aboriginal staff and community members that the school has not moved more quickly toward Aboriginal control. In fact, however, the often expressed dream of an Aboriginal-controlled, fully Aboriginal-staffed school appears to be a very long way off. Though increasing numbers of Aboriginal people are gaining skills to "Aboriginalize" the Western education system in Maningrida, the process is proceeding extremely slowly. Aboriginal people have begun to forcefully influence curriculum, staffing, and expenditure as the decision-making process has devolved and Aboriginal people are assuming an active role. Though many are content to allow the *Balandas* to "do the work," others assert their role of caretaker or "boss" of the school. But for the present, there is more rhetoric than action.

The devolution model emerged from, and has been most successful in, urban schools. There it assumes the school council members are familiar with and capable of working within the existing educational structures. But there are no Aboriginal architects, lawyers, or university graduates on the Maningrida CEC School Council, and while there are loud calls for change, few Aboriginal people are comfortable with what is, and to some extent will always be, a foreign system. Yet it is important to look at the larger picture. Some Aboriginal people charge the education department not only with failing to hand over the reins of the school but with actively thwarting attempts to put an Aboriginal administration in place; however, most are content with their consultative role. While there has been discussion in the past of developing an independent, community-controlled school in Maningrida, that initiative has never gained momentum. The reason, I would suggest, is that while some genuinely desire independent control of the school, others have learned in many subtle and effective ways to make Western education policy work to their particular ends. They have, through purposeful and strategic acts that follow their own system of situated logic, productively engaged with an alien education system and made it productive in some very significant ways. They simultaneously stand outside the system as confident, critical observers and inside from where they subvert and appropriate the system and make it serve their own particular needs.

EDUCATION: WHAT DO PEOPLE WANT?

It is easy for observers educated in Western schools to look at education in Aboriginal communities such as Maningrida and focus exclusively on the low levels of attendance, noninvolvement of parents, and low levels of academic performance. From one perspective, these are all signs of failure. Yet as Varenne and McDermott (1999) suggest, Aboriginal children are not "failing," they have been "acquired by failure." They are observed, assessed, and sorted on a day-to-day basis. Skills, abilities, and the lack thereof are "made consequential" in the school—they have no inherent meaning until they are placed in some specific context and made consequential. If there is a pervasive sense that Aboriginal children are failing, one must wonder what is being identified as consequential, under what conditions, in what ways, and for what reasons (Varenne & McDermott, 1999). These are important questions, and deserve attention. Yet there are other important questions that may be overlooked if we focus too intently on "failure." We should also be asking about what Aboriginal actors create for themselves in the process of engagement with Western educational policies and institutions. What do they lose and what do they gain as they engage with "school" and they act upon their frustrations and desires?

If consideration is given to the cultural themes that infuse the social relations of Aboriginal and non-Aboriginal people, and through which education is approached and enacted, it is possible to see additional, perhaps more subtle processes at work. Aboriginal people value Western education, but they also interpret and use the school and its policies in ways that fit their specific needs. In this way, they successfully appropriate Western education policy and make it their own.

To put this in perspective, it is useful to stop and consider what the Western educational system expects of students and communities. Australian schools, like Western schools everywhere, are typically structured around quite specific expectations of student attendance; parent and community involvement; particular, measurable levels of performance; retention; completion; and appropriate outcomes. Schools seek to nurture if not create particular types of "educated persons," individuals who are good citizens, productive, and competent. But what sort of competence? More than ever before, that answer is clear: economic competence. Schools, we are now told by the government in Australia, need to produce students who will be self-sufficient, students who have the skills to hold jobs, students who will contribute labor to build Australia's future.

Yet these notions of competence do not fit with the realities of life in a community such as Maningrida. Aboriginal people in that community view education in terms that differ significantly in both content and emphasis from that of mainstream Australia. They are steering education in particular directions, actively addressing some of the central challenges and contradictions of contemporary life. Some of these are recurring and are continually addressed in the cultural themes of autonomy, shame, sharing, and caretaking that are woven through daily life in the community and school. These cultural themes reflect and shape perceptions of opportunities, options, and choices. ~ *dilute*

Aboriginal people in Maningrida appropriate aspects of Western education where they need to and ignore the rest when it does not suit them. What they desire of education is quite different from what the Western institution expects. I would argue that they have appropriated Western education—they have created their own strategic policy—in order to secure very specific political, social, and economic ends involving cross-cultural competence, the maintenance of Aboriginal culture, material goods, and access to a range of social resources.

Cross-Cultural Competence

Paradoxically, while most Aboriginal people recognize the value of speaking English and acquiring basic literacy and numeracy skills, they do not perceive that education is urgently needed to live a fulfilling life; indeed, there is much evidence to the contrary, particularly in the homeland centers. Few Aboriginal people in Maningrida are concerned with economic competence as defined by the government. While some children and adults say they want education so they can win jobs, most see no reason to work. Few jobs are challenging and meaningful in the community and the idea of leaving the region to work makes little sense to most, since jobs have proven to be largely unnecessary in terms of surviving in the modern welfare state. Education as an investment simply does not fit with the realities of life in Maningrida. Aboriginal people do, however, recognize the importance of cross-cultural competence, and Western education does provide the means to that end. An educated person can gain competence in the cultural and bureaucratic logic of the white world. That person can gain skills necessary for negotiating with the government, for writing grant proposals, and for understanding how to fill in pension and unemployment benefit applications. These are clearly skills that empower. Indeed, some people in the region believe that education involves the revelation of the Balanda "secret language" and that with that language, Aboriginal people will gain access to the same, seemingly limitless material wealth enjoyed by white people, an analysis not without some truth. Most, however, hold an instrumental view of education and the school as the key provider of many of the skills that comprise cross-cultural competence. There is no strong perception, however, that everyone needs those skills; if some small number are able, that is sufficient.

Cultural Maintenance

The school is potentially a very effective mechanism for cultural maintenance, and Aboriginal people recognize that. The bilingual program in the school has resulted in the creation of written versions of two of the local languages, *Burarra* and *Ndjebbana*, and there is pressure on the school for expansion of the program to develop written versions of some of the other languages. There is tremendous pride taken in the fact that Aboriginal languages now exist side-by-side with English. The school also includes some traditional arts and crafts activities as part of the weekly curriculum. Elders from the community provide instruction in weaving, bark painting, spear-making, and the like. The inclusion of Aboriginal knowledge and technologies in the school curriculum provides a powerful symbolic and practical validation of Aboriginal culture.[15]

Material Goods

Aboriginal people in Maningrida recognize that the school provides an important range of material resources for the community. Food, as I have shown, is particularly significant. Hot meals, juice, fruit, soft drinks, sandwiches, ice cream, potato chips, and a range of other foods are available for sale to the Aboriginal community in the school canteen (often on credit, a situation that has created some tense cross-cultural misunderstandings), and fresh fruit is given to students several times a week as part of a subsidized nutrition program. Food is also distributed during visits of teachers to the homeland center schools in remote areas. The school vehicles are loosely controlled and provide transport for many people only peripherally involved with the school. Jobs for many Aboriginal people are provided through the school and the salaries are standardized and match those of non-Aboriginal employees in urban schools. By historical standards, the incomes of Aboriginal individuals employed as teachers, for example, are enormous. The school is thus a vital conduit for material resources in the community and Aboriginal people are adept at ensuring they have influence over the process.

Social Resources

The school provides direct access to a range of important social resources that are otherwise unavailable. Aboriginal children, like many children in other Western-style schools, often complain that daily life is boring, and so the entertainment value of the school is high. Music, art, books, computers, sports, and excursions provide stimulation and excitement. The school also facilitates special children's health programs such as hearing tests and dental checks-ups. School staff are also useful allies for interacting with the white world, and often provide assistance with filling out forms and can be useful sources for advice and cultural translation related to the workings of the non-Aboriginal world. In some instances, school staff—perceived to be powerful but less threatening than the police—have been called upon to assist in mediating disputes between Aboriginal people.[16] The school is thus an important venue for securing a variety of social resources for the wider community.

CONCLUSION

In the Maningrida region today, perceptions of education are colored by notions of equity; education is considered by Aboriginal people to be a fundamental right of Australian citizenship won in exchange for allowing non-Aboriginal people onto their traditional lands and into their world. There is insistence by Aboriginal people that they should assume a major role in steering education in their own communities. That insistence is often articulated in terms of their responsibilities as caretakers for the country and, ultimately, for the institutions non-Aboriginal people established in the region. It is crucially important that Aboriginal demands for educational equity be taken seriously. Progress toward that goal needs to be gauged in some way, but assessing the success or failure of education in Maningrida according to traditional outcome measures, such as student attendance, retention, and national performance tests, will mask some subtle and important processes. Western education is providing basic competencies in literacy and numeracy for those who want them, and facilitating the acquisition of higher-level cross-cultural skills. The school has also come to play an important role in conserving and reaffirming elements of traditional culture. In addition, it is a key site through which access to a range of vital economic and social resources is mediated. However, not all of these are primary objectives of Western educational policy. Illustrating Levinson and Sutton's (this volume) point that policy is "constantly negotiated and reorganized in the ongoing flow of social life," I have shown how Aboriginal people in Maningrida counterpoise their own version of policy based on their own cultural assumptions and principles. On a daily basis, in the context of practical engagement with Western education, they appropriate Western policy components, effectively creating their own educational policy and steering education toward their own particular ends.

NOTES

1. An earlier version of this chapter was presented at a seminar at the Centre for Aboriginal Economic Policy Research at The Australian National University and then revised for presentation at the American Anthropological Association meetings in Washington, D.C., in November 1997. I am grateful for the many useful comments provided by the participants of those sessions. I want to express my particular appreciation to Jon Altman, Brian Gray, Greg Jarvis, Bradley Levinson, Beverly Sibthorpe, and Harry Wolcott for written comments on various drafts; the analysis benefited as well from the insights of several Maningrida teachers who provided anonymous comments on an earlier version of this chapter (Schwab, 1998). Finally, I wish to acknowledge the patience and generosity of the people of Maningrida and the staff of the Community Education Centre in allowing me to carry out the research on which this chapter is based.

2. The research on which this chapter is based was carried out during three field trips to Maningrida during the academic school years of 1996, 1997, and 1998. So far, I have spent a total of 9 or 10 weeks there doing participant observation in class-

rooms—in the hub school and in various homeland center schools—on the school grounds, and throughout the wider community. I have carried out formal and informal interviews with school staff, students, parents, school council members, and other various community members and I have collected and analyzed minutes of school council meetings, studied school records on income and expenditure, and charted enrollment, attendance, and staffing patterns. I spent countless enjoyable hours in classrooms and experienced what sometimes seemed like endless drives through the savanna in four-wheel-drive vehicles packed with children and dogs, drank endless cups of tea with teachers in the school staff room, and was assured by children swimming in crocodile-infested rivers and billabongs that there was no danger because "those crocodiles *know* us."

3. See Hiatt (1965), Meehan (1982), Altman (1987), and Keen (1994) for historical and ethnographic overviews of the region.

4. Deficit models of educational failure are having a renaissance in Australia, with the arrival of a political agenda that seeks to place responsibility on individuals and promotes an ideology that decries "special treatment" for disadvantaged minorities.

5. Until relatively recently, much of Australia's educational policy relating to Aboriginal and other minority children was based on this interpretation. The answer to the dilemma of school "failure," as suggested in countless reports by indigenous education consultative and policy review committees, is contained in a set of recurring policy recommendations promoting increased indigenous involvement in decision making, increased access and participation, and equitable outcomes (Aboriginal Consultative Group, 1975; Commonwealth of Australia, 1995; Hughes, 1988; Ministerial Council on Education, Employment, Training and Youth Affairs, 1996). The catch-phrase cure is empowerment—if Aboriginal people are empowered, so the argument goes, they will succeed.

6. The approach I am taking here is influenced by Ortner's notion of cultural schemas (Ortner, 1989, 1990). More recently, she has referred to these as "serious games," highlighting their strategic character (Ortner, 1996). Cultural themes, as I am referring to them here, are essentially recurring cultural scripts that weave through daily life, ordering and structuring everyday interactions.

7. Altman (personal communication, April 1998) suggests that one reason Aboriginal parents are reluctant to "boss" their children is that children are quick to leave in anger. Because kinship is classificatory, children are never at a loss for other "mothers" or "fathers" to provide shelter and support; if they are frustrated or angry, they merely go off to stay with another "parent."

8. The non-Aboriginal teachers are increasingly aware of the nightmarish legal implications of this situation in terms of the obligation teachers have to ensure the safety and care of their students during school hours.

9. The principles of Aboriginal sharing are discussed in detail in Schwab (1995).

10. In the shift from freshly hunted and gathered foods to prepared and fried "take aways," Aboriginal people's general health levels have declined dramatically.

11. The community has recently requested an extension of open hours beyond the morning and lunch service, and a school breakfast program has been instituted.

12. A recent health screening of school children by the Community Child Health Team found 1% of the children underweight (weight for age), 12% wasting (weight for height), 8% stunted, and 10% malnourished. Of those children attending school

on the day of the screening, 40% were anemic, 12% had perforated eardrums, and 44% had skin sores, scabies, or fungal infections.

13. While it is often said that "winnings" are redistributed among community members, not all Aboriginal observers are so sanguine. Many note that with the advent of daily air service to Darwin, it is relatively easy for winnings to disappear quickly from the community, never to be seen again.

14. The notion of "boss" is multifaceted and has its roots in the ceremonial structures of the region where one group "owns" and has ultimate responsibility for a particular ceremony while a second group of ritual "managers" attends to the details (Altman, 1987; Berndt & Berndt, 1970). The owner/manager ritual moiety structure is common to many Aboriginal groups (see Strehlow [1947], Meggit [1962], and Myers [1991] for discussion of this pattern in Central Australia). There is possibly also some connection to historical experience with hierarchies in the pastoral industries, where one man assumed a supervisory role over others.

15. While most desire the school to play a role in cultural maintenance, there are exceptions. There are Aboriginal people in the region, living in remote homeland centers, who firmly believe that one day the non-Aboriginal visitors will pack up and move away.

16. In one case, two brothers had a violent confrontation at the homeland center where they both lived with their wives, children, and other relatives. To calm the situation, one brother moved his family to a neighboring center. At a school council meeting, he asked the council for assistance in resolving the dispute so he could move back to his own "country."

REFERENCES

Aboriginal Consultative Group (1975). *Education for Aborigines: Report to the Schools Commission*. Canberra: Schools Commission.

Altman, J. C. (1987). *Hunter-Gatherers Today: An Aboriginal Economy in North Australia*. Canberra: Australian Institute of Aboriginal Studies.

Berndt, R., & Berndt, C. (1970). *Man, Land and Myth in North Australia: The Gunwinggu People*. Sydney: Ure Smith.

Commonwealth of Australia (1995). *National Review of Education for Aboriginal and Torres Strait Islander People, Final Report*. Canberra: Australian Government Publishing Service.

Hamilton, A. (1981). *Nature and Nurture: Aboriginal Child-rearing in North-Central Arnhem Land*. Canberra: Australian Institute of Aboriginal Studies.

Hiatt, L. H. (1965). *Kinship and Conflict: A Study of an Aboriginal Community in Northern Arnhem Land*. Canberra: The Australian National University.

Hughes, P. (1988). *Report of the Aboriginal Education Policy Task Force*. Canberra: Australian Government Publishing Service.

Keeffe, K. (1992). *From the Centre to the City: Aboriginal Education, Culture and Power*. Canberra: Aboriginal Studies Press.

Keen, I. (1994). *Knowledge and Secrecy in an Aboriginal Religion*. Oxford: Clarendon Press.

Levinson, B., & Holland, D. (1996). "The cultural production of the educated person: an introduction," in B. Levinson, D. Foley, & D. Holland (Eds.), *The*

Cultural Production of the Educated Person: Critical Ethnographies of Schooling and Local Practice (pp. 1–54). Albany: State University of New York Press.

Levinson, B., & Sutton, M. (2000). "Introduction," in this volume.

McDermott, R. (1993). "Acquisition of a child by a learning disability," in S. Chaiklin & J. Lave (Eds.), *Understanding Practice: Perspectives on Activity and Context* (pp. 269–305). Cambridge: Cambridge University Press.

McDermott, R. (1987). "Explaining minority school failure, again." *Anthropology and Education Quarterly*, 18, 361–64.

McDermott, R. (1974). "Achieving school failure: an anthropological approach to illiteracy and social stratification," in G. Spindler (Ed.) *Education and Cultural Process: Toward an Anthropology of Education* (pp. 82–118). New York: Holt, Rinehart and Winston.

McDermott, R., & Varenne, H. (1995). "Culture as disability." *Anthropology and Education Quarterly*, 26, 324–348.

Meehan, B. (1982). *Shell Beds to Shell Middens*. Canberra: Australian Institute of Aboriginal Studies.

Meggit, M. (1962). *Desert People*. Sydney: Angus and Robertson.

Ministerial Council on Education, Employment, Training and Youth Affairs (1996). *A National Strategy for the Education of Aboriginal and Torres Strait Islander Peoples*. Melbourne: Ministerial Council on Education, Employment, Training and Youth Affairs.

Myers, F. (1991). *Pintupi Country, Pintupi Self: Sentiment, Place, and Politics Among Western Desert Aborigines*. Berkeley: University of California Press.

Ortner, S. (1989). *High Religion: A Cultural and Political History of Sherpa Buddhism*. Princeton: Princeton University Press.

Ortner, S. (1990). "Patterns of history: cultural schemas in the foundings of Sherpa religious institutions," in E. Ohnuki-Tierney (Ed.), *Culture Through Time: Anthropological Approaches* (pp. 57–93). Stanford: Stanford University Press.

Ortner, S. (1996). *Making Gender: The Politics and Erotics of Culture*. Boston: Beacon Press.

Schwab, R.G. (1998). "Educational "failure" and educational "success" in an Aboriginal community," *CAEPR Discussion Paper No. 161*. Canberra: Centre for Aboriginal Economic Policy Research, The Australian National University.

Schwab, R.G. (1995). "The calculus of reciprocity: principles and implications of Aboriginal sharing," *CAEPR Discussion Paper No. 100*. Canberra: Centre for Aboriginal Economic Policy Research, The Australian National University.

Strehlow, T. (1947). *Aranda Traditions*. Melbourne: University of Melbourne Press.

Varenne, H., & McDermott, R. (1999). *Successful Failure: The School American Builds*. Boulder: Westview Press.

11

"We Are Mountain": Appalachian Educators' Responses to the Challenge of Systemic Reform

Maureen Porter

INTRODUCTION

The Kentucky Education Reform Act of 1990 (KERA) rolled into the mountains of southeastern Kentucky like an ominous, churning thunderstorm. It brought with it a sudden change in pressure systems and let loose a torrent of new programs, funds, and requirements. Residents of the Appalachian counties in the state looked on this storm cloud with a mixture of relief and apprehension. For at the same time that it promised a windfall of resources on an unprecedented scale, the dark cloud of increased governmental control would also hang over them. Would this latest apparition be all noise and no action? Would the benefits trickle down to the neediest of children and school districts? Reform on such a large scale was an unknown. Mountaineers waited skeptically to see what it would mean for them and their homeplaces.

While policies may be written at a state level, actual reform is radically local. Negotiations about proposed changes are enmeshed in local webs of personalized relationships, power hierarchies, and long-standing paradoxes about the very meaning of education itself. These webs have repeatedly ensnared those officials who, expecting to see systemic reform proceed in a rational, impersonal manner, misjudge how strong local cultural frames of reference can be. Policymakers need a more effective, grounded understanding of the role that these resilient strands of culture play in framing local debates.

This is particularly apparent in the debate that arose over what it means to teach and learn in the mountains. The southeastern, Appalachian part of Kentucky presents a particularly challenging and fundamentally important place to look at how the politics of identity intersect with the politics of policy appropriation. In this chapter, I present a synopsis of some of the fundamental challenges faced by educators and community members as they negotiated how they would implement KERA in their schools. The data come from research conducted at "Central High" in "Hickory County" over the course of an academic year and two subsequent follow-up research periods, all of which is chronicled in the dissertation titled *Moving Mountains: Reform, Resistance, and Resiliency in an Appalachian Kentucky High School* (Porter, 1996). My goal is to provide an account that both illustrates the particularities and allows for generalization (Geertz, 1973). This analysis is deeply rooted in a particular place, but its implications do not end where the mountains recede. In the years since its completion, I have been pleased with the two-fold reception of this ethnographic portrait. First, whether I am presenting at a session on challenges of urban school reform or at an international conference on learning communities, the basic issues of ownership of change and democratization come to the fore. It seems that the challenges faced in Kentucky resonate with a much broader audience. Inner city principals have said, "That's my school, too." Appalachians, especially from Kentucky, recognize something of their own upbringing and are certain that they know which county I chose, although they are almost invariably wrong. Second, the portrait offers those who are unfamiliar with the region a metaphorically rich discourse about what it means to have "book learning'" and to "get on" in the mountains. They get a look beyond the official statistics that simplistically define this as a "persistent poverty" county to the kinds of daily, lived, personal relationships that make mountain life so richly rewarding.

Hickory Countians' responses to change were informed by their understandings of what it means to live and teach in the hills, in essence, what it means to "be mountain." This metaphor condenses profoundly important elements of their sense of place into a single phrase that was used over and over again. Lakoff and Johnson (1980) argue that our everyday conceptual systems are fundamentally metaphorical. Contests over meaning are at the root of many school encounters. McLaren (1986) stresses how the classroom is a "symbolic arena where students and teachers struggle over the interpretation of metaphors, icons, and structures of meaning, and where symbols have both centripetal and centrifugal pulls" (p. 6). Students, teachers, board members, and parents engage one another in critiquing school leaders' assertions that they are doing the best they can for the county's children, that they are preparing them to take their place within the community. I believe that delving more deeply into the implications that these metaphors have for policy appropriation is a valuable contribution of ethnographic policy analysis. That is because these ways of culturally representing the world and its actors are fertile starting places to explore the "hidden transcripts" of how local actors respond to translocal reform agendas (Scott, 1990).

I will show how "being mountain" embraces a particular set of values and codes of moral conduct that insiders link to the geography of the region. This ideal way of relating and leading has significant implications for the options that reformers can draw on when trying to motivate others to act.

"WE ARE MOUNTAIN!"

Undulating, fog-enshrouded blue mountains dominate the Hickory County skyline. They extend as far as one can see in any direction. But they are much more than a perpetual reminder of the special qualities of this Appalachian homeplace. These ancient ranges are both symbol and setting (Fitchen, 1991) of Hickory Countians' struggle to endure and to maintain a way of life that they cherish. *↗ sounds like Pike county*

The ever-present nature of mountain geography reinforces the mountains as key symbols. Hickory Countians freely use these physical elements as the raw materials for shaping metaphors that express underlying ideologies about themselves and others. In a related project that arose from the research, I specifically focus on teachers' metaphors of their work in mountain schools. These metaphors directly influence the pedagogies and the politics they choose. Some saw themselves as gardeners, tenderly pruning young saplings, others as the last true defenders of an Appalachian Alamo (Porter, 1998). In a similar way, community members of all ages metaphorically spoke of themselves as "being mountain." The direct identification with the landscape that is embedded in this statement is important. For they did not say "we are mountain people," but rather that they were in, of, and one with the mountains. Appalachia and her people share a common past and a mutually interdependent future.

Culture arises as a lived, dynamic response to both the enduring and malleable characteristics of a region. Identification with a place is not the same as essentialism. But a strong sense of self, firmly grounded in a critical sense of place, is essential if a group is to survive. Thus, to insiders, to say that a person "is mountain" draws on culturally sanctioned ways of being that are closely tied with local struggles for autonomy and cultural preservation. Someone who is paid this compliment is considered to have the following qualities: he or she is neighborly; committed to his or her family and close friends; has self-respect, yet is a humble public person; and is self-reliant and independent vis-à-vis the outside but has built extensive interdependent networks of neighbors, friends, and kin to take care of local needs. He or she is, in essence, one of the "home folks." These traits are valued all the more because they are seen as being at odds with insiders' stereotypes of urban and suburban life in other parts of the United States.

These valued traits take on even sharper relief when contrasted with its paired insult. When a person goes away, gives up the regional dialect to take on "proper" ways of speaking, and prefers new to longtime childhood friendships, he or she is said to have "lost some of the mountain." Spatially and ideologically, this person is considered to have become distant, to have "gotten above their raising," to be "uppity," to "look down on others," and "not down home." People who have "lost the mountain" are pitiable, but more important, they are suspect. Hickory Countians feel that such people cannot be trusted, as they have severed the relationships of reciprocity and respect that bind local people together over the course of a lifetime.

The mountains that rise up around Central High are also symbols of resilience. They stand as sentinels to guard against change that would come too quickly or too forcefully. In the past they have been effective buffers, holding back numerous waves of reform that may have transformed schools elsewhere. But increasingly, as Hickory County's 90-odd one-room schools were forced to consolidate into less than 10 large elementary schools, as the high school curriculum was expanded to meet state requirements, and as technology brought the outside world closer, these mountains have only slowed down the rate at which new ideas and practices filter into these rural schools.

Nevertheless, teachers, students, and staff at Central High continue to look at the solid cliffs around them as symbols of steadfastness. Although the mountains have been deeply scarred by surface mining and clear-cutting of timber, they still stand. Although streams have been polluted by strip mine runoff, irresponsible dumping of household garbage, and chemical toxins from factories lured to the region by tremendous tax incentives, they still hold out the promise of life. Residents spoke of themselves as being like the mountains, holding their ground and persevering in the face of adversity. Just as they weathered storms that arose in the Bluegrass and drifted over to the hills, so too did they persevere in the face of mandates for change that blew in on gusts of hot air from the Flatlanders. Whether or not to implement KERA was just the most recent of such challenges that they faced. It would not be the last.

The rugged, isolated terrain is the ground upon which Appalachians have constructed an origin myth that establishes them as a distinct and endangered people. A shared, generic story about how the original families came to Hickory provides a common orientation with which to locate themselves relative to the rest of the United Sates. To "be mountain" means to be a descendent, either literally or through fictive kinship, of the Anglo-Saxon Long Hunters who crossed through the Cumberland Gap into the vast and untamed western frontier named "Ken-ta-kee" at the end of the 18th century. (African-American residents had a somewhat similar exodus-like origin story, as did those who came to the mountains more recently as part of a "back to the land" movement.) Hickory Countians attribute their rugged environment with producing a separate group of people who value close ties to the land, hunting, traditional forms of Old English, and fundamental and evangelical Christianity. This history serves as a reference point against which to contrast current struggles for sovereignty and perseverance. Residents spoke proudly of conquering the original inhabitants and overcoming the dangers of the wilderness. So from their point of view, in comparison to marauding bears, how bad could KERA's state auditors be?

One of the essential components of this origin story is the central role of kinship. The success of the mountaineer family can be attributed directly to moral imperatives to stick together to face anyone or anything perceived to be a common enemy. Most students at Central came from strong and extended families, with cousins sitting with them at lunch and an aunt or neighbor at the front of the classroom. Likewise, approximately half of the teaching staff had a spouse, sibling, parent, or cousin who was also a teacher or administrator in the county, if not also at the single, consolidated high school. They knew that they could turn to a ready support system to back them up if they proposed reforms, or if they intended to see that a proposed reform failed. Thus, to "be mountain" means drawing strategically on a wide network of people bound by filial loyalty, and by giving and taking within an informal economy that supplements and often circumvents the official economy. For example, until KERA instituted antinepotism laws and new, publicly accountable procedures for hiring teachers, insiders expected—and perpetuated—a system of rewards and punishments that allocated the scarce and highly coveted teaching jobs only to strategically placed and "deserving" local candidates.

This origin myth also carries within it the idea that the long-held traditional ways of life are endangered. Certainly, adaptability and change have always been features of life on what was once the Far Western frontier. But the pace of external encroachment has dramatically increased. First river ferries, then railroads and mining camps, then state highways, and, most recently, a motor parkway designed to lure tourists to the region have all meant increasing commerce and exchange with outsiders. Not long ago, neighborhood schools and churches were the primary gathering places and purveyors of moral and social values outside the family. But greater affluence and mobility have contributed to lessened family control over teens' movements.

In addition to being a symbol, the Appalachian range is also the setting for stories that Hickory Countians tell about themselves and others. The mountains create very real boundaries, both physical and cognitive. On a physical level, the steep hollers and absence of gravel roads over the tops of ridges create effective barriers, buffering residents from direct contact with the world beyond the region. As Devon, a high school sophomore, summarized in a metaphor-generating exercise, "The mountains are closed, locked doors. They keep you in and keep everyone else out." Melissa added, "The mountains are big fences that separate us from the rest of the world. The mountains surround our region and block out all other regions. Since there are mountains, we can't see but only so far." This sense of isolation is ameliorated by the fact that now nearly all of even the poorest households have a satellite dish. Ironically, however, the mediated nature of this contact tends to magnify the sense of a fantasy world that teens believe awaits them "out there," in "the real world" beyond the hills.

The mountains provide the basis for establishing the cognitive boundaries that delineate who is "inside" and who is "outside." The 30,000 people in Hickory County form a social world in and of themselves, even though on the surface it may appear identical to neighboring counties. The county has become the basis for identity and allegiance. This is even more so the case in Kentucky than elsewhere, since most school districts are the same as the county boundaries. Mrs. Bargo, a single mother of two, a crafter and entrepreneur, explained how the mountains become the basis for labels that are linked to moral attributes:

[All these counties] are really the same place, all from the same people. But with growing up, with basketball and boundaries, you come to see people as different. You find tags to tag people with, to say they're more different. We see people in [county toward the Bluegrass] as being different, snobbish, they see us being primitive. We say people in [county to the east] are more mountain and so they're behind us. Everybody perceives the counties as different. In the old days maybe there were real political differences or rivalries with different Congressional districts dividing off districts. These divisions last. Maybe it's because there's not much contact, so people stay divided. Maybe you have a relative in the next county, but otherwise people don't like to leave their place. You hear negative things about other people. You grow up and just believe there are differences.

Differentiating between residents also is a feature of life within counties. The vast system of creeks and rivers carve out fertile valley bottoms and an intricate series of steep, wooded hollers that create niches that belong to different families and communities. Children learn in Head Start that it is as important to know which side of the mountain you are from as it is to know which patronym you carry. At Central High, teens from the Disappointment Creek end of the county are automatically branded as "hicks" or "creeks," while those from closer to the county seat are not so easily labeled with pejorative names. The distinctions between these places—and the attendant moral ascriptions—are poignant and meaningful to the Grays who call "Gray's Branch" home or the Patersons and Higgens who live up Higgens Holler.

In summary, geopolitical separations within the county, between counties, and between the mountaineers and the Flatlanders are more significant than simply locating "where a person is coming from." This process of labeling divides Appalachians from one another and drives a sharp wedge between issues perceived as mountain interests and those belonging properly to the flat Bluegrass of the central, urban part of the state. On a cognitive level, the mountains provide clear distinctions between "insiders" and "outsiders," the "home folks" and "furriners." They provide boundaries that distinguish between insiders who belong to an established place and a known people and outsiders and their suspect allegiances and motivations. These categories distinguish between insiders who belong in a teaching position at Central as a natural kind of birthright, and outsiders who are seen as unfairly infringing on a tight local job market. Likewise, the concepts of insider and outsider are extended to provide the means for deciding who is acting on reasonable family and friendship obligations and who is "being political." They differentiate between who is a "community builder" and who wants to change "what is good enough." These broad concepts can be used to create camps of those who understand "just how things are here" and defer (at least in public) to local hierarchies of power and privilege, and those who venture to take a stake in challenging problematic aspects of the status quo.

All of these streams of meaning converge in the nuanced and significant phrase, "being mountain." As a result, those who wish to implement change must do so in both a manner and for reasons consistent with the underlying mountaineer ideology. Policy that is written elsewhere, as is essentially the case with KERA, is scrutinized carefully and patiently before being adopted, even if failure to meet timelines or to comply brings the potential threat of even greater state intervention. Responses and actors must be well grounded. The Hickory Countian who can show that he or she "is one of us," and has not "gotten above their raisin'" and "lost the mountain" is the one most likely to be able to instigate the broad-based grassroots involvement needed if systemic reform of schooling is to be successful.

In the next section, I illustrate five lessons that insiders learned about implementing and adapting KERA in the mountains. Teachers, staff, and teens resisted simplistically adopting the Reform Act wholesale, and at times resisted embracing new regulations at all. Like the mountains, those who held power and privileged positions were steadfast and hard to move. Newcomers, marginalized insiders, and, indeed, some members of core families nevertheless created spaces for action. They used old styles of stories to tell new tales. They learned to present and solve problems in ways that fostered constructive responses. They learned to use numbers and written testimony without acting like the dreaded "external expert." And in each case, discussants in the emergent cultural dialogue of reform held up the yardstick of "being mountain" as the measure of their success or failure.

THE BACKDROP: KERA AND HICKORY COUNTY

KERA's passage heralded what was to be labeled the "third wave" of reform. This distinguishes itself from previous approaches to large-scale change in its integrated or "systemic" approach to using centralized resources and authority to create a more decentralized, democratic system of common schools. For example, in the Reform Act, schools would be held accountable for meeting higher standards of student achievement, but would also be given greater autonomy, resources, and flexibility to achieve standardized ends.

Public schools offer intriguing sites in which to explore the sometimes surprising twists and turns that policy implementation takes. As in many rural communities, the large, consolidated Central High School in this rugged region was the critical juncture where issues of autonomy, identity, and authority intersect. It is the single most important gathering place for teens and adults from the furthest reaches of the county. It is the place where local meets local and local engages the state. Anzaldua (1987) posits that such cultural border-lands, along the rough edges where worlds and worldviews collide, exist in a state of tensions and explicit paradoxes. These places of confluence are poten-tially creative spaces where ambivalence and negotiation can result in creative syntheses of old and new, inside and outside, mountain and mainstream. Thus, it is both fascinating and consequential to look at reform at Hickory's Central High during a time of upheaval and debate. By focusing in on a set of people who are undergoing an accelerated and/or especially fragmenting process of negotiation, this study is able to highlight those underlying issues of identity that otherwise would remain at a level of tacit understanding. When there was suddenly more at stake, what was previously understood unproblematically (or at least publicly tolerated) as "how we do things here," became a matter of public debate, derision, and division.

One of the major emphases in KERA is the cultivation of local stakeholders who have the capacity and desire to engage in public discourse and action on behalf of their schools. KERA offers, and frequently requires, site-based coun-cils, new hiring procedures, representative superintendent selection processes, teacher committees, regional educational support systems, Internet access, and more computers in the schools. New tools and ongoing training are avail-able to those who wish to take the brave step and become engaged in their schools. My focus is on this often-uneasy coupling of top-down state mandates with bottom-up advocacy and engagement. How did Appalachian educators create a basis for action? How did they understand their leadership role within a cultural framework that favors not setting oneself "above others?"

I chose a fieldsite that would be representative of common Appalachian is-sues. I came to select my fieldsite through a series of regional visits, interviews, and internships. The year prior to the actual fieldwork, I was hired as a policy analyst to do an evaluation of a statewide dropout prevention program called Destination Graduation, which paired college students with at-risk high school students in literacy, entertainment, and career guidance activities. As part of my assessment of the program's mentoring and tutoring components, I had the opportunity to meet with several program administrators and partici-pants in districts throughout the southeastern end of the state. These personal contacts, coupled with extensive research into the status of districts' participa-tion in KERA, led to several best candidates. I finally selected Hickory County as a district that was perceived "on paper" to be fully embracing the basic frameworks and new governing structures required in KERA. As residents of a persistent poverty county, educators were eligible for the very first rounds of priority support, provided it complied with the new rules of the game. The consolidated county school district also was typical of its Appalachian neighbors demographically, socioeconomically, politically, and in terms of gradua-tion outcomes and performance indicators.

WHY ETHNOGRAPHY?

Why use ethnographic tools to work in the field and to share the fruits of my labor? First, it is vital to situate systemic, standardized reform in a specific time and place, to locate it geopolitically within the overlapping spheres of power and meaning that profoundly shape the local response to externally mandated reform. Second, ethnographic conclusions are based on iterative rounds of data gathering and analysis in the field. One does not wait until the fieldwork is all over to write it up. Indeed, understanding the limitations and advantages of different kinds of instruments while still on site offers the fieldworker the op-portunity to administer improved instruments while the situation is still con-ducive to more inquiry. As I will show later, opportunities to work with educators in the site to develop instruments that would generate data that is actually useful to them greatly shaped both the quality of the results and the qualities of the relationships that I was able to forge. Third, because it is a per-sonalized, participatory approach to knowing, ethnography requires active engagement with people on an everyday basis. Actions, complaints, small tri-umphs, and concerns that would not dare be expressed in an official meeting or document reveal themselves when there is sustained contact. Fourth, ethnographers refine theories and incorporate increasing awareness of the nu-ances of significant phrases. Metaphors and images that are deeply embedded in actors' assumptions and answers only become apparent with repeated con-versations. Fifth, living in the same economy and geographic isolation drive home points like no other way of knowing can. For example, I had to drive to the next county to get my severely sprained ankle examined and casted because there were no facilities available where I lived.

I offer some of the most important methodological quandaries and solu-tions presented in *Moving Mountains* as part of this synopsis of selected sto-ries. All of those involved in the process of reform learned important lessons about appropriate and expedient ways to behave if they wanted to be heard or answered. This certainly included the resident ethnographer! In substantive ways, every day I became more and more an integral part of the scene at Cen-tral as I learned to work as an ethical and effective researcher. Through my sur-veys, interviews, and participant observation, I was a constant presence and a "sounding board" for those who needed a confidential or sympathetic ear.

As an ethnographer and policy analyst, I offer comparisons between the fieldwork dilemmas and strategies that I encountered and the parallel chal-lenges facing the teaching staff. As a novice scholar, and as novice reformers, we had to come to terms with our own limitations in implementing standard-ized requirements. We each had to find ways of making not only the final prod-uct, but also the journey toward "proficient" status, one that would satisfy both our evaluators and ourselves. We each sought to make friends and to make a difference. I had hoped that my work would be transformative on more than an interpersonal level. Just as KERA proposes to democratize the process of education, so too did I hope that my presence would contribute to a more egalitarian, open process of sharing information and crafting solutions.

FIVE LESSONS

The Kentucky Education Reform Act provided an important catalyst that sparked debate and action from the halls of the state legislature in Frankfort to the chairs of beauty salons up Bargo Branch. KERA's assessment and account-ability system, KIRIS, and the new Office of Educational Accountability (OEA), generated a sense of expediency to identify and then address items that the framers of the Reform Act defined as "problematic."

A key dimension in creating ownership of educational policies is claiming the right to define the problems to be solved. As Berger and Luckmann have noted, reality is socially constructed; these "definitions of reality have self-fulfilling potency" (1967, p. 116). Therefore, whether or not stake-holders are willing to identify a situation (or metaphor, such as "being moun-tain") as open to question is critical. Whether or not it can be treated as problematic, questionable, and hence alterable, is a matter of great impor-tance. Edelman (1988) elucidates the potential that is unleashed when some-thing is defined as a problem:

Problems come into discourse and therefore into existence as reinforcements of ideolo-gies, not simply because they are there or because they are important for well being. They signify who are virtuous and useful and who are dangerous and inadequate, which actions will be rewarded and which penalized. They constitute people as subjects with particular kinds of aspirations, self-concepts, and fears and they create beliefs about the relative importance of events and objects. They are critical in determining who exer-cises authority and who accepts it. They construct areas of immunity from concern be-cause those areas are not seen as problems. Like leaders and enemies, they define the contours of the social world, not in the same way for everyone, but in the light of the di-verse situations from which people respond to the political spectacle. (pp. 12–13)

Therefore, it is not enough for a state law to declare that the system of public schooling is unconstitutional; local people must deem this to be true for them-selves. For as Mr. Norris, a central office person, put it, "You cannot fix a prob-lem if you don't see it as one." With the arrival of KERA, local educators have more constituents to please and appease. But external pressure alone is not enough to create stakeholders who have a genuine, long-term investment in school activities. If changes are made simply for the sake of superficially com-plying with the minimal standards of the latest reform act, much of the original intent of the law will be lost. Those who take a stake in reform must also take an active role in defining their own problems and finding culturally responsive solutions.

What did it mean to juggle "being mountain" with being reformers? How did educators, community members, and students handle their competing responsibilities, allegiances, goals, and priorities? To what extent did reform take hold on a grassroots level in a way that is sustainable and culturally responsive? In this section, I profile five lessons that stakeholders learned as they responded to the challenges presented by KERA. Where appropriate, I add insights into the concurrent and entwined ethnographic research process as it unfolded in Hickory County.

Lesson One: "We Take Care of Our Own"

One of the striking things about education at Central High is the pervasive sentiment that they wish to manage their own affairs. Whether their resistance is focused against the intervention of state officials, or against local parents or business leaders, Central's teachers and staff resist external intrusion into "their" school. They wish to maintain Central as a place where they can take care of their own peers, professional lives, and their own problems.

Central High School personnel see themselves as like a family. "Everyone here is related to everyone" is the shorthand way of expressing the multiple ties of friendship, barter, church, social clubs, neighborhood, profession, and age that create many strands of connection. As a resident of the small county seat, I encountered people from work wherever I shopped, walked, or socialized. They were free to observe if I was home at night, who I ate lunch with, and, particularly important, whose turn it was to give me a ride home after a meeting. These kinds of involvements in one another's lives extend far beyond the campus but meet up again and again on the school grounds. The result is that staff and students are inextricably bound up in a Gordian knot of mutual obligations.

This understanding of being like an extended family contributes to a resilient sense that residents share something special in common. In one way or another, they are all of one people, they are all mountain. This paradigm about the world could provide the basis for collective action. Being part of a family provides an important orientation of long-term belonging, of constituting an "us" that is distinctive from people in other states, even other counties. Central High faculty do speak of "our" graduates who have achieved distinction, "brag on" "our" teams and "our mountain kids" when they do well or try hard. This paradigm can provide the basis for establishing collective responsibility for all members of the family.

Unfortunately, not all young people are equal members of the Central family. Staff resist the notion that all of the students are "our own." One may be a favorite son while another is, at best, a poor cousin. And for those Hickory Countians who are not white, race clearly marks them as being perpetual outsiders. In the narrowest interpretation, the "family" includes only closest kin and longtime friends. And, as the newest student soon learns, Hickory Countians take care of their own first.

It is not mere coincidence that it is at Central, the flagship of the Hickory County public schools, where issues of belonging, loyalty, and responsibility come to a head. Teaching is not just any job; for many, it is one of the few existing jobs in which they can locally use their advanced skills and interests in the liberal and vocational arts. One of the most important and highest profile examples of "taking care of our own" is the preference for hiring local people before outsiders, even if the local person is not quite as qualified. What gives the latter an edge is that they already belong. Residents want to invest in people who have a stake in building a life locally, and thus who will have to live with the consequences of their actions at work. Furthermore, residents want their children to "grow up knowing that there will be a place for them here."

Educational reform at Central is important for another reason. This is where young people learn the skills and attitudes that can prepare them to contribute to families, paid employment, and volunteer work that are critical to the viability and vitality of whichever communities they choose to belong to as adults. Parents at the top of the Hickory County pyramid want their children to do well. For many, this includes the preference for their own children to come back and take over the family law firm, real estate agency, elected office, educational position, or business. If the current service levels are maintained, the handful of such occupations in the county currently need only a few successors. Young people learn from experience that those who have achieved these positions of prominence seldom welcome competition. Those who are local outsiders, marginalized by race or class, learn that the future is stacked against them, that there is likely to be no place for them, even at "home."

Hickory Countians rely on a personalized understanding when generalizing local ways of working together to external agents. As seen from the mountains, "the State" is a personified, although distant, entity that, like the equally monolithic "mountaineer," is of course looking out for its own best interests. Reinforcing this conviction is a construction of the state government, the Department of Education, and the legislature's Office of Education Accountability as inherently in competition with, or at odds with, local governance. Although systemic reform requires effective cooperation between local and state levels, mountaineers in Hickory County assert that it could never be in the state's best interests to encourage autonomy and self-reliance. This line of reasoning continues to undermine the establishment of productive partnerships between the state and local levels.

In this predominantly Republican area there is a fundamental mistrust of "big government," especially government that arises from the Bluegrass. Mrs. Allen, a teacher who came of age in the mountains in the late 1960s, summed up, "We don't trust outsiders. I guess it's just the mountain attitude. It's antiestablishment. We don't trust government that they don't have an ulterior motive." Hickory Countians believed that the state has clandestine motives for proposing education reforms. And, they believed, these motives do not end with changing the way the schools are run.

One of the running jokes about my work was that I was actually a spy for the state. Although I was explicit and open about my research goals, this only fueled suspicions that I was undercover, a "state woman," or "that state spy." This label was disturbing to me until I realized its actual significance. After a while I began to realize that my joking and protesting about the label had turned it into a nickname, a new moniker for my unique role within the district. It became my "handle," a way for us to joke about the tensions and anxiety inherently present in an evaluative analysis of others. As a colleague explained, through being able to laugh at myself, and by using the assigned role to make fun of the actual state investigators, I had become one of the insiders. Mr. Hayes, a person who had used several versions of the ritual insult freely and frequently, explained the nature of the game that we shared, "People like things relaxed. People say, 'She's from the state!' to break the ice. If people were serious no one would talk to you." As an outspoken critic and leader among his peers and in our frequent chats, he confided, "If'n it was serious, I'd a not told you anything."

Lesson Two: "We Solve Things Face to Face"

Participants asked: How can a person be of the mountains yet move mountains? The second theme expresses the preferred ideal of being able to talk openly and informally with one another as equals, of addressing problems face to face. Residents prefer to keep problems within the family (literally or figuratively), rather than bringing in outside referees. Recognizing that power differentials based on family name, wealth, public office, and gender significantly undermine actual equality, this theme points to the significant gap between the ideal and actual practice.

Hickory Countians stress the importance of personal ties as the basis for approaching problems. In fact, the very success of joint problem solving is contingent upon finding a way of making a meaningful connection with others who similarly have a desire to see a particular outcome. They value being known to others as individuals rather than as a number or a statistic. When asked what they valued most about living in the country, people from all walks of life reported as their top reasons: feeling validated as a unique person, recognized for their special talents, and cherished as a friend. The primary importance of trust and being looked after was particularly pronounced when compared to the anonymity and animosity that these rural people felt was characteristic of urban life. A resident summed up the goal of knowing and being known, stating that he wanted his children to be able to walk around the courthouse square (which in many Kentucky county seats is in the center of the business district) and have people say, "That's so-and-so's son," or, "That's so-and-so's daughter." Of course, others noted, that goal is a double-edged sword—if you don't toe the line, your children will also be stigmatized.

Parties to a negotiation seek ways to create win–win situations. "I wouldn't say we have politics at our school," stated a teacher, "it's more you scratch my back and I'll scratch yours." The distinguishing features are that both parties gain something they value. Furthermore, whether or not such intervention actually occurred, the public assumes that this negotiation has taken place. Veteran teachers readily hypothesized why and how each new teacher got their job; the claim that they objectively were "the best person for the job" was meaningless as colleagues tried to guess what made them the "best" and for whom it was good. The concept that there was a neutral standard of "good" that was distinguishable from the individual was beyond nearly all people's frame of reference.

Face-to-face deals create important relations of reciprocity. By hinting that a vote for block scheduling might garner a vote for a special budget allocation later or by hinting that hiring a niece now might make it easier to hire someone else's grandson later, Hickory Countians established expectations of future returns on this investment in the relationship. In the face of limited social and economic services, residents rely on one another for the necessities of life, work, and friendship as well as access to luxury goods. They want to know that they can depend on a tangible, steady friend rather than being vulnerable to the vagaries of the economy, weather, or welfare laws. They want to know that someone will be there to defend their family name and interests. Furthermore, they want to know that leaders will work with the people who already are in Hickory County, that this is where they belong and that whatever the outside world thinks, they are not merely disposable people. They want to know that others understand and respect the local score so that patience in waiting for their turn and keeping to their place will pay off in the long run. They want to know that they have a chance.

These expectations of reciprocity further perpetuate the cycle of personal negotiations, for those who have paid in have a vested interest in maintaining the long-term payoff for their contribution. Rather than opening up the game, they want to make sure that what resources exist are doled out based on face-to-face agreements that were often established years beforehand. Thus, from this point of view, KERA's assumption that the slate can simply be wiped clean and that all community members have the same rights is dangerous. In Hickory County, reforms do not proceed on the grounds of efficiency or abstract principles. Personal considerations based on real life interactions remain primary.

The local theme of sitting down and working out mutual interests face-to-face stands in even sharper relief when contrasted with the impersonal approach exemplified by Reform Act mandates and the OEA's investigation. "You cannot mandate change!" warned one of Central's established teachers to newcomer Principal Newmann. However, the Kentucky Education Reform

Act of 1990 clearly requires specific kinds of portfolio writing, performance events, and applications of technology. It encourages consideration of dozens of other practices, from an altered school year to block scheduling. However, teachers took these required changes as insults to their authority and threats to the autonomy that they had long enjoyed. The attitude seemed to be that they would lose face if they complied. Therefore, the more the state tried to codify and regulate local actions from afar, the more noncompliance became a matter of principle. If, instead, reform had meant new kinds of collaborations that would create win–win situations, more teachers might have more eagerly come to the table.

Central teachers had shown themselves willing and determined to overturn written rules. The policy that is the most vividly recalled by school personnel, parents, and students was the Clean Indoor Air Act. Although teachers were willing to apply the ban on smoking to students, they were appalled when the administration decreed that the ban also applied to adults. Teachers and staff appealed to their superintendent on a private basis; the decision was overturned. Given this model of adult behavior, it is little wonder that many of their students saw the very existence of new dress code requirements and attendance rules as sufficient grounds for retaliation. They too set out to prove that their leaders could not write rules that they could enforce. Students saw all too many of their teachers, janitors, and bus drivers lose reports, fail to file attendance papers, and push the limits of school rules themselves (e.g., smoking on school grounds). They could see past the smokescreen. They could smell the aftereffects. All too keenly aware of the hypocrisy in this model, students dared teachers to turn them in for smoking. Most teachers, even those who did not smoke, found it easier to let these violations slide.

Furthermore, Appalachian educators believe that outsiders value official, written correspondence more than face to face direct negotiations. Writing out mandates, letters of confidentiality, official warnings, even informed consent forms for research "create an additional set of problems for us." It means substituting printed, static words for give and take, face-to-face discussions. To Hickory Countians, the author of such a document seemingly had little power if he or she could not meet the accused face to face and settle differences together. Thus, the OEA's written letters of warning were perceived as cowardly and impotent threats. The more letters were sent, the more resistance and resentment was generated. From the standpoint of Hickory County, these norms of formalizing, standardizing, and codifying rules violated valued assumptions about how people should work together. They set the scene for enmity and distrust rather than beginning from the assumption that parties could find mutual interests.

Effective face-to-face relationships were critical in conducting fieldwork. I had to make sure that I had personal references for my interviews, and met people in discreet yet public places where we could offer our hands and open our hearts to one another. Local people see written contracts as poor substitutes for genuine respect and expectations of reciprocity. The men on the superintendent selection committee felt very conflicted about writing up a formal agreement of confidentiality, asserting that a piece of paper could hardly encourage trust "if a man's handshake doesn't mean anything anymore." To them, to have to sign this statement of trust would imply a fundamental lack of it.

Furthermore, set rules violate the norm of flexibility and individualized punishments. Mountaineer ideals claim the autonomy to live as they wish and to "be their own man." Most people felt that students should be disciplined in ways that respected individual circumstances. In a parallel fashion, teachers and administrators held different standards for different students. They did not buy into the slogan that all students can be expected to achieve at high or even moderate levels. Likewise, they believed some teachers should be cut more slack than others so they would cause as little trouble as possible. In summary, to set rules of behavior and standards for achievement that all should meet would be a "problem."

What then should potential partners do? They should model the same cooperative, mutually respectful ways of working together in state–local interactions as would occur in local–local decision-making bodies; that is, practice democratization and respect at all levels. Too often, state mandates have come down to the districts in ways that feel threatening, condescending, and that denigrate or, at best, ignore local mores and traditional lifestyles. State officials eager to assert the right to mandate should use external, authoritative interventions strategically and sparingly. Local stakeholders resent the implication inherent in the state's current investigation that they are unable to govern their own affairs. Yet, many look to outside intervention (albeit on their own terms) as the only solution. However, when this external assistance is done publicly and punitively, it tends to inflame the desire to retaliate rather than cooperate.

Lesson Three: "Do Not Act Like an Expert"

This third theme addresses how one uses information in a social context dominated by personal relationships in order to successfully present and then follow through with ideas for change. Reform of what is arguably the county's most influential organization is about putting people before programs. It is about creating novel and context-specific ways for more kids to be successful. It is about continuity with the past and respect for traditional ways of knowing and ways of working together. Given these multiple concerns, those "experts" who wish to advocate reform have to walk a thin line. Theirs is a precarious balance between those who resist reform because they believe that the way Hickory County schools are run is "good enough" for them and theirs, and those who feel there remains much to be done.

Like a "leader" or "troublemaker," the label of "expert" is a symbol that expresses differently valued kinds of learning as well as moral qualities. Being an expert first requires recognition of one's status by one's peers and/or certifiers. It also requires the ability to effectively generate a following for one's proposals. This second essential component is where many external experts fall short; they lack the requisite social networks to carry through with reforms. When proposing an initiative at Central High (e.g., an incentive program linked to attendance and grades), committee members needed to seek out those colleagues who were well connected to business people who could donate prizes, civic club members who could sponsor awards, and so on. They needed to seek out those faculty and staff who had something to exchange with businesspeople and civic leaders, be it tickets to the boys' basketball games or the promise of continued patronage. While these kinds of informal bartering may seem manipulative or exploitative, they reinforce the interdependence between local (elite) groups in a county where such perks are few and are, therefore, valuable. Furthermore, these teachers' expertise in building community support that extends past the classrooms and corridors of Central is key in making the initiative work. They have the common knowledge to make the standardized book knowledge meaningful. In summary, being an expert is considerably more than a matter of diplomas; it is at heart a social role.

Those who are recognized as experts draw on sophisticated knowledge, both "book larnin'" and the "common sense" derived from everyday living in the region. Men and women with expertise in such areas as auto mechanics, hunting, gardening, child development, and carpentry are sought out for their valuable knowledge and humble manners. In the local view, common knowledge, that is, understanding the importance of obligations to people and place, is what truly makes a person an expert. For most mountain people, theory or knowledge from abstract treatises is of little value unless applied to life. From this perspective, outside experts can be compared to the protagonists in the Appalachian genre of "educated fool" parables, like the man who could talk at length about automobiles in theory but could not find his own engine if his car broke down.

In fact, being full of "book knowledge" was seen as clogging the mind, blocking out common sense. I was frequently challenged to see what I "knew" of Appalachia from my distant, worldly Stanford education, and what I had "learned" by making a life in the region. I was tested to see if I would sit on front porches and "neighbor awhile," listening to those whose "wisdom didn't come in cans." Becoming "educated" in this manner was seen as an essential part of my political readiness. In Hickory County, people are seen as only being able to absorb so much. They have to make choices. They have to take sides. Having knowledge means having responsibility.

Formal degrees may provide useful background skills or information, but they are seen as being detrimental to the extent that they undermine the person's ability to work with others in a mutually respectful manner. In fact, the person who has achieved a high degree of formal education is at greater risk of "losing the mountain," that is, acting like an expert who knows better than longtime residents, supposedly has all the answers, and does not need to listen to or work with other (rural) people. Being "mountain" means a person is respectful, especially to elders who have a great deal of "common knowledge." He or she is humble and does not put him- or herself above others on the basis of "outsider" criteria, that is, degrees or credentials. Older adults were particularly wary of the "improvements" that young or urban-educated educators supported. They felt that someone who had been successful in college, especially far away from Hickory County, might well return wanting to infuse modern assumptions about individualism, mobility, and material gain into definitions of who should be accorded respect. They feared that the person might not esteem the ties to place that had anchored Appalachians through so many a previous storm.

However, new definitions of expertise were beginning to form. In a system undergoing swift and significant change, experts are needed who have knowledge about how best to understand, negotiate, and implement KERA initiatives. Especially during this push for systemic reform with its concomitant jargon, literatures, and constant amendments to KERA, the new knowledge requirements are of a considerably different, more technical nature than that commonly shared between neighbors at the laundromat. Expertise in the Reform Act has not only great potential utility, but carries official approval; hence, it has enhanced status. Because of the increasing importance of having officially sanctioned knowledge from written sources, including books, being designated an "expert" vis-à-vis KERA has taken on increased importance.

Unfortunately, many (outside) experts are not seen as having the moral qualities it takes to effectively play this role in Hickory County. An expert, most Hickory Countians fear, is someone who prefers changes that will make Appalachian Hickory County more like mainstream white America. He or she cultivates ties and allegiances to external authorities, and does not cultivate either a network of local people or have patience for their "backwards" mountain ways. This way of constructing an expert expresses one of the most important ways that lines are drawn between "outsiders" and "insiders," those who would change the community and those who are community builders.

This profile of the external expert is clearly antithetical to the kind of relationship that an ethnographer brings to his or her work. The vast difference between my role and the external investigators' predominant approaches became all too obvious in one incident regarding dropouts. The 15% daily student absentee rate and the enduring 45% dropout rate at Central came under closer scrutiny by state investigators. State officials issued written threats of a full investigation and threatened increased visits by a program evaluator. Perplexed by the persistent nature of the problem, they launched a volley of assaults on the local bookkeeping system, dropout prevention measures, and school policies. They drove down from the city and made a day trip to the county. I encountered one of these frustrated state accountability officials walking the halls looking for the correct office. His schedule was filled with appointments to look at books and talk to senior administrators. I asked him if he would like to meet any of the "statistics" and talk to them. He could learn about why they were hard pressed to find convincing reasons to regularly attend classes at Central, what an education meant to them, how to get around being counted absent, and other topics that were regular items of my noontime "hangin' out" sessions. He did not have the time, this "expert" declared, he needed to look at more figures. How much he might have learned.

Lesson Four: "Numbers Are Legitimating"

Numbers have the power to operationalize "success," rank schools, highlight group characteristics, confer prestige, and declare bankruptcy. They legitimize intervention in "unsuccessful" districts; they justify giving rewards to "successful" ones. Because issues of assessment and accountability are so closely entwined in the Reform Act, numbers have taken on a life of their own in southeastern Kentucky.

No story of reform in Kentucky in the mid 1990s would be complete without mentioning the significant impact that KIRIS accountability test scores have had on local reform. In Hickory County, Central's low KIRIS scores were a motivating factor that gave faculty and principals ammunition in their struggle to mobilize even their most complacent colleagues into action. The danger of being declared "in crisis" was a wake-up call that got coworkers moving who would have preferred to continue what they were doing just long enough so they could retire. If they met the threshold, they could forestall unwelcome intrusion and resume their normal routines. Those who were intrinsically motivated to pursue excellence in their daily practices by conscience, professional dedication, or religious or ethical convictions also acknowledged this minimal threshold as a starting point. But they saw it as the minimum they wished to see, rather than the maximum.

Getting the entire faculty and staff of Central moving in the same direction was no simple task. From the beginning of the KIRIS assessments, those teachers at Central who felt that things were "good enough" took their cues from the district and school administration and hoped that the Reform Act would soon be forgotten. They hoped that as long as they could ignore it or do nothing to enhance its success, it would prove to be a failure and be rescinded. When funding for KERA was renewed by the legislature, they proceeded to resist preparing for the performance-based tests because the scores represented accountability to external authorities who imposed their own standards. These teachers hoped that they could contribute to the swift demise of the annoying tests if they refused to teach the skills tested or if they proved that the tests could not assess what they set out to ascertain. Faculty attempted to prove that the KIRIS assessments were worthless and that the students could not achieve high scores by telling their students that the tests were meaningless, rigged, or impossible, and that it did not matter if they tried or not. When all else failed, faculty cited the three weeks of school that the students had missed just prior to the statewide testing period because of flooding of county roads. They argued that such conditions made it impossible for them to teach or for their students to learn. The result was that scores were a better reflection of these underlying trends than a measure of either students' potential or even current abilities. The scores would have been even lower had they not been lumped in with those students whose teachers did not have such ideological problems with these accountability mechanisms, and who already included the kinds of activities KERA promotes (e.g., critical thinking, open-response questions, extensive writing, group work, and hands-on learning) in their teaching.

Although the individual test scores are the largest component, a school's total KIRIS score includes more than test results. At the high school level these include such noncognitive items as a measure of dropouts, attendance, and the variable "successful transition to adult life." These reflect choices made by both teachers and students and are the areas that have been particularly resistant to school leaders' efforts; in nearly 60 years, Central High has never graduated more than 57% of its entering 9th-grade class four years later. Nevertheless, the school as an entity is judged on achievements in these areas. Part of what motivated Central staff to try to do well on these noncognitive measures are increased financial resources available for districts through the SEEK equalization formula, and technology initiatives of KERA. Most of these resources are directly proportional to student average daily attendance. With high performance on noncognitive items, there is more money available for everything from books to lab stations, from microscopes to multimedia. Even the most complacent and resigned teachers were eager to have more supplies and aids. In faculty meetings, another concern surfaced, namely, that the number of staff a school can legitimately employ is also based on average daily attendance. In the past, the principal and superintendent had purposely kept the school overstaffed with teachers and custodians (in relation to enrollment), with the justification that the jobs were needed and they could offer better services for their students this way. However, staff were now worried that the state would take a hard line. Furthermore, if Central was to offer competitive programs that would help lure back those students who chose to attend high school out of district rather than go to Central, they needed the per-pupil money that these students currently take with them. Whereas before there were few resources and little incentive to increase daily enrollment, now kids counted.

Getting the numbers to add up was a strategic game that was not always played in the best interest of the children. The most striking example is the underlying process that resulted in increased attendance rates. At Central, some kids count more than others. My main teen respondent group was composed of those who were on the fence, not certain that there were compelling reasons to stay in high school, but not ready to give up and leave. My friendships with them and with the administrators and central office staff charged with monitoring and motivating them led to insights into the paradoxes that arose as part of the reform. Because of the way that attendance and dropout rates are computed into the school's noncognitive KIRIS index, and because of Central's high baseline of dropouts, it is actually more beneficial to remove a student entirely from the roster than to carry him or her as a chronic absentee. Faced with a precariously low noncognitive index, Central staff discussed at the faculty meetings whether it might not be beneficial to encourage troublesome students to drop out as soon as possible if they looked like they were likely to establish a pattern of frequent absences. I gathered ample and shocking evidence of the daily, direct ways that they conveyed this message to the targeted teens. In this they knew that some parents would be willing partners; every few weeks a parent would accompany a child to school on his or her 16th birthday and, as their present, legally withdraw them from high school.

Despite the important illustration above, credit has to go to those administrators, staff, teachers, parents, and students who worked hard to honestly raise the other components of the 1995 KIRIS assessments. In just one year, Central High was able to achieve nearly its entire accountability index. They lacked less than one percentage point of improvement to reach the threshold that they had two years to meet. It will require sustained effort to keep the students achieving at higher levels, but they have shown that the standards are within reach.

These results are significant. Also significant are the many things that are not accorded a number. Important changes were going on deep under the superficial gloss of averages: more people became stakeholders and identified problems that they would target, together, for reform. This is no small accomplishment. A faint afterimage of increased community involvement may appear in the KIRIS scores, but it is a weak reflection of the real changes that preceded, and indeed were prerequisites for, these improved scores. The scores were evidence of the tenacity and resilience of teachers who would not take the kids' lament of "We're just poor Appalachians, we can't do any better" for an excuse. Although the mountaineer stereotype that kids tease one another with is decidedly anti-intellectual, it is not against having intelligence. Reclaiming the intellectual aspects of mountain identity was a component of the teachers' and students' rejections of the statistics and KIRIS scores as sole definitions of either who they were or who they could be.

Indeed, in a significant reversal of authority roles, faculty effectively used these same numbers to legitimate their claims that reforms were overdue and that they as a poor, rural, mountain district should be given priority for new funds and programs. As someone who was able to be mobile and who had reasons for collecting Census Bureau and other official data about the district, I provided statistics and grant-writing expertise to those who wanted to put them to use. Teachers on the curriculum committee and staff at the Youth Service Center worked with Census Bureau and CD-ROM data about their county that I gathered. We wrote grant applications, program evaluations, and applications for awards. They used statistics that placed Hickory County among the worst in the state for teen pregnancy, dropout rates, unemployment, and underemployment. The numbers showed that problems with drug abuse rivaled that of inner cities. Writing these reports and applications meant that those using the numbers had to be willing to say that the numbers indeed represented them. They had to move from a resistance to the numbers' accuracy, to a candid realization that while they did represent the present, they need not be predictors of the future. By taking a hard, critical look at where they stood, they gained the strength to decide where they wanted to go.

Powerful.

Lesson Five: "Knowledge Is Power"

Having knowledge is powerful. Sharing knowledge generates even more strength and solidarity. Passing knowledge around until it attains the status of myth, or nostalgia, gives it potency that can last for generations.

Central High staff and faculty recall a very recent time when information was jealously guarded. An exemplary case was the district school board meetings. Past practices came to light when contrasted with how board meetings were handled by Interim Superintendent Kennedy, who replaced the previous superintendent of 27 years. Previously, board meetings were important rituals of reassurance, that is, reassurance that there was a veneer of democracy, but also reassurance that decisions were already made well before the meeting ever happened. Board members felt that they had to approve decisions without ever feeling able to ask for grounds or numbers to justify the proposal. The few spectators who bothered to show up had no idea what actually would be covered. They lacked the information about how to effectively get their concerns on the agenda. The absence of written policies reinforced the informal, insider nature of knowledge. Those who did not know the rules were afraid to ask. What rules were known (e.g., that all employment applications should be kept on file in a certain place for a certain time), were flagrantly ignored. You had to know someone in order to know what was going on. People were disengaged from formal, democratic decision-making forums.

Given the long-standing distrust of official forums, nonformal yet highly organized spaces for discourse flourished, and these provided important alternatives. Most of the dozen or so distinct communities in the county still have a gas station, laundromat, small grocery store, and at least a couple of other places of business. Scattered throughout the county are private beauty shops run by women entrepreneurs, and those also are regular nodes of communication. Most people also come to the post offices to check their P.O. box, since a sizable portion of county residents do not have an individual mailbox by their isolated homes. Each of these are important meeting places where people come not only to pick up needed supplies, but also to catch up on the news from the center of the county. Alternative spaces can also coalesce spontaneously. I got caught up in one when we had to wait an hour for a crew to teeter a mobile home off the hillside road and turn it down a gravel lane. (It was to eventually find its final spot on the far bank of the creek down in the valley below.) Motorists simply shut off their engines, got out of their cars, haywagons, and sport-utility vehicles, and got caught up. It is in such remote places, rather than through the infrequent school forums or the nonexistent school-home newsletters, that marginal participants become links in the chain of information.

What happens in the public schools, the county's largest employer and one of its most prominent institutions, is of general concern. The supposedly uneducated and "not caring" average parents ravenously consume what their neighbors and friends bring to share. What is the OEA up to? When is the state coming in? Why has my daughter's application to be a teacher been "lost," for the *third* time?!? Why was *he* selected for superintendent? The average person wants to know. In the alternative spaces, people actively create knowledge. That is, in the face of minimal official information, they generate their own understandings of what is happening. They want and need to know about the personal relationships, ties and assumed obligations, reasons, and benefits of those who are taking action. As one of the parents said, by creating a likely theory about what is happening, they gain the power to predict and cope with what they believe is coming down the line.

Furthermore, in these laundromats and stores, county residents construct a resilient sense of self that stands in opposition to what teachers "know" about them. The parents are, in their stories, the agents, the important ones in their children's education, the ones who should be listened to. Teachers tell similar stories—with the protagonists reversed. But in these scattered spaces, the speakers are the ones who hold the power to convey authority, for they hold the power to pronounce the "the truth."

A key aspect of creating knowledge is that it is not merely information, but legitimate information. "There's a difference between gossip and good gossip," stated Mrs. McCormick, "Good gossip is gossip with the facts!" What experts, outsiders, state people, even educational leaders say about what is happening is suspect simply because of who the messenger is assumed to be. On the other hand, information from one's own trusted peer group is automatically assumed to be of better quality. It seems more reliable, practical, and trustworthy. Even if the information a friend conveys is faulty or incomplete, it is assumed to be offered with the best of intentions. That is what makes it "truthful."

Because the relationship is primary, people do not publicly contradict one another's stories. While listeners may disagree, when together they will likely agree to agree. This applies whether the information shared encourages risk taking or reinforces the notion that retaliation is imminent and there is little prospect of change. Listeners reinforce the paradoxically reassuring beliefs that, for instance, the system is rigged against poor people, that there is little they can do to better their situation, that those in leadership will never listen, that their children are learning "nasty" things out behind the school. As long as there is no chance for change, they are also affirmed in their decision not to become involved. Thus, while these alternative spaces can provide opportunities for the marginal to critique those in positions of influence, they can also provide the settings for discussions that mutually reinforce the futility of becoming involved.

In a similar vein, alternative spaces for knowledge flourish within the high school. There is a widespread mistrust of information generated by the state, newcomer Principal Newmann, or other such dubious outsider sources. Staff see those who wish to press for reform of the school as only forwarding the information that supports their position. The reports they offer at faculty meetings are therefore suspect. The official accounts of what and why something happened seem to be "smokescreens" to cover "the real story" behind the scenes. Stakeholders, even those who may have agreed with the actual proposed reform (e.g., block scheduling), felt that there was more going on that they just did not know about. They resisted believing that they were being given all the information or a fair chance to become involved. This attitude enabled them to maintain the stance that what is said in public does not reflect the "true" intentions of the speaker. Moreover, from many Central staff members' perspectives, the fact that something is written should be taken as evidence that something quite different is actually meant.

Instead of creating official-sounding reports to convince peers, successful leaders adopted the revered Appalachian practice of storytelling. They adopted the content of nostalgic stories, origin myths, and the frontier family story to make modern points. These stories reaffirm that the teller and listeners share a common heritage. Such is the case with the stories told about one-room schools that persisted in Hickory until 1972. These accounts of the "old days" play a key role in generating mythical stories of a better past, a time "when we had one-room schools and the paddle" and when "teachers and parents respected each other." The underlying sense was that Hickory County used to be more cohesive, and although they had it rough, at least they were mostly in the same boat. The moral was that people pulled together and sacrificed for their local schoolhouse and teacher. "They did the best with what they had" is the proud slogan. For listeners, this nostalgic backdrop provides evidence that Hickory County schools were once equal to other rural districts, and that the ways in which they have fallen behind need only be temporary. The sense that they once had an enviable school system bolsters stakeholders' beliefs that it can be the case again.

Just like a teen growing up in the county, as an ethnographer I had to learn how to identify the "truth" in tales. I had to gain sufficient cultural knowledge about characters, places, families, and events so that I could understand the references and distill moral lessons. I enjoyed many models of how to weave a good story, a lesson that served me well in composing the tome required for my own graduation. I also learned that while the content and analysis of what I had to say is critical, perhaps the most important thing is simply sharing.

The veracity or verifiability of a statement is not what is most important. The critical element is that one is included in a circle of insiders who work together to keep one another apprised of what can be known in a situation of great uncertainty. In an interesting and significant turn of events, when the teachers asked me "to spy" on the state investigators or to follow them around, I became a counterintelligence agent. I became their ally for democratizing access. The ease with which one can find out useful information is a marker of who trusts whom and who respects whom. When committee members asked me to formally ask for official, public documents from the district, it was because they felt that I would receive it; my requests were perceived as legitimate and worthwhile (in contrast to their insider requests). I had sources there who wanted me to know, and who knew that I would share what I found in a responsible and sensitive manner.

Being part of a knowledge-sharing network can be personally empowering. Information that is reliable and worthwhile is not easy to obtain. Therefore, building coalitions in which to share information is particularly important as these become the basis for transformative action. Sharing knowledge generates strength. Knowing who would stand beside you and take your side in a faculty meeting or, for students, when called into the principal's office, was important before one entered into a risky conflict. Potential dropouts knew that I would not tell details from the interview that I conducted when I met them "laying out" at the pizza parlor. Teachers knew that I would not divulge details linked to particular names. They knew that I would be consistent and, if merited, would support their assertion that they were not alone in feeling a particular way. Knowing that there was a network of people with whom one shared a version of a story, or who would support your version, contributed to the authority and confidence with which teachers or students spoke about a policy reform, a fight, an absence from school, a conflict, or a proposal. Having and sharing knowledge created a powerful, new basis for action.

RESPONDING TO THE CHALLENGE

Reform is not about plotting abstract options on some chart of dichotomous outcomes. Reform is, at its best, a messy, passionate, political process, involving choices made by real people in real places. They are seldom either–or choices, but decisions about how best to balance the multiple interests and different individuals involved. And, in an important way often overlooked in the push for standardized reform, in Appalachia a strong sense of place infuses this struggle with meaning. "Being mountain" is more than a mere slogan, it is understood as a birthright and a legacy. Long-term commitments to a particular place inspire these Appalachians' desires to remain distinct and to act on their own behalf to create viable, vital communities that they control. These ways of understanding the interdependence of Hickory County cultures, communities, and place challenge approaches to reform that assume that these are but peripheral to the real meaning of education. In Hickory County they are central.

If sustained, thoughtful reform is to blossom, it must find suitable soils in which to grow. Change takes patience and persistent tending. Those who actively participated in the process of reform at Central High felt that they had little choice. They were investing for the future, leaving more for their children than they took for themselves. They were determined that those who came after would find something there in those very mountains that would give them hope to carry on. They were determined that their young people would find both the reasons and the means to stay. Many people in this Appalachian mountain county have deeply held commitments to both place and progeny. This is what ultimately motivated many people to take the risk of becoming stakeholders in the process of school reform. A life-long resident and father of five summed up the long-term benefits of cultivating change right there in his homeplace, "Reform is like planting a walnut tree on *your* mountain. Your *kid* is going to enjoy it."

In order for these seeds to flourish, there need to be effective partnerships between actors with different skills and resources. KERA provides the opportunity for mutually beneficial kinds of partnerships to emerge. Policy writers and policy implementers, researchers and reformers all have to work together on behalf of children. The process is an uneven one. During this first phase of reform, it often seemed that the situation had to get worse before it could get better. We should not interpret this difficult first phase as evidence of stakeholders' incapacity to change. Rather, it should be seen as the courageous struggle to personally confront the implications of working for change in a context that values continuity, public harmony, independence and autonomy, and maintenance of gender and social class hierarchies. Less unity may well prove to be a very good thing. In the past, faculty and staff had few, if any, public forums in which to meet and identify and solve problems of common concern. Decisions were made by a select few without the diverse needs and perspectives of the school in mind. Those who disagreed with these decrees all too often resisted implementing them and, when that was not enough, undermined the authority of those who made the decisions. They remained complicit in perpetuating the very problems their leaders attempted to address.

However, during the fieldwork year, Central staff and parents gained experience in taking a more active role in school affairs. Encouraged by their new administration, fewer people were satisfied to be complacent. A critical mass of teachers resisted pressures from their colleagues to conform to past levels of mediocre performance. In discussions about how to actually achieve KERA standards of literacy and numeracy, teachers wanted to find their own ways to achieve standardized ends. They resisted simply adopting what the state's experts suggested. Instead, committees and department discussions increasingly focused on devising locally relevant curricula and applications for academic skills. They wanted to articulate their own interests, define their own problems, and incorporate the ways that local people thought about the meaning and importance of "book learning." Educators who had worked hard in the past on community-based history projects or sending kids out to collect folklore for English essays found renewed impetus and acceptance of blending mountain with mainstream ways of learning.

This new enthusiasm for hands-on work carried over to the teachers' professional lives as members of a learning community. For an increasing number of teachers, the chance to take action on their own priorities became a welcome opportunity. Mrs. Atkins, a longtime teacher at Central, spoke out about the lasting legacy of learning to become a stakeholder:

In this educational reform, as in any new endeavor, to be told what to do rather than to discover problems and solutions through our own methods and resources is disheartening. Ever since Johnson's War on Poverty, some political body has been trying to "fix" the problems for us rather than assisting us in solving them ourselves, like children. . . . . To have someone who doesn't live here or understand our heritage suggest that he know what's best for both our region and schools is so demeaning and unproductive. The most positive things about KERA are that it allowed local control and tries to be nonpolitical. What a difference in focus from the usual dictation and "missionary work!"

Together, reformers made some tenuous steps from a dependency mentality in which they expressed little hope for change, to a more active sense of themselves as stakeholders in an ongoing process over which they had some control. In the process, they shifted from having a stake in the Reform Act's failure to having a stake in its success.

The metaphor of "being mountain" played a critical role in this process. It is a multivalent slogan, at once an emotional admonition to show solidarity and respect for the past and at the same time the basis for slow but significant shifts in the local story that could be told about themselves and others. Educators had to find ways to effectively combine elements of their received mountaineer heritage with new definitions of who they could be. The label reminds educators where they come from. It recalls those who have sacrificed so that they could benefit later, and reminds them that they too are bound up in intergenerational relationships of reciprocity. It challenges them to give back.

The phrase's appeal is all the more engaging because it is not one-dimensional. While they glorify independence, mountaineers are all too aware of their very real dependence on outside school funds, welfare checks, and job programs. While "being mountain" implies being a good neighbor and helping those in need, they realize that assistance seldom extends past kinship or social groups perceived as lower status. Looking to the mountains for examples of steadfastness and perseverance need not lead to the conclusion that enduring means being static. Indeed, for those with a strong sense of place, the fragile mountain ecosystem teaches a lesson about continuous adaptations to changes in the environment.

KERA opened up spaces for dialogue and action, but would have remained impotent if it were not for the real people who found and inhabited those spaces. In a like manner, ethnographic policy research offers unique spaces for dialogue and action. But it takes the concerted partnership of researchers and reformers to take advantage of the possibilities of those new relationships. I feel that in important ways I helped to break down barriers between groups and to create mutual relationships of respect. Being there on a daily basis and being involved in the school in a personal way opened up new possibilities for understanding reform that a nonethnographic approach would have simply missed. I sometimes served as a safe conduit for different groups to start to approach one another. I shared information in useful and ethical ways. I generated new facts to counter old stereotypes and assumptions. I became part of their jokes, their stories, their accounts and they became our jokes, stories, and accounts. I earned a nickname. I was invited to "stay and neighbor a while longer."

Certainly as academics, policy developers, program staff, and administrators, we can learn a great deal from colleagues who live and work in the hills of southeastern Kentucky. When developing instruments, crunching numbers, or transcribing interviews, it seems that the detailed work needed to do thorough research can be overwhelming. But working in the mountains, your view is drawn to the horizon, to the possibilities that remain hidden from view, just over the next crest. In the time that I worked at Central, it seemed that the degrees of actual change were nearly imperceptible. But, to those engaged with the process of reform, changes were significant nonetheless. Fieldwork often offers moments of respite and recreation in between the long hours of plain hard work. One such moment will remain with me forever. Standing with me on a hilltop after a particularly hard hike uphill, Mrs. Ely, a reform-weary but very determined administrator, paused to look out over the homeplace she adored. She turned to me and remarked, "You know, Maureen, reform is like moving mountains. It's grain of sand by grain of sand. You've got to take it one problem at a time." I hope that my work contributes a valuable grain to this larger project.

REFERENCES

Anzaldúa, G. (1987). *Borderlands/la frontera: The new mestiza*. San Francisco: Spinsters/Aunt Lute.

Berger, P., & Luckman, T. (1967). *The social construction of reality: A treatise in the sociology of knowledge*. Garden City, NJ: Anchor Books.

Edelman, M. (1988). *Constructing the political spectacle*. Chicago: University of Chicago Press.

Fitchen, J. (1991). *Endangered spaces, enduring places: Change, identity, and survival in rural America*. Boulder, CO: Westview Press.

Geertz, C. (1973). *The interpretation of cultures.* New York: Basic Books.

Lakoff, G., & Johnson, M. (1980). *Metaphors we live by.* Chicago: University of Chicago Press.

McLaren, P. (1986). *School as a ritual performance: Towards a political economy of educational symbols and gestures.* Boston: Routledge and Kegan Paul.

Porter, M. (1996). *Moving mountains: Reform, resistance and resiliency in an Appalachian Kentucky high school.* Unpublished doctoral dissertation, Stanford University.

Porter, M. (1998). Points of light, bridges to the future, flower gardens and the Alamo: Rural teachers' metaphors. *Journal of Teacher Education,* 185–208.

Scott, J. (1990). *Domination and the arts of resistance: Hidden transcripts.* New Haven, CT: Yale University Press.

12

Myth Making and Moral Order in a Debate on Mathematics Education Policy[1]

Lisa Rosen

INTRODUCTION

This chapter is about story making and storytelling in debates on education: how social actors create and use narratives to pursue goals; how both their goals and their stories involve other stories; and how these mutually implicating narratives structure the course and outcome of debates on education. I analyze the creation and use of explanatory tales in education as a form of modern myth making (cf., Woolard, 1989), and demonstrate the relationship of these "myths" to cherished cultural ideals about education. The analysis sheds some light on how, through cultural processes involving competitive storytelling (cf., Leach, 1954), the narrower concerns of particular interest groups are transformed into "public problems" (Gusfield, 1981) considered worthy of attention and redress. I argue that these processes and "problems" are mutually constitutive with a particular set of assumptions about schooling and achievement that I refer to as the "moral order" of education in the United States.

The discussion centers on a local policy dispute in California's Avocado Valley Elementary School District,[2] which had recently begun implementing a "reform"[3] mathematics curriculum in its schools. I analyze the debate as a public "drama of morality and order" (Gusfield, 1981, p. 82) in the explanation of academic success and failure. My analysis begins from the premise that policy is both a *process* and a *product* of constitutive cultural activity. As a process, policy is a means by which statements of value and definitions of reality are constructed, asserted, validated, and negotiated. As cultural artifacts or products, policies are the material residues of these actions; they are cultural objects that "embody the authority to define goals and command means" (Levinson & Sutton, Introduction, this volume), legitimize and reinforce particular views of reality, and grant those definitions some form of "official" (i.e., institutionalized or publicly recognized) status. This view of policy challenges the assumption that policies are external responses to problematic social conditions that exist objectively, apart from their interpretation or "objectification" in processes or products of policy. Rather, I view policy as part and parcel of how such problems are actually *constituted* (i.e., how particular conditions come to be viewed as problematic, while others are ignored or normalized).

At the same time, I also argue that policymaking is a form of ritual: that the apparatuses and practices surrounding educational policy display, enact, proclaim, and validate cultural ideals. Using the case in Avocado Valley as a focus for illuminating more general processes, I argue that the rituals of education policy are elements in the cultural production of a moral order where educational success and failure are understood in individual, meritocratic terms, as well as a natural order in which science and the state can effectively direct processes of learning and child development (cf., Gusfield, 1981; Varenne & McDermott, 1999).[4] In my discussion of the debate in Avocado Valley, I argue that those with the power to make local education policy colluded in processes of myth making that resulted in the ratification of an existing policy, on the one hand, and the validation of key aspects of the moral order of U.S. education, on the other.

The Avocado Valley controversy surrounded a recent drop in mathematics test scores, and the subsequent revelation that most teachers surveyed were not complying with the district's new policies for teaching mathematics. A series of school board meetings, from which the data for this chapter are drawn, were addressed to the controversy. In the course of these meetings, two conflicting explanations of conditions in the district were offered by competing local organizations. The debate that followed comprised a forum for the dramatic expression of competing myths of education.

Parents and Teachers for Balance—a group dedicated to defending the new mathematics program—presented an account that focused primarily on the survey finding that most teachers were not using the new curriculum. They argued that this condition indicated a problem with policy implementation. I refer to their explanation as the "myth of implementation." In contrast, local expert Vivian Smith, along with Parents that Count—a group formed to combat the new curriculum—focused their explanations on evidence from test scores. They argued that disappointing performance on recent standardized tests indicated a problem with the curriculum. I refer to their account as the "myth of curriculum." The myth of curriculum quickly became the official explanation, directing energy and attention away from alternative interpretations and becoming the taken-for-granted basis of subsequent policy activity.

This myth provided an account that reduced the complexity and ambiguity of local conditions by imposing a particular interpretive framework on those putative conditions. This evaluative stance both explained local conditions and prescribed a means for addressing them.

Two basic theoretical premises, elaborated throughout the discussion, frame my analysis. The first premise is that social reality cannot be experienced directly, but is mediated (filtered, ordered, defined, and given meaning) by processes and products of culture. These cultural processes and products allow events and experiences to make sense, and enable social life to proceed. The second premise is that these processes are active, ongoing, and constitutive of social reality. My central concern is with the moral order of education in the United States and its relationship to processes of debate and contestation, that is, with cultural ideals related to schooling, and how they are asserted, negotiated, and shored up in public debate.

My analysis is informed by 18 months of research on the ongoing debate over mathematics "reform" in California (of which the Avocado Valley controversy is a local instance). My discussion draws on data from this research, derived from participant observation at public meetings throughout the state, interviews and discussions with key players statewide, and analysis of a wide variety of texts relevant to the debate, including news reports, minutes from public meetings, public testimony, editorials, columns, letters to the editor collected from various newspapers, and other correspondence. The processes with which this chapter is concerned are illustrated primarily by data from participant observation at public meetings in Avocado Valley in the winter of 1997.

MYTH-MAKING AND MORAL ORDER IN EDUCATION POLICY

Many aspects of the educational enterprise are beyond understanding and human control. Processes of child growth, "learning," and "development" that education aims to cultivate, stimulate, nurture, and manage, are inaccessible to direct observation and rational management. We can only infer mental activity on the basis of external observed behavior, which we assume to be indexical of purported internal processes of growth and development codified in notions from psychology and culture (Walkerdine, 1984). Moreover, what distinguishes high- and low-achieving students also remains a matter of sharp debate and considerable mystery. Explanations for conditions in education thus depend not only on cultural constructs (e.g., culturally constituted notions of "ability" and "intelligence") (cf. Varenne & McDermott, 1999), but also on processes of selection and interpetation to produce coherent narratives that can account for these purported conditions. At the same time, many of the known sources of educational failure are nonetheless beyond the control of those publicly charged with the monitoring and practice of schooling. Compounding these uncertainties and limitations is the anxiety many American parents—particularly those in the "middle class"—feel in relation to perceived limitations on their ability to predict and control the future success of their off-spring (Varenne & McDermott, 1999).[5] Such parents "are anxious that their children be able to compete in what the parents perceive to be an increasingly competitive world of school and work" (Tobin, Wu, & Davidson, 1989, p. 197).

In spite (and perhaps also because) of these anxieties and limitations, policy and practice in education proceed *as if* school success can not only be fully understood, but also rationally predicted, measured, managed, and controlled. To admit our lack of control over educational outcomes would be to challenge a fundamental myth of American society—that anyone can succeed if they work hard and are given equal opportunity. Education is a crucial element of this meritocratic achievement ideology because adequate, equal education is seen as key to equality of social and economic opportunity. From this standpoint, it is not the natural order or our economic system that is seen as responsible for social inequality, but either the limitation of opportunity, or the evil and folly of human beings.

The latter beliefs are matters of faith and moral precept, rather than of verifiable fact. As such, they must be continually renewed, validated, and reinforced in the face of abundant contrary evidence and the anxieties produced by a shifting, ambiguous, and unpredictable social and economic landscape. A central function of educational policy is to thus sustain not only our belief in the American achievement ideology, but also in a more fundamental belief underlying it, the belief in "a moral order in which solutions to problems can be attained and a natural order which is not impervious to the control of science and the state" (Gusfield, 1981, p. 167). I call this idealized account the moral order of education in the United States: the tacit system of ends and means by which education is organized, particularly in the arena of public policy.

Policy activity thus performs not only the instrumental function of calculating solutions to educational problems, but also the expressive function of validating important articles of cultural faith. For example, to testify at a public meeting is an instrumental act—a means to the end of contributing to educational policy. At the same time, however, it is also *an end in itself*. The mere act of testifying validates the beliefs that ours is a democratic society comprised of rational, self-determining agents, that educational achievement (and therefore social mobility) is predictable and controllable, and that the means of this control is both individual agency and "sound policy." The whole range of public discourses and practices surrounding education policy—the perpetual gathering and public presentations of data; commissioning of studies and establishing of committees; writing of standards and issuing of reports; sounding of alarms and calls to "reform"; and convening of summits and other official gatherings—reinforces this belief system as well. These activities validate the ideas that academic success and failure are amenable to technical procedures of policy administration, and that social advancement and mobility (linked to education in our national ideology) can also be rationally managed and controlled.

The endemic uncertainties of education and social mobility magnify the drive for order and meaning—of which the rituals of public policy are an expression—that is intrinsic to human cultural activity. Another means by which actors create order and meaning is through narratives. In the domain of education, when we perceive that children or schools are not performing as we imagine they should, we seek or construct stories to explain why, and to orient our efforts at addressing perceived problems (cf., Krasniewicz, 1992). Education policy is implicated in these myth-making processes: any plan of action, recommendation for change, or statement of goals involves (either explicitly or implicitly) an account of purported conditions and a set of recommendations for addressing them. Thus, policy debate often involves competition between advocates of conflicting myths for the (actual or perceived) power and legitimacy accorded by having one's own account institutionalized in the form of public or "official" policy. Narratives, like rituals, also validate cultural ideals by presenting reality in a manner that eliminates qualifications and uncertainties, and denies the conflict between the ideals of the moral order and the reality "on the ground."

Although myth, tale, narrative, story, and account are used interchangeably throughout the discussion, my analysis foregrounds the classic anthropological concept of myth. I do so in order to highlight the relationship of the explanatory tales under consideration to moral order (i.e., to the "sacred") in education: beliefs that are "removed beyond the limits of doubt and questioning, accepted on faith alone" (Bailey, 1977, p. 8).

A myth tells what one should desire . . . and how to get it; the way people are and how they should be; the reasons why things happen the way they do, especially when they go wrong; in short, myths provide values and meaning and ideas and plans and stratagems and alternative forms of social organization. (Bailey, 1977, p. 7)

Cultural systems are collections of myths. The coexistence of multiple, competing myths concerning any single social domain (e.g., education) requires adherents of any particular myth to develop means for persuading others, and sometimes even themselves, of the truth of their own accounts. The discussion below illuminates these rhetorical processes, and analyzes their relationship to the course and outcome of debates on education. I show how actors in such debates create and use narratives to order and construct reality, explain and orient their own and others' behavior, and pursue interests, and I analyze the connections between these narrative processes and cherished cultural beliefs about education and achievement. My analysis regards these processes as forms not only of constitutive social action (i.e., as means of constructing and negotiating educational reality), but also of ritual (as ways of asserting, displaying and reinforcing cultural ideals) (Gusfield, 1981; Leach, 1954).

THE MYTH OF CURRICULUM VERSUS THE MYTH OF IMPLEMENTATION

The first meeting in which the Avocado Valley school board addressed the mathematics controversy was billed as simply a forum for airing concerns—an opportunity for the trustees to receive input from their constituents. At this meeting, members of Parents That Count criticized the newly implemented mathematics program as the cause of academic decline in the district. They presented the board with 300 signatures petitioning for the reinstatement of "traditional" mathematics as the core curriculum. A leader of Parents That Count told the board:

I have 300 signatures from parents, community members, and businesspeople asking for the traditional math to be brought back and more coming in everyday. There were some coming in on my fax tonight as I was walking out the door. If you want 500 signatures, we'll give you 500. If you want 1,000, we'll give you 1,000.

Many people also spoke in favor of the program, arguing that it was simply not being implemented properly. They argued that the board's attention should be focused on obstacles to implementation rather than on evaluating the curriculum, which had already gone through a comprehensive and inclusive evaluation process prior to its adoption. A few teachers also gave demonstrations of "reform" mathematics lessons as evidence of the merits of the newly adopted program.

The curriculum nonetheless quickly emerged as the primary focus of the board's attention and concern, in spite of efforts by the program's defenders to direct attention elsewhere. The latter challenged the claim that there was ever a problem with the curriculum, and instead argued that the district's real problem stemmed from ineffective leadership. The central focus of their arguments was the actions of the board itself. This ultimate curricular focus is evident in remarks by Janet Mitchell, the president of the school board, at the end of the forum. Referring to the agenda for the upcoming meeting, she suggested:

I think we should have a goal for the workshop on what I am calling the math controversy. The situation is unmanageable. . . . We are assessing the value of the program. The workshop will need to answer some questions for us as a board: Is the curriculum the best way to meet our stated objectives, our grade level standards? Is it balanced? Does it need to be supplemented? We need input from our teachers, . . . from our staff, parents, and community members, particularly parents, as our clients. We have several options: Keep the current program, replace it, or supplement it.

One week later, the board held a crowded special meeting, which they dubbed a "math workshop," to determine the direction of the district's math program. Members of Parents and Teachers for Balance wore green neon badges with the organization's name emblazoned above an old-fashioned scale to demon-

strate their support for the current program. At this meeting, 26 people testified in favor of the program, while 13 spoke against it.

Those in favor argued that the current program was "balanced" because it
integrated basic skills, conceptual understanding, and problem solving. Critics
of the program argued that it did not sufficiently emphasize basic skills and
computational proficiency. Public testimony, such as the following, was typical
of arguments that the newly adopted curriculum was the cause of the turmoil
in the district: "I'm gravely worried about my child. My daughter's scores
plummeted in two years from the 99th to the 26th percentile. . . . When you
have an overachiever and an enthusiastic teacher and scores like this, it's time
to question the curriculum." Referring to the survey finding that roughly half
of the district's teachers were not using the new materials, another parent publicly reasoned, "If you have half of the K–12 teachers saying they're not using
the new curricula, then the problem is with the curriculum itself." Another
protester suggested that professional educators had betrayed the public trust
by choosing an inferior curriculum: "Once I showed people my daughter's
6th-grade math textbook, they were eager to sign [the petition]. People are
angry—angry that this is what their tax dollars are being spent on, this un-
tested, uneconomical [program]. . . . Parents are losing faith in the system."
Vivian Smith, a local expert and community member, presented a detailed
technical report critiquing the program. Smith's report was both a centerpiece
of the "math workshop" and a recitation of the myth of curriculum. As such, it
is worth describing at some length.

Smith began her presentation by stating the diverse credentials that comprised the grounds for her expertise, and claiming a position of both professional authority and political neutrality:

I want to be clear that I am not involved with any group in favor of or opposed to the
New Math. I have completed independent research for two reasons. First, a board
member requested my reflections of the "math" dilemma because of my background.
Second, my broad experience (with the children, their parents, their present and future
teachers, their community schools and the curriculum used to teach them) has given
me a unique perspective that I believe could benefit our community as it makes critical
decisions regarding the math program.

Smith's opening remarks also summed up the current state of mathematics education in the words of California Assemblyman Steve Baldwin, who has been
an outspoken critic of mathematics "reform":

"Teachers have adopted the gimmicks, processes and procedures of Constructivist
Math, but *without* the advance in *conceptual understanding* the best of the old math
practitioners sought and that constructivists *promised* would come with conversion to
their classroom techniques." Baldwin describes the new math: "Child-centered discovery learning where the teacher asks unknowing students, 'What do you think?'"

Her report focused on examples from documents and texts (e.g., the 1992 California Mathematics Framework, which articulates the official state philosophy for mathematics education, and the Avocado Valley School District's standards and curricula for mathematics); theory and statistics about learning, cognition, and child development; and assertions about both the nature of young children and the appropriate relationships between teachers and students.

She also critiqued materials for each grade level, and made technical recommendations in the areas of testing, standard setting, and the selection of materials. For example, she presented a chart that systematically compared the district's mathematics standards and materials against the objectives of the MAT 7 exam, a standardized test correlated with expectations for "traditional" mathematics education. She pointed out discrepancies between the district's standards and materials on the one hand, and the MAT 7 objectives on the other, arguing that the district program failed to challenge students adequately when measured against the expectations for the MAT 7.

Smith took particular issue with the following characterizations of students and teachers from the 1992 California Mathematics Framework:

Teachers are facilitators of learning rather than imparters of information. . . . Our classrooms can be student-oriented, self-directed, and nonauthoritarian. We can drop the role of a figure who passes judgment on what is right and wrong . . . authority is designated to students and to groups of students. . . . Students need to verify their thinking for themselves rather than to depend on an outside authority to tell them whether they are right or wrong. . . . An excellent approach . . . . is to have students participate, letting them help define the criteria for good work and then evaluating student work (their own or that of colleagues) in comparison with those criteria. . . . What is the goal for students' disposition? How do ideally disposed students feel and act?. . . they are critical of their teachers and the program if they are given assignment without purpose, are left alone, or are given too many answers.

Smith argued that such recommendations were illogical and inappropriate because they defied "common sense" about children, teaching, and learning:

These directives are alarming. Parents and teachers both want children to develop greater independence and responsibility, as well as a conscience sensitive to right and wrong. But we still insist on responsible, well-trained adults as classroom teachers. Why? Because most sensible citizens agree that it is a privilege for a student to glean wisdom and knowledge from a well-seasoned teacher. Though children have an innate sense of logic and conscience, they are in school to learn. If they could learn by their own goals and agenda, we would not send them to school. Students cannot evaluate their own work or that of their fellow students with the same expertise as a teacher. Teachers and parents *should* be imparters of information and knowledge.

She argued that the Framework's recommendations for student-directed classroom inquiry were not only academically ineffective, but also socially damaging:

Authority should come from the teacher. Lack of an authority figure results in chaos. We do a great disservice to our children if we teach them to be actively critical of their teachers. This can only lead to disrespect for authority. An employee who repeatedly questions and criticizes *will* be fired.   →✓ Hmm

She expressed similar concerns about the "project" method typical of "reform" pedagogy:

Many of the large projects proposed in today's math classes do not have clear answers. Steve Baldwin contends that such pointless exercises do not prepare students for college or the working world. He quotes a parent: "When people are building bridges, we want them to have the right answers, and in math there is a right answer. What we want is a rigorous computation, not the touchy-feely stuff. With all the recent talk of building bridges to the 21st century, I just hope we will still have the ability to build them correctly."

Smith argued that schools must cultivate particular attitudes and dispositions in children, which "traditional" mathematics education reinforce and "reform" practices undermine. Smith's criticism of the Framework's views on "group work" demonstrate this position:

Steve Baldwin puts it in perspective: "In actuality, adults who do math in organizations rarely do so in a group setting. However, with mixed abilities in an academic setting, the faster learners do most of the work. Regrettably, what we have is a group of students who only learn to split up the work and then copy the answers." . . . Another negative outcome is the feeling of frustration for the student whose grade is lowered because of another student's laziness.

Smith's response to the Framework's recommendations for calculator use indicate similar concerns:

As adults, we do not always have access to a calculator. Maybe we have misplaced it or maybe the batteries have run out! It is not prudent to have calculator-dependent children. . . . Students should be forced to do mental calculation, instead of allowing a gadget to do the work for them. Children will always take the easiest route available.

She also insisted on the necessity of drill and practice to the development of "basic skills":

Most children need daily drill or "rote" learning to master their [math] facts. Children learn through repetition. Throwing a multiplication fact into an investigation or using computation in "appropriate contexts," as elaborated in the State Framework, does not actively teach the facts; it only reinforces what the child should have already learned through drill. No, drill is not always fun. Neither are showers and table manners.

Near the end of the heated meeting, the board held a straw vote to determine the direction of the program. Three out of five board members indicated that they would vote to replace the current program and reinstate a "traditional" curriculum, despite the fact that only two of the trustees had actually seen the program in action. The president of the board then asked the superintendent for his opinion on the potential consequences of such a vote. The superintendent's pessimistic response swung the vote of one member. Just before midnight, at the conclusion of a tense, standing-room-only meeting, the board voted 3–2 to keep the current program. However, they also voted to establish a committee of parents, teachers, and community members that would assess the program, identify its weak areas, and choose supplementary materials to compensate for them. The board ultimately determined that parents who objected to the existing program could request "traditional" instruction for their children, although placement in a "reform" class remained the default option in the district.

MODES OF OBJECTIFICATION IN COMPETING MYTHS OF EDUCATION

The conditions of mathematics education in Avocado Valley were uncertain, and the evidence for each myth both ambiguous and incomplete. Any single, coherent narrative that purported to account for these conditions had therefore to depend upon processes of selection and interpretation to assign meaning and value to them. These processes produced coherent "storylines" that reduced ambiguities and compensated for gaps in evidence by presenting interpretations that highlighted some aspects of those conditions, while directing attention away from others.

The coherence of a narrative comes from its consistent themes or common threads. Those threads are woven out of the elements of other narratives. In the two myths at stake in the present case, these common threads correlated with four dimensions of variation that distinguished the myth of curriculum from the myth of implementation. These variations comprised regularities in each myth related to (1) the allocation of responsibility, (2) modes of presenting information, (3) means of grounding assertions, and (4) modes of representation.[6] Along each dimension, the two myths drew upon existing cultural meanings that reinforced the truth status of their respective claims and gave them the appearance of external reality (i.e., objectivity). The discussion below describes the common threads that differentiated the two myths along each dimension.

Allocation of Responsibility

The previous description of Smith's report (essentially a recitation of the myth of curriculum) made clear that the curriculum myth allocated responsibility for problems in the district to the curriculum. By contrast, the implementation myth allocated responsibility for the controversy to the trustees' failure to adequately support and train teachers to manage the transition to a new mathematics program.

A mathematics educator from a local university explicitly contested the curriculum-centered account and suggested that the board's attention had been misdirected, insisting, "the focus should be on staff development not curriculum." Others made similar claims, such as the teacher who suggested: "I believe that what we need in this district is support and staff development." Many argued that a lack of sufficient support and training had prevented teachers from fully or properly implementing the program, and that the curriculum could not therefore account for the conditions in the district (because it was not actually being used). Referring to survey results that showed that barely half of the district's teachers were actually using the new materials, one teacher challenged: "How can we judge the merits of a program that is being used by only a small percentage? . . . We need full participation to judge its value." The same data that her opponents cited as evidence of a problem with curriculum, she cited as evidence of problems of leadership. She urged the trustees to redirect their attention away from the curriculum and instead "focus on the obstacles to implementation." Several teachers and parents reminded the board that the curriculum had been adopted only after it had been exhaustively reviewed by all stakeholders. A respected teacher who had recently been awarded a prestigious teaching honor testified: "As a teacher I am disturbed by the lack of support from the board for a process that many teachers worked long and hard on." Another admonished the trustees, "Refocus on your district objectives and implement the program you voted for."

The conduct of one of the trustees provided additional grounds for the argument that the school board, rather than the curriculum, was the source of the district's problems. In the period between the two meetings, trustee Barbara Mayfield told a local newspaper reporting on the controversy: "Group math is like group sex. Nobody gets the attention they deserve." Her comment was featured prominently in an article released on the morning of the second board meeting. Parents and teachers lined up to publicly rebuke Mayfield for her "irresponsible" conduct. For example, the vice president of the PTA admonished, "To say group math is like group sex, that's disgusting." Another parent told the trustees that Mayfield's comment was "vulgar and unacceptable," adding, "to have any activity my child is engaged in compared to group sex is appalling. . . . I think you owe each child in our district an apology." A teacher who had been an outspoken advocate for the existing curriculum testified that she was embarrassed to tell people she was from Avocado Valley because of the behavior of the school board. She added,

I know a teacher that uses the newspaper in her class everyday. She didn't use it today. I hope you find in your heart a way to see that your first responsibility as a policymaker is one of integrity and modeling. . . . I am embarrassed at the sensationalism that the [newspaper] deemed fit to print. . . . I regret their error. And I regret yours.

Several other pro-"reform" audience members gave similar testimony, comprising a chorus of condemnation that not only claimed a moral high ground for their position, but also supported the effort to shift attention from issues of curriculum to issues of leadership.

As part of this effort, they argued that the trustees had wasted the community's resources, not only by failing to enforce policies for which they had voted (i.e., the decision to adopt the curriculum), but also by paying too much attention to the concerns of a vocal minority. As one parent contended:

The arguments we've heard say more about the board than about the curriculum. The board can't enforce its decisions. . . . That is bad management. It has wasted our district staff's time and money. . . . If this district was running a for-profit company, we'd be bankrupt. . . . Our children will be bankrupt if you react this way to every emotional plea.

Trustee Marsha Lewis agreed that the district's problems were managerial and political, rather than curricular. Halfway through the second meeting, she reminded her colleagues of their own contributions to the situation at hand, and admonished them to accept greater responsibility for their part in creating it:

We did adopt this program, . . . but to this day we still have little idea of what's really going on in the classrooms. . . . We need to recognize our part in the turmoil in which we find ourselves. . . . This board voted unanimously for [reform] math. . . . We have to step back, be leaders, and assume responsibility for that which we've created. . . . It's embarrassing to sit here and say that we really don't know what is going on. . . . As a board, our failure to stand behind our decision plays a large part in the turmoil in which we presently find ourselves. . . . Some teachers don't want to bother learning to teach the new curricula because they think that we're going to just dump it anyway.

Her comments echoed the argument that the board's own actions (i.e., their failure not only to enforce their decisions, but also to foster the trust and respect of their employees and to adequately monitor the implementation of their policies) were responsible for the controversy. She agreed that the board had helped to create their current circumstances (i.e., confusion and mistrust among both teachers and parents, and lack of compliance with the board's decisions). However, Lewis's views held little sway with her colleagues, who persisted in making the adequacy of the *curriculum* their primary concern.

Modes of Presentation

Both myths were narrated in disparate episodes of oral testimony and conversation, and both were augmented with visual props such as printed literature. In addition, however, the curriculum was also retold in uninterrupted form by an authoritative narrator (in the form of Smith's technical report), and re-presented symbolically in the parent/community petition. Both Smith's report and the petition pointed clearly to the curriculum as the single cause for disappointing achievement scores, and posed a clear solution: the reinstatement of a "traditional" curriculum.

By contrast, the unique modes in which the implementation myth was presented neither communicated a single causal argument nor offered a single clear solution. Rather, they suggested several possible reasons for the failure of implementation (e.g., poor leadership, insufficient training, etc.) that implied a more complex vision of education and change. Likewise, the green badges worn by members of Parents and Teachers for Balance communicated their support for the curriculum, but did nothing to directly shore up their argument that it was not being implemented properly. Their demonstrations of "reformed" mathematics lessons also communicated the value of the curriculum, but did not offer a solution to the purported implementation problem.

Modes of Representation

The respective myths also differed in how they depicted children, learning, and the enterprise of education. The curriculum myth represented education in technical, scientific, quantitative, and utilitarian terms, using idioms of objectivity, neutrality, and rationalization (such as "rigor" and "efficiency"). In contrast, the implementation myth was narrated in a combination of everyday language (using subjective, qualitative idioms of relatedness, commitment, self-expression, and personal experience) and terms from the progressive educational lexicon (e.g., "critical thinking," "learning how to think," "figuring the concepts out for themselves," "hands-on learning").

The latter modes of representation depicted education as an ideally pleasurable, natural, and active process, not all aspects of which are amenable to measurement, control, and rationalization. Comments by the curriculum's defenders suggested that learning can and indeed *should* occur automatically and pleasurably, as an expression (rather than by the inhibition) of children's natural intellectual and creative impulses. Claims about the need for children to appreciate, understand, feel comfortable with, and enjoy mathematics dominated the statements of Avocado Valley parents and teachers who favored the existing program.

Grounds of Assertions

Both myths grounded assertions in appeals to cultural authorities, moral obligations, and social imperatives (e.g., the need to prepare children for college and/or work). However, only the curriculum myth was grounded in "scientific" evidence, invoking abstract and quantitative data as evidence for its causal assertions. These data were derived from systematic, though indirect evaluation of the curriculum by means of documents, texts, test scores, and survey data. Advocates of the implementation myth, by contrast, grounded assertions primarily in concrete and qualitative evidence from direct, though unsystematic observations of student work and student behavior. They also grounded claims in cognitive and emotional imperatives (e.g., the need for children to "understand" and/or "feel good about" what they are learning) and indirect assessments of children's internal states (based on either observations or on children's reported thoughts and feelings).

The emphasis on pleasure and enthusiasm in the following testimony is typical of statements by advocates of "reform," not only in Avocado Valley, but in the statewide debate as well: "I am excited about the program and my students are excited about this program"; "My son likes building big numbers (and) my daughter likes tackling work problems (as a result of 'reform')." Statements such as the latter were offered as evidence of the benefits of mathematics "reform." The program's defenders argued that academic failure is the result not of insufficient effort on the part of students, but of insufficiently motivating curricula and methods. They claimed that "traditional" curricula give short shrift to "conceptual understanding," "critical thinking," "active learning," and the "relevance" of subject matter to students' lives. They argued that "traditional" mathematics education alienates, dulls, and stifles (rather than engages, stimulates, challenges, and motivates) children's intellect and creativity. The resulting failure damages children not only academically, but also emotionally, compounding failure with further impediments to effort and achievement.

The pattern of grounding assertions about the mathematics program in evidence from children's feelings is demonstrated by comments such as the following:

Our son has been tested for special education. . . . The tester was impressed by his very advanced math skills. . . . He had learned the ability to take some advanced principles and apply them. . . . He had experienced enough success at doing this to be comfortable enough to try new things in a new and stressful environment.

Other parents who testified grounded their assertions in a similar fashion. For example: "Any program that can get them enthusiastic about math and seeing why they're learning the basics, that's terrific"; and "My third grader has learned how to think and loves math." The latter statements imply that how students *feel* (not only about the subject, but also about themselves) is as relevant as what they *know*. The authors of the implementation myth argued that if children enjoy their schoolwork, they will be motivated to work hard and will have the self-confidence to tackle difficult tasks.

On the other hand, the contention that mathematics "reform" promotes false self-esteem was a consistent theme in the myth of curriculum, whose adherents argued that "reform" curricula gives students a false sense of accomplishment by lowering standards for achievement. As one parent declared: "You shouldn't give them false praise. . . . This is affirmative action math." She told me that "parents of low achievers love the ('reform') curriculum" because their children succeed in it, but that their success is an illusion created by low-ered standards.

A defender of the existing program argued that the district's adopted math program "is like a plate of pasta, and if you try to take the individual strands out it falls apart. . . . Basic skills, conceptual understanding, and problem solving are thoroughly integrated." To this an irate parent responded: "Math is not a plate of spaghetti. . . . Math is about order and logic. . . . My daughter's educa-tion is more important than feel-good rhetoric."

The following exchange between trustees Mayfield, Lewis, and Mitchell typifies the self-esteem/rigor opposition that distinguished the myth of imple-mentation from the myth of curriculum:

Mayfield: I thought that everyone wanted to look to tests to measure the bang for their buck. . . . I feel that I have factual evidence [from test scores] that our standards do not meet our stated objectives. . . . If we as a district do not want to use nationally normed testing, we shouldn't do testing. . . . How can you enter a game and not want to win that game? . . . The game of testing bothers me. Either we play the game to win, or we choose another game. . . . I wanna win this game. I want our kids to learn. . . . It's not fair to subject our district to bad press and declining real estate values. . . . I want some-thing to sell newspapers about.

Lewis: I don't care so much about selling newspapers. I want something our kids can feel good about—

Mitchell: I don't care if they feel good. I want them to learn.

Mayfield: People at Haight-Ashbury felt good all the time [*laughter*]. I want something measurable. . . . I just want to know I live in a school district that is competing well with other districts. . . . Kids need to be able to go out and compete for jobs. . . . Nationally normed tests tell you that.

Mayfield voiced sentiments central to the curriculum myth: that defenders of "reform" have lower standards for academic performance; that they care more for how children feel than what they know and are able to do; that they mislead and manipulate children into acquiring a false sense of self-esteem based on il-lusions of achievement produced by lowered standards; and that advocates of "reform" care more for their own ideologies than for the practical challenges children will face in their futures. — *could this self-esteem translate into improved outcomes*

POLICYMAKING AS CONSTITUTIVE SOCIAL ACTION

The "facts" of education (to borrow Gusfield's metaphor)

are not shiny marbles lying on the beach and awaiting only the sharp eyes of skilled men and women to be found. They are picked out of a pile, scrubbed, polished, highlighted here and there, and offered as discoveries in the context of the particular and practical considerations of their finders. (1981, p. 20)

Constitutive social processes not only shape the interpretation of intrinsically ambiguous conditions, but also assign *facticity* (status as factual accounts) to interpretations that become objectified by those processes. Both myths involved processes of interpretation and selection by which a particular set of meanings was simultaneously constructed and presented as an objective account of purported conditions. However, the curriculum myth alone acquired the status of truth (i.e., it became a "social fact"). The authors of the curriculum myth assigned particular meanings to ambiguous circumstances and then "enrolled" others in the truth of their account, such that they came to relate to those constructed meanings *as if* they were objective facts. Thus, while the "curriculum problem" did not exist as an objective fact (i.e., apart from the interpretation assigned to it), the "problem" was nonetheless *objectified*.

The discussion below examines this objectification process with particular attention to the way in which the trustees—as policymakers with the authority to establish the conditions of the debate—colluded in actually *making* the "problem" to which their policy-activity was ostensibly addressed. The board's own role in creating "the turmoil in which they found themselves" (in Lewis's words) was not limited to the creation of a particular set of circumstances (i.e., adopting a policy and then not enforcing it). The trustees also helped to *assign meaning* to those conditions, coauthoring an official account that assigned fault primarily to inadequate texts, while ignoring pertinent factors that could warrant alternative interpretations.

First, they allowed Smith's technical presentation disproportionate time on the agenda. Every other speaker, regardless of status or position in the debate, was permitted only a few carefully timed minutes in which to address the trustees, according to the conventions for general public testimony. Smith, however, was allocated 15 minutes on the agenda, and then permitted to exceed her allotment by an additional 10 minutes (objections to which were silenced by the board president). Smith's language, her reliance on abstract evidence, her visual props (i.e., charts and diagrams), and her privileged position on the agenda reinforced both the authority and the facticity of her account. The distinction between a "single, seamless performance delivered to a rapt audience" and fragmented, episodic narration often demarcates the narratives of the powerful from those of the weak (Kondo, 1990, p. 260). Authoritative narratives command prolonged attention, while narrations of weaker myths are more often interrupted, hurried, and/or restricted to limited, marginal spaces and times.

Second, data from the teacher surveys were presented as if they constituted objective evidence of a problem with the mathematics program. Yet, not only the survey itself (which focused on issues of curricula rather than of training or leadership), but also the board's choice to conduct it (rather than to take some other action, such as observing classroom instruction) presupposed a problem with the curriculum. This presupposition predetermined the interpretation of the "facts" that the survey "revealed." The survey itself was thus part of a circular process by which the official account of the situation was constructed and then validated.

The board's decision to *keep* the reform curriculum did not challenge the truth status of the curriculum myth. The vote seemed to have been motivated by a variety of concerns, among them consolidating their own authority (by enforcing their original decision to adopt the program) and conserving district resources (by avoiding another costly and time-consuming adoption process). The decision to keep the program was contingent upon its evaluation by a committee that would identify and correct its flaws. More importantly, the trustees did *not* appoint a similar committee to study questions and problems related to implementation, training, or other issues, nor did they indicate any intentions to do so in the future. Instead, all of their attention and energy was focused on the curriculum itself, and directed away from other possible explanations for conditions in the district.

Thus, the decision that the program was worthy of *keeping* was itself structured by the myth of curriculum. Once the decision to keep the program had been made, the "problem" (presumed to be the curriculum) was treated as "addressed" (presumably by the appointment of the committee to evaluate and address its weaknesses). In other words, the process by which the "curriculum problem" was both constructed and addressed (Gusfield, 1981, pp. 6–8) presupposed the conclusion it ultimately validated: that the curriculum was the appropriate object of collective attention and concern.

To see a set of conditions as a problem is to direct attention away from other conditions, which are thereby "granted immunity" from concern (i.e., not viewed as problematic) (Edelman, 1987, pp. 7–8). Sufficient evidence existed to warrant multiple interpretations of the facts of education in Avocado Valley; the trustees could have plausibly concluded that the district's problem was one of policy implementation, training, leadership, management, and/or communication. Yet, the processes by which the trustees addressed the problem maintained attention primarily on issues of curriculum, thereby helping to contain and exclude alternative interpretations.

Moreover, the manner in which the trustees approached the controversy helped to ratify a broad array of taken-for-granted beliefs, practices, and institutional arrangements in education. For example, the board could have regarded the test scores as evidence of a problem with either the tests themselves, or with the practice of standardized testing altogether. By instead treating them as evidence of a problem with the curriculum, the trustees both presupposed and validated the range of assumptions surrounding standardized testing (i.e., tacit beliefs about knowledge, learning, and how to measure and assess them, and about the validity of using such tests to competitively assess and rank students by purported ability).[7]

Likewise, by evaluating the program primarily on the basis of survey data, public testimony, and instructional materials (rather than direct observation or samples of student work), the board also validated a particular, deterministic view of education: that learning occurs by the relatively unmediated transmission of knowledge from the teacher or the text to the child. Their mode of addressing the problem ignored dynamics of teaching and learning in context (i.e., the specific, situated interactions between and among particular teachers, students, and texts), consideration of which would challenge the "cultural transmission" model of education (Kohlberg & Mayer, 1972, pp. 452–454) implied by that mode. The trustees' manner of addressing the controversy thus created a self-fulfilling prophecy: it predetermined an account (the "curriculum problem") that, by finding responsibility for educational outcomes with the curriculum, validated the presupposition that curricula determine learning.

The interpretation that there was a problem with the mathematics curriculum provided a clear, concrete focus for concern. This story both simplified and accounted for local conditions, reducing their complexities to a single, manageable source: the relatively simple matter of textbook selection. At the same time, this account also diverted attention away from other, more nettlesome conditions. By contrast, to suggest that the implementation of educational change requires greater support for teachers, stronger leadership, and attention to complexities of teaching, learning, and institutional and conceptual change is to advance a far more complex view of schooling than that implied by the myth of curriculum. The curriculum problem thus symbolically resolved the ambiguities of education, while leaving unquestioned the broad array of institutionalized beliefs and practices surrounding education in Avocado Valley.

CULTURAL MYTHS AND POLICY RITUALS

The behavior described in this chapter presumed a clear and orderly world in which the facts of education can be objectively known, and educational outcomes can be directed and predicted by means of "sound" (i.e., factually based) curricula and policy. The realities of education, however, are far more messy, confusing, and ambiguous. A complex interaction of economic, social, emotional, developmental, and cognitive factors play into a child's educational success or failure; even those aspects of the process that we may know and understand better than others (e.g., the relationship between poverty and school failure), we often cannot control. Reality seldom corresponds to idealized accounts of it, and frequently contradicts them.

The moral order nonetheless imposes a coherence on the chaotic reality of social life: The heart of the matter is a tension between certainty and uncertainty. We pin things down intellectually—we escape chaos—by making intellectual models that identify patterns of events and, beyond the patterns, their causes. These models let us recognize what has happened, tell us what is the appropriate action, and even sometimes allow us to shape future events—at least to plan to do so. . . . Each of these models both explains past and future events and suggests appropriate action, both immediate and in the future. They are, to use Ibsen's splendid phrase, . . . the "lies that make life possible." They are only lies in the sense that they are, each in themselves, incomplete explanations of experience. Each explanation leaves a great deal unsaid. (Bailey, 1994, p. 82)

Elmore Backward mapping

At the same time, the rituals of public policy deny the situation of conflict between the ideals of the moral order and the reality "on the ground." To acknowledge this conflict would be to admit the mythical status of the moral order itself. Instead, the rituals of public policy work at shoring up cultural ideals "against the awesome skepticism of unending alternatives, ambiguous facts, and the confusion of the concrete and the particular" (Gusfield, 1981, p. 170).

All of these practices work to comprise a public "drama of morality and order" (Gusfield, 1981, p. 82) in the explanation of school success and failure. Their social significance lies in the extent to which they help maintain a sense that the world is an orderly, logical, just place, and that we have some control over our own and our children's lives and futures. Within this moral drama, it is neither the "natural order" nor the unequal distribution of social and material resources that determines educational success and failure. Rather, it is the incompleteness of our scientific understanding, the inefficiency of our institutions, the inadequacies of our policies, or the actions of individuals that are responsible for educational success or failure.

To the extent that it validated the latter assertions, the curriculum myth was thus a morality tale in a scientific idiom. However, the moral dimensions of how its authors constructed both the "problem" and the "solution" were obscured by the manner of its presentation: the rhetoric of science. This language gave the myth's moral assertions the aura of truth, producing "the illusion of certainty, of being accurately in correspondence with an objective world" (Bailey, 1994, p. 83), and constructing a "cognitive and moral order which appears external and unyielding to human choice and design" (Gusfield, 1981, p. 18). Scientific language "both enlist(s) and generate(s)" an interpretive context that assigns facticity to arguments framed in its terms (Gusfield, 1981, pp. 107–108), while concealing their moral and cultural dimensions. This interpretive frame is comprised of the imagery, language, and symbolism of objectivity, neutrality, and technical expertise.

The curriculum myth also validated the ends and means (i.e., order, truth, utility, efficiency, self-reliance, self-discipline, initiative, hard work, competition, technology, precision, and standards) dictated by metanarratives of science, policy administration, and American capitalism. Its emphasis on "facts," "rigor," "individual effort," "results," and "measurability" were elements in the construction of a natural and moral order in which educational outcomes could be precisely measured and predicted through the technologies of science and administration, on the one hand, and individual sweat of brow, on the other (Varenne & McDermott, 1999,). In so doing, the curriculum myth reduced the intrinsic uncertainties of education; it created an illusion of control by prescribing precise solutions for the problems it constructed.

cruelly.

The curriculum myth likewise validated foundational values of American capitalism and its "competitive *laissez-faire* system of status allocation" (Kahne, 1996, p. 14). For example, the emphasis on academic performance as measured by test scores reinforced the values of competition and "meritocracy" central to public schooling in the United States (Kahne, 1996, p. 17). The notion that self-esteem should be an educational objective challenges that value orientation. Its critics assert that praise should be given to students only when they "earn" it because "false praise" will lead to complacency and discourage students from working hard. Smith's assertion that "drill and practice are not always fun [but] [n]either are showers and table manners" hints at the moral dimensions of the work/play dichotomy in "traditionalist" narratives: hard work is necessary to curb children's base natural tendencies through the imposition of discipline and constraint. Concerns that "reform" curricula and methods encourage laziness and dependence, and discourage individual initiative and effort, reflect these same commitments.

Both the curriculum and the implementation myth were situated local narratives. Each expressed and validated particular historical and cultural myths about educational achievement and social mobility. However, the moral and subjective biases of the implementation myth were more explicit, leaving its authors open to accusations that their views were grounded in emotion and "ideology" rather than reason and "factual evidence." Moreover, the implementation myth threatened the moral order because it amplified the endemic uncertainties of education by focusing on the complexities of concrete experience in classrooms and schools. This threat was compounded by the context of current economic transitions that also magnify the uncertainties of social mobility. At the same time, the implementation myth's reliance on idioms of feeling and experience (which lack authority as grounds for truth claims in the context of public policy administration) also made it vulnerable to ridicule. When viewed from this perspective, it seems evident that the curriculum myth acquired much of its power from how its authors drew upon authoritative cultural narratives not only to deride the myth of implementation, but also to shore up the illusions of certainty and control that are, to adapt Ibsen's phrase, the "lies" that make policy possible.

NOTES

1. I wish to thank F.G. Bailey and Hugh Mehan, for guidance and support throughout the research and writing of this chapter; Bradley Levinson, for detailed comments on several drafts; and Steven Fram, for editorial assistance and support. The larger project from which the data for this chapter are drawn was funded by a Doctoral Research Fellowship from the American Educational Research Association and the Spencer Foundation in 1996–1997, and a Dissertation Fellowship from the Spencer Foundation in 1997–1998. I am grateful for their generous support.

2. Names of places and individuals are pseudonyms.

3. Throughout the discussion, the terms "reform" and "constructivist mathematics" refer to a set of recommendations embodied in both the *Mathematics Framework for California Public Schools* (California Department of Education, 1992), and the *Curriculum and Evaluation Standards for School Mathematics* (National Council of Teachers of Mathematics, 1989), on which the California framework is based. These recommendations have met with resistance from groups of parents and politicians in various parts of the state, who argue for the restoration of "traditional" mathematics instruction. Both "traditional" and "reform" are presented in quotation marks to foreground their role in the politics of representation at play in the debate, a central concern of the larger study (Rosen, n.d.) from which data for this chapter are drawn.

4. In formulating my argument, I was influenced by Gusfield's (1981) study of the "problem" of drinking and driving in the United States, which suggested how traditional anthropological concepts could be applied to the study of contemporary educational "problems" and the policies addressed to them. At the same time, my discussion also furthers the line of argumentation in Varenne and McDermott (1999), showing how the "success/failure system" they illuminate (what I have chosen to call the "moral order" of education) is reproduced, naturalized, and validated in local arenas of education policy.

5. See Varenne and McDermott (1998) for a discussion of the relationship between middle class parents' anxiety about their children's achievement and the success/failure system that structures American education.

6. My discussion in this section reflects the influence of two sources: Gusfield's (1981) analysis of the allocation of responsibility in rituals of law and policy surrounding drinking and driving in the United States; and Mehan's (1993) case study of the politics of representation surrounding competing accounts of student behavior and "ability" among differently situated actors in schools. Mehan's argument supplied some of the framework for my analysis (i.e., the focus on differences in the manner of presentation, modes of representation, and manner of grounding assertions among the two accounts), which also supports some of his findings regarding the relative power of different modes of representation in education (i.e., that the interpretation that ultimately prevailed among competing accounts employed idioms of objectivity and neutrality associated with technical expertise; was grounded in abstract, quantitative evidence; and was narrated seamlessly rather than episodically).

7. For a more detailed analysis of the relationship between this range of beliefs and practices, on the one hand, and the moral order of education, on the other, see Varenne and McDermott (1999, pp. 106–108, 115–116).

REFERENCES

Bailey, F. G. (1977). *Morality and expediency: The folklore of academic politics.* Oxford, UK: Basil Blackwell.

Bailey, F. G. (1994). *The witch hunt.* Ithaca, NY: Cornell University Press.

California Department of Education. (1992). *Mathematics framework for California public schools.* Sacramento: California Department of Education.

Douglas, M. (1973). *Rules and meanings: The anthropology of everyday knowledge.* Harmondsworth, Middlesex, UK: Penguin Books.

Edelman, M. (1987). The construction of social problems as buttresses of inequalities. *University of Miami Law Review, 42*(1), 7–28.

Gusfield, J. (1981). *The culture of public problems: Drinking-driving and the symbolic order*. Chicago: University of Chicago Press.

Kahne, J. (1996). The politics of self esteem. *American Education Research Journal, 330*(1), 3–22.

Kohlberg, L., & Mayer, R. (1972). Development as the aim of education. *Harvard Educational Review, 42*(4), 449–496.

Kondo, D. (1990). *Crafting selves*. Chicago: University of Chicago Press.

Krasniewicz, L. (1992). *Nuclear summer: The clash of communities at the Seneca Women's Peace Encampment*. Ithaca, NY: Cornell University Press.

Leach, E. (1954). *Political systems of Highland Burma*. Boston: Beacon Press.

Mehan, H. (1993). Beneath the skin and between the ears: A case study in the politics of representation. In S. Chaiklin & J. Lave (Eds.), *Understanding practice: Perspectives on activity and context* (pp. 241–268). Cambridge, UK: Cambridge University Press.

National Council of Teachers of Mathematics. (1989). Curriculum and Evaluation Standards for School Mathematics. Reston, VA: NCTM.

Rosen, L. (2000). *Calculating concerns: The politics of representation in California's "Math Wars."* Unpublished doctoral dissertation, University of California, San Diego.

Tobin, J., Wu, D., & Davidson, D. (1989). *Preschool in three cultures*. New Haven: Yale University Press.

Varenne, H., & McDermott, R. (1999). *Successful failure: The school America builds*. Boulder, CO: Westview Press.

Walkerdine, V. (1984). Developmental psychology and the child-centred pedagogy: The insertion of Piaget into early education. In J. Henriques, W. Hollway, C. Urwin, C. Venn, & V. Walkerdine (Eds.), *Changing the subject: Psychology, social regulation and subjectivity* (pp. 153–202). London and New York: Methuen.

Woolard, K. (1989). Sentences in the language prison: The rhetorical structuring of an American language policy debate. *American Ethnologist, 16*(2), 268–278.

Index

About the Editors and Contributors

DONALD K. ADAMS is professor emeritus of the University of Pittsburgh. His international experience includes work with the Asian Development Bank, USAID, World Bank, and UNESCO in educational planning, policy analysis, and evaluation in over 25 Asian, African, and Latin American countries. He is author of several books and over 100 articles, book chapters, monographs, and reports. He is an Honorary Fellow and past President of the Comparative and International Education Society.

NTAL-I'MBIRWA ALIMASI is a Ph.D. candidate in the Department of Administrative and Policy Studies at the University of Pittsburgh, Pennsylvania, specializing in International and Development Education. He has consulted for various national and international organizations in management and community development, and taught and trained educators across Africa and in the United States. His current research interests and social concerns are perhaps best summarized in the working title of his dissertation proposal, "Development Assistance and Empowerment: A Bystander Reading of Instantiated USAID Education Assistance Rhetoric in Guinea and Mali." He is currently assistant to the co-directors of Pittsburgh's Institute for International Studies in Education.

KATHRYN M. ANDERSON-LEVITT is a professor of anthropology at the University of Michigan-Dearborn and the editor of the *Anthropology and Education Quarterly* (1995 through 2000). Her ethnographic and comparative research on teachers' knowledge has appeared in *The Elementary School Journal*, the *Anthropology and Education Quarterly*, and *American Ethnologist*, and will appear in *Teaching Cultures: Knowledge for Teaching First Grade in France and the United States* (2001). She has also conducted research on girls' schooling in Guinea and on "sheltered workshops" for mentally retarded adults in the Detroit area.

ISABELA CABRAL FÉLIX DE SOUSA earned her bachelor and professional degrees in Psychology at the State University of Rio de Janeiro, and her doctoral degree in International Education at the University of Southern California. She has been working since 1996 as a research fellow of CNP at LEAS-IOC, Oswaldo Cruz Foundation (FIOCRUZ), Rio de Janeiro, Brazil. Her research interests are in health education, women's education, and social development.

SANDRA L. CADE has recently joined the faculty at Olivet College in Michigan as assistant professor in the Education Department, where she will research implementation of the College's Institutional vision of Education for Individual and Social Responsibility. Prior to her arrival at Olivet, Sandra served as a Senior Research Associate at the David C. Anchin Center, University of South Florida—Tampa. Her professional interests include immigrant and women's education, professional development, and home–school relations.

THOMAS CLAYTON is assistant professor of English and Linguistics at the University of Kentucky. His interests include educational and language policies in world-system context. His book *Education and the Politics of Language: Hegemony and Pragmatism in Cambodia, 1979–1989* will be published by the Comparative Education Research Centre, University of Hong Kong, in 2000.

MARK B. GINSBURG is a professor of Comparative Sociology of Education, in the Departments of Administrative and Policy Studies and Sociology at the University of Pittsburgh (USA). He is also co-director of Pittsburgh's Institute for International Studies in Education (IISE). He has written *Contradiction in Teacher Education and Society: A Critical Analysis* (1988); *Understanding Educational Reform in Global Context: Economy, Ideology, and the State* (1991); *The Political Dimension in Teacher Education: Comparative Perspectives on Policy Formation, Socialization, and Society* (1995); *The Politics of Educators' Work and Lives* (1995); and *Cuba in the Special Period: Cuban Perspectives* (Third World Studies/1997 and Editorial de Ciencias Sociales de Cuba/1998). He was co-director of IISE's subcontract on USAID's first Improving Educational Quality project (IEQ1) and serves as director of IISE's subcontract on IEQ2. He has done extensive fieldwork in Mexico, focusing on teacher education, and has spent time in the field in China, Cuba, Egypt, Indonesia, Korea, Nicaragua, and South Africa.

BRADLEY A. U. LEVINSON is assistant professor of Education in the Department of Educational Leadership and Policy Studies, School of Education, Indiana University, where he also holds an adjunct appointment in the Department of Anthropology. He is editor (with D. Foley and D. Holland) of *The Cultural Production of the Educated Person* (1996) and *Schooling the Symbolic Animal* (2000), and author of *We Are All Equal: The Play of Student Culture at a Mexican Secondary School and Beyond* (2001). His articles have appeared in *Anthropology and Education Quarterly*, *Comparative Education Review*, *American Anthropologist*, and the *Journal of Contemporary Ethnography*. Most recently, he has turned his attention to developing an ethnographic approach to the study of public policy and public spheres, especially in relation to new immigrants in Indiana schools and communities.

MARTHA E. MANTILLA is a doctoral candidate in the Department of Administrative and Policy Studies, School of Education, University of Pittsburgh. Her area of concentration is Social and Comparative Studies in Education, with specialization in International and Development Education. She has special interest in the Latin American region and most of her research has been in Guatemala. She is particularly interested in the participation of actors who have traditionally been at the margin of the decision-making process, namely, teachers, parents, and students.

KHAULA MURTADHA-WATTS is an assistant professor of Educational Leadership and Policy Studies at Indiana University. Her research interests include urban school leadership and women as leaders of organizational change.

MAUREEN PORTER is an assistant professor in the Social and Comparative Analysis of Education program in the Department of Administrative and Policy Studies, School of Education, University of Pittsburgh. She also has an adjunct appointment in the Department of Anthropology. She does research and teaching in the areas of sense of place and the politics of identity, gender, and education; rituals and community-building; (women's) communities of practice; service-learning and cross-cultural exchanges; and the balance between standardized testing and local, culturally grounded pedagogy. She has been invited to be a keynote speaker at regional conferences and international symposia on sustainable, regional development, identity politics and educational reform, service learning in the global village, and coming-of-age rituals. She recently enjoyed a summer as a visiting professor at the University of Augsburg, Germany.

PAMELA ANNE QUIROZ is an associate professor in the Department of Policy Studies, College of Education, University of Illinois at Chicago. Her main research interests are the sociology of education, educational reform, ethnic identity, and schooling. She has published extensively in *Sociology of Education* and the *Journal of Contemporary Ethnography*.

LISA ROSEN is a research associate at the Center for School Improvement, University of Chicago. Her dissertation is an ethnographic study of the politics of representation in the debate on mathematics education policy in California. Her main research interest is in the intersections between public debates on education, on the one hand, and the social construction and transformation of metanarratives for schooling in the U.S., on the other. She is particularly interested in the emergence of "mobility" or "market" narratives of public schooling in the context of recent debates on education reform.

R. G. SCHWAB holds a research position as fellow at the Centre for Aboriginal Economic Policy Research, The Australian National University. His Ph.D. is in anthropology and he has conducted research related to educational issues in Australia, the United States, the United Arab Emirates, and Egypt. His research has focused on literacy (especially early literacy), educational development (in schools and for academic staff in higher education), and program planning and evaluation. Most recently, he has pursued research interests and has written extensively on indigenous education and training in Australia, addressing theoretical, practical, and policy issues.

SUSAN STREET is a full time researcher-professor at the Centro de Investigaciones y Estudios Superiores en Antropología Social (CIESAS)—Occidente (Center for Higher Studies and Research in Social Anthropology—Western Branch), in Guadalajara, Mexico. Her research on Mexican educational policy is from a "social actor" perspective, specializing in teachers' organizations and in struggles for democracy. More recently, she has been doing ethnographic research on "teachers' work, school reforms, and regional diversity" in western Mexico. A political anthropologist of education, Street has published widely in numerous books and journals.

JUDY SYLVESTER is a teaching fellow of Social Foundations of Education in the School of Education of the University of Pittsburgh. Her scholarship and research are in the fields of international development education and teacher education. She has worked for UNICEF as a staff member and a program consultant in both emergency relief and rehabilitation and development programs.

MARGARET SUTTON is an assistant professor of Educational Leadership and Policy Studies at Indiana University. Her work focuses on the construction of social realities, by both authoritative and by ordinary practices. She has worked extensively as a practitioner in the field of education and development, and has written about social scientific knowledge in post-colonial settings, gender and education, and curricular practices in international and global education.

YIDAN WANG is training and learning specialist at the Asian Development Bank Institute in Tokyo, Japan. She received her Ph.D. in international and development education at the University of Pittsburgh. She has worked for several international agencies, including ADB, UNESCO, UNICEF, and USAID. Her recent publications include "Providing Teacher Training through Educational Television, The China Experience"; and "Public-Private Partnerships in the Social Sector: Issues and Country Experiences in Asia and the Pacific."